500 PRAYERS

FOR THE CHRISTIAN YEAR

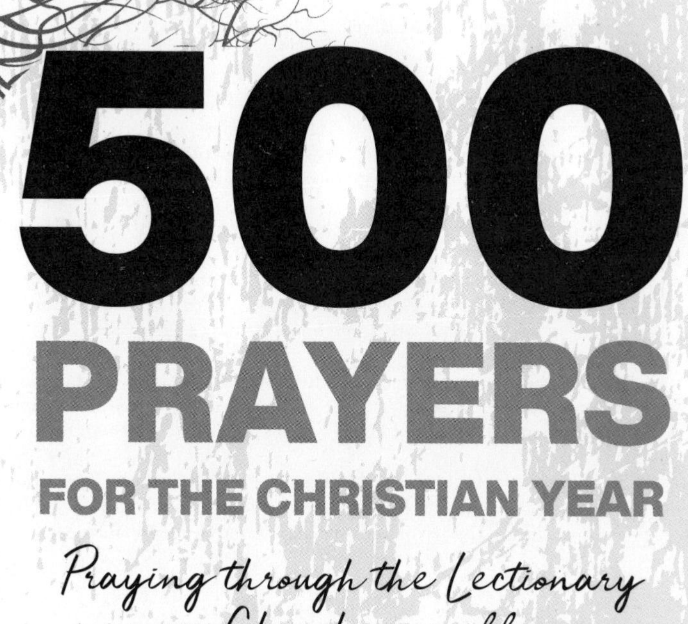

500 PRAYERS

FOR THE CHRISTIAN YEAR

Praying through the Lectionary for your Church or small group

DAVID CLOWES

DAVID C COOK™

transforming lives together

500 PRAYERS FOR THE CHRISTIAN YEAR
Published by David C Cook
4050 Lee Vance Drive
Colorado Springs, CO 80918 U.S.A.

Integrity Music Limited, a Division of David C Cook
Brighton, East Sussex BN1 2RE, England

ISBN 978-0-8307-8246-8
eISBN 978-0-8307-8247-5

The Team: Ian Matthews, Megan Stengel, Jo Stockdale, Jack Campbell, Susan Murdock
Cover Design: Pete Barnsley

Printed in the United Kingdom
First Edition 2020

1 2 3 4 5 6 7 8 9 10

090120

CONTENTS

INTRODUCTION

It was January 1968 when I discovered the joy and the responsibility of leading the people of God in conversation with their Maker. My church background was firmly in the camp of extemporary prayer. That I started to write my prayers down was due in part to nervousness but mainly because my preaching mentor insisted on a careful and prayerful approach not only of the hymns, readings and the sermon but also of the prayers.

The first book, *500 Prayers for All Occasions*, was itself a journey of the Christian year. The second book, *500 More Prayers for All Occasions*, was more of a patchwork quilt covering a whole range of styles and themes of prayer. The new book in the series, *500 Prayers for the Christian Year*, provides prayers based on the Revised Common Lectionary covering the complete three-year cycle. With each of the prayers for a particular Sunday you will find the biblical text which has been the inspiration for that prayer. There are three prayers for every Sunday, each of which is either a prayer of approach, praise, thanksgiving, confession or intercession. Because they use the same lectionary readings each year, the prayers for Christmas Eve, Maundy Thursday, and Good Friday are collected in the appendix.

As previously, the prayers are set out in verse form which is intended as an aid to leading the prayers in worship. They are also not written in formal church style of language, but in the language we speak every day. The purpose of this means that they are more easily 'prayed' and not simply 'read'. I fully expect that those who use these prayers will amend the words and phrases in ways with which you are not only more comfortable but are more appropriate in the context in which you are using them. It is worth noting that the prayers of intercession have more stanzas than would normally be used in any one service but are there to be used selectively.

Many of the prayers of intercession are responsive. In the previous books I severely limited the range of responses used. In *500 Prayers for the Christian Year* I have allowed myself to be a little more expansive, and to have a broader palate as it were, on which to draw. This is, in part, because of the wider use of video projection in services. This means that a congregation can see the responses they are being invited to make.

It is one of those strange experiences of life that some of the most moving moments in my prayer-life have been as I have clicked away with two fingers on the keyboard of my computer. I have no doubt that those prayers which you will find most helpful and meaningful are the very ones which for me were 'gifts' I received through the grace of God. I do believe that prayers for use in public worship are not the same as those used in our private devotions. Nevertheless, many of the prayers included in this third volume of prayers have indeed 'found their life' during those precious moments in God's presence. They have come in the early morning before the day began or when the house was silent and still at the end of the day. It would also be true to say that many of the prayers, particularly those of intercession, find their roots in over forty years of pastoral ministry.

I am grateful for the guidance, help and support of Ian Matthews and Jack Campbell who provided the opportunity to share my prayers with a far wider congregation than I ever imagined possible.

David Clowes
Stockport, April 2020

YEAR A

FIRST SUNDAY OF ADVENT

Prayer of Approach

Psalm 122:1

Lord,
we have come at your invitation
to meet together to offer
heartfelt thanks and praise.
By your Holy Spirit, enable us
to celebrate your glory
with joy. **Amen.**

Praise

Isaiah 2:2–3

Lord,
we praise you because you
know everything.
You know when the sun and
moon first appeared
and when all the planets
took to their orbits.
You can look back to when
all things began
and you hold forever in
your gaze the moment
when the final curtain will fall
upon your handiwork.

Lord,
we praise you because you
know everything.
You know the journey we have made
and the pathways we
have yet to walk.
You know when we stand fast
and when we fall.
You know when we speak the truth
and when we allow honesty
to be hidden away.

Lord,
we praise you because you
know everything.
You know that the words of
judgement in Scripture
are in truth the promise that
we can begin again.
You know that every word of warning
holds the offer of forgiveness
and renewal.

Lord,
we praise you because you
know everything.
You speak to us of the days of Noah,
that we may hear your offer
of love and freedom.
You remind us of the
challenges to come
and of the choices we
must make now.

Lord, precious Lord,
we praise you because you
know everything.
We know now that if there was
one thing you didn't know
you would not be God.
All-knowing God,
in Christ you offer the
promise of freedom
and through your Holy
Spirit you set us free.
All-loving God,
in Jesus you hold our hands
and guide our footsteps
and by your holy presence you
clothe our days in hope.

Lord,
we praise you because you
know everything—
and you know us!
And knowing us, you love us;

and loving us, you gently
lead us home to you.
We praise you, our all-
knowing God. **Amen.**

Intercession

Matthew 24:36

For those facing a time of
uncertainty about their health
as they prepare to keep that
hospital appointment
or they await the results of tests
with apprehension and dread;
for those whose days are troubled
with anxiety and despair
and for those experiencing a
loss of confidence and joy.
Let us pray to the Lord
with assurance and hope.

For those facing a time of uncertainty
with their employment
and for those who have already
lost their jobs and their status;
for those experiencing rejection,
bitter disappointment, and fear
as they are left wondering how
they will support their family
and for those who are in danger of
losing all sense of self-worth.
Let us pray to the Lord
with assurance and hope.

For those facing a time
of uncertainty with
their relationships
as the demands of work and
family mean there is less
time for one another;
for those homes and families
under strain of conflict
and misunderstanding
as they struggle with broken
promises and the pain
of trust that is lost
and for those now left alone
with precious memories of
relationships of love.
Let us pray to the Lord
with assurance and hope.

For those facing a time
of uncertainty in their
concern for the world
as all they see and hear speaks
of a world which is daily
tearing itself apart;
for those filled with anguish
for the millions who are
hungry and starving
as they watch in despair a
world that seems to care
little for people or planet
and for those who ache
for the thousands killed
by war or disease.
Let us pray to the Lord
with assurance and hope.

For those facing a time of
uncertainty with their faith
as the familiar landscape of
church, Bible, and Christian
faith are ridiculed;
for those who have lost the faith
they received as a child
as they forgot the need to nourish
it with worship and fellowship
and for those whose faith
has withered through the
failure to use it each day.
Let us pray to the Lord
with assurance and hope.

For those facing a time of
uncertainty with themselves
as they have lost their way
on the journey of life;
for those who no longer know
their own name or the
names of those they love
as the years have stolen their
memories of people and
places once precious
and for those, young and old,
who are simply longing
to make a new start.
Let us pray to the Lord
with assurance and hope.

In the name of Jesus, the source of
all hope and assurance. **Amen.**

Confession

Lord,
we confess
that we need your light
to heal our brokenness;
to restore our relationships;
to show us the way;
to cleanse and renew us;
to enable us to offer
forgiveness to those
who have hurt us most;
and to receive the forgiveness
that you give to those who come
confessing their need of your light.

Lord,
we confess our need of your light,
trusting that you will
light up our lives
with your grace. **Amen.**

SECOND SUNDAY OF ADVENT

Prayer of Approach

Isaiah 11:1–2

Lord,
they tell us that there is a
time for everything.
We have a time to pray
and a time to praise;
a time to give thanks
and a time to give honour;
a time for fellowship
and a time for worship;
a time to confess
and a time to pray for others.

Lord,
for us, this is the time to be
still in your presence
and a time to give you
the adoration of hearts
that love you deeply. **Amen.**

Praise

Psalm 72:18–19

Lord,
why is it that we are
moved with wonder
by a starlit sky
or by a snow-covered view?

What is it that touches us so deeply
in the song of a bird
or the laughter of a little child?

What is the reason for that
warm glow within
when we know that a
job is well done
or when we have been able to
help someone in need?

Why do we experience
 a sense of peace
on the mountaintops of life
or find hope even in its valleys?

How is it possible to be
 so overwhelmed
as we look at the face of the hungry
or to be by the despair
 of the homeless?

What is it that enables us to
love the unlovely,
care for the careless,
touch the untouchable,
search for the lost,
welcome the stranger,
give to the hungry,
and to forgive the unforgiveable?

Is it because of you, Lord?

Is it because you are Lord
of all your creation
and that everything we see and hear
owes its being to your lordship?
Is it because you are Lord
of our hearts and minds
that our responses are always
fashioned and shaped by
 your presence within?

Lord,
we praise you because you are Lord
and because your lordship
is the sole reason for all that is.

We praise you because
you are Lord of our lives
and because your lordship within
is our sole reason to give
 you thanks and praise.

It is because you are our Lord
that by the presence and power
 of your Holy Spirit
our eyes are opened
to see your presence
everywhere and in everyone;
to be aware of your working
through those who know you
and through those who don't.

Lord,
fill us now with your Holy Spirit
that we may take hold
of every facet of life
and offer it, by your grace,
 for your glory.

We bring our praises
in the name of Christ,
who is Lord of all. **Amen.**

Intercession

Matthew 3:1–2

We pray for those who are
 ready to be different;
for politicians ready to
 sacrifice their own career
in pursuit of the truth;
for those who refuse to
 follow the party line
when it conflicts with the
 needs of the poor;
for those who speak out
when others would rather
 they were silent.
The Lord hears our prayer.
Thanks be to God.

We pray for those who are
 ready to be different;
for those who like John the Baptist

stand firm when their faith
is ridiculed or denied;
for those who are ready
to pay the price
of naming Jesus as
Saviour and Lord;
for those who face hostility,
rejection, and death
in their witness for the
Saviour of the world.
The Lord hears our prayer.
Thanks be to God.

We pray for those who are
ready to be different;
for those who work in the media
who daily face the challenge
of decency and truth;
for those who are a lone voice
in the morass of innuendo and lies;
for those who refuse to stay silent
when to compromise would
save them great pain.
The Lord hears our prayer.
Thanks be to God.

We pray for those who are
ready to be different;
for those who are employed
in the health service
and for whom it remains
more than a job;
for those whose care
and compassion
brings hope, comfort, and
courage to many;
for those who serve at great
cost to themselves
as they offer dignity and
wholeness to others.
The Lord hears our prayer.
Thanks be to God.

We pray for those who are
ready to be different;
for those who work in care
homes for the elderly
and for those who show respect for
those who cannot remember;
for those who care for the
aged in their own homes
and for those whose daily visits
are coloured with love;
for those who demonstrate
the love of God
to those who are bitter,
selfish, or confused.
The Lord hears our prayer.
Thanks be to God.

We pray for those who are
ready to be different;
for those who care for the careless
and who seek to support
those who have nothing;
for those who work with
no home of their own
and for those who offer practical,
costly compassion;
for those who are able to seek
beyond the dirty exterior
and discover the person of
worth hidden within.
The Lord hears our prayer.
Thanks be to God.

We pray for those who are
ready to be different;
for those whose lives
are a battlefield
as they strive to overcome
disability of body or mind;
for those who still smile through
the pain and concern

and for those whose death and
dying give hope to us all;
for those whose lives are a source
of courage and strength
and whose way of living makes
the presence of God real.
The Lord hears our prayer.
Thanks be to God.

We pray for those who are
ready to be different;
for ourselves as we face the
challenges and changes around us
that we might be beacons of peace,
hope, and joy for our neighbour.
In a moment of silence, let us
reflect on those areas of our lives
where God may be calling us
to be ready to be different.

silence

The Lord hears our prayer.
Thanks be to God.

In the name of Christ, whose
difference nailed him
to the cross. **Amen.**

THIRD SUNDAY OF ADVENT

Prayer of Approach

Luke 1:46b–47

Lord, we have not come
to sing hymns,
nor are we here to say prayers
and to listen to your Word.
We are here to praise
the living God
and to do so with every fibre
of our being. **Amen.**

Confession

James 5:7

Father,
we confess that we live in
an instant world,
a society that wants everything,
and wants it now!
We are offered success in a moment
and a wealth of possessions paid
for with 'plastic money'.

We assume that all our
problems will end with the
snapping of our fingers
and our worries will disappear
like the morning mist.
We thought our step of faith
would mean our questions
would be answered
and all our doubts would
be a thing of the past.

Father,
forgive our lack of patience
in our walk of faith
and our failure to take you
on childlike trust.

Father,
forgive our wanting to know every
twist and turn of the pathway
before we will risk taking
the first step.

Father,
Forgive our fine words of
faith, hope, and love
which too easily slip through
our sieve-like trust
as we continue to insist on knowing
the 'day and the hour'.

We pray, *maranatha*. Come,
Lord Jesus, come.
But teach us to be patient
as we eagerly await your
coming. **Amen.**

Praise

Isaiah 35:1–2

Lord,
nothing seems to last;
everything is changing;
everywhere the old,
familiar landmarks
are being torn down, removed,
or simply trodden under
the foot of progress.

The mighty oak that stood
strong and true
for hundreds of years
falls beneath the forester's saw.
The house that was home
to succeeding generations
has long since found itself
in the path of the
unrelenting bulldozer.
Our idyllically remembered
childhood,
filled to the brim with endless
long, hot summers
and endless days of fun
and laughter,
has given way to failing eyesight,
weary limbs, and senior moments.

Lord,
everything is changing;
nothing remains the same.
But you tell us that is how
you designed it all to be.
For that which does not change
ceases to be alive.

And yet, Lord,
in the midst of our chaotic lives,
the endless round of
changing seasons
gives us cause to praise you—
the one true, living God.
You do not change
but are the source
of the hope of renewal and life.

Lord,
we praise you that in the midst
of all that we are facing
we can trust you to be at
the heart of all things.
For you are the God
who has promised to make
all things new.

In the name of Christ
we praise our renewing God. **Amen.**

Intercession

Matthew 11:2

Lord,
we pray for those in a prison of fear;
those for whom each day
is a day of dread
and every moment seems to be
filled with things to avoid;
for those who long to step out in faith
and to face each day with the
freedom they long for.
May the presence of Christ
be their sign of hope.

Lord,
we pray for those in a prison of pain;
for those who live with pain
of body, mind, or spirit
and for whom the door of
release is but a dream;

for those whose every movement
comes at great cost
and for those who are always busy
to keep hurtful memories at bay.
May the presence of Christ
be their sign of hope.

Lord,
we pray for those in a
prison of poverty;
for those who are members of
the world's forgotten poor,
and for those who have
lost everything in the
latest world tragedy;
for those who had nothing of
value to lose, only themselves,
and for those who seek an
equal opportunity to share
in the good things in
God's wonderful world.
May the presence of Christ
be their sign of hope.

Lord,
we pray for those in a prison of illness;
for those whose days are no
longer filled with laughter
and for those whose sickness
is crippling their days;
for those trying to overcome the
burden they carry within them
and for those who count the days
they know they have left.
May the presence of Christ
be their sign of hope.

Lord,
we pray for those in a
prison of riches;
for those who trust in the wealth
they can touch and handle
and for those who find it
hard to trust in the one
who is seen only by the eye of faith;
for those who have possessions
in abundance
but who will arrive empty-handed
before the throne of grace.
May the presence of Christ
be their sign of hope.

Lord,
we pray for those in a prison of doubt;
for those who long to experience
the joy of the warmed heart
but are finding the cost of a step of
faith a price they cannot pay;
for those with genuine questions
and uncertainties
and who are failing to grasp
this is part of the journey
we all must take.
May the presence of Christ
be their sign of hope.

Lord,
we pray for those in prison
like John the Baptist;
for those facing years of
internment without a fair trial
and for those who languish in jail
for the faith they proclaim;
for those looking for signs of
hope and encouragement
and for those who are blind to the
love and the power of God.
May the presence of Christ,
be their sign of hope.

We bring our prayers in the
name of the Lord of hope,
the one who by grace offers
true freedom to all. **Amen.**

FOURTH SUNDAY OF ADVENT

Prayer of Approach

Psalm 80:7

Wonderful, wonderful God,
you are almighty in power,
truth, and love.
You hold all things and all people
in the palm of your hand
and we have come to
worship you. **Amen.**

Praise

Romans 1:2–4

All praise to God
and all thanks to the King.
We worship our creator
and give thanks for the love
that holds us and heals us
every moment of every day.
Sovereign Lord,
King of all majesty,
and the source of all
goodness and truth.
Jesus Christ, whose life,
death, and resurrection
acts as a mirror to the
heart of the Father.
No words we can use
are too high for your glory.
No act of devotion
bows too low before your throne.
We come in the name of the Lord
who is almighty
to declare together
our adoration and love.
In the name of Christ. **Amen.**

Confession

Lord,
we confess that we find it so hard
to stand up and to stand out
for what we know is right.
Lord,
we confess that in Joseph's place
we would probably have
taken the easier option.
No one would have blamed us
and the law would have
been on our side.
But you require us to
take steps of faith
to have the courage to listen to you
and not to the clamour of the crowd.

Forgive us, Lord,
and, by your Holy Spirit,
renew our faith
that we may walk in the footsteps
of your faithful people
of every age and in every
place. **Amen.**

Intercession

Isaiah 7:3–4

Lord,
we pray for those who
clamour for peace;
for those who live out their lives
in the midst of civil war
and whose days are punctuated
with abuse and violence,
with injury and death;
for those who are
traumatised with fear
and for those left as orphans
and homeless
by the fighting they are
powerless to end.
Lord of all creation,
hear our prayer.

Lord,
we pray for those who
clamour for hope;

for those who seek to
bury their despair
under their addiction
to work and to leisure,
to home and to family,
to drink and to drugs;
for those who have no purpose in life
and for those whose hopes
have been lost
in a well of selfishness,
self-centredness, and self-sufficiency.
Lord of all creation,
hear our prayer.

Lord,
we pray for those who
clamour for life;
for those who have lost everything
in [*name any recent tragedy*]
that has robbed them of
home and family
and for those whose lives
now hang by a thread,
as with empty stomachs
and unseeing eyes
they wait the promised aid
that will allow them to cheat death
for one more day.
Lord of all creation,
hear our prayer.

Lord,
we pray for those who
clamour for others;
for those who cry out for those
whose voices we have not heard;
for those who long to trade fairly
without the need for charity;
for those whose presence
stays hidden
beneath the cardboard
shelters they call home;
for the work of Christian
Aid, Save the Children,
Tearfund, Action for Children,
Amnesty International,
and Shelter.
Lord of all creation,
hear our prayer.

Lord,
we pray for those who
clamour in silence;
for those who ache deep inside
and for those whose hurt,
pain, and sorrow
are beyond what mere
words can tell;
for those whose voices are still
and for those who would cry out
if only they could still
remember their name;
for those who clamour for
justice for others
and for those who feel
love and forgiveness
has left them behind.
Lord of all creation,
hear our prayer.

Lord,
we pray for ourselves
and the clamour we
should be making
in the name of our God
whose love never ends;
of our Saviour whose sacrifice
is our pathway to hope
and of the Holy Spirit
by whose presence and power
we can clamour at all.
Lord of all creation,
hear our prayer.

Lord,
if you were not our hope,
our peace and our life
our clamour would be in vain;
our prayers, empty mutterings,
and our deepest longings
would remain unfulfilled.
But you are the
sovereign, Saviour, and Lord
who has promised to be with us
to the end
and beyond.
Lord of all creation,
hear our prayer. Amen.

CHRISTMAS DAY

Prayer of Approach

John 1:14

The Christ-child has come
and we will sing his praises.
The Christ-child has come
and we will confess his glory.
The Christ-child has come
and he is Immanuel.
The Christ-child has come
and he is the Prince of Peace.
The Christ-child has come
and he will reign for ever and ever.
The Christ-child has come
and he comes that we might
know the Father.
The Christ-child has come
and now he waits
for us to make him room
in our lives today.
The Christ-child has come
and he will come again
as Lord. **Amen.**

Praise

Isaiah 9:6

Lord,
every year it's the same;
our thoughts are guided to that event
two thousand years ago.
We sing our familiar carols
and they warm our hearts.
We listen to the story
of an angel, of shepherds,
of Mary and Joseph,
and a baby in a manger.

And every year it's the same:
we are left a little unsure
of just what we are doing—and why!

Somewhere deep inside we are aware
that we have reduced your Christmas
to tinsel, turkey, and a
time of 'good cheer'.
It is our annual escape
from the troubles and problems
we face in our world for
the rest of the year.
It is as if the story of
Christmas is true—
only so long as we sing our carols—
but we obstinately refuse to allow
the birth of the Christ-child
to lower the drawbridge to
the castle of our life.

We have not only locked you out
of our Christmas celebrations,
but we even look forward
to when 'everything will
be back to normal'
and 'Christmas is over
for another year'.

But you are Immanuel.

You came and you did not go.
You came and you lived and
died and rose again.
You came—and your coming means
that nothing can ever really
be the same again.

Come, Lord Jesus, come.

Come now, come again.
Come that your coming will mean
that the whole world will confess that
Jesus Christ is Lord,
to the glory of God the
Father. **Amen.**

Confession

Isaiah 9:2

Lord,
forgive us when we try
to celebrate Christmas
but give no thought
to your coming.

Lord,
help us to keep the wonder
of Immanuel
at the heart of all
that we allow to fill our Christmas.

Lord,
enable us to give you
the thanks and praise
that you deserve,
for your love that was made real
in the coming of the Christ-child.

Lord,
give us that assurance
that as your coming
as the babe of Bethlehem
was the fulfilment
of your promise given long ago,
so we can trust your promise
to come again. **Amen.**

Intercession

Luke 2:6

Think of someone you know
who will be on their own
this Christmas
and ask for God's peace
to be upon them.

Think of someone you know
who has lost their job
and who will be facing an
uncertain Christmas.

Think of someone you know
who will be celebrating 'Xmas'
but will give no thought to
the King of Kings.

Think of someone you know
whose days are filled with
sadness and pain
and who needs the touch
of love and kindness.

Think of those around the world
whose Christmas will be filled
with hatred and war
and who have yet to know
the Prince of Peace.

Think of those who will be
sleeping rough this Christmas,
those many people in our local
community without a home
and for whom like their Saviour
there is still no room.

Think of those we have been
asked to remember …

Think of yourself and all
that you must face
in the coming days of this week
in the knowledge that the
Christ-child has come.

We bring our prayers in
the name of the one
who was, is, and always
will be Immanuel,
and Jesus is his name. **Amen.**

FIRST SUNDAY OF CHRISTMAS

Prayer of Approach

Psalm 148:1

Lord,
as we come to lift up our
voices in praise
and our hearts in thanksgiving
we join with the billions
of worshippers
across the centuries and
around the world
and all the hosts of heaven
as we bring our sacrifice of praise
to the living God. **Amen.**

Meditation

Isaiah 63:7

When you are facing difficulties
at work or at home
say, 'Immanuel,
God is with me.'
When your family is under pressure
and you don't know
which way to turn
say, 'Immanuel,
God is with me.'
When you are at odds with yourself
and feeling lost and alone
say, 'Immanuel,
God is with me.'
When those you love
and for whom you are concerned
are facing sadness, sorrow,
and all kinds of opposition
say, 'Immanuel,
God is with me.'
When you have questions
for which you don't have the answer
and you have no answer
for those who are asking
the questions of life
say, 'Immanuel,
God is with me.'
When you are filled with
hope, peace, and joy
and when the bottom drops
out of your world
don't forget to remember to say,
'Immanuel,
God is with me
always.' **Amen.**

Intercession

Matthew 2:10

Lord, we light this candle
and we pray for those
who are ill or in hospital
and who do not know
what the future holds for them.
May the light of the Christ-child
give us hope.

Lord, we light this candle
and we pray for those
who live in the midst of war
and every moment is
dark with danger.

May the light of the Christ-child
give us hope.

Lord, we light this candle
and we pray for those
whose homes are filled
with the darkness
of sadness and loss;
for those who remember with tears
those they have loved but see no more.
In a moment of silence we pray
especially for those known to us
whose life and witness for Christ
has filled many lives with the light
and the love of God.
May the light of the Christ-child
give us hope.

Lord, we light this candle
and we pray for those
who have lost their jobs
and are facing times of great hardship.
May the light of the Christ-child
give us hope.

Lord, we light this candle
and we pray for ourselves,
for those things we face
at home, at school, or at work
that make each day seem very dark.
May the light of the Christ-child
give us hope.

Lord, we light this candle
and we pray for those known to us;
for those who are near to us
but are not yet near to you;
for those for whom we are concerned
and whose lives are coloured
by darkness.
May the light of the Christ-child
give us hope.

We ask our prayers in
the name of Jesus,
the light of the world. **Amen.**

SECOND SUNDAY OF CHRISTMAS

Prayer of Approach

Psalm 147:1

Lord,
your name is honoured
in all the world
and your praises will last for ever.
By your Holy Spirit,
may we offer worship to
the King of Kings
and celebrate the glory of your
wonderful name. **Amen.**

Praise

Jeremiah 31:10–12

What name shall we give him
and how shall he be made known?
We call him our friend
and our Saviour;
to us he is master and King.
Shall we declare him as
sovereign, almighty,
and the source of joy never-ending?

The God that we worship
is more than the sum of all
that we can proclaim.
His wisdom is too great
for mere finite minds
and his mercy leaves us
breathlessly asking for more.
His grace is utterly overwhelming
and his power beyond
all we can imagine or sing.

But his love is the reason for
our peace and our joy
and his presence is the driving force
of the worship we offer.

What name shall we give him?
He is the Lord—
in whose name we offer
all our worship
and our prayers of praise. **Amen.**

Confession

Matthew 2:2

Lord,
we confess that like the wise men
we set out with great hope
and determination
to follow wherever you
might lead us.

But once we take our eye
from the light of Christ
we find ourselves
wandering aimlessly.
We almost forget the reason
why we are here
and we lose sight of the
purpose of our lives.

Lord,
we confess that you are the
light of the world
and we commit ourselves to follow
in the footsteps of your wise men.
We know that only as we open our
hearts and lives to you once more
will our lives be engaged in
that purpose for which
you gave us life. **Amen.**

Intercession

John 1:9

Prepare a set of ten candles. Light a new candle as you begin each prayer.

We light this candle
for those whose lives are in
the darkness of pain—
of body, mind, or spirit;
for those who ache within as a sign
of their anguish and deep concern.

silence

We light this candle
for those whose memories are
covered in darkness;
for those who are still hurting inside
because of what was said or done to
them or denied them years ago.

silence

We light this candle
for those whose future looks very dark;
for those facing the cost
of wrong decisions
and the bleak horizon of
emptiness and loss through
no fault of their own.

silence

We light this candle
for those who are overwhelmed by
the darkness of the sickness within;
for those whose lives will
never be the same
and for those who have
little future left.

silence

We light this candle
for those who are
darkening their lives
with the addiction to drugs,
drink, or gambling;
for those whose lifestyle is clouding
the lives of those nearest to them.

silence

We light this candle
for those who daily face the
darkness of hopelessness;
for those who sleep rough,
and for those on the downward
spiral that is leading to
a life on the street.

silence

We light this candle
for the darkness of nations;
for those who see no alternative to
violence and the terror it creates,
in what they see as their struggle
for justice and freedom.

silence

We light this candle
for those whose darkness
is all in their minds;
for those who are so overwhelmed
by life and by living
they see only the darkness
that shuts out the light.

silence

We light this candle
for those who hide from the
darkness and pretend all is light;
for those who close their eyes to
the hurt of their neighbour
and the cry of the poor.

silence

We light this candle
for ourselves as we offer to
God our darkness within;
we leave our unspoken hurt,
sadness, and loss
with the one who is forever
the light of the world.

silence

Lord,
you are the light in our darkness
and our hope in times of despair;
you are our courage when we
know we have failed;
you are the way when the
pathway is unclear;
you are our strength when
we might fall;
and you are our Lord
and the light that conquers the
deepest darkness of all.

We bring our prayers in
the name of Christ,
the world's light and ours. **Amen.**

FIRST SUNDAY IN ORDINARY TIME

Prayer of Approach

Psalm 29:2

Lord,
by your Holy Spirit, enable
us to give you glory;

by the power of your grace may
we worship you as you deserve.
Your name is the Lord Almighty
and you reign over all things.
Teach us to sing your praise
as we join with the hosts
of heaven. **Amen.**

Praise

Isaiah 42:9–10a

Lord,
how can we not sing our
song of glory?
How can we not give you
our heartfelt thanks and praise?
How can we not long to
know you more
and trust you with the
whole of our lives?

Lord,
we sing because you are
our great creator.
Everything we see and hear,
everything we touch and hold,
everything we watch and
think we understand,
everything that is good
and true and worthy
finds its origins in the
heart of our God.

Lord,
we sing because you are
our great sustainer.
Every moment of every day,
every breath we breathe,
every discovery we make,
every good deed and kindness,
every helping hand,
every time someone cares,
understands, and loves
finds its origins in the
heart of our God.

Lord,
we sing because you are
our heavenly Father.
Your almighty power and presence,
your compassion for all
that you have made,
your unfailing mercy
and forgiveness,
your love that reaches out
and welcomes us home,
your Holy Spirit who enables
us to begin again,
your coming to us in the one
who taught us to call
you 'our Father'
find their origin in the
heart of our God.

Lord,
we come to sing our song of glory.
We come to give you our
heartfelt thanks and praise.
We come because we long
to know you more
and trust you with the
whole of our lives.
All praise and thanks to our God.
In the name of Jesus. **Amen.**

Intercession

Acts 10:47

Prepare a bowl of water and seven pebbles. Place a pebble in the water as you finish each prayer.

Lord,
your baptism was the sign of
your eternal sonship

and of your entering into all
that life means to us.
So we bring our prayers in the
knowledge of your glory
and in our experience of
your humanity.
Lord of the waters of baptism,
come and refresh your world.

Lord,
we pray for those who are
hungry in a world of plenty
and for those who have nothing
whilst others have everything;
for those who have lost all that
was precious to them
and for those whose hands reach
out for help to rebuild their lives.
Lord of the waters of baptism,
come and refresh your world.

Lord,
we pray for those who are
longing to learn
and for those with no one
to teach them;
for all teachers, lecturers, and
ministers of education,
that there will be equal
opportunity for everyone.
Lord of the waters of baptism,
come and refresh your world.

Lord,
we pray for those who care
for those in need
and for those whose life of service
brings dignity to others;
for those who give of themselves
in care homes and hospices
and for those whose lives are
enriched by their caring.
Lord of the waters of baptism,
come and refresh your world.

Lord,
we pray for those who serve the
nation as members of parliament
and for those whose faithful service
goes unnoticed by the media;
for those whose passion for truth
and for justice is undimmed
and for those in high office who
carry great burdens for us all.
Lord of the waters of baptism,
come and refresh your world.

Lord,
we pray for those who hold office
in the life of your church
and for those who work unseen
and unknown for your glory;
for those whose pastoral care is an
expression of their love of Christ
and for those who share the love
of Jesus in all they do or say.
Lord of the waters of baptism,
come and refresh your world.

Lord,
we pray for those who work
for closer relationships
between churches
and for those whose daily
prayer and service is that
we may all be one;
for those who reach out across
the foolish barriers we erect
and for those whose life in the
Spirit destroys the stumbling
blocks we protect.
Lord of the waters of baptism,
come and refresh your world.

Lord,
we pray for ourselves
and our church,
that you will touch us and mould
us, hold us and love us.
We pray, renew your church in
the baptism of the Holy Spirit,
that we may worship and witness
to the Lord of all glory.
Lord of the waters of baptism,
come and refresh your world.

In the name of Christ, Son of
God, source of grace. **Amen.**

SECOND SUNDAY IN ORDINARY TIME

Prayer of Approach

Psalm 40:11

Your hands upon our
lives give us hope
and your gentle touch shows us
the way that we should go;
your ever-seeing eye warns us
of the paths of danger
and your grace-filled heart is
always reaching out in love.

Father, our Father,
we come to praise you for who you
are and for all you have done
and we cannot hold ourselves back
from offering you the worship of
our thankful hearts. **Amen.**

Thanksgiving

Isaiah 49:5–6

Lord,
we have come to thank you
for the multitude of grace-gifts
that flow from your hands.
From the beginning
it was your purpose that we
should know and love you
at the very heart of our being.

When you granted us the gift of life
it was in order that we might
experience that fullness of joy
that comes from walking step
by step and day by day
in the presence of our living God.

Lord,
we are overwhelmed with a gratitude
that is impossible to put
into mere words
and a thankfulness that springs
from the very depths of our lives.

We thank you, Lord,
that you have given our lives
a purpose vast and wide
and a hope that alone
finds its fulfilment
in your grace-filled majesty
and holiness.

It seems almost too simple a
thing to say thank you
and an injustice to your glory
to sing your praises.
But you delight in our love
and you rejoice in our worship.
By your Holy Spirit, our words
are filled with your glory
and our praises are lifted to
your throne of grace.

We bring our thanks and our
praise in the name of Jesus,
the source of your grace and the
reason for our thanksgiving. **Amen.**

Intercession
John 1:43–46

Lord,
we pray for those who are losing hope
and for those who can see no way out
of the difficulties they are facing;
for those who are battling with
depression, anxiety, and despair
and for those who feel as if
they are losing the fight;
for those struggling with the onset
of life-threatening illness
and for those filled with
uncertainty as they await
their medical diagnosis.
May the healing love of God
flow through their lives.
The Lord hears our prayer.
Thanks be to God.

Lord,
we pray for those who are
longing for peace
and for those still seeking
the pathway
to reconciliation and renewal;
for those who find themselves
trapped in the midst of a war zone
and for those who yearn
for their homes
to become an oasis of tranquillity
and their hearts a place
of contentment.
May the renewing love of God
flow through their lives.
The Lord hears our prayer.
Thanks be to God.

Lord,
we pray for those in positions
of leadership and authority
and for those who are daily
making decisions
that will affect people's lives
for good or for ill;
for those who find their
choices are limited
by the demands that others
lay upon them
and for those whose desire to
be of service to others
has been lost in their quest
for personal power and glory.
May the cleansing love of God
flow through their lives.
The Lord hears our prayer.
Thanks be to God.

Lord,
we pray for our nation torn
apart by its divisions
of wealth and poverty, of
colour and gender
and for the continuing slide
into a secular void
as God's presence is usurped by
the gods of status and power;
for those whose behaviour and
attitudes are tearing families apart
and for those whose desire to
treat anything as acceptable
is undermining the need
for responsibility at the
heart of everything.
May the transforming love
of God flow through the
heart of the nation.
The Lord hears our prayer.
Thanks be to God.

Lord,
we pray for those whose lives
are weighed down

by the pressures they face by
the demands of their work
and for those sinking under
burden of their concern for
their home and family;
for those whose search for
meaningful employment
has come to nothing
and for those whose exclusion
from the opportunity to
use their gifts and skills
means they are losing their sense of
well-being and purpose in life.
May the hope-filled love of God
flow through their lives.
The Lord hears our prayer.
Thanks be to God.

Lord,
we pray for those in our world who
are still waiting to have a share
in its wealth and rich resources
from which they are excluded
and for those who know
they have no part in its
abundant opportunities;
for those who are disabled and
are trying to live in a world
designed for the fit and well
and for those who are single
and feel excluded
in our family-orientated
communities.
May the courage-giving love of
God flow through their lives.
The Lord hears our prayer.
Thanks be to God.

Lord,
in your presence we pray for those
for whom we are concerned.

silence

We also pray for ourselves,
for the memories that haunt us,
for the future that concerns us,
and for the present that at
times overwhelms us.

silence

May the amazing love of God
flow through our lives.
The Lord hears our prayer.
Thanks be to God.

We bring our prayers into the
presence of the living God,
whose love and grace changes
everything. **Amen.**

THIRD SUNDAY IN ORDINARY TIME

Prayer of Approach

Psalm 27:1

Father, our Father,
we have not come to escape
from the world
or to hide from the darkness
and despair all around us.
We are here to praise you,
the Lord of glory and the sovereign
at the heart of creation.
In your presence we glimpse
something of your light and hope
for you alone are the
stronghold of our lives.
May our worship reach to
the heights of heaven
that we may be light, hope,
and strength for our
neighbour. **Amen.**

Thanksgiving
Isaiah 9:2

Lord,
we thank you for the way you
are light to each of us
and shine your love upon
all our lives.
We live in a world made dark
by greed, selfishness, and indifference
to the needs of others.
All around we see the evidence
of broken hearts, broken minds,
and broken promises.
Each day we are bombarded with
images from your world
of the hurt, loss, and devastation
which is the experience of so many.
We thank you that, like the Father
of Compassion you are,
you speak tenderly to
all your creation
and you reach out with a touch of
gentleness to your broken world.
We thank you that you have not only
brought light and hope to our lives
but you have done so that
we may be channels of
grace to our neighbour.
We thank you that in Jesus we
have made it crystal clear
that your word of grace will always
be your final statement of hope
and his living presence the sign
of peace for all nations.
Our hearts overflow with
joy and thankfulness
as we remember Jesus came as the
window into the heart of God
and as the sign that always and
everywhere we live and die
in the presence of the one whose
love is for all and for ever.
Lord,
it is only when our hearts
are flooded with gratitude
for your grace
and our lives awash with
thankfulness for the blessings
we have received
that your Holy Spirit can
transform our words of praise
into an act of worship that is worthy
of your mighty name. **Amen.**

Intercession
Matthew 4:12–23

Hold in your mind those who are
facing the darkness of hunger;
those who do not know where their
next meal will come from—
or if it will come at all;
for those who feel starved
of love, joy, and hope.
May the Lord bring light
to those in need.

silence

Hold in your mind those
overwhelmed by the
darkness of bereavement;
those who have lost the one with
whom they shared life's memories
and with whom they experienced
each day's ups and downs;
for those trying to come to terms
with the end of a relationship
or the loss of employment
and the sense of failure and
rejection they feel.
May the Lord bring light
to those in need.

silence

Hold in your mind those engulfed
by the darkness of depression;
those who wrongly blame
themselves for their pit of despair
and long for the colours of
the rainbow to replace
their shades of grey;
for those who feel trapped by the
panic that overwhelms them
and for those unable to
break out into the life God
planned for them.
May the Lord bring light
to those in need.

silence

Hold in your mind those who live
their lives in the darkness of war,
those whose every day is surrounded
by suffering and death
and for young children forced
to leave their time for play
to become soldiers;
for those who are working to
bring peace and reconciliation
and for those whose sole purpose
is to bring terror and fear.
May the Lord bring light
to those in need.

silence

Hold in your mind a friend
or a neighbour walking in
the darkness of doubt;
those for whom life never seems
to be easy and straightforward;
those who have been let
down again and again
by those they thought
they could trust
and those whose experience
of abuse and rejection
makes it hard for them to trust
anyone again, even God.
May the Lord bring light
to those in need.

silence

Hold in your mind those who are
facing the darkness of disaster;
those who have lost everything and
everyone that mattered to them
through the earthquake, fire,
flood, or drought that has
wrecked their lives;
those who are risking their
own lives as they enter
the darkness of others'
and those who are seeking to reach
out with the love of God
as they speak of Christ, the
light of the world.
May the Lord bring light
to those in need.

silence

Hold in your mind the times
of darkness you are facing
and give thanks for those who are
sharing the journey with you.
Hold in your mind the darkness
of those around you.
In the stillness hold them before
God as you promised,
as you now reach out and
hold them in love.
May the Lord bring light
to those in need.

silence

In the name of Christ, the light and the hope of the world. **Amen.**

Dismissal

1 Corinthians 1:18

The Father sends us out in
the name of his Son,
in the power of the Spirit,
and in the light of his grace
and love. **Amen.**

FOURTH SUNDAY IN ORDINARY TIME

Prayer of Approach

Psalm 15:1–2

Lord,
we have come into your presence
and we know that you are holy.
Everything you say and do is right
and we are overwhelmed
by your glory, your power,
and your majesty.

We come painfully aware that we
simply have no right to be here;
nothing we can say or do,
no catalogue of our acts of
love and kindness,
can qualify us as those who are
worthy of your invitation.

Lord,
we come here in the name of Jesus,
who alone can open the way into
the presence of our King.
It is only through his death
and resurrection
that we can be grace-cleansed
and, by your Holy Spirit,
empowered to worship
the one who is Lord of all. **Amen.**

Praise

Micah 6:8

Father,
we praise you for the journey of life
and that you have promised
we will not journey alone.
Each of us longs to find the way
through with a life that satisfies
and the pathway that is
filled with peace.
You have given us your word
that hope, meaning, and purpose
begin and end in your presence.

Through plans, dreams,
and achievements
people of every age and generation
have sought the road
that leads to the ultimate
sense of fulfilment.
All of us allow ourselves to be
lulled into a false security
through the things we
have and hold.

We too have gathered our
wealth and possessions
in the foolish assumption
that these are the things
that mark the road to joy
and contentment.
There are times when even our
gathering for worship
has been a mask to hide our
inner disappointments.

We live in a conditional world
where all too often
help, acceptance, and support
are offered only in response
to standards reached, grades
achieved, requirements met.

Our value and worth are seen in
what we have, and what we are
is tested by earthly and
not heavenly values.

We praise you, our Father,
that you do not withhold
your love from us
until targets are reached
or goals attained.
You do not wait for our commitment
before you desire to soak
us in your grace,
and our lack of confession
does not diminish your
longing to forgive.

We praise you, our Father,
whose love is unconditional
and whose grace, mercy, and
peace are without end.
We are lost for words to express
our joy in your presence
and your faithfulness that goes with
us to the end of every journey.

Your requirement that we
fashion our whole lives
on your merciful and
compassionate nature
is simply the key that
unlocks the door
to your unconditional love,
mercy, and grace that we
can never deserve. **Amen.**

Intercession

1 Corinthians 1:27

Let us hold up before God
the leaders of nations;
those whose foolish greed, self-
interest, and love of power
are robbing their people of the hope
and joy that should be theirs;
and those who are taking seriously the
responsibilities laid upon them.

silence

Let us hold up before God all judges,
magistrates, and probation officers;
those whose task is to apply the law
to those who have acted foolishly,
as they seek to balance justice and
truth with mercy and hope,
and those who find themselves
seeking wisdom in the
hardest places of all.

silence

Let us hold up before God the
young people of our world;
those who are just setting out
on the journey of life
and those who are uncertain which
pathway they should take;
those being drawn by peer pressure
and the lure of a good time
to foolishly sacrifice their
health and their future.

silence

Let us hold up before God
those in life's later years;
those who look back to
opportunities foolishly missed
and those are who still looking
forward to new avenues to explore;
those for whom their age is a barrier
and their health a burden
and those who see each day as the
chance to walk wisely with God.

silence

Let us hold up before God homes
and families near and far;
those relationships that by jealousy,
selfishness, and angry words
are daily being undermined and the
fragility of trust is put to the test;
those whose only concern is to find
food to fill empty stomachs
and those where unconditional love
wisely binds family together.

silence

Let us hold before God those for
whom we are concerned;
those facing times of stress,
illness, or bereavement;
those struggling to cope with
loss of employment;
those whose love of their
Lord has grown cold
and those whose experience
of grace is daily renewed.

silence

Let us hold up before God ourselves
and our lives of each day;
the foolish mistakes we still
grieve over instead of wisely
accepting forgiveness;
the things that hold us back
from deeper commitment to
one another and to God;
the dreams we still have and
the hopes we still hold
that by the grace of God may
yet come to fruition
and bring him the glory and
thanks he deserves.

silence

We have held up our prayers to the
God who listens and answers
and will now trust him and
praise him in the name of
Jesus, our Lord. **Amen.**

FIFTH SUNDAY IN ORDINARY TIME

Prayer of Approach

Psalm 112:1–2

The Lord is our God
and we will praise him.
The Lord gave us life
and he is our Father.
The Lord is our hope
and in him we have placed our trust.
The Lord is the Lord over
all things and for ever
and he is the one alone whom
we worship. **Amen.**

Praise

Isaiah 58:10

Father, we praise you for the
way you have made us;
you have designed us to be a
reflection of your grace.
It is no accident that we are
moved to feed the hungry
or that our hearts ache for those who
struggle on the journey of life.
When we show concern for the lost,
the broken, and the hopeless
it is then that we are looking
through the eyes of our
heavenly Father.

We praise you that we have
been made in your image

and that you intended us to be a
sign of your loving-kindness;
the heavenly mould you used to
fashion and shape our lives
declares the purpose for which
each one of us was created.

We thank you, Father, for showing
us your will for all humankind
and demonstrating your eternal
plan for your precious creation.
From the beginning you
intended the whole of life to
be the arena for worship
and it was your plan that
everything in all creation
should sing your praise.

When you gave us life you planted
within us the desire to worship
and you surrounded us with
a world of beauty to draw
forth our praises.
We experience an emptiness when
we do not focus our lives on you
and a sense of futility when we allow
earthly things to take your place.

Our greatest pleasure is to join
in that endless song of praise
and to add our voices to the
eternal crescendo of glory
that is your worth.
Now you declare your word of
truth and require us to respond;
now you touch our hearts
and seek our love;
now you open our eyes and
show us your mercy;
now you unlock our ears and
demand that we hear the
cry of our neighbour;
now day by day you stand
in our midst that we may
not hide from you;
now you embrace us with
grace that all our days will
be an act of worship.

Father, you never intended
that our praises should be
imprisoned within these walls
or that our worship should cease
at the door of the church.
You call us together, in the name of
your Son, to sing, pray, and praise
so that everything we say and do—
our work and our leisure,
our giving and our caring,
our silence and our speaking,
our aloneness and our embracing,
our trusting and our forgiving,
our serving and our sharing—
have, through the life, death,
and resurrection of Jesus,
been transformed in
all things, everywhere and for ever,
to be part of our song of glory.

Father, receive our song through
Christ, who taught us to
sing your praises. **Amen.**

Intercession

1 Corinthians 2:2

Lord of the empty cross, we
pray for your world,
where civil war and terrorism
crucify the innocent
and the guilty alike.
We pray for those who, through
no fault of their own,
are caught up in fighting,
bloodshed, and ethnic cleansing

and for those so damaged
and traumatised by all
they have experienced
that for them life will never
be the same again.
Lord of the empty tomb,
come heal our brokenness.

Lord of the empty cross, we
pray for our neighbour,
for whether they live next door,
across the road, or across the world
you have made them our
responsibility.
We pray for those with no hope,
no purpose, and no love
and for those whose bitterness and
closed hearts and closed minds
have built a wall of self-centredness
that nothing seems to penetrate.
Lord of the empty tomb,
come heal our brokenness.

Lord of the empty cross, we pray
for the children of your world
whose experiences will go with
them through the years;
for those who have been so
badly used and abused
they have become case-hardened
to love and compassion;
for those starved of food for their
bodies and for their minds
and for those deprived of
unconditional love that would
have given them hope.
Lord of the empty tomb,
come heal our brokenness.

Lord of the empty cross, we pray
for the families of your world,
where relationships, once secure,
are now under great strain;
for those in danger of losing
their jobs and their homes
and for those already facing
the indignity of being
made redundant;
for those who have joined the
world of the 'have nots'
created by the irresponsibility, self-
interest, and greed of the 'haves'.
Lord of the empty tomb,
come heal our brokenness.

Lord of the empty cross,
we pray for the leaders of
nations of your world;
for those whose genuine
concern for their people
shines as a light of hope
in a world turned an ugly grey
by the corruption and self-
centredness of others;
for those whose decisions will
change the lives of millions
and for those weighed down
by the choices they know
they must make.
Lord of the empty tomb,
come heal our brokenness.

Lord of the empty cross, we pray for
the sick and dying in your world;
for those who today will suffer and
die alone with no one to care
and for those in hospital or hospice
who are surrounded by the
compassion that should
be offered to all;
for those badly injured as they
answered the call of duty
here and around the world

and for those who today will receive
the news of a lost loved one.
Lord of the empty tomb,
come heal our brokenness.

Lord of the empty cross,
we pray for ourselves
and those for whom we
are concerned;
for members of our church, our
community, and our family
that the name of Christ crucified
will be their hope and their light;
for all that we know we must face
in the coming days and hours,
that the presence of Jesus will
mean that we journey in faith.
Lord of the empty tomb,
come heal our brokenness.

We bring our prayers in the
name of Christ crucified,
risen, and ascended,
our hope and the hope of
the world. **Amen.**

SIXTH SUNDAY IN ORDINARY TIME

Prayer of Approach

Psalm 119:7

Lord,
we have gathered for worship
but it is your Word that
brings us hope;
we have come to sing your praises
but it is your almighty power
that declares your glory;
we have come in the name of Christ,
your word in human guise,
whose living presence transforms
our imperfect offering
into songs of heaven from
hearts made new by the
Word of God. **Amen.**

Confession

Matthew 5:23–24

Father,
we delight in your love and
rejoice in your kindness,
and your grace all but
overwhelms us.
You are our creator, our
sustainer, and our Saviour,
the one to whom we owe thanks
and praise for all eternity.

But, Father, your Word teaches
us that you are a holy God
who demands that we are holy,
set apart for your service.
You have left us no room
for compromise
and second best is not something
for which you will settle.

We confess that deep within us
we know how we fall short
of being the reflection of your
holiness we were intended to be.
There are times when your presence
makes us feel uncomfortable;
when we are reminded of how
little of your love shines
through our darkened lives
and how much we allow our
bitterness, our grudges, and
broken relationships
to remain a barrier to our praises
reaching the heights of heaven.

By your grace enable us to deal
with the barriers we have built,

that through your Holy Spirit
we may become channels of
reconciliation and hope.

We ask our prayer in the
name of Christ,
who died for all. **Amen.**

Praise

Deuteronomy 30:19

Lord,
the whole earth sings your praises
and everywhere we look
shouts your glory.
Again and again you direct our gaze
to the wonders that flowed
from your hands
and you leave us breathless by
the scale of your universe.
Songs of thanksgiving are the
only responses we can make
and words of praise tumble
uncontrollably
from lives touched by your grace
and hearts set on fire by
your Holy Spirit.

There is nowhere we can look that
doesn't speak of your grace
and wherever we travel you remind
us that you are with us.
Our greatest desire is that our every
word would speak your glory
and that all our thoughts would
bring honour to your name.
We long for the day when our
praises will be truly worthy of you
and the whole of our lives will
be a song to your majesty.

We know that no song of
praise is too great for you
and every prayer adds to the
totality of creation's devotion.
You speak into our hearts
the word of grace
and an anthem of thanksgiving
wells up within us.
In those moments when your
presence presses close upon us,
even in times of stillness
and quietness,
we experience a sense of being
truly alive as never before.

So you issue your mighty challenge
that rings from one end of
eternity to the other
and your call reaches out
and touches the very
heart of our existence.
Again and again you have
affirmed your love for us
and in Christ demonstrated its
reality in flesh and blood.
If we had dared to ponder what
might be the limits of your grace
your crucified Son provides
the ultimate answer.

You offer us life, hope,
peace, and fulfilment
and you desire that we
should be set free from all
other entanglements.
You long for us to focus our
praises and our worship
solely on your glory
and to ring-fence our devotion
in the name of your Son.

Lord,
we want to choose the life and the
blessings you have promised

and to have our lives filled to
the brim with your love.
We will listen to your voice and
seek to hold fast to you,
not simply for our blessing, but
for the honour and the glory
of your wonderful, wonderful
name. **Amen.**

Intercession

1 Corinthians 3:9

Our prayers are for those who
are God's fellow workers—
those who know him and
those who don't;
those whose service is a sign of
their love and commitment;
and those who even though
they are unaware of it are
also God's fellow workers.

Let us pray.

We pray for those whose work of
caring is in the wider community;
for those who work in nursing
homes and homes for the elderly
as they seek to provide an
atmosphere of peace
and understanding;
for care workers, social workers,
and meals on wheels volunteers,
whose support enables
many to continue to live
in their own homes.
Lord, your sovereign love
knows no limits
and your grace is for all.

We pray for those who work
with young people;
for youth workers, church
family workers, and Sunday
school volunteers
who seek to support and share
faith with those in their charge;
for the leaders of youth groups,
youth fellowships, and
all uniformed groups
whose generous giving of
their skills and their time
is a blessing to others.
Lord, your sovereign love
knows no limits
and your grace is for all.

We pray for those whose work is
a blessing to the community;
for those who serve as police officers,
magistrates, and probation officers
who seek to bring change to
the convicted and hope and
peace to the community;
for those who are vital to
the continued health and
well-being of us all
as they recycle our waste, clean our
streets, and collect our rubbish.
Lord, your sovereign love
knows no limits
and your grace is for all.

We pray for those who work in
the National Health Service;
for physiotherapists, occupational
therapists, audiologists,
and radiographers
and for porters, cleaners, and
secretaries who silently
work in the background;
for health visitors, midwives,
GPs, health centre staff,
opticians, and dentists

and for doctors and nurses
and all who care for the
health of the nation.
Lord, your sovereign love
knows no limits
and your grace is for all.

We pray for those involved
in education;
for examiners, lecturers, and
college and university staff
and for full-time and part-
time students in the
challenges they face;
for primary and secondary school
teachers, teaching assistants
and for those who work with
those with special needs.
Lord, your sovereign love
knows no limits
and your grace is for all.

We pray for all who care
for the planet;
for those involved in scientific
study and research
and for those who make us aware of
our impact on the environment;
for those who discover the
wonders of the universe
and for those who help us to see the
hand of our creator in all things.
Lord, your sovereign love
knows no limits
and your grace is for all.

We pray for those who offer care
to the wider church family;
for pastoral visitors,
ministers, and deacons
who offer fellowship, a listening
ear, and love to the members
and for every church member who
is a source of blessing to others
as they seek to offer Christian
love to their neighbour.
Lord, your sovereign love
knows no limits
and your grace is for all.

Lord, we are all your fellow workers
and we offer our prayers as
servants of Christ. **Amen.**

SEVENTH SUNDAY IN ORDINARY TIME

Prayer of Approach

Leviticus 19:1–2

Lord,
to enter the presence of
the living God
is the most powerful experience
we can ever know;
to offer worship to the
Lord of all creation
is the highest task to which
we can ever attain;
to allow you to speak and for
us to listen to your voice
can be the most awe-inspiring
moment of our lives.

Lord,
your call to be a holy people
living holy lives—
hearts and minds and lives
set apart for you—
is only possible when you
dwell within us
and, by your Holy Spirit, empower
us for holiness. **Amen.**

Praise

Matthew 5:41

Father,
we praise you that the lifestyle
to which you call us
and the way of life that
you require of us
is nothing short of an utter
and total revolution.

You do not ask that we live
lives improved by religion
or to allow our behaviour
and our attitudes
to be modified by the outward
rituals of worship.
It was never your will that we
should try harder to be kind
or that by dint of our own effort
we might somehow be able to satisfy
the standard your love demands.

We remember the lesson
that Samuel was shown
all those years ago,
that while we see only the
outward appearance,
you alone can see the heart
of our inward desires.
We praise you that though
you see us as we really are
and you know us more fully
than we know ourselves,
you still long to dwell even within
such poor vessels as ourselves.

You are the God of grace
and it is because of your
undeserved love
that it remains your will that we
should be mirrors of your grace.
You are the master builder
of all things
and the architect of all that
was, and is, and will be.
You are the Father of creation
and nothing and no one can
escape the gaze of your
love upon their lives
or the grace-touch that can
make them whole.

You are our amazing God
who not only sets the bar of your
life-requirements so very high
but, praise be to you, Lord,
your grace makes it possible
for us to reach the heights
and your indwelling Spirit alone
can heal the brokenness within.

You do not measure our lives by the
standards of your fallen world
but by the life of Christ—
crucified, risen, and ascended.
Your grace is for all and
your grace alone
can liberate us from our
earthly shackles,
that we might live the new life
and live it for your glory. **Amen.**

Intercession

1 Corinthians 3:18

Lord,
we pray for those that the
world counts as fools;
for those who seek to act
as peacemakers
between the Israelis and
the Palestinians
and for those who work for
harmony and understanding

where none seems to exist.
Lord, in your wisdom,
teach us to be fools.

Lord,
we pray for those that the
world counts as fools;
for those who try to be good
Samaritans to their neighbours,
even in the midst of
painful rejection,
and for those who continue
to offer God's grace
in the face of misunderstanding
and ridicule.
Lord, in your wisdom,
teach us to be fools.

Lord,
we pray for those that the
world counts as fools;
for those who are ready
to offer forgiveness
to those who have hurt them most
and for those who are prepared
to take the initiative
to bring reconciliation and
healing at great cost.
Lord, in your wisdom,
teach us to be fools.

Lord,
we pray for those that the
world counts as fools;
for those whose hearts go out
to the lost and the broken,
as they reach out to those
with no home,
and for those who no
longer count the cost
of what it means to be a
servant of Christ.
Lord, in your wisdom,
teach us to be fools.

Lord,
we pray for those that the
world counts as fools;
for those who offer
compassion and dignity
to those who no longer remember
who they really are
and for those whose words and
deeds are a sign of hope
to those overwhelmed by
doubts and depression.
Lord, in your wisdom,
teach us to be fools.

Lord,
we pray for those that the
world counts as fools;
for those who have fought
against injustice
and have brought hope and
purpose to those around them;
for those who have coped with
rejection and broken promises
and who, by God's grace,
have attained a peace that
seemed beyond them.
Lord, in your wisdom,
teach us to be fools.

Lord,
we pray for those that the
world counts as fools;
for those who take the name
of Jesus on their lips
as a sign of their love of Christ
and their neighbour
and for those who bring light,
peace, and courage

to those overcome with the
darkness all around them.
Lord, in your wisdom,
teach us to be fools.

Lord,
we pray for those that the
world counts as fools;
for ourselves and the pride
and fear of rejection
that prevent us living each
day as Christ's fools
and for those moments at
home and at work
where we might offer the
foolishness of God's love.
Lord, in your wisdom,
teach us to be fools.

We bring our prayers in
the name of Christ
who was and is the foolish
wisdom of the Father. **Amen.**

TRANSFIGURATION SUNDAY

Prayer of Approach

Psalm 99:3

Lord,
our worship can never reach
the heights of your glory
or sound the depths of
your love and mercy.
You are the Holy One,
whose greatness is beyond
understanding
and whose grace enables us to
stand before the Lord.

Lord,
hold us in your grace,
lift us by your mercy,
and may the awesomeness
of your name
transform our praises for
your glory. **Amen.**

Adoration

Matthew 17:1–2

Lord,
there is a song in our hearts,
a song of adoration.
We long to know you more
and experience your presence
every moment of every day.

Lord,
there is a song in our hearts,
a song of adoration.
We cannot contain our joy
as we look into the manger
or stand at the foot of
the empty cross
and the empty tomb.

Lord,
there is a song in our hearts,
a song of adoration.
Here and now
and everywhere we go
we will sing in adoration of
your holy name. **Amen.**

Intercession

2 Peter 1:16

Prepare a small table on which to place items as you pray.

Newspaper

Lord,
we pray for the world;
the hurt and pain,
the suffering and loss,

the deceit and the despair,
the success and the failure,
that are recorded on these pages.
Each report of robbery and violence,
every story of delight and disaster,
touches the lives of the famous
and impacts the days of
the unknown.

silence

Lord, we pray for your world,
that Christ may reign there.

Bowl of food

Lord,
we pray for those who are hungry;
for those in a world of plenty
who have no idea when
they will eat again;
for those who daily depend
on the work of the aid agencies
for whatever food they are given
and for those who must
watch helplessly
as their children swell up and die;
for those who are being
robbed of their future
by corruption or civil war.

silence

Lord, we pray for your world,
that Christ may reign there.

Walking stick

Lord,
we pray for the elderly
and for those left behind
in a society that despises old age,
that is designed for the
young and successful;
for those who feel they are forgotten
in a world that prizes
success at any price
and those who through
the weakness of age
are experiencing the indignity
of dependency on others.

silence

Lord, we pray for your world,
that Christ may reign there.

Mobile phone

Lord,
we pray for those who live
and die in isolation
in a world that thrives on
communication;
for those who by their disability
are trapped in their own
dark, silent world;
for those who have no one who cares
what happens to them
and have no one with whom
they can share their hopes
and their fears.

silence

Lord, we pray for your world,
that Christ may reign there.

Bottle of medicine

Lord,
we pray for those who are
ill or in hospital
and for those who work

to restore them to health;
for those who took
their continued health and
fitness for granted
and for those now robbed
of the years they thought
would be theirs;
for those faced with the
responsibility
of caring for loved ones
and for those who know they
may soon be alone.

silence

Lord, we pray for your world,
that Christ may reign there.

Book

Lord,
we pray for those involved
in the world of education;
for teachers, lecturers,
writers, and students
and for all who are involved
in learning;
for those with no qualifications
and for those, who through
no fault of their own,
are unable to read or write;
for those whose skills are
no longer required
in our modern technological society
and for those marginalised
by the information highway.

silence

Lord, we pray for your world,
that Christ may reign there.

Door key

Lord,
we pray for those whose homes
are places of love, trust, and joy;
for those where there is
stress, anger, and bitterness
and for those being brought
to the point of breakup
or breakdown;
for those with no place to call home
and for those whose home
is a cardboard box
and whose bed tonight will
be the pavement.

silence

Lord, we pray for your world,
that Christ may reign there.

Address book

Lord,
we pray for all those we
know and love
and for any we know to be
in special need of any kind.

silence

Lord,
we pray for ourselves
and all we are facing and
all we must face
in the days and weeks that lie ahead.

Lord,
we pray for any we know
who do not know you as
Saviour and Lord

and for those who once
worshipped with us
that they may yet return to
the throne of grace.

silence

Lord, we pray for your world,
**that Christ may reign
there. Amen.**

FIRST SUNDAY IN LENT

Prayer of Approach

Psalm 32:11

Lord,
how can we not give thanks
and how can we not offer praises
to the King of Kings
and the Sovereign of all that
was, and is, and will be?

We have come,
not to sing hymns and to
say our prayers;
our reason for being here
is not that we might feel better.

We are here to declare our love,
to proclaim your glory,
and offer adoration
as we worship you with hearts set
on fire by your grace. **Amen.**

Confession

Matthew 4:1

Lord,
we confess that sometimes we
walk with unseeing eyes
and with ears that are closed
to the wonders
you have placed all around us.

We thank you for opportunities
simply to 'be';
to be aware of your presence
in the majesty of the trees,
the softness of the undergrowth,
and the vibrancy of birdsong
that fills the air.

We confess that it is for all
too brief a moment
you have captured all our senses.
It is as if our sight is clearer,
our hearing so much sharper,
and the aroma of the woods and fields
fill us with unspeakable joy.

Lord,
we confess that we see
your fingerprints
not only in the world around us
but in the love, care, and skill
of those who serve you in
the care of others.
We confess that we take all
these blessings for granted
and we fail to be truly
grateful to those
to whom, each day, we are
utterly dependent.

May your grace sustain
them in their service
and us in our thankfulness
that your love may flow in all
we do in your name. **Amen.**

Thanksgiving

Romans 5:19

Lord,
once more your love, mercy, and grace
leave us completely stunned.
Every day you seek to open our eyes

to see, as if for the first time,
the glories of your creation
and to experience the sheer joy
of witnessing your touch
on every facet of life.

Again and again you open our ears
to the sounds that break upon us
and the gentle music of life with
which your handiwork abounds.
The ripple of a mountain
stream, the breeze that
moves amongst the leaves,
and the beating of the waves
upon the shore.

Everywhere we look the colours
we see beat upon our eyes
and enrich our pathway through
life each day in your world.
The music of a thousand
musicians and the work of
artists down the centuries
has added more to our lives
than we could ever find the
words to express our joy.
Writers and painters, singers
and dancers, poets and those
who seek to entertain us
have added more to the totality
of our lives than we could
have hoped to have received.

The customs and culture of
every nation add to the
kaleidoscope of life
and each voice is part of
the rich tapestry that
constantly surrounds us.
The friendly smile and the hand
that welcomes carries an
important message of peace
to tell us we are not alone,
that we belong and we
matter to someone.

Lord,
it is the colour of your grace
that enriches the soul
and the warmth of your love that
makes each day worthwhile.
No song we can sing is too great
to offer you in thankful praise
and no word of prayer and
worship is too rich to be meat
at the table of your mercy.

You are the one who reigns forever
supreme in the heavens of all ages;
there has never been a God
like you from one end of
eternity to the other—
and there never will be.
You alone are the Lord of
time, space, and eternity.
You are the Lord who is sovereign
over all things, and for ever.

We thank you that your
sovereignty is shot through
with the grace that sets us free
and the love that brings healing,
renewal, and wholeness.
When you blessed us with the
precious gift of free will
it did not take us long to pollute
your gift with our selfishness
and to destroy its possibilities
for good with our determined
self-centredness.
Today we bow before you,
the Lord of creation, and
confess with gratitude
our hope is found in Christ alone.

Thank you for Jesus;
thank you for his victory;
thank you for the hope he brings;
thank you that through his
death and resurrection
he reclaims and restores what was lost.

All thanks and praise to our
life-renewing Lord. **Amen.**

Intercession

Genesis 2:15

Lord,
we pray for those whose whole
world has been torn apart
and for those who have lost
everything and everyone
that mattered to them;
for those who have lost
home and family through
earthquake, cyclone, or flood
and for those whose way of life and
livelihood have been destroyed.
Lord, whose presence
is our strength,
teach us to help and to care.

Lord,
we pray for those whose lives are
blighted by sickness and disease
and for those who live in places
where there is no help for
those who can't pay;
for those suffering the
effects of HIV/AIDS
and for those whose disability
robs them of the freedom
to work and to play.
Lord, whose presence
is our strength,
teach us to help and to care.

Lord,
we pray for those who bear a
burden of concern for the planet
and for those whose research
demonstrates the damage
we have done;
for those with the power and
the authority to influence our
care for the environment
and for those whose actions are
robbing future generations
of the resources they need.
Lord, whose presence
is our strength,
teach us to help and to care.

Lord,
we pray for those who are
numbered among the millions
with no voice and no home
and for those whose colour
or low status has left them
without hope or real purpose;
for those who have little
or no share in a world of
wealth and possessions
and for those whose earthly
success blinds them to the care
they owe to their neighbour.
Lord, whose presence
is our strength,
teach us to help and to care.

Lord,
we pray for those whose whole lives
are focused on the here and now
and for those whose hopes
are anchored on what they
can see and touch;
for those who forget to walk in the
garden of life with their Lord

and for those who yearn for hope
and for purpose but fail to
look to the source of all life.
Lord, whose presence
is our strength,
teach us to help and to care.

Lord,
we pray for those who work
in the garden of life
and whose task is to ensure that
there is food for us to eat;
for those who farm the land or the
seas at great risk to themselves
and for those whose work
brings food to our homes.
Lord, whose presence
is our strength,
teach us to help and to care.

Lord,
we pray for ourselves and for those
for whom we are concerned;
for those facing a painful
journey or a period of life-
changing decisions;
for those struggling with doubt,
despair, or depression
and for those weighed down
with a sense of guilt that
is false or is real.
Lord, whose presence
is our strength,
teach us to help and to care.

We bring our prayers in the
name of the One, who gave
us the garden of life
and whose promise—'I am with you
always'—remains true. **Amen.**

SECOND SUNDAY IN LENT

Prayer of Approach

Psalm 121:1

Lord,
we have come to lift up our eyes
that we may see your
world in a new way;
we have come to lift up our minds
that our thoughts may be
transformed by your love;
we have come to lift up our hearts
that we might be made
whole by your grace;
we have come to lift up
our voices in praise
that we may worship you for
ever and ever. **Amen.**

Confession

Genesis 12:1

Lord,
we confess that we have
often heard your call
and we have simply closed our ears.
We know that you have spoken
in the cry of the children
and made your will plain
in the faces of the poor,
but we have turned away
and pretended that you
had not spoken.

Lord,
we confess that we are afraid
that you will go on calling us
until we turn, open our
hearts and minds,
and allow you to use us
as channels of your grace.

Lord,
we confess that we can
resist you no longer!
Come, Lord Jesus, come—
and, by your Holy Spirit,
cleanse, renew, and empower us
for the service to which you
are now calling even us.
In Christ's name. **Amen.**

The Lord says,
'I have heard your confession
and now by my grace
you are forgiven.
Go now—serve in my name
and live to bring me glory.'

Praise

Romans 4:3

Lord, we stand in awe of you—
the mighty King and
sovereign Lord
of all that was, and is, and will be.

You spoke, and the universe
came into being.
You spoke, and your ten
words of command
gave us the guidelines for life.
You spoke, and prophets,
priests, and kings
brought us your word of
challenge and hope.
You spoke, finally and completely,
through your Son.

Lord, we stand in awe of you—
the God who spoke
and the God who still speaks.

You speak, and our hearts
are filled with praise.
You speak, and we bow in
adoration before you.
You speak, and we are
overwhelmed by your grace.
You speak, and you call us by name.

Lord, we stand in awe of you.
How can it be
that you should love us
unconditionally
and long to fill our lives
with your peace?

How is it possible
that our mighty King and
sovereign Lord
should, through Christ,
come as one of us?

How can we comprehend the mystery
that through his life, death,
and resurrection
we, even we, can become your
sons and daughters,
born anew by the power
of the Holy Spirit?

Lord, we stand in awe of you—
that the mighty King and
sovereign Lord
should now reach down
to call and equip us in
the service royal.

Come, Lord Jesus, come.
Receive our praises
and rejoice in our adoration.

Come, Lord Jesus, come
and touch our hearts again
that we may answer the call of grace
and seek to give you all the glory.

Lord, we stand in awe of you—
the mighty King and sovereign Lord
of all that was, and is, and will be.
We do so now,
and we will do so for ever
and ever. **Amen.**

Intercession

Genesis 12:1

Let us pray for those who
answer God's call to serve
in the local community;
for those who are local councillors,
magistrates, and social workers
and for those who are teachers,
lecturers, and administrative staff.
May they know that in serving
others they are serving
him who called them.

silence

The Lord hears our prayer.
Thanks be to God.

Let us pray for those who answer
God's call to serve him in
the church community;
for those who are church
stewards, welcome stewards,
and pastoral visitors
and for those who work with
young people on Sundays
and in midweek activities.
May they know that in serving
others they are serving
him who called them.

silence

The Lord hears our prayer.
Thanks be to God.

Let us pray for those who
answer God's call to serve
him in the task of healing;
for those who are doctors,
nurses, radiographers,
and physiotherapists
and for those who are GPs,
community nurses, and all who
support the work that they do.
May they know that in serving
others they are serving
him who called them.

silence

The Lord hears our prayer.
Thanks be to God.

Let us pray for those who
answer God's call to serve
him where they live;
for those who are street pastors
or run neighbourhood
watch schemes
and for those who seek to
be a good neighbour or to
make a friend for Jesus.
May they know that in serving
others they are serving
him who called them.

silence

The Lord hears our prayer.
Thanks be to God.

Let us pray for those who answer
God's call to serve him in
some form of ministry;
for those who are local
preachers, deacons, ministers,
or lay church workers

and for those who are volunteers
or serve as mission partners
here or overseas.
May they know that in serving
others they are serving
him who called them.

silence

The Lord hears our prayer.
Thanks be to God.

Let us pray for those who
answer God's call to serve
him in their daily life;
for those who work in an office or
factory, in commerce or in industry
and for those who work in IT,
the media, or as parents to the
family they have been given.
May they know that in serving
others they are serving
him who called them.

silence

The Lord hears our prayer.
Thanks be to God.

Let us pray for ourselves and for
anyone we know, that we may
hear and answer God's call;
for those moments when we are
aware that he is speaking our
name and the call is for us
and for those opportunities
to be the channel for God's
voice to someone we know.
May we know that in serving others
we are serving him who called us.

silence

The Lord hears our prayer.
Thanks be to God.

We bring all our prayers in the
name of the God who calls,
and goes on calling. **Amen.**

THIRD SUNDAY IN LENT

Prayer of Approach

Psalm 95:1

Lord,
by your Holy Spirit,
transform our words of praise
into songs of joy;
our prayers that are spoken
into a deep conversation with our God
and our gathering together
in your name
into an expression of the
love we have for you
and for one another. **Amen.**

Praise

John 4:13–14

Lord,
you are the King of all creation
and the source of life itself.
Without your stupendous
power nothing would exist
and unless you had breathed out
your power upon all things
there would have been a void;
no experience of the life
that you had planned.

Glorious God,
almighty Lord and sovereign
over all things,
in awesome wonderment
we bow before the one who
alone is the Lord.

It is you, Lord, who has
graciously soaked our lives
with the greatest bounty of
gifts that could be given
and placed within us and around
us such a harvest of joy
that will forever be beyond
our deserving.

From your hand we have not
only received the gift of life
but the offer of new life.
You have not only given us
eyes to see your world
but inward sight to recognise
your presence all around us.
The richness of your gifts of
hearing, touch, and speech
are only outweighed by the grace
that allows and enables us
to hear your voice, experience
your touch upon our lives,
and to know the thrill of
communicating through prayer
with the God who holds all things
in the hollow of his hand.

But it was when Jesus met
the woman at the well
we realised for the first time in our
lives something of the richness
that you are offering to all
who listen to Jesus.

We praise you that your gift
is not simply of life
nor simply of life improved
by the teaching of Jesus.
We come with songs of thanksgiving
and hearts set ablaze by your grace
that through your Holy
Spirit you are desiring
to bless, heal, and transform
as you become the very
touchstone of our lives.

Lord,
we rejoice that in you there is
hope, life, and renewal
that is not for this life only
but for now and for ever
and for all eternity.

As your people we will sing
praise to the King of life
and to the Lord of new life who is
our hope and our joy. **Amen.**

Intercession

Romans 5:1–2

I am a world leader
and I live and work in
a world at war.
Everywhere I look I see people
fighting each other
and everything I hear speaks
of just how inhuman
human beings can be.
The cry is for peace and for justice
and I long to do more
to bring it about.
But deep down I know there
will only be peace on earth
when we are at peace with our Maker.
Pray for me.

silence

I am a member of a family
but the truth is we haven't
been a family for as long
as I can remember.
We fell out some time ago
over something so trivial

that now no one can remember what
was the cause of the family rift.
The years have rolled by and
I long for harmony
and for us to live in peace and love.
But deep down I know there
will only be peace on earth
when we are at peace with our Maker.
Pray for me.

silence

I am an old person;
my years have come and gone.
I look at the pictures of my
family all around me
and they bring me great joy.
But I would rather they come and
listen to my old memories
and allow their being with
me to bring me peace
in my twilight days.
My hours of loneliness steal my peace
and I sit in my chair and
feel I have no value.
But deep down I know there
will only be peace on earth
when we are at peace with our Maker.
Pray for me.

silence

I am a member of the church
which I have attended
for many years.
Lately I have taken a step back and
reflected on just who we are
and thought deeply about what
we are seeking to achieve.
Somehow or other my church
friends seem unable to
think outside their box
and every attempted change
or fresh expression is forced
through the sieve
which is labelled 'what suits me'.
But deep down I know there
will only be peace on earth
when we are at peace with our Maker.
Pray for me.

silence

I am a charity worker
and my work takes me to some of
the poorest places on earth.
It never ceases to amaze me
how self-centred we can be
and how easily we think that a
coin in an envelope means
we have done our duty.
If only I could take you to walk
where I have walked and
seen what I have seen,
you would never again rest in
peace until you had accepted
your responsibility
to bring hope, justice, and peace
to those who long for the
chance to help themselves.
But deep down I know there
will only be peace on earth
when we are at peace with our Maker.
Pray for me.

silence

I am a person who is dying.
My terminal illness has cut me off
from friends and colleagues
and from those with whom
I brushed shoulders in the
daily routine of life.

You have no idea how desperately
I long for the word of hope
and how much I would appreciate
the touch of your hand.
I am finding this final journey
such a lonely affair
and I would find so much peace if
you would come and pray with me.
But deep down I know there
will only be peace on earth
when we are at peace with our Maker.
Pray for me.

silence

I am an entertainer,
whether in sport, films, or on
television doesn't really matter.
All you see is the glitter and
the outward gloss
and you do not realise the emptiness
and the loneliness that is mine.
On the field and on the
stage I play my part
but when the final whistle
blows and the curtain falls
I find I have the adulation and
the riches but little else.
I have my medals and my memories
but peace is at a premium.
But deep down I know there
will only be peace on earth
when we are at peace with our Maker.
Pray for me.

silence

I am a retired person.
Finishing work was something
to which I looked forward
and doing things I wanted to do
was the prize I had grasped.
But somehow I miss the daily
banter with my colleagues
and the sense of purpose and
meaning work gave to each day.
I am glad I retired, but I long to
find a new purpose in life
and to discover a pathway to
peace that doesn't fade.
But deep down I know there
will only be peace on earth
when we are at peace with our Maker.
Pray for me.

silence

I am myself.
I come with all my hopes
and my problems
and with my bucketload of
questions and doubts.
To everyone else I seem fine and I
don't have a care in the world
but there is a sadness and hurt deep
inside that just won't go away.
I'm ashamed to admit my need
of help, love, and support
and often people seem to think
I can cope with everything
life throws at me.
But deep down I know there
will only be peace on earth
when we are at peace with our Maker.
Pray for me.

silence

We bring our prayers in the
name of the One,
who knows and cares. **Amen.**

FOURTH SUNDAY IN LENT

Prayer of Approach

Psalm 23:1–3

Lord,
we come for your name's sake
to give you all the glory;
we come because you are
the source of stillness
that helps us begin all over again;
we come to meet with the
shepherd of our lives
for you alone are the Lord who
leads us into life. **Amen.**

Confession

1 Samuel 16:1–13

We confess, Lord, that we are afraid
and that we would rather you didn't
look deeply into our lives.
It makes us feel uncomfortable
when we realise that you
comprehend our motives
and you are never fooled by our
outward show of holiness.
We are so adept at allowing other
people to think well of us—
it comes as a timely reminder that our
whole lives from beginning to end
are an open book to you.

We confess, Lord, that we are not
the people we would like to be
nor are we the people
others think we are.
And we are certainly not the
people you meant us to be.

It is the knowledge that you
look within us through
the eyes of grace
and it is your love that burns its way
through our shell of pretence
that fills us with hope and the
assurance of your forgiveness.

So look within us, Lord, and heal,
restore, and renew our hearts
that our words and deeds
may be worthy of you
and our way of life bring you the
honour that you deserve. **Amen.**

Praise

Ephesians 5:8

Lord, from all eternity you
are the almighty one
and from the beginning you are
sovereign over all things.
You are our creator,
sustainer, and Saviour
and it is to you we look to find the
source of our life and our being.

Everything we have and are we
owe to your amazing generosity
and each step we have taken is
surrounded by your grace.
There is nothing and no one with
whom you share your glory
and your holiness demands our total
obedience to your loving will.

Father, day by day you open
our eyes to your goodness
and around every corner of our lives
we see signs of your compassion.
Until we allowed you to walk
into our lives it was as if we
were walking in darkness
and it is your holy presence that rips
the cataracts of sin from our eyes.

Without your grace we have no hope,
no joy, and no true destination

and we journey in darkness unless we
surrender ourselves to your love.
Your desire is to light up our
lives from beginning to end
and to restore us completely, that
we might seize that purpose
for which you gave us life.

We praise you, the God of all that
is good and true and worthy
and we honour you above all others
for the light that you are.
With our voices we celebrate
your holiness and truth
and with our lives, by your grace,
we will live for your glory.

Lord, we want nothing more
than to sing your praises
and to live so that the whole
world will join in our
hymn of thanksgiving.
Gently you shower us with the
power of the Holy Spirit
and, beyond our wildest dreams,
you fan the flames of our joy.

Come, Holy Spirit, and shed
your light upon our lives.
Come, Father of love, and infuse
our hearts with your grace.
Come, Lord Jesus, come, that our
praises may be worthy of you.
Come, Lord Jesus, come. **Amen.**

Intercession

John 9:5

Think of someone who is in
the darkness of despair;
whose whole life has been
turned upside down
and for whom each day is a
struggle just to cope.
May Christ be the light of their world.

silence

Think of someone whose days
are darkened with fear;
whose every waking moment is
coloured by their anxiety
and who find themselves locked
in by their attacks of panic.
May Christ be the light of their world.

silence

Think of someone who is facing
the darkness of hunger;
whose only thought each new day
is finding food for their family
and for those for whom this will be
their last day, for they have no food.
May Christ be the light
of their world.

silence

Think of someone facing the
darkness of persecution;
who lives each day surrounded
by hatred and anger
and whose only crime is that
they know Jesus as Lord.
May Christ be the light of their world.

silence

Think of someone weighed down
by the darkness of bereavement;
who knows the pain of the loss
of employment, of hope,
or of one who was loved

and the sense of regret of what
they did or failed to do
that still haunts them.
May Christ be the light of their world.

silence

Think of someone whose
life has been coloured by
the darkness of abuse;
whose memories of childhood are of
things they would rather forget
but who still long to find
someone they can trust to hear
of their darkness within.
May Christ be the light of their world.

silence

Think of someone in the deep
darkness of loneliness;
who longs for a phone call
or a friendly face to break
into their aloneness
but whose words, deeds, and
attitude have long since
driven others away.
May Christ be the light of their world.

silence

Think of someone in the darkness
of frustration and emptiness;
whose plans, hopes, and dreams
have come to nothing
and who have yet to hear the
voice of Jesus, to open their
hearts and find life.
May Christ be the light of their world.

silence

Think of yourself and the
times of darkness that still
cloud your relationships.
Ask Christ to fill your home
with his presence and your
speech with his grace
that you may be a source of hope,
love, and light to your neighbour.
May Christ be the light of their world.

silence

We bring our prayers in
the name of Christ,
the light of the world. **Amen.**

FIFTH SUNDAY IN LENT (PASSION SUNDAY)

Prayer of Approach

Psalm 130:1–4

Lord,
from the depths of our despair
to the pain of our heartfelt longings—
we look to you.

Through tears of joy
and in the midst of sadness
that tears us apart—
we look to you.

With eyes wide open to our weakness
and our tongues ready to make
genuine confession—
we look to you.

Lord,
our God, our Saviour, and our joy,
you are the reason for living and
the object of our worship—
we look to you.
Only to you. **Amen.**

Thanksgiving

Romans 8:11

Wonderful, wonderful God,
you are the almighty one
and you are our crucified
and risen Lord.

We thank you that we do
not offer our prayers
in the name of a long-dead hero,
nor do we worship a teacher
whose only gifts
are the guidelines for living
on a printed page.

We thank you that your promise is
for life that transcends the grave
and a hope that not even death
itself can ever extinguish.
You are our living Lord who
alone can grant that most
precious of gifts—
that quality of life that can only be
lived in the presence of our God.

Majesty! Majesty! Majesty!
Our hearts cry out majesty,
honour, and glory.
We cannot be silent and our
lips will not be still.
How can we do other than
sing your praises
and allow the whole of our lives
to be a song of thanksgiving?

Wonderful, wonderful God.
Come live within us;
come hold us in your grace;
come infuse our prayers
with your Holy Spirit;
come and make your
home in our hearts.

On this Passion Sunday we fix
our eyes upon the cross
and remember again that you
died for us in our place.
On this Passion Sunday
we give thanks
that the cross was not the
end but the beginning.

You are our timeless Lord
and through your dying and rising
you have opened the door
to the heaven of your love.
Now receive our thanks and praise
for holding our hands as you
lead us by your Spirit
into the kingdom of your
grace. **Amen.**

Intercession

John 11:35

Lord,
we pray for those who weep
over lost dreams
and for those whose hopes and
plans have come to nothing;
for those who never had a dream,
a hope, or a sense of purpose
and for those now filled with regret
over what might have been.
Lord of the broken-hearted,
come wipe our tears away.

Lord,
we pray for those who weep in fear
and for those overwhelmed by
what their future may hold;
for those who have lost the will to live
and for those facing the uncertainty
of serious health problems.
Lord of the broken-hearted,
come wipe our tears away.

Lord,
we pray for those who weep
over their relationships
and for those whose words
and deeds are destroying
even the love that is left;
for those whose ability to
trust has been damaged
and for those whose self-centredness
is the cause of much weeping.
Lord of the broken-hearted,
come wipe our tears away.

Lord,
we pray for those who
weep for the lost
and for those torn apart by their
child's damaging addiction;
for those who once walked
all their days in the
knowledge of God's grace
and who have allowed the
world's pleasures to silently
steal them away.
Lord of the broken-hearted,
come wipe our tears away.

Lord,
we pray for those who
weep for the world
and for those who ache for
the victims of war;
for those who see Christ crucified in
the violent work of the terrorist
and for those who shed tears daily for
those with no food or no home.
Lord of the broken-hearted,
come wipe our tears away.

Lord,
we pray for those who weep
for your creation
and for those who warn
of the damage we are
doing to your world;
for those who close their
eyes and shut their ears
to their responsibility
and for those who resist
anything that would require
a change in their lifestyle.
Lord of the broken-hearted,
come wipe our tears away.

Lord,
we pray for those who weep
for those they have lost
and for those whose sense of hurt
is too deep to put into words;
for those who cry all alone where
no one can see or hear
and for those who long for someone
to come and share their tears.
Lord of the broken-hearted,
come wipe our tears away.

Lord,
we pray for those who
weep for the broken
and for those whose lives have
been destroyed through
no fault of their own;
for those whose homes,
places of work, all of life's
landmarks, and loved ones
have been carried away through
earthquake, fire, or flood.
Lord of the broken-hearted,
come wipe our tears away.

Lord,
we pray for those who
weep for themselves

and for those who hurt so much
they can weep no more;
for ourselves as we remember those
for whom we personally weep
and the times of emptiness,
brokenness and anxiety
that no one else sees.
Lord of the broken-hearted,
come wipe our tears away.

We bring our prayers in
the name of Jesus,
who wept and still weeps
for us all. **Amen.**

SIXTH SUNDAY IN LENT (PALM SUNDAY)

Prayer of Approach

Psalm 118:1–2

Let thankfulness well up within us
and our voices be filled
with songs of praise.
May our hearts overflow
with deepest joy
and our worship be a sign
of our true devotion.
As the pilgrims who waved
palm branches as they sang,
we declare the glory of our
Palm Sunday Lord. **Amen.**

Praise

Zechariah 9:9

Lord,
we simply cannot imagine what
it must have been like
to walk into Jerusalem on
that Palm Sunday.
We have no idea how the
pilgrims must have felt
as they prepared to welcome
their humble King.
Your disciples must have been
overwhelmed by the experience
as together that mobile
congregation sang your praises.

We have celebrated so
many Palm Sundays
and we have heard the incredible
story of your entry into Jerusalem
but we sometimes fail to grasp the
joy and the wonder of it all.
On this day, we are given a graphic
demonstration of worship
and a powerful reminder of what
praising you should really mean.

We have substituted joyous
thanksgiving with our
formal worship
and we have settled for the
outward act of praise
in place of an overflowing sense of
the presence of almighty God.
Instead of hearts warmed by the
knowledge of your glory,
we seek to comfort ourselves that
our corporate words and actions
are worthy of you and have somehow
reached the throne of grace.

Lord,
on this Palm Sunday we have
come ready to open our
hearts to your power
and to allow our self-effacing King
to ride victoriously into our lives.
We, like the pilgrims and the
disciples, lift our voices to
celebrate your presence

and we lay our lives at your feet as
a sign of our love and your glory.

We praise you for the way that the
Holy Spirit sets us free to worship
and for the Spirit's renewing grace that
transforms everyone he touches.
You are more worthy of our worship
than our hymns can ever say
and our songs can never truly tell of
the glory and mercy that are yours.

So come, our Palm Sunday King,
seal our worship with your love
and, by your Holy Spirit, make
it a fit vehicle for you to
ride to your coronation,
where you will be declared
to be sovereign Lord of all
and for ever. **Amen.**

Intercession

Matthew 21:2

The following prayers are intended to involve several people bringing forward items that represent various aspects of the life of the community. These can be adapted to include anything thought most suitable.

Introduction

As the man with the donkey
gave Jesus what he had, so
our prayers are that we and
others may do the same.

Newspaper

I bring a newspaper.
I ask your prayers for those
who work in the media;
for those whose work in
television, in the cinema,
through the printed word,
and the internet
to touch and change the
lives of many people.

silence

For the praise of Jesus the King,
may they offer to God what they do.

Waste bin bag

I bring a waste bin bag.
I ask your prayers for
those we rely on to
take away the rubbish
from our homes;
for those who clean our
streets, recycle our waste,
and whose unseen work
prevents so much disease.

silence

For the praise of Jesus the King,
may they offer to God what they do.

Child's toy

I bring a child's toy.
I ask your prayers for those who
care for young children;
for all parents and grandparents and
members of the wider family
and those who work in
preschool play groups
who together share responsibility
for moulding young minds.

silence

For the praise of Jesus the King,
may they offer to God what they do.

Hymn book

I bring a hymn book.
I ask your prayers for those
who serve within the life of
the church community;
for those who lead worship,
provide music, or offer pastoral
support to those in need
and for those responsible for
leadership, the finances,
or the property,
that together we may provide a place
of welcome, worship, and service.

silence

For the praise of Jesus the King,
may they offer to God what they do.

Tool

I bring a tool.
I ask your prayers for all who
work with their hands;
for mechanical and civil engineers,
for plumbers and electricians
and for all those on whom
we rely to mend our roads,
our cars, and our homes,
that they may feel valued for
the work they do in the
life of the community.

silence

For the praise of Jesus the King,
may they offer to God what they do.

Bottle of medicine

I bring a bottle of medicine.
I ask your prayers for all who care
for the health of the community;
for doctors, nurses, and
pharmacists, and those who
provide vital support services,
that together with hospital auxiliary
and cleaning staff and paramedics,
the provision of healthcare
and support may be
freely available to all.

silence

For the praise of Jesus the King,
may they offer to God what they do.

Laptop computer

I bring a laptop computer.
I ask your prayers for all who work
in information technology;
for those whose unseen work
provides services for our
homes and our community
and for those who develop the
technology we use in our
homes and our hospitals,
and the communication made
possible through the internet
and mobile phones.

silence

For the praise of Jesus the King,
may they offer to God what they do.

Person

I bring myself.

I ask your prayers for one
another and for each member
of our community;
for those we know to be
in particular need of
help and support
and for those who live alone and
feel they have nothing to offer,
that every person may be valued,
single or married, old or
young, female or male.

silence

For the praise of Jesus the King,
may they offer to God what they do.

We bring all our prayers in
the name of the King,
who longs to use us all in his
kingdom of grace. **Amen.**

EASTER SUNDAY

Prayer of Approach

Psalm 118:22–24

The Lord is risen!
He is risen indeed!

We meet to celebrate a living Lord
and to praise the one who has
been raised from the dead.
He is rejected by many but
worshipped by millions.
He is dismissed as just a good
man or spiritual teacher
but we who have met him have come
to give praise to the one who
will always be Lord. **Amen.**

Praise

Acts 10:40

Gracious God, we cannot
find the words
that will adequately express
the wonder and joy that we feel.
The empty cross speaks
of a loving Saviour
and the empty tomb is forever
the symbol of hope
that declares the truth of
our living Lord.

We praise you for the hope you
have offered us through your Son.
In his death you have promised not
only that we can begin again
but that all our self-centredness
and self-interest
can be wiped from the
record of our lives.
It is your grace that oozes
from the cross
bringing joy, hope, and peace to
all who step into its flow.

We stand amazed at the
mind-blowing wonder
of the Easter story
and we are enthralled by
your assurance
that it isn't just a story—but the
truth which gives us life.
If the story of Christ's
resurrection is simply a story
then there would be no hope, no
joy, no reason to celebrate.
But the truth on which the people
of faith have always stood
is that Christ has died, Christ is
risen, Christ will come again!

We praise you that our faith in the
resurrection is not a question
of trying to believe the unbelievable.
We have the solid evidence of the
disciples' report in the Bible
and that not even Christ's
enemies ever denied that
the tomb was empty.
The change in the disciples
from weak, frightened men
into bold witnesses
speaks of the truth of the impact of
the risen Lord upon their lives.
Our presence is the greatest
evidence of the truth of
the Easter message;
our being here means we too
are witnesses to the reality
of the empty tomb!

We worship you, Lord Jesus
Christ, our risen Saviour.
Your resurrection confirms your
work of grace upon the cross
and demands our celebration in the
defeat of death in your rising.
When we wonder if this life
is all that there is to life
and that death is simply the end,
the empty tomb gives us hope.
When we are accused of being
out of touch with reality,
the empty tomb gives us hope.
When we are filled with uncertainty
and are afraid of death,
the empty tomb gives us hope.
When the world scorns our faith
and ridicules what we hold dear,
the empty tomb gives us hope.
When our journey is hard and
the way strewn with sadness,
the empty tomb gives us hope.

We praise you that we can
live in the knowledge
that the power that raised
Christ from the dead
is the same grace-energy
that raises us now
and will raise us for ever.

By the power of the Holy Spirit,
we praise you, our risen Lord,
for all eternity. **Amen.**

Intercession

John 20:2

I ask your prayers for those in
the darkness of depression
and for those who feel entombed
by anxieties that are very real;
for those who long to break out
of the shackles that hold them
and for those who feel foolish
and guilty for an illness
that isn't their fault.
May the joy of the empty
tomb bring them hope
of peace yet to come.
The Lord hears our prayer.
Thanks be to God.

I ask your prayers for those
in the darkness of hate
and for those whose bitterness
is the source of pain and
suffering for others;
for those whose actions are
designed to terrorise others
and for those who show no
remorse for the death and
destruction they caused.
May the love from the empty
tomb heal the bitterness
they feel within.

The Lord hears our prayer.
Thanks be to God.

I ask your prayers for those in the
darkness of a stress-filled life
and for those whose every
waking moment tightens
the bonds around them;
for those whose work or home life
drains them of energy and peace
and for those who feel stressed
through the loss of employment.
May the peace of the empty
tomb hold them in times
of stress and despair.
The Lord hears our prayer.
Thanks be to God.

I ask your prayers for those facing the
darkness of life-threatening illness
and for those whose anguish is
deepened by the uncertainty
about tomorrow;
for those reassessing their whole
lives as a result of serious injury
and for those who still face the
confusion of not knowing
what the future may bring.
May the light from the empty
tomb give them hope for
the journey to come.
The Lord hears our prayer.
Thanks be to God.

I ask your prayers for those facing
the darkness of leadership
and for those overwhelmed by the
choices that they have to make;
for those who are finding the
role of leadership lonely
and for those who still seek to serve
with integrity and compassion.
May the faith which flows from the
empty tomb give them strength.
The Lord hears our prayer.
Thanks be to God.

I ask your prayers for
those surrounded by the
darkness of hunger
and for those for whom finding
the next meal for their
family is their only task;
for those who are thankful
for the aid that comes from
charities and governments
and for those who simply
long for the freedom to be
able to help themselves.
May the truth which echoes from
the empty tomb ring in the
hearts of those with power.
The Lord hears our prayer.
Thanks be to God.

I ask your prayers for those in
the darkness of loneliness
and for those who feel forgotten
by family and friends
who no longer visit;
for those in the twilight
of their years who have
only their memories
and for those who simply long
for someone with whom
they could share them.
May the joy of the empty tomb
give them comfort and hope.
The Lord hears our prayer.
Thanks be to God.

I ask your prayers for those
in the darkness of loss

and for those whose homes have been
swept away by storm or by flood;
for those whose whole
community has disappeared
through earthquake or fire
and for those left with no family
or friends with whom to start
to rebuild what was lost.
May the love which flows from
the empty tomb give them
the courage they need.
The Lord hears our prayer.
Thanks be to God.

I ask your prayers for those whose
days are filled with darkness
and for those who experience an
emptiness nothing can heal;
for those who search in vain
to find the faith, hope,
and love that satisfies
and for those who will look
anywhere but in the empty tomb,
where true hope is found.
May the blinding light of the
empty tomb be the place where
trust and hope are found.
The Lord hears our prayer.
Thanks be to God.

We bring all our prayers in the
name of our risen Lord,
who is himself the light and the
power of the empty tomb. **Amen.**

SECOND SUNDAY OF EASTER

Prayer of Approach

Psalm 16:1–5

You are our Lord and we
will praise you.
You are the Holy One and
we will adore you.
You are the mighty God and
we will honour your name.
You are the source of all that is
good and true and holy.
You are the centre of our lives and
we will praise you for ever. **Amen.**

Praise

1 Peter 1:3–9

Almighty God, our heavenly Father,
you have infused our hearts with
a joy that is beyond words
and with a peace that nothing
can ever take away.
Since you made yourself
known to us,
we experienced such an overflowing
sense of wonderment
that we find our greatest pleasure
in giving you thanks and praise.

To offer you worship has
ceased to be a mere duty
and to praise you is indeed the
high point of our life.
Gone is the sense of your
being remote from us
and never again will we consider
our lives in isolation from you.

Lord, we have been blessed
far beyond our deserving
and we have received a life-
transforming hope at your hand.
You have made it possible for us
to start our lives all over again
and you have lifted us out of
the pit of despair into which
we had dug ourselves.

There is no God like you
and we would have no other
god besides you.
You are the only God that there
has ever been or ever will be
and you alone shall be the sovereign
Lord of our days and hours.

You have given to us the hope—
that deals with the past,
that transforms the present,
and that acts like a bridge
into the future
in the kingdom of your grace. **Amen.**

Intercession

John 20:24–25

Prepare a set of six candles. Light a new candle as you begin each prayer.

We light this candle for those for
whom life in our age of science
makes faith in the unseen
God hard to believe;
for those who see only a conflict
between science and faith
and for those who are
discovering that only as they
complement each other
can we truly know God and
give him true worship.

silence

Lord, in your mercy,
hear our prayer.

We light this candle for those who
find that the life of the world,
with all its wickedness and
evil, makes it so very hard to
believe in a loving God;
for those who can see only
the hunger and suffering
but are unable to open their eyes
to the compassion of God
through those who know him
and through those who don't.

silence

Lord, in your mercy,
hear our prayer.

We light this candle for those
for whom the church,
with its weakness and hypocrisy,
is a barrier to faith in the
God they worship;
for those who find it hard
to cope with the certainty
faith seems to imply,
that seems to have no room for
honest doubts and difficulties
and for those of faith and of no
faith who have forgotten
God gave us minds to think
and to ask questions.

silence

Lord, in your mercy,
hear our prayer.

We light this candle for those
with closed minds
and for those afraid of the changes
to life that faith might bring;
for those who are longing
to experience the joy
and the love of God,
that they have seen in the lives
of those whom they trust,

and for those whose words and deeds
are making it easier for others
to hear the knocking of Christ
on the door of their lives.

silence

Lord, in your mercy,
hear our prayer.

We light this candle for those
whose personal pain and loss
is in danger of robbing them
of the faith they once had
and for those who have turned
their backs on their Maker
when he failed to fulfil what they
thought was their right;
for those of our family and friends
who long to know Christ
and for those hands we are
being called to take hold of,
that they too may know
the joy of our Lord.

silence

Lord, in your mercy,
hear our prayer.

We light this candle for all those
for whom we are concerned,
that the presence of the
Father may hold them,
the grace of the Son may renew them,
and the power of the Holy
Spirit may empower them.

silence

Lord, in your mercy,
hear our prayer.

We bring our prayers in
the name of Christ,
whose risen presence lights
up our world. **Amen.**

THIRD SUNDAY OF EASTER

Prayer of Approach

Psalm 116:13–14

Wonderful, wonderful God,
everything we have and are;
every good thing we see or hear;
everything of worth or lasting value;
every hope, every joy, and
every blessing;
absolutely everything—
even life itself—
flows from your generous hand
and your loving heart.

We have come to give you the
thanks that you deserve
and the praises that we
have promised.
As your people, gathered
in your name,
we declare: you are worthy! **Amen.**

Praise

1 Peter 1:23

Lord,
we praise you for the way you have
touched and changed our lives
and for the promise to go on
renewing us day by day.
It was your plan from before
the dawning of time
that we should walk in the
presence of our God
and that our days should be
overshadowed by your grace.

When we filled our lives with
the possessions of the earth
you lifted our eyes to see the
promised kingdom of grace.
When we spent our days listening
to the voices all around us
you opened our ears to the call
of your renewing love.
When we allowed our senses
to be imprisoned by the
ways of the world
you reached out grace-soaked
hands to set us free.

We praise you for challenging us to
look beyond the here and now
and to discover that life is more
than we can touch and hold.
We are filled with renewed
hope and purpose
for you have shown us how to
live out our days on earth,
but always with our eyes firmly
fixed on the heaven of your love.

To have received the gift of
life is something that is
extremely precious,
but to be offered life that simply
cannot be lost by death
is the most wonderful present we
could ever possibly be granted.
Now we know that the one we
worship is not only Lord of life
but you are also the sovereign
over death and for all eternity.

Come, sovereign Lord, and
receive our praises.
Come, Saviour God, as we gather
to offer you heartfelt thanks.
Come, Holy Spirit, and enable
us to offer the thanks and
praise that you deserve.
Come, Lord Jesus, come. **Amen.**

Intercession

Luke 24:21

We pray for those whose hopes for
a healthy life have been dashed
and for those whose lifestyle has
robbed them of the health
they might have enjoyed;
for those who through
the passing years
are struggling to cope with the
loss of physical well-being
and for those whose loss of sight,
hearing, or mobility is a burden
almost too hard to bear.

silence

On the journey of life,
the Lord renews our hope.

We pray for those whose hopes for
a peaceful life have been wrecked
and for those who are still
trying to put their broken
lives back together;
for those who live in the midst of
civil war or terrorist attacks
and for those whose homes
have become a battleground
of anger and abuse.

silence

On the journey of life,
the Lord renews our hope.

We pray for those whose
hopes for home and family
have been destroyed
and for those whose longing for
parenthood has come to nothing;
for those whose singleness means
they are outsiders in our
family-orientated society
and for those whose home
and family were lost in an
earthquake, flood, or fire.

silence

On the journey of life,
the Lord renews our hope.

We pray for those whose hope of
employment has been lost
and for those whose job
was the only thing that
gave meaning to life;
for those who are trying
to come to terms with
redundancy or retirement
and for those whose work is
a burden from which they
see no way of escape.

silence

On the journey of life,
the Lord renews our hope.

We pray for those whose hope
of freedom has disappeared
and for those whose behaviour
has landed them in prison;
for those who are filled with remorse
for what they did or failed to do
and for the victims whose lives
have been damaged by the
addictions of others.

silence

On the journey of life,
the Lord renews our hope.

We pray for those whose hope of
fulfilment has been satisfied
and for those whose meeting
with the risen Christ has
transformed their days;
for those who by God's
grace have risen above
their suffering and loss
and for those whose love
and joy touches the lives
of those they meet.

silence

On the journey of life,
the Lord renews our hope.

We pray for ourselves and the hopes
and fears we still carry within
and for the unfulfilled dreams
and the 'might have beens'
that never go away;
for a renewed sense of our own
worth and a new purpose in life
and for the courage and
strength to begin again, even
when we don't want to.

silence

On the journey of life,
the Lord renews our hope.

We bring our prayers in the
name of the risen Christ,
who is our hope on the
journey of life. **Amen.**

FOURTH SUNDAY OF EASTER

Prayer of Approach

Psalm 23:5

Lord,
you are at the heart of all things
and your grace is the source
of life and hope.
You are the God who is ever-present
and the Lord whose love soaks
into the very essence of life.
Nowhere can we go, but you
are there to meet us
and your blessings come to us
through nail-printed hands.
In the midst of the darkest hour,
you prepare a banquet of hope
and as we gather for worship you are
here to receive our praises. **Amen.**

Praise

1 Peter 2:21

Lord,
we praise you that wherever we go
you are there
and whatever we face
we know you are standing beside us.
You alone are the one
who understands
what it means to face the darkness,
and you yourself have experienced
a sense of loneliness and rejection
too deep for words.

Lord,
you are more than an
example of courage
and in the face of hatred
and betrayal
you exceed every model of love.
We simply cannot take it in
and our minds are overwhelmed
by the wonder of who you are
and what you have done.
From all eternity you are
God's only Son
and all the glory of heaven
was yours by right.

Lord,
we are told that in your
death and resurrection
you have left us an example
of what love can do;
how it can triumph when
faced with those
whose lives are overflowing
with bitterness and evil.
Yet we praise you more that
you do not simply provide
a template to cope with suffering,
a pattern to deal with the
pain and hardship,
or a handbook of teaching to
strengthen our commitment.

Lord,
wherever we go—you are there
and whatever we face we know that
you will be standing beside us
with your arms around us
and your peace, power, and
love deep within us.
We praise you, our sovereign Lord,
that you are our light
in the darkness
and our hope now and for
evermore. **Amen.**

Intercession

These prayers should be used with two voices, one for the Scripture verses and one for the prayers.

Acts 2:42–47

Verse 42

I ask your prayers for those
who help us to know God
and for those whose words and
deeds make God real for us;
for those who write poetry,
songs, and Christian books
and for the work of the Bible
Society and the Wycliffe
Bible Translators
who open our hearts and minds
to the purposes of God.
The Lord hears our prayer.
Thanks be to God.

Verse 43

I ask your prayers for those
whose lives are a witness
to the love of God
and for those whose words are
filled with the grace of God;
for those who are prepared
to risk everything
to be a good neighbour
regardless of colour or creed
and for those whose selfless
words and ways
bring others hope in the
darkness of tragedy
and a peace that only
Christ can give.
The Lord hears our prayer.
Thanks be to God.

Verse 44

I ask your prayers for those
who open their homes for
times of fellowship
and for those whose faith and
love are a beacon of hope
to their neighbours;
for those who give a high priority to
meeting with those who believe
as they seek to deepen their
knowledge of Jesus
and for those who are content to
stay in the shallow waters of belief
that they may discover the joy and
strength of fellowship in Christ.
The Lord hears our prayer.
Thanks be to God.

Verse 45

I ask your prayers for those
whose generosity puts
our giving to shame
and for those who have little of
this world's prized possessions
but whose open hearts and minds
are full of the riches of heaven;
for those who have the
power and resources
to feed the hungry, clothe
the naked, heal the sick,
and help the prisoner
but who lack the will and the love
to reach out in compassion;
for the work of the agencies
such as Christian Aid, Save
the Children, and Tearfund
and the hope they bring in place
of hopelessness and despair.
The Lord hears our prayer.
Thanks be to God.

Verse 46

I ask your prayers for those who
believe but never worship
as they see no need to meet together
to praise the living God
and for those whose faith is a
formal belief in their heads
and not the vibrant resource
that rekindles hope and
overcomes disaster;
for those whose lives are filled with
the good things of this life
but who have no hope of the
joy of life yet to come
and for those whose hearts are
filled with thankfulness and joy
but have yet to find faith in
God, who is the source
of all good things.
The Lord hears our prayer.
Thanks be to God.

Verse 47

I ask your prayers for the
whole people of God,
that churches of every
denomination and in every place
may be a magnet of hope, faith,
and love to their community
and that our worship may be so
infused by the Holy Spirit
that all who enter this place may
be touched by the love of God;
may our welcome be genuine and
our praises come from the heart
that people will say of us,
'see how those Christians
love one another,'
and so Christ will continue to
draw all people to himself.
The Lord hears our prayer.
Thanks be to God.

We bring all our prayers in
the name of Christ,
the Lord of life and the hope
of the world. **Amen.**

FIFTH SUNDAY OF EASTER

Prayer of Approach

Psalm 31:16

Touched by your grace
and challenged by your love,
we worship you.
Cleansed by your mercy
and held in your peace,
we worship you.
Called to be your servants
and empowered by the Spirit,
we worship you.
Overwhelmed by your presence
and adopted as your children,
we worship you.
Lord, shine upon us now
that we may worship you. **Amen.**

Praise

1 Peter 2:4

Father,
we have no right to be here in
the presence of the King
and we have nothing of ourselves
that would claim our place
before the sovereign of eternity.
Your almighty power holds all things
in the purposes of your will
and your never-ending love
encompasses every living thing.

We stand in awe of you, our Father.
We stand in awe of you.

Our minds cannot comprehend the
sheer magnitude of your being
and our puny thoughts cannot grasp
the tiniest detail of your presence.
Our assumptions of your glory
cannot reach the gates of heaven
and the greatest claims we can
make for your authority
do not even reach the foothills
of the mountain range
of your sovereignty.

And yet your invitation is
to come to you—
not in doubt,
not in fear,
not by right,
and not by our own worth.

We praise you, Father,
that we come through Christ,
who opened the way to
your presence
and paid the price of our coming
to the throne of grace.

We come to offer our
thanks for Jesus
and his willingness to be himself
the vehicle of our renewal
and our living hope.
We are here to praise him—
that he should give himself for us
is a holy blessing that simply
takes our breath away.

We, like the prodigal child,
have been drawn home
by the overwhelming
love of the Father.
We, like the prodigal child,
come ready to be servants
but, by your mercy, find ourselves
reinstated into the family of grace.
As your children, made precious
at the cost of your Son,
we come with grace-touched lives
to give praises to the Father
of life, love, and hope
in whose presence all things
are made new. **Amen.**

Intercession

John 14:1–14

Lord,
we pray for those who carry
a burden of loneliness
and for those whose days
are spent in isolation;
for those, who with the
passing years,
are left alone and whose
friends are gone
and for those with only memories
and no one with whom
they can share them.
Lord, you are the way, the
truth, and the life;
be our way home to the Father.

Lord,
we pray for those who carry
a load of worries
and for those whose days are
crippled by anxieties;
for those facing an uncertain future
without work, home, or family
and who are fearful of just
how they will cope
and for those who daily struggle
with the darkness of despair
and depression
from which they can find
no way of escape.

Lord, you are the way, the
truth, and the life;
be our way home to the Father.

Lord,
we pray for those who face
the very real threat
of imprisonment because
of their faith in Jesus
and for those locked away
from the world's eyes
for daring to believe in justice,
democracy, and truth;
for those with the courage to
stand up and be counted
in the face of injustice
and corruption
and for those who speak out in the
name of Christ and his people
at the cost of their personal
liberty and hope.
Lord, you are the way, the
truth, and the life;
be our way home to the Father.

Lord,
we pray for those who are no
longer the people we once knew
as their health has declined and
the years have taken their toll;
for those who are locked
up in their bodies
but whose minds have ceased
to recognise the ones
that they once loved;
for those who sit at the bedside
and must speak as if to a child
and for those left feeling
bereft and alone
when they visit the person
they once knew
but who treats them as a member
of staff or a stranger.
Lord, you are the way, the
truth, and the life;
be our way home to the Father.

Lord,
we pray for those who no
longer answer our call to
renewal of relationship
and for those who ignore every
email or letter we write;
for those with whom we once
shared laughter and friendship
but who now treat us as
strangers they never knew;
for those of our family who reject
every offer of reconciliation
and for those who respond with
one rebuff after another.
Lord, you are the way, the
truth, and the life;
be our way home to the Father.

Lord,
we pray for those who are
condemned to live in a
home made of cardboard
and for those with no real
home of their own;
for those who live out their
days in the poverty of the
latest shanty town
and for those whose addiction
to drugs or to alcohol or
their own inadequacy
means that they now sleep rough
on the streets of our cities;
for those who seek to offer the
hand of friendship and the
chance to begin again

and for those with the power, but not
the will, to help those in great need.
Lord, you are the way, the
truth, and the life;
be our way home to the Father.

Lord,
we pray for ourselves as we
face the challenges and trials
on the journey of life
and for those, who by your
grace, have laid themselves and
their needs on our hearts;
for ourselves, in the face of the
stresses and the pressures of life,
that we may, by your grace, learn to
love our neighbour and ourselves
and for those relationships,
once precious and loving
but now under strain,
and for those where reconciliation
seems a far-off dream.
In the stillness we bring before God
those for whom we are concerned.
Lord, you are the way, the
truth, and the life;
be our way home to the Father.

We bring our prayers in the
name of the One,
who alone is the way home
to the Father. **Amen.**

SIXTH SUNDAY OF EASTER

Prayer of Approach

Psalm 66:8–9

Lord,
we have come not to
receive a blessing
but that we might bless you.
We have come not for
our own benefit
but that you might receive glory.
We have come not for
fellowship with each other
but that together we may
praise your name. **Amen.**

Praise

John 14:19

Lord,
we praise you for the incredible
promise you have given to us
and for the assurance that
your plan for life,
and for our lives, reaches on
beyond life as we now know it.
This has stopped us in our tracks
and you have forced us to
begin to rethink
those things that seemed to
be the boundaries of life.

We had been led to believe
that when we die
we would simply be history
that was marked by the
RIP on our grave.
We were told that science
had all the answers
and that any hope of a future-life
was simply 'pie in the sky'.
The world around us and
its tunnel vision
is focused on the things we
can have and hold now.
So many of our friends,
neighbours and colleagues
have a vague hope that
death is not the end
but they possess no solid assurance
of a place prepared for them.

If we are honest, Lord, on our
days of darkness and doubt
we too are overwhelmed
by our uncertainties
and we allow our faith in
you to be crowded out
by our questions and misgivings.

Then comes your word of hope
as once more you place our
feet on solid ground
and you anchor us again to
your promise in Christ.
In Him you offer us not a wistful
hoping for better things
nor some craving for an
'end of life solution'
to reverse all the injustices of this life.
But we praise you that the
promise that we shall see Jesus
and that we shall be with
him for all eternity
comes not as a reward
for the righteous
but as a gift of grace that
is received by faith.

Lord,
yet again you move us to
praise and thanksgiving.
Once more your Spirit blows
away the fear of not knowing
as faith overcomes doubt and
trust replaces uncertainty.
We acknowledge that we have but
the word pictures in the Bible
which give but a sketch
outline of your heaven.
We confess that though
we may not know
the geography or the
architecture of heaven,
you alone remain the highway
to the throne of grace.

By your grace we shall see
you face to face
and the praises we offer
here on earth
will be transformed by the
glory that is yours.
We have your promise.
We live by your grace.
We live on earth, but
with our eyes fixed
on the heaven of your love. **Amen.**

Intercession
John 14:16
I am a child and I have no voice,
no one to speak for me.
I live in Haiti.
My parents are both dead,
they died of HIV/AIDS.
I live on the street and my daily task
is to hunt for the scraps of food
other people have thrown away.
I have no one to care for me,
no one to be my voice,
no one to speak for me.
Pray for me.

silence

I am an old woman and
I have no voice,
no one to speak for me.
I live alone,
four bare walls with no
hope of freedom.
I do have a family,
they live not far away
but they never visit.
No one calls.

I'm just a statistic and one
  that can be ignored
by the community and
  politicians alike.
I have no one to be my voice,
no one to speak for me.
Pray for me.

silence

I am a teenager and I have no voice,
no one to speak for me.
You see I've even lost my name.
I have a one size fits all label.
Having a label means I
  get all the blame
and none of the praise.
When I try to speak up
I'm told I don't understand
and when I protest
I'm then labelled as antisocial.
Were the powers that be never young
just wanting to be heard?
I have no one to be my voice,
no one to speak for me.
Pray for me.

silence

I am a Christian who is
  persecuted for my faith
and I have no voice,
no one to speak for me.
I cannot understand just how easily
you take your freedoms for granted.
For me to declare my faith in Jesus
means instant arrest
and attacks from my so-called
neighbours and friends.
For simply attending an
  act of worship,
I risk losing my job, my
  home and my family.
My hope is in Christ and
  his love for me,
his Holy Spirit floods into my heart.
But I have no one to be my voice,
no one to speak for me.
Pray for me.

silence

I am a businessman and
  I have no voice,
no one to speak for me.
Every Sunday I attend worship
and wait for the moment
  when we pray for others.
Again and again we pray for
  anyone and everyone
but not for me,
the one whose work brings
  wealth to the community.
I am the 'fall guy' when
  things go wrong,
the one to blame for the
  ills of society.
Whether I'm a banker,
  manufacturer or a service provider
like you we have all made
  our greedy mistakes.
It would help to feel if not loved,
at least appreciated and respected.
I have no one to be my voice,
no one to speak for me.
Pray for me.

silence

I am a childless woman
  and I have no voice,
no one to speak for me.

You have no idea of the
ache within me
the deep, deep longing
that tears me apart.
When I hear others speak
of the right to a child
and the wonder and joy
of parenthood
I want to scream—but
what about me?
I am just part of that hidden army
of 'would be, but can't be' parents.
I'm happily married
but we never expected our 'family'
to remain just the two of us.
I have no one to be my voice,
no one to speak for me.
Pray for me.

silence

I am a victim of a disaster
and I have no voice,
no one to speak for me.
When the disaster struck
we were headline news.
You couldn't move for TV crews
and newspaper reporters.
But whatever the disaster—
earthquake or tsunami, wind or fire
once they have their sound bites,
we are history and forgotten
in the rush for something
more newsworthy.
But my home is destroyed,
my family are dead
and my community has
disappeared.
I have no one to be my voice,
no one to speak for me.
Pray for me.

silence

I am myself and have no
one to be my voice,
no one to speak for me.
In the stillness—
hold up before God
your pain and your sorrow;
your sadness and loss;
your fears and uncertainties
and your longing to be heard.
I have no one to be my voice,
no one to speak for me.
Pray for me and pray for yourself.

silence

We bring all our prayers
in the name of the One
who knows our name
and asks the Father
to give us another Advocate
to be with us forever. **Amen.**

SEVENTH SUNDAY OF EASTER

Prayer of Approach

Psalm 68:34–35

How great is our God,
he is the Lord over all things.
How great is our God,
he is sovereign over all creation.
How great is our God,
all time and eternity sit in
the palm of his hand.
How great is our God,
there is none like him.
How great is our God,
and we have come to praise him,
and he is worthy. **Amen.**

Praise
John 17:1–14

Lord,
there are many things with
which we fill our days
and there are a host of things
that consume our thoughts;
there are times when we
are overwhelmed by the
concerns around us
and there are moments when we
cannot think outside the box
of constricting pressures.

It is at precisely these times when we
need to step aside to focus on you
and to allow your grace to
calm our troubled minds;
It is when we are at our lowest
we urgently need to turn
again to the fountain of life
and yield to your loving-
kindness which overflows
with your healing mercy.

Lord,
remind us yet again that
though there are many
calls upon our time
your call to offer you the worship
of our lives is paramount
and even when our minds are in
turmoil and our hearts are restless
your invitation is to find the
very peace that passes all
human understanding.

The world in which we live makes
many costly demands of us
and the lifestyle we have allowed
ourselves to create, squeezes
the joy of life out of us;
So easily we permit the pressures
of home and family and
of work and leisure
to usurp the time and space
in our lives that was meant
to have been yours.

Lord,
as Jesus looked up to heaven so
lift our hearts and minds to
recognise your presence
and place upon our lips words
of praise and a true expression
of the joy we feel;
Remind us all over again that
we may have many concerns
but only one task
which is to offer you thanks
and praise and to worship
the Lord of glory.

We praise you that your
almighty presence is ready
to touch us once more
and that your extravagant love
is sufficient to hold and to
heal us no matter what.
It is when your glory is the focus
of all we do and say that life
will be a song of praise
and the concerns of our days
will be set in the midst
of our Father's grace.

Come, let us praise the Lord
whose love and grace bring
healing and hope
and whose presence can redeem
the darkest day and the
most troubled heart.
You are the Lord of all glory and
we have come to praise you;

You are the Lord and we your people
are here to worship you. **Amen.**

Intercession

1 Peter 4:12–13

You need some pebbles—one for each prayer. Hold the pebble as you pray, then place it in front of a small cross.

Lord,
we place this pebble at the
foot of your cross
as we pray for those whose lives are
being torn apart by civil war
and those whose lives have
been broken by the ruthless
actions of terrorists.

silence

Come and hold them in
your grace-filled hands.

Lord,
we place this pebble at the
foot of your cross
as we pray for those whose homes
are blighted by jealousy, broken
trust or the desire to control
and for those whose selfish
and violent actions cause
others to be overwhelmed
by insecurity and fear.

silence

Come and hold them in
your grace-filled hands.

Lord,
we place this pebble at the
foot of your cross
as we pray for those whose whole
lives have been swept away
by earthquake, wind or fire
and for those whose lives have been
crippled by redundancy and
their future by foolish choices.

silence

Come and hold them in
your grace-filled hands.

Lord,
we place this pebble at the
foot of your cross
as we pray for those around the
world persecuted for their
faith or political beliefs
and for Christians struggling to bear
witness to Jesus to their affluent
and indifferent neighbours.

silence

Come and hold them in
your grace-filled hands.

Lord,
we place this pebble at the
foot of your cross
as we pray for those who are
facing life-changing situations
and for those whose life-
threatening illness leaves
them counting their days.

silence

Come and hold them in
your grace-filled hands.

Lord,
we place this pebble at the
foot of your cross
as we pray for those with the power
but not the will to rescue their
people from grinding poverty
and for those who face ridicule
and hostility as they seek to
speak for those with no voice.

silence

Come and hold them in
your grace-filled hands.

Lord,
we place this pebble at the
foot of your cross
as we pray for your church, here
and around the world as we
seek to be the face of Jesus
and for those who know the name
but not the power of Christ to
bring hope to a hopeless world.

silence

Come and hold them in
your grace-filled hands.

Lord,
we place this pebble at the
foot of your cross
as we pray for young people
who are facing the pressure
of their peers to conform
and for those whose bright futures
are lost in the haze of the
addictions they can't break.

silence

Come and hold them in
your grace-filled hands.

Lord, in your mercy,
hear our prayer. **Amen.**

Dismissal

Acts 1:8

Go in the grace of the Lord.
Go in the Love of the Father
Go in the power of the Spirit.
Go, and wherever He sends you,
live and serve in the presence
of the Father, the Son and
the Holy Spirit. **Amen.**

PENTECOST SUNDAY

Prayer of Approach

Psalm 104:1–3

Lord,
you open our eyes
that we might be witnesses
to your fingerprints over every
part of your creation;
you open our ears
that we might tell of the song
at the heart of all things;
you open our lips
that we might not remain silent
but sing a song of your glory;
you open our hearts
that we might worship the Lord of
glory with every fibre of our being.
Bless the Lord, O my soul;
your greatness and majesty
demand our praises! **Amen.**

Praise

John 20:21–22

Lord,
we praise you, the giver of peace—

through the cross you healed our
relationship with the Father;
because you died in our place,
we can begin again;
knowing that the tomb was empty,
today overflows with hope;
but it is through your gift
of the Holy Spirit
we can experience the
heights of grace
your living presence offers
and the depths of peace
with our God
that the gift of the Spirit guarantees.

We praise you for the knowledge
Christ gave of the Father
and of the mind-blowing
truth of his love.
We bless you now and
always for opening the
doorway to his presence
and for being the way into
his kingdom of grace.
We honour you for the riches
of joy, wonder, and love you
have showered upon us
and for the daily experience of the
Spirit's touch upon our lives.

Come, Lord, breathe upon us again
and indelibly mark our lives
with your indwelling Spirit.
Come, Lord, and flood our
hearts with your presence
that our words and deeds, what
we say and what we do,
may shout aloud that our
sovereign Lord reigns within
and that he will do so for
all and for ever.
In the name of Christ,
the Lord of life
and the source of the Spirit. **Amen.**

Confession

Acts 2:2–3

Lord,
come with the wind of change
and renew our lives;
come with fires of holiness
and cleanse our hearts;
come with the breeze of hope
and refresh our worship with
the joy of heaven;
come with the blazing
power of the Spirit
and make us new, make us strong,
and make us holy. **Amen.**

Intercession

Acts 2:4

Prepare a small table on which to place items as you pray. As different members of the congregation bring each item forward they should briefly hold them for the congregation to see what they have brought before placing it on the table.

Candle: Light in people's darkness

Lord,
we pray for those whose lives
are filled with darkness
and for those whose days are
shadowed with despair;
for those whose eyes are closed
to the hope of your presence
and for those whose words
and deeds darken the lives
of their neighbour.

Come, Holy Spirit,
and set the world on fire.

Newspaper: Need for honesty and truth

Lord,
we pray for those who
work in the media
and for those we trust to
bring us the news;
for those who share the news of
events here and around the world,
that they will do so with
honesty and integrity.
Come, Holy Spirit,
and set the world on fire.

Money: The economic situation

Lord,
we pray for those on the bottom
rung of life's ladder of hope
and for those who have
reached the top
without regard for those who
are still struggling;
for those who are counting
the pennies
and for those with too many
pennies to count.
Come, Holy Spirit,
and set the world on fire.

Bread and water: The hungry and starving

Lord,
we pray for those who do not know
where their next meal
is coming from
and for those who wonder
if it will come at all;
for those whose health is suffering
because they are drinking too much
and for those still thirsty for
life with real meaning.
Come, Holy Spirit,
and set the world on fire.

Tools/computer: Those who have lost their job

Lord,
we pray for those who set out
with such high hopes
and for those whose house of cards
has come crashing down;
for those whose work brought
them satisfaction and fulfilment
and for those now paying the
price of others' extravagance.
Come, Holy Spirit,
and set the world on fire.

Key: Homes and relationships under threat

Lord,
we pray for those whose homes
are a daily battleground
and whose promises to love
have been broken;
for those who still long to
find reconciliation
and for those who are discovering
the pain of learning to trust again.
Come, Holy Spirit,
and set the world on fire.

Pebbles: Those facing hard times, difficult choices

Lord,
we pray for those for whom each
day seems harder than the last

and for those wrung dry by
the pressures of life
and the struggle just to live;
for those who feel let
down by a society
that promised peace and security
and for those who are
discovering the emptiness
of the trinkets it offers.
Come, Holy Spirit,
and set the world on fire.

Bible: The Word of life and hope

Lord,
we pray for those who are
looking earnestly for
purpose and meaning
and for those who are finding it in
Jesus, the living word of God;
for those who are acknowledging
the promise of life to come
and for those who have received
the gift of the Holy Spirit
and are now seeking to live
and speak for their Lord.
Come, Holy Spirit,
and set the world on fire.

We bring our prayer in
the name of Christ
and in the power of the
Holy Spirit. **Amen.**

TRINITY SUNDAY

Prayer of Approach

Genesis 1:1–4

Father of creation,
we bring you our worship;
Lord of the heavens,
we come with songs of praise;
Spirit of light, truth, and glory,
we seek your presence to enable us
to worship the Father, the Son,
and the Holy Spirit. **Amen.**

Praise

Psalm 8:1–6

Lord,
we stand in awe at the
wonder of your glory!
There are no words we can find
that will offer the praises that
your majesty deserves.
It is as if our whole being is blinded
by the light of your presence
and we feel compelled to
bow before your glory.

Lord,
we cannot grasp but the tiniest part of
what it means for you to be God
and we can only scratch the surface
of the truth that is yours.
We lift our eyes and survey
the heavens you have
brought into being
and its vastness simply takes
our breath away and we
are lost in adoration.

Lord,
as we contemplate your glory and
wonder at the power that is yours
we are utterly overwhelmed
by your deep concern for
all you have made.
We are moved by your love that
is deep and vast and wide
and we are staggered by the
extravagance of your grace

that is forever flowing to
even the least deserving
person who ever lived.

Lord,
how can it be that you who
are the mighty one
and whose power, glory, and
majesty simply know no bounds
should long to know our love
and seek to bring us into
your living presence?
This is love beyond our
understanding
and grace we cannot comprehend.
It is love, hope, and grace
that we can only receive
and give you thanks and praise
from hearts in love with you.
We praise you in the name of
Christ the Lord. **Amen.**

Intercession

Matthew 28:18–20

Lord,
we pray for those who look back
on their lives with sadness
and for those who only
remember their 'if onlys'
and 'might have beens';
for those whose dreams
have come to nothing
and for those who never
dreamed at all.
May their experience of
Christ's presence
heal their wounds and
bring them hope.
Lord of today and every day,
hear our prayer.

Lord,
we pray for those who look
to the future in fear
and for those whose days are
clouded with uncertainty;
for those whose days are filled with
forgetfulness and confusion
and for those who are still seeking to
offer love, care, and compassion.
May their experience of
Christ's presence
heal their wounds and
bring them hope.
Lord of today and every day,
hear our prayer.

Lord,
we pray for those for whom each
new day is filled with despair
and for those whose search for
employment seems endless;
for those for whom today is filled
with only their memories
and for those who know that
they will spend it alone.
May their experience of
Christ's presence
heal their wounds and
bring them hope.
Lord of today and every day,
hear our prayer.

Lord,
we pray for those whose lives have
been engulfed in civil war
and for those who have lost
everything through earthquake,
hurricane, or fire;
for those whose lives have been
wrecked by the work of terrorists
and for those whose homes have
been washed away by flood.

May their experience of
Christ's presence
heal their wounds and
bring them hope.
Lord of today and every day,
hear our prayer.

Lord,
we pray for those who are
facing times of great stress
and for those who are facing
situations with which
they can't cope;
for those who are finding their
relationships falling apart
and for those who are filled
with regret for what they
did or failed to do.
May their experience of
Christ's presence
heal their wounds and
bring them hope.
Lord of today and every day,
hear our prayer.

Lord,
we pray for those in positions
of leadership in the life
of their nations
and for those with the power
but not the will to bring
hope to their people;
for the leaders of churches who long
to witness renewal and growth
and that all their members
might grasp the vision of
sharing their faith.
May their experience of
Christ's presence
heal their wounds and
bring them hope.
Lord of today and every day,
hear our prayer.

Lord,
we pray for ourselves and
the burdens and hopes
we carry within
and for the plans we have
and the choices we must
make in the days ahead;
for those concerns that we
have for our world, our
nation, and our church
and for the needs of those that God
has laid on our hearts and minds.
May our experience of
Christ's presence
heal our wounds and bring us hope.
Lord of today and every day,
hear our prayer.

We bring our prayers in
the name of Christ,
the one who heals wounds and
restores hope. **Amen.**

EIGHTH SUNDAY IN ORDINARY TIME

Prayer of Approach

Psalm 131

Lord,
we have come into your presence
that you might open our eyes;
we have come into your presence
that you might open our ears;
we have come into your presence
that you might open our hearts;
we have come into your presence
that our hearts might be set
on fire with your grace,
our ears might hear the cry
of those without hope,

and our eyes might see
your fingerprints
in every part of your creation
as you open our lips to sing of your
praise and your glory. **Amen.**

Thanksgiving

Isaiah 49:8–11

Father,
it is when we come with hearts
overflowing with thankfulness
that we see for the first time
the wonder of your grace.
We thank you that in times
when all seemed dark
your love washed over us and
we walked in your light;
when we experienced an emptiness
that nothing would fill
we discovered your extravagant
grace that changed everything.

We thank you that you have
touched our eyes
and as the scales of doubt and
despair were wiped away
it was as if we were seeing the glory
of your creation for the first time.
We thank you because
you longed to enter
the throne room of our days
and we have your
unbreakable promise
that we shall find our end in you.

It is from the abundance of
your grace-filled hands
that we have received far
richer blessings
than the world could ever offer.
It is because of your desire that
we should know your love
that our lives have been transformed
and our days renewed by
your living presence.

Thank you for those who met
with us on our journey
and spoke your name
and demonstrated your
love in their lives;
for those whose courage
challenged us to continue
to walk in faithfulness
and for those who have
shared our tears of sadness
and our tears of joy.

Thank you for Jesus who is the
heart and centre of your grace
and for his life, death,
and resurrection
which is the guarantee
of your promise
to make all things, even people
like us, completely new.

Come, Father, receive
our thanksgiving
for it comes from hearts set ablaze
by the living Christ. **Amen.**

Intercession

Matthew 6:25–26

Lord,
we pray for those who are
worried about their lives
and for those whose days are
crippled by unknown fears;
for those whose concerns rob
them of joy and peace
and for those who live out their
days filled with doubt and fear.
Lord of life,

hear our prayer.

Lord,
we pray for those who
worry about the past
and who are haunted by the
mistakes they have made;
for those who carry burdens that
no one knows anything about
and for those who are ashamed
of the things they have said
or done or thought.
Lord of life,
hear our prayer.

Lord,
we pray for those who worry
about tomorrow
and are overwhelmed by their
fear of the unknown;
for those whose depression and
anxiety is stealing their hope
and for those whose painful
memories cloud their
thoughts of the future.
Lord of life,
hear our prayer.

Lord,
we pray for those who
worry about today
and for whom each day is
a struggle to survive;
for those whose very real concerns
for their health weigh them down
and for those who know that
their days are too few.
Lord of life,
hear our prayer.

Lord,
we pray for those who have faced
the tragic loss of home and family
and for those who worry where
they will live and how they
will feed their family;
for those who feel torn apart by
the loss of paid employment
and for those who feel they have been
left behind by an uncaring society.
Lord of life,
hear our prayer.

We pray for those who have no
worries that disturb their daily lives
and for those who close
their eyes to the pain and
suffering around them;
for those known to us who have
a burden of concern that is
too heavy to carry alone
and for ourselves and the worries,
fears, and concerns for which
Christ is the answer.
Lord of life,
hear our prayer.

We bring our prayers in
the name of Christ,
the Prince of Peace and the
hope of the world. **Amen.**

NINTH SUNDAY IN ORDINARY TIME

Prayer of Approach

Psalm 46:1

Lord,
we have come to worship you
and not to run away
from the world;

we have come to enjoy
your presence
and not to escape from the
pressures of daily life.

Lord,
we have come to confess your glory
and not to feel self-righteous
by our coming;
we have come because you are
the source of all that is good
and the centre of every
heartfelt desire for peace;
we have come, and in our
coming, it is true
that we find a contentment and
a joy we find in no one else;
we have come because you, and
you alone, are our hope
and the hope of all the
world. **Amen.**

Thanksgiving
Genesis 8:15–16

Lord,
you are our song and the
heart of our praises;
from deep within us there
rises up such a longing
that nothing and no one
can ever satisfy;
you are the most holy God,
our wondrous Lord,
and our greatest pleasure is to
honour your mighty name.

You are the King of glory and
the centre of all creation.
Everyone, everywhere finds
their meaning and purpose,
their hope, and their salvation
in you, and in you alone.

The day that is not filled with
the knowledge of your
love remains empty
and the hour that is not focused
on your grace loses meaning.

To say that you are worthy of our
praises is a vast understatement
and to look elsewhere for hope and
satisfaction is a useless exercise.
Holy God, wonderful,
wonderful is your majesty
and your transcendent being
holds all things in the
hollow of your hand.

Lord,
where would we be
without your favour
and where would we experience
hope apart from your grace?
Never for an instant are we
far from your thoughts
and not for a moment are we
a thousand hairsbreadth
from your mercy.
If we could travel for a billion
years at ten thousand
times the speed of light
we would remain for ever at
the centre of your blessing.

Lord,
when we become engrossed
in the things of earth
and allow our thoughts to
be dominated by what
we have and hold,
you hold us gently and lead us
to the foot of the cross.
It is then that once again you
whisper in our hearts:

'In the time of my favour
I will answer you,
and in the day of salvation
I will help you.'

It is then as we see Jesus, and
look upon his brokenness
and suffering,
we know that Christ marks
the time of your favour
and this is the day when you
come to heal us and hold us
and make us whole.

From the depths of our
being we cry,
'Holy, holy is the Lord
God Almighty.
He is our King, our sovereign,
and our Saviour.' **Amen.**

Intercession
Genesis 7:24
We pray for those whose lives are
overwhelmed by darkness;
for those who have lost everything
through earthquake, storm, or fire
and for those whose home and
family have been swept away
by forces of nature beyond
their control.
Lord, in the darkness,
come as the light.

We pray for those whose lives are
overwhelmed by darkness;
for those who are anxiously waiting
for the doctor's diagnosis
and for those who are coming to
terms with the knowledge
that their days of life are more
limited than they ever imagined.
Lord, in the darkness,
come as the light.

We pray for those whose lives are
overwhelmed by darkness;
for those whose journey has drained
every experience of hope
and for those whose minds are full
of questions they can't answer
as they struggle to hold on to their
faith in the midst of the storm.
Lord, in the darkness,
come as the light.

We pray for those whose lives are
overwhelmed by darkness;
for those whose lives are blighted
by the addictions that hold them
and for those who have
yet to acknowledge how
far they have fallen
or to honestly seek the help
they so urgently need.
Lord, in the darkness,
come as the light.

We pray for those whose lives are
overwhelmed by darkness;
for those left with the feelings of
aloneness at the loss of a loved one
and for those still experiencing
a deep sense of rejection
through the indignity of
redundancy or the pain
of broken promises.
Lord, in the darkness,
come as the light.

We pray for those whose lives are
overwhelmed by darkness;
for those whose dreams were
destroyed by a terrorist's bomb

and for those whose faithful service
in the name of their country
is paid for daily through
their broken bodies and
shattered hopes.
Lord, in the darkness,
come as the light.

We pray for those whose lives are
overwhelmed by darkness;
for those whose daily life remains
a constant battle with anxiety
and for those whose childhood
memories and experiences
mean that peace and joy seem
to be forever out of reach.
Lord, in the darkness,
come as the light.

We pray for those whose lives are
overwhelmed by darkness;
for those we know for whom
each day is a journey of
doubt and despair
and for ourselves as we cope
with the worries and
fears we carry within
that we find hard to acknowledge
even to the Lord.
Lord, in the darkness,
come as the light.

We bring our prayers in the name
of the One, who is the light
and whose grace alone can
lighten even the darkest
places of life. **Amen.**

TENTH SUNDAY IN ORDINARY TIME

Prayer of Approach

Psalm 33:20–22

Lord,
we come in faith;
we come in hope;
we come in expectation;
we come in worship;
we come intent on singing
your praises;
we come because we know
you as Lord. **Amen.**

Thanksgiving

Genesis 12:2

Father,
we have gathered to offer
you heartfelt thanks
and the worship of lives set
on fire by your love.
We are here not simply by your
call of duty upon our lives
but because we cannot withhold
the longing to give you the glory
as a result of your grace which has
flooded our hearts and lives.

You are our creator and
the source of all life
and day by day we rely utterly
on your sustaining grace.
With the eye of faith
we feel bombarded by
more and more signs
of your fingerprints over every
part of this vast universe.

We give thanks for the
work of scientists
whose discoveries continually
inspire our wonderment

and undergird our worship,
joy, and thanksgiving.
Wherever we look we are
left breathless at the reach
of your sovereignty
and songs of praise and glory
well up within us
as, once again, we discern the loving
touch of our mighty God.

Father,
we thank you for the witness
of all your faithful people
who, like Abraham, proved
your faithfulness;
for those whose path has been
strewn with times of hard testing
and who have known the
assurance of your loving-
kindness through it all.

Today we honour you, our faithful
God and our loving Lord,
and we thank you that
there is nowhere we can
go, but you are there
and there is nothing we face but you
have promised to share it with us.
Wonderful, wonderful God,
how can we not thank you?
For you alone are the one who never
lets us go and never lets us down.
In Jesus' name, we give you our
thanks and praise. **Amen.**

Praise

Matthew 9:16

Lord,
you are the one who makes
all things new
and in your presence nothing
is ever the same again.
In Christ's life, death,
and resurrection
the past is healed, the future
is seen in hope,
and each day is renewed in
your living presence.

You touch our lives—and
we can begin again.
You hold us gently—and
our hope returns.
You speak in grace—and we
experience forgiveness.
You listen to our worries—and our
fears are surrounded by love.
You call us by name—and we
know we have a purpose
in your kingdom.

Lord,
we praise you that you have a
purpose that is vast and wide
and there is nothing and no
one who cannot experience
your renewing grace.
It began in the heart of the Father
before creation was born
and it will reach its zenith
before the throne of grace.
From before the beginning of all
things your love was reaching out
and it has always been your
ultimate purpose
to bring everything and everyone
everywhere to confess that
Jesus Christ is Lord.

Lord,
we praise you that through Jesus'
life, death, and resurrection
we can be healed,
lives can be restored,

forgiveness can be experienced,
wholeness can be entered into,
unconditional love can make all
things and all people new.

How can we not praise you—
life-giving, life-renewing,
life-affirming Lord?
No title is too high;
no praises too great;
no honour too worthy;
no name more wonderful than his!

Lord,
we praise you now and we
will praise you for ever,
for you alone are worthy of
our praises. **Amen.**

Intercession

Genesis 12:4

Lord,
we pray for those whose
journey is hard and long
and for those whose path is one
of sadness, pain, and fear;
for those whose home and
family have been lost in
[*name any recent tragedy*]
and for those who feel they
can struggle no more.
May they be held in the hands
of God's grace-filled people.
Lord, in your mercy,
hear our prayer.

Lord,
we pray for those who have chosen
the wrong path through life
and for those whose life of
crime has brought heartache
to their victims;
for those who have nowhere to
go, no place to call home
and for those whose home is a
cardboard box and they make
their bed in a shop doorway.
May they be held in the hands
of God's grace-filled people.
Lord, in your mercy,
hear our prayer.

Lord,
we pray for those who feel they
have travelled in vain
and for those whose determined
efforts to succeed have
ended in failure;
for those who have nothing and
are labelled scroungers by
those who have too much
and for those who are driven
to despair by their poverty
in a rich person's society.
May they be held in the hands
of God's grace-filled people.
Lord, in your mercy,
hear our prayer.

Lord,
we pray for those who daily face
the evils of terrorism and war
and for those who see no way
to reach the place of peace
for which they long;
for those living under corrupt
and violent governments who
murder their own people
and for those who still hope that the
world leaders will come to their aid.
May they be held in the hands
of God's grace-filled people.
Lord, in your mercy,
hear our prayer.

Lord,
we pray for homes where
anger, bitterness, and abuse
are all too common
and for those whose innocence
has been taken away by those
who should have cared;
for homes where love is paramount
and each member is cherished
and for those struggling to
cope with broken promises
and fragile trust.
May they be held in the hands
of God's grace-filled people.
Lord, in your mercy,
hear our prayer.

Lord,
we pray for those who have
heard God's call to set out
into the unknown
and for those who have responded
to his challenge to serve
him in unexpected ways;
for those who seek to serve
Christ in their daily work
and for those called to be beacons
of hope in their community
or across the world.
May they be held in the hands
of God's grace-filled people.
Lord, in your mercy,
hear our prayer.

Lord,
we pray for those who feel they
have no special gifts and
have lived ordinary lives
and for those who are now
beginning to discover God
is calling even them;
for those who look back to
opportunities missed and
challenges ignored
and for those who are finding
that he can use them in
ways they never expected.
May they be held in the hands
of God's grace-filled people.
Lord, in your mercy,
hear our prayer.

Lord,
we pray for ourselves and the
journeys we have taken and
obstacles we have faced
and for those for whom we
are concerned and the
paths they now tread;
for a renewed awareness that, like
Abram, we do not travel alone
and for God's grace as we seek
to share our journey of faith
with our neighbour.
May they be held in the hands
of God's grace-filled people.
Lord, in your mercy,
hear our prayer.

We bring all our prayers in
the name of Jesus,
who promised to be the beginning
and end of all our journeys. **Amen.**

ELEVENTH SUNDAY IN ORDINARY TIME

Prayer of Approach

Psalm 116:12–14

Lord,
our songs are not worthy
and our voices not strong enough;
our prayers are not trusting

and our faith is too weak;
our minds are full of our plans
and our hopes are not
focused on you;
our words are too often empty
and do not speak of your majesty.

So, Lord, by your Holy Spirit,
set us on fire so that
our songs and our voices,
our prayers and our faith,
our minds and our focus,
our words and our praises,
will give you the glory
that you deserve.

Come, Lord Jesus, come,
for we are here to worship
you. **Amen.**

Thanksgiving

Genesis 18:1

Father, we thank you for
those moments
when we have been overwhelmed
by your presence
and joy, peace, and hope have
welled up within us;
for those experiences of
your abounding grace
that have captured our hearts
and flooded our minds.

We thank you that again and again
you have shown yourself
to be present
not only in the stillness
but also in the storm;
not simply when all is well,
but also when our lives
are falling apart;
not just in the cool of the morning
but also in the heat of
the troubled day
and the sleep-starved night.

Father, we thank you
for giving us shelter in the storm
and rescuing us from danger,
lifting us up when we have fallen,
forgiving us when we were wrong,
cleansing us when our
lives were in a mess,
touching us when we felt so alone,
and holding us when we were afraid.
We thank you for being an oasis in
the desert moments of our lives:
when we felt spiritually dry
you quenched our thirst for hope;
when all seemed dark and empty
you drenched our weary
lives with joy;
when, in times of barrenness,
we had lost our way
you came and showed
us your rainbow
and led us to an empty cross
and an empty tomb.

Father, Son, and Holy Spirit,
we thank you for who you are,
and for all you have been,
and for all you will be. **Amen.**

Praise

Romans 5:8

Father,
we praise you for this
beautiful world
where there is so much to see,
to learn, and to discover.
When we feel the gentle
breeze upon our faces
it speaks to us of your tender touch;

when we hear the singing of the birds
our minds are filled with words
of praise for your love;
when the cool water of the stream
flows through our fingers
we give thanks for the life-
cleansing work of Christ;
when the air is filled with the
scent of many flowers
and our walk through the
forest assaults our senses
we long to experience the
fragrance of Jesus all our days.

Father,
we live in a world where our
acceptance is provisional
and our being included
often seems to depend
on who we are, the colour of our
skin, and what we have achieved.
We live in a nation where the
rich are becoming richer
and the poor even poorer—and
no one seems to care.
In our society we prefer to keep
ourselves to ourselves
and would do anything rather
than play the Samaritan.

Father,
we confess that we are utterly
overwhelmed by your grace
and your desire for our love
leaves us breathless.
There is nothing we can do to
make you love us more
and there are no good things
we can say or do
that can possibly mean we qualify
as worthy of your love.

We praise you that your love
is strong, demanding,
and all-embracing.
It is not condemning but it is
never weak and condoning.
Here is love that is free,
real, and eternal.

We praise you that your
love is unconditional
and that there is absolutely
nothing we can ever do
to deserve even a glimpse of
your loving-kindness.
Our affirmation that
Christ has died, Christ is risen,
and Christ will come again
is the sign of our thanks and praise for
your unconditional love. **Amen.**

Intercession

Matthew 9:37–38

Lord,
we pray for those who told
us the story of Jesus
and whose faith awoke in us
the desire to serve him;
for those whose words and deeds
spoke of their discipleship
and for those whose lives
demonstrated their love
for their Lord.
May the love of God
touch all our lives.

Lord,
we pray for those whom you
have called to serve you
and for those who live out their
response in their daily lives;
for those who serve as chaplains in
hospitals, prisons, and industry

and for those who risk their lives as
chaplains in the armed forces.
May the love of God
touch all our lives.

Lord,
we pray for those who each day
answer your call to discipleship
and for all who live as ambassadors
for Christ in their place of work;
for those who serve Christ in
the life of the church and
in their community
and for those sent overseas
with the message of hope,
healing, and grace.
May the love of God
touch all our lives.

Lord,
we pray for those who reach out to
those who have lost everything
and for those who stand alongside
those with no hope;
for those who offer compassion
and care to the homeless
and for those who get their hands
dirty in the name of Christ.
May the love of God
touch all our lives.

Lord,
we pray for those engaged in
planting new congregations
and for the opportunities of creating
fresh expressions of being church;
for those who nurture the work
and mission of the church
in their community
and for those who serve as local
preachers, pastoral visitors,
and evangelism enablers.
May the love of God
touch all our lives.

Lord,
we pray that each of us will seek
opportunities to share our faith
and for the Holy Spirit to
give us the courage to speak
the name of our Lord;
for every church to give a
higher priority to reaching
out to its local community
and for every member to have
a new desire to share God's
love with their neighbour.
May the love of God
touch all our lives.

Lord,
we pray for those for whom
we are concerned
and remember especially those we
love who are yet to know Christ;
for ourselves, that we may
be filled to overflowing
with the love of God
and that sharing this love will be the
most natural thing in the world.
May the love of God
touch all our lives.

We bring our prayers in the name of
the Lord of the harvest. **Amen.**

TWELFTH SUNDAY IN ORDINARY TIME

Prayer of Approach

Psalm 86:2–4

Lord,
to gather to worship you is the most
important thing in our lives

and to sing your praises
gives us joy forever;
we are here to pour out
the thankfulness that
wells up within us
and gathering in your name is
a sign of our love for you.
Fill us, Lord, with the Holy
Spirit that our praises
may be worthy of you
and our prayers of adoration will
rejoice your heart. **Amen.**

Thanksgiving

Genesis 21:8

Father,
it is because we have experienced
your love in our lives
that we have discovered the
joy of thankfulness;
it is because we have
counted our blessings
that we know just how much
we have received.

Again and again when we
take time to consider
the precious gift of life you have
permitted us to experience,
we are moved deep within with
the desire to offer you the
love of thankful hearts.
Again and again you have
touched us with your grace
and you have changed the
purpose and value of our
lives with your peace.
Again and again when we felt
an emptiness and a dryness
that could not be healed by
anything the world can offer,
you renewed our hope and
transformed our lives.

Father,
we came to you when our
faith was fragile
and like a father with his child
you lifted us when we fell, you
wiped away our tears,
and you taught us how to
walk in your ways.
When in our childish tantrums
we turned away in anger
and frustration,
like the prodigal's father
you reached out and
welcomed us home.

So, Father,
we have come to offer you a
feast of thanksgiving
and a table spread with songs of joy.
Our prayers are like presents
offered in love
and our celebration is an
echo of the praises
we long to offer around
your throne of grace.
We bring our thankfulness wrapped
up in the love of Jesus. **Amen.**

Praise

Romans 6:4

Father,
again and again we have tried
to change our ways
to be more caring, more
understanding, more forgiving.
But we find that the harder we
try the more we seem to fail
and each time we commit
ourselves to change

we find ourselves slipping all too
easily into our old ways.

We point the accusing finger
at our neighbour
and hide our eyes and our ears
that would accuse us too.
We comfort ourselves that we are
no worse than those around us
and we measure our lives against
those who, like us, have fallen.
It is when we stand next to Christ
that we know for certain
just how weak and feeble our
attempts to change really are.

Father,
we praise you that your call is not
to change, but to be changed,
to be transformed by the grace
of the Lord Jesus Christ,
and to be renewed by the power
of the Holy Spirit within.
Through your word in the Bible
we have your promise:
'Behold, I make all things new.'

Father,
we praise you for your offer
of new life in Christ
and that through his life,
death, and resurrection
we can experience the life-changing
power of the Holy Spirit.
We stand at the foot of the cross in
wonder, amazement, and hope
as Christ declares, 'It is
finished,' and we know
his victory was for us
and his word of assurance echoes
in our hearts and minds.

We praise you that in Christ's
victory on the cross
our new life has begun and our
hope has been restored.
At last we can know that the
struggle to be accepted is ended
and the arms of our heavenly
father are reaching out
and calling our name and
welcoming us home.

We praise you, our Father,
that this new life is no
prize we have won,
nor is it evidence of something we
have attained by our own effort.
It is entirely a gift of your
amazing grace
and yet another sign of your
extravagant love.

Father,
we can now call you Father
because, by your Holy Spirit,
we have been born anew, a new
creation born of grace.
By your Holy Spirit, fill our
hearts with joy unending
and our lips with songs of praise.
May the praises we offer
you here today
ring through all the world and
to the end of our days,
that one day they may be joined
to the songs of heaven.
This we ask in the name of Christ,
whose grace has set us free and
made us new. **Amen.**

Intercession
Matthew 10:29–31

Lord,
we pray for those with no voice
as their poverty silences
their cries for help
and for those whose skills are
no longer required in our
technological world;
for those who feel abandoned
by a society more concerned
with profit than with serving
and for those whose disabilities
make it harder to compete
with those who don't care.
Lord of compassion and caring,
we pray in hope.

Lord,
we pray for those with no
memory of who they are
or what they have been
and those they loved but who
now seem like strangers;
for those who feel they
have been forgotten
and who spend their days alone
with their memories—
but with no one with whom
they can share them.
Lord of compassion and caring,
we pray in hope.

Lord,
we pray for those who are unable
to see the beauty of your world
and for those who close their
eyes to the brokenness
of their neighbour;
for those whose world is being
destroyed by war and by famine
and for those whose greed
and ruthless ambition
are destroying a world
that isn't theirs.
Lord of compassion and caring,
we pray in hope.

Lord,
we pray for those who cannot
hear the song of a bird or
the voice of their child
and for those who close their
ears to the cry of those who
simply long for justice;
for those who give of themselves
to support those with no
home and no food
and for those who are deaf to
the longings of the poor
to have a chance to share in the
bounty of those who have
more than they need.
Lord of compassion and caring,
we pray in hope.

Lord,
we pray for those who feel they
are lost and worthless failures
and for those who find it hard
to love their neighbour
because they have forgotten
how to love themselves;
for those who are labelled
shirkers in a society
that judges our value by what we
have and by what we own
and for those who are strivers,
that they too will discover
their true value to God.
Lord of compassion and caring,
we pray in hope.

Lord,
we pray for those who live
alone and have no one with
whom to share their stories
and for those whose aloneness
is the result of bereavement
or broken promises;
for those whose days are filled with
'if onlys' and 'might have beens'
and for those who feel guilty
for the depression and anxiety
that cripples their days
and for those who have yet to
understand deep within
that they are not to blame.
Lord of compassion and caring,
we pray in hope.

Lord,
we pray for ourselves and our
weaknesses that others don't see;
for the worries and fears that leave
us damaged and struggling;
for the knowledge we carry within
of words we wish had
never been spoken,
of hopes that still remain unfulfilled,
of concerns for those we love deeply,
of doubts that undermine our
already fragile faith and assurance,
and for the promises of God's
love, peace, and forgiveness
to transform what we have
been, who we are, and
who we will become.
Lord of compassion and caring,
we pray in hope.

We bring our prayers in the
name of the One,
who was somebody,
who became a nobody,
that we might become the
someone we were always
planned to be. **Amen.**

THIRTEENTH SUNDAY IN ORDINARY TIME

Prayer of Approach

Psalm 13:5–6

Father,
prepare us to sing a song of hope
and to offer prayers of thankfulness;
teach us to come into your
presence in expectation
and to seek to give and not
simply to receive;
empower us to worship you
with our whole being
and enable us through your Holy
Spirit to lose ourselves in you.
We ask this in the name
of your Son, Jesus,
the heart and centre of
our praises. **Amen.**

Thanksgiving

Genesis 22:14

We live in a world of
beauty and wonder
that enriches and encourages
us to be thankful again.
There are rivers and streams
and valleys and mountains.
There are trees and flowers
and there are creatures that
swim, fly, walk, or crawl.
But we have not made them,
they are gifts from our Lord.

We live in a world of
sight and of shapes

that constantly bring
excitement and challenge.
There's a rainbow of colours
that dazzle and shine
and each day we experience
a vast array of designs.
Together they brighten our days
and light up our world
enriching all that they touch,
wherever they are found.
But we have used them forgetting
they are gifts from the Lord.

We live in a world of
noise and of sound
that break up the silence and
can thrill our hearts.
The sounds of laughter and
music, of singing and storm,
of the voices and footsteps
of those that we love
transform our experience
wherever they are heard.
But they would be impossible
without the gifts from our Lord.

We live in a world of
invention and science
that brings amazing discoveries
that are changing our lives.
The advances in medicine,
we can fly to the moon,
the speed of our travel in
time and in space,
computers and the internet that
have opened new worlds.
But all this is possible because
of the gifts of our Lord.

We live in a world of hope and
despair, of love and of friendship
that brings meaning and purpose
to our life on this earth.
Through the life, death, and
resurrection of Jesus
we are offered new life and the
promise of heaven to come.
Knowing Jesus as Saviour and
the Spirit's presence within
is only possible because of
the gift of Jesus as Lord.

We bring our prayer of thankfulness
for God's great provision
in the name of Jesus, the
greatest gift of all. **Amen.**

Praise

Romans 6:4

Lord,
we praise you for the love
that reaches out
to touch, change, and
renew our lives.
There is nothing we can
do to deserve
even one second of your
unconditional mercy.
We can never, ever live
the kind of lives
and walk a path of perfection
that will be worthy of
your acceptance.

You are an amazing God!
From the least to the greatest,
we are utterly dependent
on your grace.
It reaches down to the depths
to which we so easily fall
and like the prodigal's father
you come to meet us before
we have seen you

and to welcome us home
even before we knew we were lost.

Lord,
your grace comes to us at
such a great cost
and carries the cross of
forgiveness as a sign of hope.
How can we not turn to you
in praise and adoration
for the sacrifice of grace on Calvary?
How can we not sing of
your glory and majesty
as we stand and wonder at the
grace that sets us free?

You are an amazing God!
From all eternity you were,
are, and will be
sovereign of time and space.
You are the Lord of all things
past, present, and to come.
You hold all things in this world,
and worlds of which we
know nothing,
in the palm of your hand.
And yet this amazing
God comes close
to hold even us in hands
full of grace.
You did not have to love us
and there is no earthly reason
why you should love us
unconditionally.
But you are the God of grace
and though our sin creates
a barrier between us
your hand of grace reaches
us through the cross.

Our amazing God with the
grace-filled hands,
receive our prayer of praise
in the name of Christ,
the sign, symbol, and channel
of your grace. **Amen.**

Intercession

Matthew 10:29–30

We pray for those who are worth
more than the sparrows
and for those who have
yet to discover it;
for those who are homeless,
whose bed is a cardboard box
and who are covered with
a blanket of newspapers
and for those who simply walk
past on the other side
without a thought or a care
for those without hope.

silence

Lord, in your mercy,
hear our prayer.

We pray for those who are worth
more than the sparrows
and for those who have
yet to discover it;
for those who cry deep inside because
of the abuse they have suffered
that continues to damage
their lives today
and for those who called
it their 'little secret'
without any consideration for those
whose lives they had wrecked.

silence

Lord, in your mercy,
hear our prayer.

We pray for those who are worth
more than the sparrows
and for those who have
yet to discover it;
for the students who have
worked hard to qualify
but are labelled as 'shirkers'
when no work can be found
and for those on the bottom
rung of life's ladder
who pay the price of the mistakes
that others have made.

silence

Lord, in your mercy,
hear our prayer.

We pray for those who are worth
more than the sparrows
and for those who have
yet to discover it;
for those who sweep our streets
and remove the rubbish
from our homes
and for those who do not recognise
the valuable work they are doing
in removing the possible
source of infection.

silence

Lord, in your mercy,
hear our prayer.

We pray for those who are worth
more than the sparrows
and for those who have
yet to discover it;
for those who are social workers
who, when something goes wrong,
face the brunt of the media's wrath
and for those whose lives
have been enriched
by the help and support
that they give.

silence

Lord, in your mercy,
hear our prayer.

We pray for those who are worth
more than the sparrows
and for those who have
yet to discover it;
for those in the midst of a war zone
or whose home and family
have been destroyed by
the work of terrorists
and for those whose only ambition
is to find food for their
family for today.

silence

Lord, in your mercy,
hear our prayer.

We pray for those who are worth
more than the sparrows
and for those who have
yet to discover it;
for those who have lost everything
in [*name any recent tragedy*]
and have nothing left
that they value
and for those whose life
feels empty and lonely
as they grieve the loss of the
ones that they loved.

silence

Lord, in your mercy,
hear our prayer.

We pray for those who are worth more than the sparrows
and for those who have yet to discover it;
for those who have been made to feel worthless
and still find it hard to love themselves,
for ourselves when our worries and fears overwhelm us
and we are made to feel foolish because of our faith in Jesus.

silence

Lord, in your mercy,
hear our prayer.

We bring our prayers in the name of Jesus,
who counts the hairs on our heads
and knows when each of the sparrows falls down. **Amen.**

FOURTEENTH SUNDAY IN ORDINARY TIME

Prayer of Approach

Psalm 45:17

Lord,
we come to share our memories of your grace
and to sing of your mercy that makes us whole.
We come empty, searching, and longing for your touch
as we celebrate the glory of your name.
We come to recall all you have done for your creation
and to worship you for the freedom that was bought through Christ.
We come, not out of duty but with hearts overflowing with praise
and as your people simply longing to worship the Lord.
We come, not in our own name but in the name of Christ alone. **Amen.**

Thanksgiving

Romans 7:24–25a

Lord,
we sit and wait.
Daily we find ourselves
in a world that is in too much of a hurry—
weighed down by responsibilities too great,
hopes too weak,
and for whom peace is a distant memory.

Our world searches in vain for meaning and purpose
and too often finds itself looking for the wrong things
and in the least helpful places.

At times we too discover we have filled our days
with pleasure which lasts but for a moment
and all too soon is gone for ever.
We have permitted our days to be submerged
under the weight of material possessions
and precious moments of our lives to be lost

in the barren wastes of self-
centredness and self-interest.

Lord,
we thank you that you continue
to search the horizon
like the prodigal Father you are;
by grace you reach out to take hold
of all that we have been, all that
we are, and all we will be.

We thank you, Father
of endless love,
that you come to meet us,
not to judge, but to welcome,
not to highlight our mistakes,
but to renew us,
not to ignore our falling
short, but to pick us up,
not to make us pay for
our prodigal lives,
but to hold a party to celebrate
that through Jesus
we can come home—not
as fearful slaves
but as your precious
children of grace.

Father, our Father,
we thank you and we worship
you with songs of joy
and we honour you, the
King of all creation,
who by grace has made us
your sons and daughters.

We bring our prayers
of thanksgiving
and our songs of praise in
the name of Jesus,
who alone enables us to sing
the song of grace. **Amen.**

Confession

Matthew 11:17

Father,
we have spent our days
seeking fulfilment
only to discover we have
an emptiness within;
we long to know that our
lives have a purpose
but we lose our way in our
assertion of self-sufficiency;
we invest our time and our
energy in things of no value
and we arrive empty-handed
at the throne of the King.

We confess often our focus has
been on the things of earth
and we have forgotten to lift
our eyes to heaven.
Our plans and dreams, our
hopes and our aspirations
have pleased no one but ourselves
and we have abandoned
our walk of faith
to the side streets of our lives.

Father,
come forgive, cleanse, renew,
and reclaim us as your own
that we, by your grace, might
once again enter your
presence with joy. **Amen.**

Intercession

Genesis 24:34

I am a servant of the Lord
as I seek to serve the community.
The work of a police officer,
magistrate, and probation officer
can make the difference, enabling
a person to start again

and to live a life of value
and purpose.
Pray for me as I seek to
serve the Lord
as I serve the community.

silence

I am a servant of the Lord
as I seek to serve young people.
Teachers, lecturers, and
careers officers
have a vital role to play in
the future of our youth.
Pray for me as I seek to
serve the Lord
as I serve the community.

silence

I am a servant of the Lord
as I seek to serve those
who elected me.
Members of parliament
and local councillors
seek to use our gifts and
the resources we receive
for the benefit of all.
Pray for me as I seek to
serve the Lord
as I serve the community.

silence

I am a servant of the Lord
as I seek to serve as the
best parent I can be.
The care and nurture of family
life is of vital importance
for the future of a society
where everyone is valued.
Pray for me as I seek to serve the Lord
as I serve the community.

silence

I am a servant of the Lord
as I seek to serve as a member
of the armed forces.
Our role of peacekeepers in
the world's trouble spots
brings hope in place of strife and
rescue for those in danger.
Pray for me as I seek to
serve the Lord
as I serve the community.

silence

I am a servant of the Lord
as I seek to serve the needy and
the hungry around the world:
bringing food to the starving and
medicine to the sick and
teaching them to care for themselves
and to produce their own food.
Pray for me as I seek to
serve the Lord
as I serve the community.

silence

I am a servant of the Lord
as I seek to serve those
who have lost hope:
reaching out to those whose
home is a cardboard box
and whose dependence
on drink and drugs has
stolen their self-worth.
Pray for me as I seek to serve the Lord
as I serve the community.

silence

We are servants of the Lord
as we seek to serve our neighbour
by sharing the love of God.
In the stillness remember before him
those his grace has laid on your heart
that we may have the courage and
sensitivity to name Jesus as Lord.
Pray for yourself as you seek
to serve the Lord
in his name.

silence

We bring our prayers in the name
of the Servant King. **Amen.**

FIFTEENTH SUNDAY IN ORDINARY TIME

Prayer of Approach

Psalm 119:105

Lord,
we have come to hear your Word;
open our ears to its promise of grace.
We have come to be fed
by your Word;
open our hearts that we might
be nourished by your truth.
We have come to be guided
by your Word;
focus our minds on the
way of Christ.
We have come to be embraced
by your Word
that Christ may be the way, the
truth, and the life for us. **Amen.**

Thanksgiving

Romans 8:1–2

Father,
we can use words of thanksgiving
and sing songs of praise;
we can use lofty sounding phrases
as we seek to declare your glory.
All the time deep down we know
that we have barely scratched
the surface of your majesty
and that your glory extends from
one end of eternity to the other.

So great is your power and authority,
your sovereignty and majesty,
that even the whole universe is
not sufficient to contain you.
We look up and see the stars
stretching out far beyond
our comprehension.
It is then that the mind-blowing
truth dawns upon us—
we can talk in person with the
God who holds all things
in the palm of his hand!

Father,
we come not simply with
words of thanksgiving
but with hearts overflowing
with a gratitude
and a sense of joy and wonderment
too deep for mere words.

How can we not thank you?

In Jesus you came and shared
all that life means to us
that we might experience a life
that is soaked in your grace.

How can we not thank you?

You did not wait until
we turned to you
or lived our lives in ways
that brought you glory.

You did not come to lay a
heavy load upon us
but to set us free from all
that weighed us down.

How can we not thank you?

Through Christ's life, death,
and resurrection
you unlocked the door
of our prison cell
that we might walk with
you from now
until we meet you face to face.

Father, we bring our prayer
in the name of Jesus
and overwhelmed with
thankfulness. **Amen.**

Confession

Genesis 25:34b

Father,
forgive us that we are so careless
in the way we treat your world
and for the little thought we give
as to how our choices today
will impact on the lives of
others around the world.
Forgive us that we spend so little
time alone with you in prayer
and that we would rather read the
daily paper than read your Word.
Forgive us that we fail to
take account of the effects
our words and deeds
daily have upon those around us
and that we are so anxious to
highlight each other's failings
that we easily overlook the
times when we fall short of
living to bring you glory.

Father,
we ask that you will not
only forgive us,
but that we may know what
it means to start again;
may we experience the joy of
your renewing Spirit
and we ask that you will enable
us to forgive one another.

We ask our prayer in
the name Christ,
who died to make us new. **Amen.**

Intercession

Matthew 13:17

Father,
we pray for those who sow seeds
of care and compassion
and bring hope, peace, and
security to those they serve;
for those who plant seeds of care
in homes for the elderly
and for those whose presence
enables many to remain
in their own home.
May those who sow in love
reap a harvest of hope.

Father,
we pray for those who sow seeds
of support and understanding;
for those who serve as chaplains
planting seeds of hope
in hospitals, colleges,
universities, and prisons;
for those whose work seems
to go largely unrewarded
and for those reaping a harvest
through their sharing of faith.
May those who sow in love
reap a harvest of hope.

Father,
we pray for those who seek to
sow seeds of knowledge;
for those who work with children
in preschool play groups
as they encourage little ones
along the path of discovery;
for teachers, teacher's assistants,
college and university lecturers
as they show their students
how to dig for even
deeper understanding.
May those who sow in love
reap a harvest of hope.

Father,
we pray for those who seek to sow
seeds of a good neighbour;
for those who visit the sick, the
bereaved, and the lonely
and for those who refuse to
allow their own needs to stifle
the growth of compassion;
for GPs, practice nurses,
receptionists, and all the staff
of the local health centre
and for the staff of Citizens
Advice and Victims Support
as they reach out to those
in great need.
May those who sow in love
reap a harvest of hope.

Father,
we pray for those who seek
to sow seeds of justice;
for those who speak out for
those with no voice
and for those who ensure that
the cry of injustice is heard;
for those with a mission to those
whose home is a cardboard box
and for those who show
compassion to those with
no past and no future.
May those who sow in love
reap a harvest of hope.

Father,
we pray for those who seek to
sow seeds of faith and hope;
for those who serve as street pastors
as they witness to the love of God
and for those who are
pastoral visitors who care
for the body of Christ;
for those who counsel the ones
whose days are crippled by
anxiety, fear, and depression
and who walk with those
who still carry their times
of abuse within them.
May those who sow in love
reap a harvest of hope.

Father,
we pray for those who seek to
sow seeds of truth and love;
for the church to declare the
good news and not echo
the agenda of the world
and that its witness to the timeless
truth of God will be rooted
in love for the broken;
for each Christian to sow
seeds of hope in the soil of
a materialistic society
and to witness with joy to
the challenge of Jesus who
heals and restores.
May those who sow in love
reap a harvest of hope.

Father,
we pray for those we know
to be in need of hope,
healing, and renewal.

silence

May they know the presence of
Christ and his grace in their lives.
We pray for ourselves, that we
might be agents of Jesus
as we witness to the love of God
in all we say and do and are.
May those who sow in love
reap a harvest of hope.

We bring our prayers in
the name of Jesus,
who sows the good seed of his grace
for a harvest of eternal life. **Amen.**

SIXTEENTH SUNDAY IN ORDINARY TIME

Prayer of Approach

Psalm 139:1–4

Father,
you are utterly amazing!

You are sovereign of the universe
and the Lord of history;
there is nothing you do not know
and there is no one you do
not fully understand.

Father,
you are utterly amazing!
And we have come to worship you,
our amazing God. **Amen.**

Praise

Genesis 28:16

Lord,
we think we know how
Jacob must have felt
when he discovered your presence
when he least expected.
You were there with him,
leading him, guiding him—
being the way for him.
But when he woke up to
knowing you were there
he knew deep within himself—
he simply had to worship you.

We praise you for the way you
make each day so special
and how, even on the darkest day,
just to know you are there
is so important.
The day may be dreary,
it may be full of problems
and sorrows,
we may feel small and insignificant,
and we may be wondering
how we will cope.

But your being there,
offering us the gift of a new
day, changes everything,
and to have the assurance
that whatever we face
we will never have to face alone—
because we have discovered
the living God of all creation
changes everything.

And so we praise you!

We praise you for the
glimpse caught of you

in the sad eyes of the old
lady now alone;
in the laughter of the small child;
in the joy of the mother as she
held her newborn baby;
in the sense of contentment
on the grandparent's face;
in the gold of the lingering sunset;
in the majesty of the towering peaks;
in the satisfaction of a job well done;
in the memories of people and
places that meant so much.

We praise you most when we
stand before the empty cross
and peep in amazement
into the empty tomb
then find our hearts filled with
the Holy Spirit's presence.

And so we praise you!

What else can we do once
we have discovered
that we are for ever in the
presence of the living God—
who loves us beyond all expectation?

Praise the Lord. **Amen.**

Confession

Romans 8:12–17

Father,
how patient you are with us
and how understanding
even when we fail you.

You offered us life and we
have settled for existence.
You promised us a new beginning
but we resisted being changed.
You gave us everything but we
thought it had to be earned.
You promised a place in your
heaven but our focus is
on the things of earth.
You call us to follow you, to
take up our cross, to bear
witness to your name
but we have allowed ourselves
to be content with our
limited discipleship.

Forgive us, Lord, and call
us again to trust you with
the whole of our lives,
that by your grace we may yet
become the disciples you
always meant us to be.

In the name of Christ, who calls
and goes on calling. **Amen.**

Intercession

Matthew 13:24–26

Think of someone, you don't
know their name—
just another person whose
home has been flooded.
Think of how you would feel,
how you would respond
to see everything you cherished
completely ruined.
Hold them now in the
presence of God.

silence

Think of someone, you may
not know their name—
someone who longed for the
parenthood that never happened.

Think of what it would mean to you
to see your dreams unfulfilled
and your deepest desire left
as an ache within.
Hold them now in the
presence of God.

silence

Think of someone, you may
not know their name—
someone who spends their days
locked in a prison cell.
Their prison bars may be made
of their fears and anxieties
but their inner pain bars the way
to a life of joy and freedom.
Hold them now in the
presence of God.

silence

Think of someone you may
know by name—
someone who can't remember
who or what you are;
the dementia has not only
impacted their whole life
but also everyone they knew
and loved feels the pain.
Hold them now in the
presence of God.

silence

Think of someone, you may
not know their name—
the abuse they suffered robbed
them of their innocence;
you cannot see them, but they
still bear the scars within
and every relationship is touched by
the shame they ought not to feel.
Hold them now in the
presence of God.

silence

Think of someone, you may
not know their name—
just someone living in the midst
of [*name any recent tragedy*].
Their first thought of the day:
Will there be anything to eat?
They do not know how long their
malnourished child will survive.
Hold them now in the
presence of God.

silence

Think of someone, you may
not know their name—
a local councillor or a
member of parliament
who felt called by God to
serve him as a politician.
The call is real and the
challenge is still there
as they seek to balance their
principles with the party line.
Hold them now in the
presence of God.

silence

Think of someone, you may
not know their name—
just a child who would love to
have their own parent.
They see pictures of families
enjoying being together

and they long to have a mum
and dad of their own.
Hold them now in the
presence of God.

silence

Think of someone you
know by name—
remember those who are troubled
by the doctor's diagnosis.
Think of those whose whole life is
being changed by their illness
and also those who know their days
are shorter than they had hoped.
Hold them now in the
presence of God.

silence

Think of yourself and all you will
be facing in the coming days—
remember you are being held
in the presence of God.

silence

We bring our prayers in
the name of Christ,
whose love is great enough
to hold us all. **Amen.**

SEVENTEENTH SUNDAY IN ORDINARY TIME

Prayer of Approach

Psalm 86:11–12

Lord,
as we gather for worship
remind us that praising you is
not for an hour a week.
You require it to be our
whole life experience
and a daily expression of our
joy in your presence.
Come speak with us, Lord,
and make us whole.
Come touch our lives that
we may honour you.
Come fill us with the Holy Spirit
that our songs, prayers, and praises
may we be worthy of you. **Amen.**

Thanksgiving

Psalm 105:1–2

Father, we have a thankfulness
that at times is overwhelming
as it seems to permeate every
part of our being.
We sing, not simply songs of praise,
but to thank you for who you
are and what you have done.

You are the one who gave us life
and in Jesus, your Son, you
have given us new life.
Every time we look at the cross
and remember his sacrifice
we hear you whispering in our ears,
'This is how much you matter to me!'

We live in a world where many
people feel unwanted and unloved
and many are aware that they don't
count and are not valued.
In this world we are judged by who
we are and what we have achieved
but at the cross all barriers
have been destroyed.
As we look to Jesus on the cross
we hear God saying to us,
'You matter because you
matter to me.'

Thank you, our creator God,
for becoming in Jesus the
source of our hope
and the one in whom we
can begin again.
Thank you for touching our
lives with your grace
and drawing your prodigal
children home.
Thank you that again and
again when we fall
you reach down, hold our
hands, and lift us up.
Thank you that there is
nothing we can say or do
that will make you love us more,
and there is nothing we can say or do
that will ever stop you loving us!

Wonderful, wonderful God,
we praise you for who you are
and we thank you for all you
have done to make us whole.
We bring our prayer in
the name of Jesus,
in whom you have shown us a
love that never ends. **Amen.**

Intercession

Matthew 13:31

Lord,
we pray for homes that have
become a battlefield
and for relationships that are
in danger of falling apart;
for places where there are
endless arguments
and where trust has been broken
and forgiveness forgotten.
Come, Lord, and plant the
seed of your kingdom.
The Lord hears our prayer.
Thanks be to God.

Lord,
we pray for those whose choices
have led them to a prison cell
and for those who seem unable
to do the right thing;
for those who turn to crime
to fund their addiction
and for those who have no conscience
as to whom they are hurting.
Come, Lord, and plant the
seed of your kingdom.
The Lord hears our prayer.
Thanks be to God.

Lord,
we pray for those who once
walked faithfully with Christ
but who have long ago left behind
the faith they once had;
for those who no longer meet
for worship and fellowship
and for those who long for someone
to invite them to come home.
Come, Lord, and plant the
seed of your kingdom.
The Lord hears our prayer.
Thanks be to God.

Lord,
we pray for those who work in
manufacturing industries
and for scientists, chemists,
physicists, and engineers
on whom we depend for the
wealth of the nation;
for those whose research opens
doors to new discoveries
and for civil servants who
serve the community.

Come, Lord, and plant the
seed of your kingdom.
The Lord hears our prayer.
Thanks be to God.

Lord,
we pray for those on whom
we depend for our safety;
for police officers, the fire brigade,
and for lifeboat crews
and for judges, magistrates,
and probation officers
who are responsible for dealing
with those who get it wrong.
Come, Lord, and plant the
seed of your kingdom.
The Lord hears our prayer.
Thanks be to God.

Lord,
we pray for those facing times of
ill-health and of weakness
and for those whose days are filled
with pain and discomfort;
for those whose eyesight, strength,
and mobility are failing
and for those coming to terms with
the limited number of their days.
Come, Lord, and plant the
seed of your kingdom.
The Lord hears our prayer.
Thanks be to God.

Lord,
we pray for those mourning the
loss of someone they loved
and for those for whom the
feeling of aloneness is hard;
for those unable to leave
their home unaided
and for those who resent losing
their independence.
Come, Lord, and plant the
seed of your kingdom.
The Lord hears our prayer.
Thanks be to God.

Lord,
we pray for ourselves and
those known to us
as we seek your blessing on
those in great need;
for a new realisation that you
have planted gifts in our lives
and for a willingness to use them
in the service of your kingdom.
Come, Lord, and plant the
seed of your kingdom.
The Lord hears our prayer.
Thanks be to God.

We bring our prayers in
the name of Jesus,
who is the King of the
kingdom of God. **Amen.**

EIGHTEENTH SUNDAY IN ORDINARY TIME

Prayer of Approach

Psalm 17:6–9

Lord,
you are our strength
and you are our hope;
you are our Saviour
and you are our God.

You are the one whom we worship
and you are the one whom we love;
you are the one whom we pray to
and you are the one who listens.

Lord,
by your Holy Spirit,

enable us to worship you
our strength, our hope, our
Saviour, and our God. **Amen.**

Praise

Matthew 14:14

Father,
we praise you that you
never turn us away
and you never reject us
or refuse to listen;
when we are in need we know
we can come to you.

You are our creator, sustainer,
and redeemer.
Through your sovereign will you
brought all things into being.
Everything that has ever been
finds its origin in you
and everyone who has ever lived
has received life by your grace.
Moment by moment, all
life depends on your
sustaining power;
each new day is a free gift from
your grace-laden hand.

We praise you, our holy God.
There is no God like you and
there is no God besides you;
you alone are sovereign
over all things.
In you there is no evil and in your
presence nothing evil can exist.
You are holy beyond our
understanding
and you are God beyond
our comprehension.

Father, we must make you smile
when we begin to think we know
who you are and what you can do.
You know the truth:
that when we gather together the
totality of all that we know
we have yet to scratch the surface
of your knowledge of all things
and we have not even made a
mark on all that you are.
You are our God and your knowledge
of who we are is complete
and your desire that we should call
you our Father is paramount.
We praise you, our holy,
self-giving God,
who in and through Christ
you have done everything
to meet our need of hope,
forgiveness, and renewal.

We praise you, our God of all grace.
We praise you, our God who
makes all things new.
We praise you, our God whose
love for us is overwhelming.
We praise you, our God. **Amen.**

Intercession

Genesis 32:27–29

Father,
we bring before you those
for whom your name
is a term of abuse and not
a song of praise.
May they know you and love you,
their heavenly Father.

silence

Lord, in your mercy,
hear our prayer.

Father,
we bring before you those for
whom life is a struggle
as each day they fight the
battle against addiction.
May they know you
and find in you
the strength to overcome.

silence

Lord, in your mercy,
hear our prayer.

Father,
we bring before you those for
whom life is an empty void
as they are overwhelmed with
depression and anxiety.
May they find in you the
greater comforter
who can heal the
emptiness within.

silence

Lord, in your mercy,
hear our prayer.

Father,
we bring before you those who
have lost home and family
through the work of the
terrorist's bomb or civil war.
May they experience in you the
peace that passes understanding
and the hope that never fails.

silence

Lord, in your mercy,
hear our prayer.

Father,
we bring before you the needs of
our neighbour, wherever they live,
as they seek justice, freedom, and
the chance to start again.
May they discover in you the
one who stands with them
and who remains faithful in the
midst of all that they face.

silence

Lord, in your mercy,
hear our prayer.

Father,
we bring before you those whose
lives have been wrecked by abuse
as they still feel the pain of their
childhood or the internet
hate mail they received.
May they know that your love
can heal the deepest wound
and that your grace can heal their
scars and remove their shame.

silence

Lord, in your mercy,
hear our prayer.

Father,
we bring before you those who have
been devastated by serious illness
and those who are haunted by their
'if onlys' and 'might have beens'.
May they experience that
life-changing grace that
opens closed doors
and discover that you still
have a purpose for them
that is vast and wide.

silence

Lord, in your mercy,
hear our prayer.

Father,
we bring before you the hopes and
the fears of those we know
and the concerns, doubts,
and questions we find
in our own hearts.
May we know you as Father, not
just in words but in truth
and may you equip us to speak of
the one who makes us whole.

silence

Lord, in your mercy,
hear our prayer.

We bring our prayers in
the name of Jesus,
the Father's Son, who is in the midst
of all our struggles. **Amen.**

NINETEENTH SUNDAY IN ORDINARY TIME

Prayer of Approach

Psalm 105:1–4

Lord,
we have come with problems
in our minds
and deep concerns in our hearts.
We have come with questions
we can't answer
and hopes that forever
seem out of reach.
We have come to seek you, Lord,
and to sing your praises.
We have come to give you thanks
for all that we have received
as children of grace.
We have come, not for ourselves,
nor that we might find our
problems solved,
our questions answered, and
our hope restored.
We have come to give you
the worship, honour, and
glory you deserve
and to do it in Jesus' name. **Amen.**

Thanksgiving

Matthew 14:30–31

Lord,
we thank you that in the
midst of our fears
you hold our hands
and that when we have reached
the end of our tether
you are never far away.

The disciples were afraid of
the wind and the waves
and they had lost all confidence
in saving themselves.
They had recognised the
limits of their abilities
and they, in desperation,
turned to you.

We thank you that when
we feel we are sinking
your strength holds us fast.
When we know we cannot
sink any lower
it is then we discover underneath
are the everlasting arms.
When we feel that we have reached
the end and can go no further
it is then we hear your word
from the empty tomb

that declares you turn our ends
into new beginnings!

We thank you that again and again
you meet us in the depths
and raise us to the heights.
You are the God who meets us at
the moment of our greatest need
and promises, 'Lo, I am
with you always.'
We thank you that there is
nowhere we can go and
you will not find us
and that it is when we acknowledge
our own weaknesses and failures
that you can lift us, hold us,
heal us, and change us.

Lord,
hold us in the midst of our
storms of doubt and fear
and be there to hold us in
your mighty grace.
May we for ever praise
and thank you,
our living Lord and Saviour.

In Jesus' name. **Amen.**

Confession

Genesis 37:2–3

Father, we confess
that too often we love our
possessions more than we should
and honour your name far
less than we ought;
that we have a deep desire
to be well thought of
and a weakness for seeking
praise we don't deserve;
that our focus is on ourselves
and our own needs
and not on the needs of others
and the glory of your name;
that like Jacob we have allowed
our attitudes to hurt others
and like Joseph we have damaged
relationships by our behaviour.

Father, we confess
our need of forgiveness that is more
than wiping the slate clean
but that which heals relationships
and restores hope for all.

The Father says,
'By grace you are forgiven and by
grace you are made whole,
now live in my grace that my
forgiveness may flow out
through you.' **Amen.**

Intercession

Romans 10:9

I ask your prayers for those
who answer God's call to
share their faith in Jesus
and are prepared to serve him
at home and overseas;
for those who still go to the
remote places on earth
to bring healthcare, agricultural
skills, and the good news of Jesus
that hope, strength, and
self-sufficiency in place
of aid is possible.
May all that we do
bring glory to God.

I ask your prayers for those who
witness to Christ where they are
and for those who lead
worship and preach the good
news of our Saviour;

for those who share their faith with
children and young people
and for Sunday school
teachers, youth workers,
and university chaplains.
May all that we do
bring glory to God.

I ask your prayers for those who
witness to their faith in Christ
and do so at great risk to themselves;
for those have lost home and family,
their work, and their lives
and for those whose passion
and commitment are a
challenge to us all.
May all that we do
bring glory to God.

I ask your prayers for those
imprisoned for their faith
and for all who have taken a stand
against injustice and corruption;
for those who still languish in
detention without trial
and for those whose faith, love, and
forgiveness in Christ's name
touch those whose job
is to guard them.
May all that we do
bring glory to God.

I ask your prayers for those involved
in the work of Bible translation
and for those whose obedience,
skill, and commitment
enables more and more
people to have a Bible in
their own language;
for those who risk their lives as
they transport Bibles in secret
and for those whose faithful witness
means more and more are
naming Jesus as Lord.
May all that we do
bring glory to God.

I ask your prayers for those
who work out their
faith in their homes
and for those who are ready to
name Jesus in their place of work;
for those who live out their faith
as sports men and women
and for those who witness to
Christ as local councillors or
members of parliament.
May all that we do
bring glory to God.

I ask your prayers for those
who demonstrate their
faith in their daily life
and for those whose response
to serious illness and death
remains a powerful witness
and a challenge to us all;
for those whose witness rings true
because they are so filled
with the love of God
and for those whose experience
of God's grace
can offer forgiveness and love to
those who have hurt them most.
May all that we do
bring glory to God.

We bring all our prayers in
the name of Christ,
our crucified, risen, and
ascended Lord. **Amen.**

TWENTIETH SUNDAY IN ORDINARY TIME

Prayer of Approach

Psalm 133:1

Lord,
we have assembled in your name
and we have come to
sing your praises.
May everything we say and do
bring honour to your name
as, by your Holy Spirit, you make
us one in Christ. **Amen.**

Praise

Romans 11:27

Father,
how can we not praise you,
for you are the Lord of life and
the King of the kingdom;
how can we not worship you,
sovereign over all things—
Lord of time, of history,
and of eternity;
how can we not praise you for
all you have done for us,
bringing hope to the hopeless
and light in the darkness?

Father,
your grace, your undeserved
love is what makes us whole
and it is your covenant
promise that sets us free.
You are truly amazing for the
way you reach out to the lost
and bring home those who
would be prodigals.

Your Word overflows with
your promises
and in Christ we find the
fulfilment of them all.
He is the focal point of all
that you have promised
and the fulcrum of your
never-ending grace.

We praise you for your firmness
in dealing with our sin
and your gentleness in your
compassion for the sinner.
Though you are holy beyond
our comprehension
and your majesty and sovereignty
outstrip all our words,
you are faithful to your
covenant promise.
In Christ we are washed clean and
stand before you as your children.

Covenant Lord, we praise you
that as Isaiah declared,
'Though our sins were as scarlet,
we can be as white as snow.'
We praise you that though you take
our sinful lives very seriously
your grace-love and your
cleansing power are sufficient
for all our needs.
In Jesus we can have the assurance
that we are accepted
and that because of your covenant
promise we can be certain
that Christ has gone to
prepare a place for us in
the heaven of his love.

Covenant God, receive our
praises as a down payment
of the worship we long to offer
before the throne of grace.

In the name of Christ, our
covenant Saviour. **Amen.**

Intercession
Genesis 45:4–7
Prepare a set of six candles. Light a new candle as you begin each prayer.

We light this candle for
those who seek to help
those who are hungry
and to bring hope to those who
have no food for their children;
for those who seek to change
the giving of short-term aid
into fairer trading for those
countries squeezed out by
the larger monopolies.

silence

May the light and love of Christ
change hearts and minds.

We light this candle for
those seeking to help those
affected by disaster
and for those who give of their
time, skills, and themselves
to rescue others;
for those facing the latest
earthquake zone, forest
fire, or dangerous flood
and for those who put their
own lives at risk to save
those in greatest danger.

silence

May the light and love of
Christ be their reward.

We light this candle for those
diagnosed with a terminal illness
and for those overwhelmed
by the news and have no
one to share it with;
for the support from medical staff,
Macmillan nurses, and hospices
and for a new sense of peace and a
renewed sense of God's presence.

silence

May the light and love of
Christ bring hope.

We light this candle for those
whose relationships are at
the point of breaking
and for those still seeking to
restore the love and trust
that once was there;
for those who live alone, by design
or the result of bereavement
and for those who are grieving
and for those with only
their memories to share.

silence

May the light and love of
Christ bring peace and joy.

We light this candle for those living
rough on the streets of our cities
and for those with no past or
no future as today is all with
which they can cope;
for those who reach out with
food and warm clothes,
with friendship and faith
and for those who remind us of
the wealth that is ours compared
to paupers around us.

silence

May the light and love of Christ
change hearts and minds.

We light this candle for those
known to us for whom we
have promised to pray
and for ourselves and the concerned
in our hearts and minds.

silence

May the light of Christ
transform our days. **Amen.**

TWENTY-FIRST SUNDAY IN ORDINARY TIME

Prayer of Approach

Romans 12:1

Our worship is not simply
in words of faith
but in deeds of love and
compassion.
Our praises are not confined
within the doors of the church
but must flow out in acts of grace.
Our thanksgiving must
flow from our hearts
but must touch everyone we meet.
Our meeting is not for a
blessing for ourselves
but that we may give honour
and glory to God. **Amen.**

Praise

Psalm 124:8

We praise you, Lord, that
we can look to you as the
source of everything good
and the fount of all that is
really important in our
life in this world.
You were there before
the dawn of time
and no big bang could have been
without your authority.
Your power echoes through
this world and worlds
beyond our own.

We praise you that who and what
you will be for ever is beyond us
and that ultimately our tiny finite
minds cannot grasp your majesty.
We worship you for the
awesome God that you are
and we are here to celebrate some of
how utterly amazing you really are.

Sovereign, Saviour, King, living
God, author of creation,
master of the universe,
we simply run out of words that
will do justice to who you are.
Nothing we can say will ever
gather up the multitude of
your gracious blessings
and no words or thoughts of
ours can make sense of all
you have done for us.

When we consider the wonder
of every planet in our galaxy
our praises are yours by right
of your creative word
and every star in every universe
that lies beyond our human eyes
challenges us to offer you
glory in recognition of
your colossal energy.

It is then that it dawns upon
us that the most amazing,
mind-blowing thing of all

is that you want to receive the
praises of your creatures
and you are thrilled with our
songs of adoration.
We are utterly staggered
as we try to understand
something of your desire
that we should walk hand in
hand with you our God,
the King of creation.

All we can say, in the words
of the psalmist:
'Our help is in the name
of the Lord,'
the maker of heaven and earth,
the Lord who has done
all things well.
Let us praise the Lord. **Amen.**

Confession

Exodus 1:8

We confess that we have many
kings that rule our lives
and many things we allow to take
precedence over you, Lord.
We give more of our time and
energy to pleasing ourselves
and we forget that the purpose of
our creation was to please you.
We confess that we have
kept ourselves busy with
so many things;
too busy to pray, too busy to
worship, too busy, busy, busy
but achieving nothing of lasting
worth—and we are sorry.
So come, Lord, take your place once
more on the throne of our lives
and by your grace reschedule
our days according to
your grace. **Amen.**

Intercession

Matthew 16:15–16

I am a medical scientist.
I am committed to my research
to find new and better treatments
for cancer, MS, dementia, and AIDS.
I work under enormous pressure
not just from myself
but also from the cries for help
from the victims of disease.
People look to science
and to scientists;
they expect us to solve all
their problems.
But I am not superhuman,
just a person seeking understanding
and longing to help others.
Pray for me.

silence

I am an environmentalist.
With my colleagues
I have done a great deal of research
and studied the data.
I truly believe that we
cannot continue
to pollute God's world the
way we are doing.
It is almost too late to save the planet
from the damage our
lifestyles are doing.
But how can I prevent
serious repercussions
when governments around the world
and those whose decisions
could make a difference
are pushing heads in the sand
and refusing to act?
Pray for me.

silence

I am a teacher.
I came into the profession
because I wanted to see children
reach their potential.
For me it was almost a calling,
a kind of thank offering for
all I had received.
To see a child's blank face
suddenly light up
as they now understood
was sufficient reward in itself.
But now I am treated as if I
don't know how to teach
and ridiculed by governments
and parents alike.
I'm expected to fulfil the roles
that once were the parents',
teaching social skills, good
behaviour, and safe sex.
But I'm only a teacher, a
good one perhaps—
but I am not the saviour
of the community.
Pray for me.

silence

I am a prison officer.
I work with the lowest of the low.
The prisoners that I deal with
should not be in prison at all.
Many are mentally ill or simply
can't cope out in the world.
There are others who are evil
and have lost any conscience
that perhaps they once had.
Some blame it on their
abusive childhood
and it seems they have been affected
by all they suffered then.
But they still had choices to make
and they have made the wrong ones.
It is hard in this repressive
environment
not to become cynical and hard.
But I'm just a human being
so don't blame me when things
don't go as was planned.
Pray for me.

silence

I am a politician.
Whether I serve as an MP
or local councillor
I still see my role as a servant
of the community.
My life as a politician is not easy
as I try to balance my vision
of hope for my people
and the party line which I am
often condemned to obey.
There are always difficult
decisions to be made
and there isn't a bottomless
pit of resources.
How can anyone know
which choices will prove
right in the end?
It will only be when we look
back from the future
that we will understand the
history we are still writing.
I do not profess to know
all the answers
and I, like everyone else,
can get things wrong.
But I'm expected to be omniscient
then ridiculed when my words
prove that I'm not!
Pray for me.

silence

I am a charity worker.
I travel the world taking
food to the starving
and medicines to the sick.
There are times when I feel
out of my depth
and utterly overwhelmed by
the scale of the need.
You have no idea of the anguish
when a tiny, helpless child
dies in your arms.
They are not sick, just dying
needlessly of hunger.
We just need a little more aid.
Too much of the resources donated
are confiscated by corrupt officials
to sell for profit on the black market.
I know times are hard
and it costs more to do
what we want to do,
but each of us are wealthy beyond
the dreams of these children.
I don't have all the answers
and I can't do everything
that's needed.
They need us all to be saviours
so they can live before they die.
Pray for me.

silence

I am a church leader.
Whether I'm a pastor, a
priest, or a minister
we all face the same dilemmas.
I truly believe that God called me
to serve him and his
people on earth.
I'm expected to be a kind of
spiritual jack of all trades
when in truth I have some
of the gifts needed
but not all of them.
I always understood from the Bible
that we are the body of Christ.
So how is it assumed I
can do everything?
I believed I was called to pastor
the flock, preach the gospel,
and care for the needs of
the community.
Now it seems I must allow the
world to teach me the truth
and God's word in the
Bible is out of date.
But there are some things
that don't change
and God's will and God's love
in Jesus are paramount.
It is Christ who is Saviour,
and him alone.
Pray for me.

silence

Lord, in your mercy,
hear our prayer. Amen.

TWENTY-SECOND SUNDAY IN ORDINARY TIME

Prayer of Approach

Psalm 105:8

Our God always keeps his promises
and will never forget those
who worship him.
The psalmist sang with joy
in the assurance of God's blessing.
He reminds us that there
is simply no end
to his word of compassion
for all he has made.
He is the Lord and we celebrate
his goodness to us

and we have come to
remember his love
because he has promised to
remember us. **Amen.**

Thanksgiving

Exodus 3:4–5

Lord, like Moses we too
have discovered
that you are a holy God
and that your presence in our midst
is our reason for worship.

We come with thanksgiving
that you are not remote,
unknown, and unknowable.
Again and again you make
your presence felt
and your being there
changes everything.
Again and again you
burst into our lives
and when you do, you turn
our lives upside down.

We thank you that you do not wait
for us to come looking for you
for you are the God who
takes the initiative
and you bring us hope.
We thank you that even when we
were not aware of your glory
you made the first move and in
Jesus declared your grace.

No wonder Moses was overwhelmed
when you spoke to him.
We are not surprised that his
experience at the burning bush
remained a lasting memory
on his journey with you.
He received no warning that
you would be there
and that he would be ordered to
prepare himself to meet his God.
We want to thank you for every
experience we have had
when we just knew you were with us.
We are still greatly moved when
we remember those moments
when we felt your hand
upon our lives
and our hearts were strangely
warmed by the love of Christ.

Thank you most of all that your
purpose is to share our pain
and to enter into the journeys
that we must make.
That, like Moses, you speak
to us by name.
Your word of hope, love,
forgiveness, and grace
is written in the wounds of Jesus.

Thank you for who you are
and for your presence
that changes our lives
and fills our days.

In the name of Christ,
who is always Immanuel,
God with us. **Amen.**

Confession

Matthew 16:24

Lord,
if we are honest we are
happy to follow you
but we would rather it could
be on our own terms.
Being a disciple of Jesus is
something we would embrace

but we are not too happy with your
requirement about carrying a cross.
We confess that we often want to be
followers but without the pain;
to be Christians but
without the cost.

We are not very good at
denying ourselves
and we do wonder just how you
can expect anyone to do that.

And yet, Lord, if you are Lord
then we know you do have the
right to set the agenda.
Who are we to say what makes
a Christian in your eyes?

Lord,
we confess that we have been
looking at discipleship
in the totally wrong way.
We have been seeing everything
from our own point of view
and not yours!
Forgive us our audacity in thinking
we know better than you
and we repent of our arrogance
for failing to be the disciples
you always meant us to be. **Amen.**

Intercession
Romans 12:17–18

Lord,
we pray for peace between nations,
that you will move the
leaders of nations
to seek to end the struggle for power
as they bring an end to the
corruption and injustice
which fan the flames of war
and are a barrier to peace.
Come, Prince of Peace,
and heal your world.

Lord,
we pray for peace in our homes,
that your grace will transform
our attitudes to one another,
and that we shall learn to treat
each other with respect;
for homes where there is
bitterness and anger
and for families where only
harsh words are ever heard.
Come, Prince of Peace,
and heal your world.

Lord,
we pray for peace in our
communities
that are places where inequalities
create resentment
and where people feel excluded
from life's opportunities;
for places where poverty and
lack of employment
leave many feeling unwanted,
unnecessary, and inferior
and for communities where
drugs rule the streets
and violent crime is easily bred.
Come, Prince of Peace,
and heal your world.

Lord,
we pray for peace in the
dark places of life
where people are hurting and
no one seems to care;
for those whose lives are in
turmoil at the death of
someone they loved

and for those who have lost a child
to drink or to drugs or to crime;
for those whose longing for a
child has remained unfulfilled
and for those who are single in
our family-orientated society.
Come, Prince of Peace,
and heal your world.

Lord,
we pray for peace in the
life of your church
as we find ways to accept and
affirm one another;
for an end to the false divisions
of faith we erected
and a removal of the barriers
we still retain;
for an end to the sin of
separation we perpetuate
and a new openness for everyone
at the table of the Lord.
Come, Prince of Peace,
and heal your world.

Lord,
we pray for peace in our
hearts and minds
and a new assurance of our place
in the kingdom of God;
for a renewal of that experience
that brings cleansing and hope
and for the knowledge that
peace in the Bible
means that, by grace, all is well
between me and my Lord
and that we constantly give thanks
that all peace begins and ends
at the foot of the cross and at
the door of the empty tomb.
Come, Prince of Peace,
and heal your world.

Lord,
we bring before you those known
to us who long for peace
and for those whom your love
has laid on our hearts.

silence

We also pray for ourselves,
that we may experience
the peace that passes all
understanding
that comes from the
heart of the Lord.
Come, Prince of Peace,
and heal your world.

We bring all our prayers for peace
in the name of the Prince of Peace,
Jesus Christ our Lord. **Amen.**

TWENTY-THIRD SUNDAY IN ORDINARY TIME

Prayer of Approach

Matthew 18:20

Lord,
remind us that we are not simply
a group of like-minded people
nor are we here because we have
some things in common;
we have gathered together not because
we can but because we must.
Deep within us we know that
this is the house of God
and he is here!

Lord,
you are no respecter of
persons or numbers
and the setting can be informal,
traditional, or radical

and you will be there.
For you are there when we
feel small in number
and when we are in a huge crowd.
For you are no gatecrasher
but it is yourself who
invited us to come.

Lord,
we are here by your holy invitation
and in your presence we are
gathered to worship. **Amen.**

Praise

Psalm 149:1

Father,
we often fill our lives with
many concerns
and we flood our days with the
foolish things of earth.
There are times when we feel
completely overloaded
and when we have too little
time to do a great deal.

But the truth remains
that you have given your church
on earth just one task
and that task must be
all-consuming.
There is for us nothing more vital,
more important, more urgent
than offering thanks, praise, and
glory to the living God.

The song we sing to him is not new—
it is as old as creation itself;
we sing to the praise of the
King of creation
as together we worship one
who is Lord of all.

We sing of the one who gave us life
and in Christ gave us new life.
Our song is the old song made
new by the grace of the Lord
and the joy that we can
sing it together
as we meet in the name of the King.

We sing of our God who is
the one Lord of all,
who in Christ came and lived
among his creation;
our praises are focused on
the one who is Saviour
and the desire of our worship is to
celebrate his wisdom and glory.

Never for a moment must the praise
of the living God come to an end
for the whole world who
knows his name is a part of
the Lord's congregation;
whenever we meet, the hosts
of heaven gather with us
and together we offer thanks,
praise, and adoration to the
one who is Lord. **Amen.**

Intercession

Romans 13:8

Lord,
we pray for those who are
hopelessly in debt
and for those who see no way
to pay what they owe;
for the impact on families with that
albatross around their necks
and for the fears that they
may lose their home.
May they find the help they need
to pay the debt that they owe.

Lord, in your mercy,
hear our prayer.

Lord,
we pray for those to whom
we owe a debt of gratitude
for keeping us safe
and for those who come to our aid
when things have gone wrong;
for those who serve in the police
force or the fire brigade
and for the staff in the local
hospital and those we meet
in our health centre.
May we remember to thank those
who seek to restore us to health.
Lord, in your mercy,
hear our prayer.

Lord,
we pray for those who are
paying their debt to society
and for those behind bars whose loss
of freedom pays what they owe;
for those who have robbed someone
of their peace of mind,
their comfort, and precious
memories as well as
things they stole
and for those whose debt
to their victims will be
hard for them to pay.
May they find a new beginning in
Jesus and a new pathway in life.
Lord, in your mercy,
hear our prayer.

Lord,
we pray for those who have
been snared by a loan shark
and for those whose debts are
now growing by the day;
for the work of Citizens Advice
who offer guidance
and for those whose debts mean
they have already lost everything.
May they find the help they
need to start again.
May they find the help they need
to pay the debt that they owe.
Lord, in your mercy,
hear our prayer.

We pray for those who
are recognising their
indebtedness to God,
for the gift which we can not earn or
deserve in life now and to come;
for those yet to experience the joy
and the freedom of forgiveness,
knowing that it is Christ's
death on the cross that
wiped the slate clean
and for those still burdened by their
feelings of guilt and remorse.
May the love of God set them free.
Lord, in your mercy,
hear our prayer.

Lord, we pray for ourselves,
that we might experience
a deep cleansing within,
a forgiveness that is real,
a joy unending,
and a peace that passes
all understanding,
because our debt has been paid.
Lord, in your mercy,
hear our prayer. Amen.

TWENTY-FOURTH SUNDAY IN ORDINARY TIME

Prayer of Approach

Matthew 18:21–22

Come to worship knowing
you are forgiven.
Now is the time to go and forgive.
Come and know you have
been made clean.
Now is the time to let go of the
hurt that still holds you.
Come and celebrate the power
of the Holy Spirit.
Now is the time for the Spirit
to bear fruit for the praise
of the Lord. **Amen.**

Praise

Psalm 114:7–8

Almighty God, our heavenly Father,
we, like the psalmist of old,
tremble in your presence.
We too come ready for
your refreshing Spirit
to wash over us and cleanse
us completely.

Lord,
too often we live out our days
in the lukewarm waters of the past
when all the time you are offering
us the chance to begin again.
When the past haunts us and
the future frightens us
we need to remember that
today is all we may have
and it is your special gift to us—
empowering us for your glory.

When, like the people of
God in the wilderness,
we are hungry and thirsty and we
know we have lost our way
you reach out in love and
draw us to yourself.
By grace you feed us on
the Word of God
and by the Holy Spirit we
are never thirsty again.

Lord, so great, so understanding.
Lord, our sovereign and Saviour.
Lord, you deal with our
hunger for life.
Lord, you quench our
thirst for life eternal.
You are like a spring of cool water
that refreshes us heart and soul.
You are like manna in
the wilderness;
we feed deeply on the
God made flesh.
You remind us to return again and
again to the place of refreshment
and you call us home
to drink deeply
at the wells of salvation,
renewal, and hope.

Lord,
we praise you that by your
grace we can be filled
and through your Holy Spirit
we can be restored.
Wonderful, wonderful God,
we praise you for offering to
deal with the struggles of
our hearts and minds.
You are the endless
source of supply
of all that matters as we give thanks
to the Lord of all glory. **Amen.**

Intercession
Romans 14:7–8

I ask your prayers for those who
have been used as slaves
as they have been held against
their will for many years;
for those trapped in an
abusive relationship
and are too afraid to leave and
find hope and freedom.

silence

The Lord hears our prayer.
Thanks be to God.

I ask your prayers for those who are
slaves to obsessive behaviour.
Their lives are ruled by a strict
pattern they must follow
and they are unable to break the
cycle of things they must do.

silence

The Lord hears our prayer.
Thanks be to God.

I ask your prayers for those at risk
from those closest to them
who accuse them of bringing
dishonour to their family.
For those too afraid to speak
out and seek help.

silence

The Lord hears our prayer.
Thanks be to God.

I ask your prayers for those who
are slaves to illegal drugs;
for those who are enslaved to
alcohol and drugs on prescription
and for those simply
striving to be free.

silence

The Lord hears our prayer.
Thanks be to God.

I ask your prayers for those
addicted to a life of crime;
for those whose whole life has been
on the wrong side of the law
and for companies and
bankers who act as if they
are outside of the law.

silence

The Lord hears our prayer.
Thanks be to God.

I ask your prayers for those who
are slaves to gambling;
for those whose family are paying
the price of their addiction
in the financial problems and
the constant stress they face.

silence

The Lord hears our prayer.
Thanks be to God.

We bring our prayers in
the name of Christ,
who offers to break all the chains
that would hold us. **Amen.**

TWENTY-FIFTH SUNDAY IN ORDINARY TIME

Prayer of Approach

Psalm 105:1

Lord,
we come with a deep longing
to meet with you
and to declare again that
you are Lord.

We come with songs on our
lips to give you glory
and with hearts set on fire by
your grace and power.

We come not to receive but to give,
not for our own benefit but for
the honour of your name.

We come with hearts and lives
overflowing with thankfulness
and with a deep desire that
the whole world
should join in the song of praise to
the one who is Lord of all. **Amen.**

Thanksgiving

Matthew 20:16

Father,
we come as the children of grace
to give thanks for the
extravagance of your love.
As we gather in your name
we are once again
utterly overwhelmed by the
sum of your blessings
and the super abundance of
your love and mercy.

We have no words that can do
justice to the thankfulness we feel
and every time we survey the
beauty of your world
we are forced to our knees
in humble gratitude.

If we stand before you in silence it
is the wonderment we experience
that closes our lips but floods our
hearts and minds with joy.
We simply cannot comprehend
how the creator of the universe
should humble himself and enter
fully into our life on earth.

Once more in your presence we
discover a sense of meaning
that we can find nowhere else
and as we come with our worship
songs and our feeble words of praise
we enter into your purpose
for our lives.

It is as we offer you thanksgiving
and celebrate your glory
that we are reminded that it is
only through the Holy Spirit
that our words and actions are
transformed into praise.
For you are the God who changes
hearts and renews minds
as you turn our attitudes and
values upside down.

Having met in your presence
we cannot help seeing the world
and the things of the world
in a whole new light.
You open our eyes
to see our world of materialism
as the empty, weak, and
valueless thing it really is.

You open our ears
to hear the cry of the poor
and the disadvantaged,
the focus of your grace.
You open our minds
that we might begin to rethink the
people we count important
and to discover that you are
gracious with your blessings,
when and to whom you choose.

Lord,
how can we not thank you,
our grace-filled God,
as you long for your world
to be awash with your
mercy and love?

We bring our thanksgiving
in the name of Jesus,
the centre and source of
your grace. **Amen.**

Confession

Exodus 16:8

Father,
forgive us whenever we close
our eyes to the hungry
and shut our ears lest we hear
their cry for justice.

Forgive us whenever we are dazzled
by human achievement
and fail to give thanks for your
gifts that make things possible.

Forgive us whenever our focus
is on bread for the body
and our relationship withers
through lack of spiritual
nourishment.

Forgive us whenever we allow
ourselves and our needs
to become the centre of our
concern and our service
and fail to look up to the
one who is Lord of all.
Come, Lord Jesus, come, and
make us new. **Amen.**

Intercession

Philippians 1:21–22

Father,
we pray for those who
just live for today
without a thought for
anything or anyone else
and for those who simply struggle
to find enough food and water
for their family to exist
another day.
Lord of all life,
may we live for Christ.

Father,
we pray for those who are
ruining their lives today
as they give no thought
for tomorrow
and for those who are
abusing their bodies
through the misuse of drugs,
alcohol, or tobacco
and are yet to discover
that their lifestyle
is robbing them of the future
that might have been theirs.
Lord of all life,
may we live for Christ.

Father,
we pray for those who are
finding life hard today
as all the dreams they once had
have long since been broken
and for those who today
are filled with regret
for the dreams they never had,
and the 'might have beens'
that they allowed to slip
from their grasp.
Lord of all life,
may we live for Christ.

Father,
we pray for those who
have treasured memories
of healthier times
and carefree days when the sun
always seemed to shine;
for those whose only wish is to
be free of pain and worry
and for those who long to
be free to walk unaided,
whenever they want.
Lord of all life,
may we live for Christ.

Father,
we pray for those who live
their lives giving little or
no thought or space
in their busy lives for the Lord
who gave them their life
and for those still searching for a
meaning and purpose to their days
but look anywhere except the
grace of God in the empty
cross and the empty tomb.
Lord of all life,
may we live for Christ.

Father,
we pray for those whose lives are
filled with anger and hatred
as they live the life of a
terrorist bringing fear and
despair into the world
and for those whose lives are
being torn apart by evil deeds
as they count the cost in the loss
of home and family and peace.
Lord of all life,
may we live for Christ.

Father,
we pray for those whose
days are clouded by fear,
anxiety, and depression
as each day becomes a
struggle just to survive
and for those who spend their
days feeling ashamed
for the illness for which
they are not to blame.
Lord of all life,
may we live for Christ.

Father,
we pray for those weighed down
by the pressures of leadership
and the choices they face that will
impact the lives of millions
and for those who close their eyes,
their hearts, and their minds
to the decisions they need to
make no matter the cost.
Lord of all life,
may we live for Christ.

We bring our prayers in
the name of Christ,
in whom all life that is real
always begins. **Amen.**

TWENTY-SIXTH SUNDAY IN ORDINARY TIME

Prayer of Approach

Psalm 78:1–4

Lord,
how can we not listen to you
for you have the words of eternal life?
How can we not worship you
for you have put a song of
praise in our hearts?
How can we not declare
our love for you
for you are the source of
love and life for us all?
How can we not speak of your glory
for you have commanded
us to tell the world
of your love for all
humankind? **Amen.**

Praise

Philippians 2:6–11

Lord,
we praise you for you are
the King of creation,
the Lord of history,
and the sovereign over all things
and all people.

Yet even as we offer these
words of praise
the truth dawns upon us
that even our greatest thought
cannot but scratch the surface
of the worship that is your due.

Our deepest sense of your presence
and the most profound
longing for you
cannot plumb the depths
of your majesty.
Our experience of your love
and our declaration of
your compassion
cannot ever possibly do
justice to your grace.

Our words of your holiness
and our knowledge of
your sovereignty
cannot be more than a
feeble muttering
in the praise of our God.

Lord,
we live in a world
and we are surrounded by a society
that has turned its back on you
and has erected for itself idols
of power, possessions, and
self-satisfaction
to which it gives its devotion.

But you alone are God,
you alone are sovereign
over all things
and all people for all time.

You have promised that
ultimately everyone
who has lived,
is living now,
or will live sometime in the future
will one day
bow the knee to Jesus Christ.

The one who lived, died,
and was raised again
is already Lord.
We praise you that his lordship
will be for ever the hallmark of
your glory and your grace.

For now,
our worship is a poor reflection
of what you truly deserve.
We look forward to that moment
when by grace we kneel before
the throne of grace
and worship you our Lord. **Amen.**

Confession

Matthew 21:32

Father,
we come to worship
and we use words to tell
of your worth.
We come to praise you
for all you are and all you
have done for us.

But we confess that too often
our words do not match
our worship
and our lifestyle does not
speak of your love.
We ask that you will not
only forgive us
but, by your Holy Spirit,
you will renew who and
what we are—
that all we say and do
will declare the glory and love
of our Lord. **Amen.**

Intercession

Exodus 17:2

We offer our prayers as we reflect
upon the news of the day.

We begin with an article
about our health
and the needs of the National
Health Service.
We pray for everyone who
works within it—
those on the front-line, on the
wards, or behind the scenes.
We also remember those
involved in research
that will lead to improved treatments
and a better quality of life for us all.
We pray especially for those
who are seeking ways
to enable the care of the
nation's health
to be available to all from
the cradle to the grave.
When our lives are tested to the full,
let us trust in the Lord.

Now a story about the
huge sums paid
to men and women in
different areas of sport
and to those in the various
fields of entertainment.

We remember athletes
who demonstrate
the true meaning of commitment
and dedication
which comes as a challenge to us all.
We pray for those who in
the eyes of many
receive much more than
their real worth
and for those who do not receive
the thanks, appreciation, or rewards
that their service to the
community deserves.
When our lives are tested to the full,
let us trust in the Lord.

The abuse and misuse of illegal drugs

can always be found in
our newspapers.
They remind us of the
lives being wrecked,
relationships broken, and
homes torn apart.
Whilst many are discovering
the long-term damage
their addiction is storing
up for the future,
there are those who grow
ever wealthier
on the backs of those who
are ruining their lives.

We pray for those who track
down the ones responsible
for the supply of this life-
destroying trade in drugs
and for those seeking to help those
overcome their addiction.
When our lives are tested to the full,
let us trust in the Lord.

Concern for the problems
of the wider world
is never far from the
pages of the news.
We read of the impact our
lives and our lifestyle
have on the lives of millions
around the world.
Whilst our problem is often obesity
as we have too much available to eat,
many around the world
simply wonder
where they will find food
for their family today.
There are the mansions of those
who have everything
right next door to the shanty
towns of those in poverty.
There are times when we feel
part of a world under threat
by the onslaught of violent
terrorism and radical extremists.

We pray for the leaders of
nations to respond
to the desperate plight of the poor
and to end the scourge of violence
that ruins people's lives.
When our lives are tested to the full,
let us trust in the Lord.

We read the reports of the
impact our lifestyle is having
as gradually the effects of global
warming are challenging us all.
We are told that action is
urgently needed now
for the sake of generations of
children yet to be born.
Reports tell us that many of the
world's birds and wild animals
are in serious danger of extinction
by the demands we make
and the lives we live.
This world is a special place—
the blue planet—
and we see its fragile beauty when
viewed from perspectives of space.

We pray for those with the
power, that they will act now
as we remember that this
is God's world
and we are simply his stewards.
When our lives are tested to the full,
let us trust in the Lord.

Education continues to
be an item of news

as we are reminded of
the importance
of every child having an
equal opportunity
to reach their full potential.

We pray for teachers in schools
and lecturers in colleges
and universities
as they feel overwhelmed by the
ever-increasing demands
of their time, commitment,
and service.
We pray too for the young
people who leave school
without a qualification
to their name
and for those who have studied hard
and are now disillusioned
when they discover
that their skills and their training
mean they are still without work.
We pray for all who have a part to
play in the realm of education,
that the future of our young
people will be paramount
in all the choices they make.
When our lives are tested to the full,
let us trust in the Lord.

We bring all our prayers to the Lord,
who is the best news that the world
has yet to know. **Amen.**

TWENTY-SEVENTH SUNDAY IN ORDINARY TIME

Prayer of Approach

Psalm 19:14

Lord,
we use many words when
we come to praise you
and we have many thoughts
in our minds.
We sing many songs and
offer many prayers
but the focus of all we say or
do is your praise and glory.
You, Lord, are the heart and
centre of our worship
and without you and your
presence in our midst
our praises would be an empty
shell and a useless ritual.
By your Holy Spirit, fire our
words with your power
and our hearts with your life-
renewing grace. **Amen.**

Thanksgiving

Philippians 3:14

Lord,
every time we focus our
thoughts on you
we cannot hold back our desire
to offer you the thanks of our hearts
and the praises of our lips.
What a privilege is ours as
we meet in the presence
of the Lord of all creation and
the sovereign over all things.

Lord,
too easily we take your
grace for granted
and too readily do we assume
that we have a right to
experience your love
at the very centre of our being.
Teach us again, Lord, not only
to remember your love
but to affirm from the rooftops
that we have no right in ourselves
to be loved by you.

That you love us is a miracle
of grace alone
and that you long to
receive our worship
must be one of the most
amazing things
in this truly astounding universe
that snuggles deep and safe in
the hollow of your hand.

To say thank you for your grace
seems to be almost too
easy a thing to do.
Perhaps that is why you call us
to worship you in word and deed.
That how we live and
how we behave—
that our caring and our serving—
confirm the reality of the
thankfulness that wells up within us
whenever we consider the wonder
of your grace-filled heart.

We have done nothing whatsoever
to deserve your love
and there is nothing we can say or do
that makes you stop loving us
or makes you love us more.

Your call is to a discipleship
that doesn't cease
at the close of our act of worship.
The call to a grace
relationship with you
carries within it the challenge
and the expectation
that, like Paul, we will press on
to take hold of your grace
so that more and more we
may live the kind of life
that causes your praise to ring
to the ends of the earth.

We thank you, Lord, for
you have loved us
and through your love
and by your love
we will offer you thanks and
praise all our days. **Amen.**

Confession

Exodus 20:4

Father,
you said, 'no idols'
and you meant it.
But we thought you were speaking
of idols of wood and stone.
We never imagined that an idol
could be anything and anyone
that we allowed to have a
more important place in
our lives than you.

We confess that we have made
idols of our possessions
and we have placed
our earthly security, our
place in society,
and even our family
on the altar of our lives.

Come, Father, and renew your
claim upon our lives.
Come, Lord, and reign supreme.
Come, Holy Spirit, and enable us
to worship the Lord our God,
and him alone. **Amen.**

Intercession

Matthew 21:45–46

Lord,
we pray for the prophets
of our generation.
For those who call us to
care for your world

and for those who warn us
of the damage we are doing
to your creation;
for those who know you
and those who don't
and for those whose
words remind us
that ultimately we are answerable
to you, the Lord of all creation.
The Lord hears our prayer.
Thanks be to God.

Lord,
we pray for the prophets
of our generation.
For those who cry out for
those with no voice
and for those who speak up
for the poor, the marginalised,
and the broken.
For those who know you
and those who don't
and for those who remind us
that only those who work
out their faith
as they care for the hungry,
the prisoner
and give a cup of water
in your name
will enter the kingdom of God.
The Lord hears our prayer.
Thanks be to God.

Lord,
we pray for the prophets
of our generation.
For those who open our eyes to see
the ever-widening chasm between
the 'haves' and 'have nots'
and for those who refuse
to allow us to ignore
the cry for a just and equal sharing.
For those who know you
and those who don't
and for those who are hurting
that they may reach out with hope
to those overwhelmed with
anxiety, despair, and depression.
The Lord hears our prayer.
Thanks be to God.

Lord,
we pray for the prophets
of our generation.
For those who speak of their
concerns for young people
growing up in a society that
doesn't seem to care
and for those who were encouraged
to study and gain qualifications
who now feel abandoned
as their only reward
is to join the endless queue
of the unemployed.
For those who know you
and those who don't
who warn us of the peer
group pressures
our young people are facing
and how hard it is for
them to just say no
to a lifestyle that will rob them
of their health and future.
The Lord hears our prayer.
Thanks be to God.

Lord,
we pray for the prophets
of our generation.
For those who challenge our
focus on our individual needs
and neglect our corporate
responsibility for one another
and for those who speak up

for those who are single or live alone
in our family-orientated society.
For those who know you
and those who don't
who expose the emptiness
of our materialistic and
godless society
and for those who call
us to lift our eyes
and acknowledge the Lord
of our creation
to whom we owe everything
we have and are
and before whom, one
day, we will answer
for all we have done or failed to do
with the days and years we
have been granted.
The Lord hears our prayer.
Thanks be to God.

Lord,
we pray for the prophets
of our generation.
For those with deep concern
for the elderly and infirm
and for those with so many
happy memories
but who have no one with
whom they can share them.
For those who know you
and those who don't
who are filled with compassion
for those who can no
longer remember
the names and the faces of
those they once knew
and for those they loved
who sit and wait and wonder
and weep inside.
The Lord hears our prayer.
Thanks be to God.

Lord,
we pray for the prophets
of our generation.
For those who speak to our hearts
on behalf of the sick and the dying
and for those who call us
to share the burden
of those who are suffering
deep inside,
whose pain is such that
it cannot be seen,
only heard by whose with
empathy and love.
For those who know you
and those who don't
who refuse to allow us
to forget those
whose lives are crippled by
the shame they still feel,
for the anxiety, despair,
and depression
that limit their horizons,
and for those still carrying the scars
of the abuse they have suffered
that continues to rob them
of the peace, hope, and joy
that should have been theirs.
The Lord hears our prayer.
Thanks be to God.

In the name of Jesus,
our eternal prophet and priest,
our Saviour and Lord. **Amen.**

TWENTY-EIGHTH SUNDAY IN ORDINARY TIME

Prayer of Approach

Psalm 106:1–2

Lord,
what a joy,
what a privilege,

what a wonder
to gather in your name;
to offer you thanks and praise
and to experience all over again
that love which never ends
and to rediscover the power
of your presence
to heal, to bless, and to draw forth
the adoration of our hearts.
Come, Holy Spirit,
and empower us to worship the
Lord of eternity. **Amen.**

Praise

Philippians 4:8

Father,
how easily we take each
day for granted
and how readily we assume
that we will have a
tomorrow to enjoy.
We take for granted the care,
love, and support we receive
from those around us
and we assume
that the world will be beautiful,
that the sun will still shine,
that the rain will refresh the earth,
and that your love will never end.

Your Word reminds us that all
the good things we enjoy
are a daily gift from your
hand of grace.
Not a second, not a
minute of our days,
not a month, not a year of our lives
comes by dint of our own
efforts or our deserving.
All, all is of grace.

When we reflect, as Paul directs us, on
'whatever is true, whatever is noble
whatever is right, whatever is pure,
whatever is lovely, whatever
is admirable,'
the truth is we find ourselves
utterly overwhelmed
with the deep desire
to praise you for the
sheer extravagance
of your grace-filled love towards us.

Wonderful, wonderful God!
It is all too easy to be dragged down
by the dark things in our world
and to fill our minds
with the evil that so easily
captures our attention.
We know we should never
allow ourselves
to hide from the realities around us
and that you call us again and again
to pray for the healing
of your world.
Yet you still call us to give
thanks and praise
not only for the ability to enjoy
the beauty around us
but for the inspiration it gives
to sing your praises.

Yet it is in and through Jesus
that our eyes are opened
and through the Holy Spirit
that we are empowered
to worship you.

We stand before the throne
of grace and bless you
for the one who died in our place,
who was raised from the dead,
and is here now in the
midst of our praises

and enjoying the worship of hearts
set on fire by your grace.
In Christ's name. **Amen.**

Confession

Exodus 32:1

Lord,
we are ashamed
that even in the face of your
goodness and love
we so easily turn our backs on you.
We, like your people in
the wilderness,
are effortlessly led astray
to find security
in the works of our hand
and the things we can
touch and hold.

We are like children for whom
everything must be now;
to wait patiently in hope
appears to be beyond us.
Your people lost sight of
your majesty and glory.
They substituted a thing
of their own making
for the one to whom they owed
their very existence and
their freedom.

Lord,
be patient with us because
we fall so easily
and we turn our backs on you
when the going gets tough.
Forgive us and draw us
back to your side,
that our eyes might
behold your glory
and our hearts worship your
eternal presence. **Amen.**

Intercession

Matthew 22:8–10

Think of someone who is
facing a crisis in their life
and for whom the path ahead
is full of uncertainty.
May they find courage
in the invitation
to the feast of the lamb.

silence

Think of someone who is struggling
with problems with their health
and for whom the uncertainty
and the treatment
is a burden they bear every day.
May they find strength
in the invitation
to the feast of the lamb.

silence

Think of someone who works
in a home for the elderly
and for those whose contribution
seems to go unnoticed.
May they find joy in the invitation
to the feast of the lamb.

silence

Think of someone overwhelmed by
the demands of work and home
and for those whose responsibilities
are bringing them
to the end of their tether.
May they find peace in
the invitation
to the feast of the lamb.

silence

Think of someone who appears
to sail through life
without a care of concern
and for those case-hardened
to the problems and struggles
others are facing.
May they find their eyes and
hearts opened in the invitation
to the feast of the lamb.

silence

Think of someone whose
life has been wrecked
by the actions and
attitudes of others
and for those whose homes
have been destroyed
as a result of war or the
action of terrorists.
May they experience hope
in the invitation
to the feast of the lamb.

silence

Think of someone—the
face of a hungry child or
a starving community
and for those who do not
want to rely on aid
but long for the opportunity
to provide for themselves.
May they find a new beginning
in the invitation
to the feast of the lamb.

silence

Think of someone you know
who is struggling
on the pathway of faith
and for those among your
family and friends
whose lifestyle has crowded
God out of their lives.
May they find the way home
in the invitation
to the feast of the lamb.

silence

We bring all our prayers in
the name of the lamb,
who invites us all to his
feast. **Amen.**

TWENTY-NINTH SUNDAY IN ORDINARY TIME

Prayer of Approach

Psalm 99:2–3

Lord, we come again to worship,
to prepare our minds,
to reach out to know you,
and our whole being celebrates
your greatness, your wisdom,
your awesome power, and
your limitless glory.

We have come into the presence
of the King of all creation,
the author of salvation,
and the one who is exalted
over all things.

Lord,
prepare our hearts to fall
in love with you
all over again. **Amen.**

Thanksgiving
Exodus 33:18–19

Father,
we thank you that you have
revealed your glory to us
in the life, death, and
resurrection of your Son.
From the very beginning
it was your purpose
to make yourself known.
Though you hid your
face from Moses,
you have always been determined
to demonstrate to those
with eyes to see
your presence, power, and glory.

We thank you that the whole of
creation sings your praises
and every facet of this world
speaks of the wonder of its creator.
From the trees of the smallest wood
to the depths of the
rainforests of Brazil;
from the pool of water alive
with tadpoles and insects
to the mighty oceans that teem
with creatures great and small;
from gently rolling meadows,
to lofty mountain heights,
together they join in a
massive demonstration of
your power and glory.

Faith declares that everywhere we
see the fingerprints of our God.
We looked and we saw
hints of your majesty,
power, and authority.
But then you took our breath away
and you did that which many
thought to be impossible.
In Jesus you broke the
barrier between us
and you stepped into our
world—as one of us.
When Jesus came he was
flesh of our flesh
as he entered all that life means to us
that we might experience all
that life might mean
to live in your presence.

So we come with thanksgiving
that you have not left us
to simply wonder
who and what you are.
Neither have you left us in the
dark as to your purposes
for us and all your creation.
You made it clear from
the very beginning
that we can only find our
joy and fulfilment
and experience life as you
meant it to be
when through Jesus we find our
relationship with you restored,
and we walk each day in fellowship
with you, our living Lord. **Amen.**

Intercession
Matthew 22:20–21

Lord,
it's all about the journey.
We pray for those whose
journey is hard
as each day brings greater
stress than the last
and for those who do not know
how they will feed their family
today or tomorrow.
Let us give as we should
to God and our neighbour.

Lord,
it's all about the journey.
We pray for those whose
every step is a struggle
and for those whose footsteps
are reduced to a shuffle
because of their pain or
their weakness or age.
Let us give as we should
to God and our neighbour.

Lord,
it's all about the journey.
We pray for those who give
of their time and their skills in
the life of the community
and for those who volunteer
for victim support
within the Health Service,
their local school,
or within the life and witness
of their church.
Let us give as we should
to God and our neighbour.

Lord,
it's all about the journey.
We pray for those whose journey
is limited by the four
walls of their room
and for those who long for someone
whose coming, for a moment,
opens a new window of hope.
Let us give as we should
to God and our neighbour.

Lord,
it's all about the journey.
We pray for those who
have no home
to which they can return
and for those whose
homes are an arena
of bitterness, criticism, and a
failure to love and forgive.
Let us give as we should
to God and our neighbour.

Lord,
it's all about the journey.
We pray for those whose journey
is burdened with times of ill-health
and numerous hospital
appointments to keep;
for those who fear their earthly
journey is almost over
and for those who know that it is.
Let us give as we should
to God and our neighbour.

Lord,
it's all about the journey.
We pray for those whose
hopes and opportunities
have been taken from them
by the corruption and
decisions of their leaders
and for those who have taken
the pathway to crime
and are reaping the reward of the
foolish choices they have made.
Let us give as we should
to God and our neighbour.

Lord,
it's all about the journey.
We pray for those for whom
we are concerned
who are facing pain, sorrow,
or deep questions of faith
on the journey of life.

silence

And for ourselves as we tread
the pathway of discipleship
and walk in the footsteps
of the Master.
Let us give as we should
to God and our neighbour.

We bring our prayers in
the name of Jesus,
who has promised always
to walk with us
on the journey of life. **Amen.**

THIRTIETH SUNDAY IN ORDINARY TIME

Prayer of Approach

Psalm 90:1

Father,
we reach out to adore you
for your love that never ends.

Jesus,
we bow down to adore you
for the grace that lifts us up.

Holy Spirit,
we reach up to adore you
for your life-transforming power.

Father, Son, and Holy Spirit,
we meet together to adore you
for you are our dwelling place
on earth and in heaven,
for ever and ever. **Amen.**

Thanksgiving

Matthew 22:36–37

Father,
Jesus told us to love you
with all we have and with all we are
and our fellow human beings
as we love ourselves.
He said that these are the
greatest commandments
you ever gave us to keep.

Yet there are moments when
it feels less of a command
and more like an albatross
around our necks!
As we struggle and strain
to obey your Word
you whisper in our ear
that what you are offering us
is the greatest privilege the
world has ever known.

Amazing, wonderful, gracious God,
we thank you for the opportunity
not only to worship the King of Kings
but to enter into a personal,
loving relationship with you.

God of all grace, we are
utterly overwhelmed
by the dawning realisation that
by your commandment
our worship is changed
from a mere duty
into an experience of meeting with
the one who loves us most.
Our gathering together in
the name of Jesus
is no longer in the realm of a mere
ritual or an act of obedience.
It is a meeting with the one
who is our heavenly Father
and in a relationship that is
of eternal proportions.

We thank you too that
as we experience

more and more of your
grace-filled presence
we shall find that we are able to
love the unlovely, forgive
the unforgiveable,
and reach out with arms of
compassion and understanding
to those who have hurt us most.

Father, we thank you that by
your love for us in Jesus
you flood our hearts, minds,
and lives with your grace.
We thank you that again
and again your grace
transforms our worship,
empowers our service,
and renews our commitment.
Now, at last, we find that
we can love you
with our heart, soul,
mind, and strength
and our neighbour as
ourselves. **Amen.**

Confession

1 Thessalonians 2:1–6

Lord,
we confess that there are times
when our lives do not
reflect your presence
and our lifestyle does not
speak to others
of your hand upon our
words and deeds.

Lord,
we confess that too often
we live as though
Christ has not been born
and that he has not died
to set us free.
Too many times the way we
face each day's concerns
does not demonstrate the
truth of his resurrection.
Even our worship often fails
to be shot through
with the power and presence
of the Holy Spirit.

So come, Lord,
set us free,
place the stamp of your
presence on our daily lives
that we might become a true
reflection of what it means
for us to be the body of
Christ. **Amen.**

Intercession

Deuteronomy 34:4–6

You do not know my name
but you see me everywhere.
I am one of the world's
forgotten children.
Our family were forced
to flee our home
and our country.
We walked hundreds of miles
just to escape to a place
away from the fighting
and the killing.
I just want to go home;
to be safe
and to see if any of my
friends are still alive.
Pray that I may receive
the gift of hope.

silence

You do not know my name
but you see me everywhere.

For years I lived a full life,
my work was a pleasure
and my family a joy.
I was full to the brim with
happy memories
of people I knew and
places I had seen.
But now I sit and feel alone.
It's as though I'm locked in
and I can no longer make contact
with those all around me.
I see faces that are vaguely familiar
but have no idea who they are.
I cannot remember their names
though they seem disappointed
that I no longer know them.
Pray that we may receive
the gift of peace
and contentment in just
being together.

silence

You don't know my name
but you meet me every day.
I sweep your road
and remove the rubbish
from your bins.
You don't really see me—
I'm just there!
I don't have a face
and within a minute you have
forgotten I ever existed.
I am ignored by everyone
but without me and the work I do
there would be sickness and
death everywhere.
Please pray that I may receive
the gift of someone's smile
and even a word of gratitude.

silence

You don't know my name
but you see me every day.
Turn on your television
and I am there.
I'm a member of parliament.
When I was elected I
had such a vision
of helping the poor;
finding work for the unemployed;
improving health, education,
and opportunities for all.
I dreamt of building a fairer,
more equal society.
But somewhere along the line
the vision was undermined by
commitment to the party
and now I find myself
toeing the line.
Please pray for the gift of wisdom,
that my original vision
might be restored.

silence

You don't know my name
but you see me everywhere.
There I sit in my wheelchair.
Nobody sees me, they
see only the chair.
Oh yes, I get the occasional smile—
more of pity than a
greeting of persons.
But that's the problem.
To everyone else I'm only
half a person—
I'm incomplete, I'm a reject.
But I'm not!
I am a person just like you
and that's how I want to be treated.
If only you would come
down to my level
and speak to me as you would

to a person not in a
wheelchair like me.
Pray that I may receive the gift of
being treated as a real person
instead of something on wheels.

silence

You don't know my name
but you see me every day.
Whether I am
a nurse or a paramedic;
a teacher or a social worker;
a police officer or a care worker—
all you see is the job
but you never see me.
If you did take the time
and the patience
you might not be ready to
criticise my human failings
and you might even turn
and say thank you.
But I am a person, just like you.
I have feelings and failings;
I have worries and problems;
I have a family or I live alone.
If only you would see me as me!
Pray that I may receive the gift
of being a person
and not just a job title to
take for granted.

silence

You don't know my name
but you see me every day.
I'm your neighbour,
next door or down the street.
We came to live here when these
houses were first built.
It's where our children grew up
and in those days I knew
everyone by name
and they knew me.
Now I'm on my own
and the family have long
since left home.
Everything has changed,
and now I know no one and
no one knows me.
I potter in the garden
hoping someone will stop
and share a word.
But people don't do that anymore.
It's not that I'm lonely,
I simply hate being alone
with no one to share my
memories anymore.
Please pray that someone
will receive the gift
of looking beyond the elderly
person—and see me.

silence

You do know my name
and you know who I am.
I am a member of your family
or your circle of friends.
We haven't met or spoken for years.
I still don't know what went wrong—
was it something I said
or did we just get much too busy?
All I know is this unspoken barrier
has been unbreached
for far too long.
One of us needs to step out in faith
and take the risk of another rebuff.
Perhaps the time has come for me
to pick up the phone or
knock on your door.
Someone has to do it—
it might as well be me.

Please pray for the gift of
faith, hope, and love
that, as we are promised,
breaks down
all the barriers we erect.

silence

Lord,
there are so many people
we meet each day.
We don't know their name
or their story.
We pray, grant us the gift
of compassion
and the willingness to
make time and space
in our self-orientated lives
to see one another as you see us—
those precious people for
whom Christ died. **Amen.**

THIRTY-FIRST SUNDAY IN ORDINARY TIME

Prayer of Approach

Joshua 3:9

Lord,
we draw near to hear the
words of faith
and to open our hearts to
respond in trust.
We draw near to acknowledge
you as Lord
and to celebrate your
limitless knowledge.
We draw near to worship
your holy name
and to offer the praise and
thanksgiving you deserve.
We draw near to our God
because he has called us
and we declare his living presence
in our midst. **Amen.**

Thanksgiving

Psalm 107:1–2

Sometimes, Lord, we feel
utterly overwhelmed
by your love and patience towards us.
We simply cannot
contain our desire
to offer you the praise of
thankful hearts.
We remember the many,
many times
your grace has touched
us, changed us,
and opened our eyes to see a
little more of your glory.

To see the moonlight shimmering
across the still waters of a lake;
to watch the white sea horses
as the ocean breaks upon the shore;
to watch the myriad of
tiny creatures
gather nectar from a flower;
to experience the sublime
joy and wonder
of a newborn child—
these and a thousand wonders of life
mean that the song of
thankfulness in our hearts
cannot be contained a
moment longer.

And yet these times of gratitude
pale into insignificance when we
pause and consider your
love towards us.
No wonder the psalmist
commanded us
to give thanks to you, Lord.

Nothing would hold back his
praises when he remembered
how you made his nation
your 'special possession'
and he reflected on your saving
grace that set them free.
It is hardly surprising that he
challenges us to praise the Lord.

But it is when, and only when,
we kneel at the foot of the cross
and confess that Christ has
died in our place
that we too experience again
that overwhelming,
uncontrollable longing
to give you thanks and praise.

Receive our prayer of praise
and thankfulness
as a sign of the wonder and joy
which well up within us when we
come in Christ's name. **Amen.**

Intercession

1 Thessalonians 2:9

We pray for those on whose
labours we depend;
for those who work on oil
rigs or in hydroelectric
and nuclear industries
to provide the fuel we use
every day of our lives
and for those who erect the pylons
and lay the pipes and the cables to
bring the power to our homes.
The Lord hears our prayer.
Thanks be to God.

We pray for those on whose
labours we depend;
for those who work in factories
creating the cars we drive,
the planes that fly,
and the vast range of things with
which we fill our homes
and for those unknown and unseen
but on whose skills we rely
for the new things
that are changing our lives.
The Lord hears our prayer.
Thanks be to God.

We pray for those on whose
labours we depend;
for farmers who care for
their livestock
or reap the harvest of the land
and for those whose labours
bring to our table
the fruits of the orchard and
of far-distant lands.
The Lord hears our prayer.
Thanks be to God.

We pray for those on whose
labours we depend;
for the staff at our local
health centre
and for dentists, opticians,
and physiotherapists
who are there when we
need them to help us;
for doctors, surgeons, and
nurses who use their skills
to care for us when we are ill
and for radiographers, porters,
and all the ancillary staff
whose work in the background is
forgotten and often unseen.
The Lord hears our prayer.
Thanks be to God.

We pray for those on whose
labours we depend;
for those who care for
the community;
for police officers, local councillors,
and the members of parliament
and for those who
repair our roads,
build new houses and keep
our streets clean;
for those who oversee
neighbourhood watch schemes
to help us feel safe in our homes
and for those who provide
help for us
through the work of Citizens
Advice and Victim Support.
The Lord hears our prayer.
Thanks be to God.

We pray for ourselves and our
labours on which others depend;
for those who work at home to care
for the needs of their family
and for those who provide support
for parents who are out at work;
for those who give of their
time and their skills
to visit the sick, the housebound,
the lonely, and the alone
and for all who serve in the
church and community
as part of their offering
in God's name.
The Lord hears our prayer.
Thanks be to God.

We bring all our prayers in
the name of the Lord,
whose presence and power
enable us all to offer what we have
and are in his name. **Amen.**

THIRTY-SECOND SUNDAY IN ORDINARY TIME

Prayer of Approach

Matthew 25:13

Lord,
this is the time and this is the place
and we are here to worship you.
This is the time and this is the place
and we are here to focus on
you, and you alone.
This is the time and this is the place
and we are here to seek your presence,
to acknowledge your glory,
and to rejoice in your love. **Amen.**

Confession

Joshua 24:14–15

Lord,
we know that you are holy
and that there is no stain
or sin in you.
You are utterly pure,
glorious, and righteous
and our worship affirms
your sovereignty.

But we confess that too often
our focus is not on giving you praise
but on meeting our need
of fellowship.
We come with our hymns and songs
of thanksgiving and adoration
but we confess that there
are times when
our thoughts are not on
you and your glory;
they are controlled by our
doubts and our fears.

You call us to declare your name
and to do so in everything
we say or do or are.

Yet the way we live and speak
must make it almost impossible
for our friends and our neighbours
to hear your word of love.

By your Holy Spirit,
renew our hearts and minds;
cleanse our every thought
and transform our words and deeds.
Do this that your true name of love
may be heard this day. **Amen.**

Intercession

1 Thessalonians 4:13

Lord,
we pray for those who have lost hope;
for those whose home and family
have been destroyed by [*name any recent tragedy*]
and for those who do not know
how they can put their lives
back together again.
May they receive hope to begin again.
Lord, in your mercy,
hear our prayer.

Lord,
we pray for those who
are losing hope;
for those who are awaiting
their doctor's diagnosis
and are concerned what it might
mean for their future
and for those who already
know that they are facing
a period of painful and
unpleasant treatment.
May they find hope in the
presence of your love.
Lord, in your mercy,
hear our prayer.

Lord,
we pray for those who have lost
the hope they once had;
for those who never seemed to
have a care in the world
but have lost their veneer of
peace and tranquillity
and for those who are now
overwhelmed by anxiety
as the darkness of depression
colours their day.
May they find hope in
God's healing love.
Lord, in your mercy,
hear our prayer.

Lord,
we pray for those who
have no hope left;
for those whose every job
application receives no reply
and every attempt to find
work is rejected
and for those whose experience
of unemployment
means they are losing their sense
of purpose and self-worth.
May they find hope in the
assurance of God's power.
Lord, in your mercy,
hear our prayer.

Lord,
we pray for those whose
hope is fading;
for those whose children
have now left home
and are losing any real sense
of meaning in their lives
as they struggle to learn to be
parents in a whole new way

and for those, who with
the passing years,
find their failing eyesight
and lack of mobility
leave them feeling isolated
and worthless.
May the ever-present peace of
God renew their hope.
Lord, in your mercy,
hear our prayer.

Lord,
we pray for those whose
hope is daily renewed;
for those whose walk with God
is the strength of their lives and
an inspiration to others
and for those whose words of hope
bring courage and encouragement
to everyone they meet.
May the hope of God radiate
through their lives.
Lord, in your mercy,
hear our prayer.

Lord,
we pray for those we know
who are losing hope;
for a friend, a neighbour, or
a colleague at work
whose life is in turmoil and they do
not know which way to turn.

silence

And we pray for ourselves,
that in the darkest times
we may hold fast to Christ
who has promised
to hold fast to us—no matter what;
that we may spend time
in his company,
that he may lead us into the
light and to new hope.
May the presence of Jesus
be our hope.
Lord, in your mercy,
hear our prayer.

We bring all our prayers in
the name of Christ,
the light and the hope of
the world. **Amen.**

THIRTY-THIRD SUNDAY IN ORDINARY TIME

Prayer of Approach

Psalm 123:1

Lord,
lift our eyes to see something
of your glory;
open our minds to grasp a little
more of your sovereignty;
move within us that
we might know
that we are gathered in
the presence of
the Lord of time and space
and all eternity.
Then, by your Holy Spirit,
empower us to worship you
as we have never worshipped
before. **Amen.**

Praise

1 Thessalonians 5:23–24

Father,
how can we not praise you?
Your endless love surrounds
us day by day
and your grace is the touchpaper
that sets all our hopes
and praise ablaze!

When we first became aware
of your grace for us
we were stunned into silent wonder.
We were so overcome
it felt as if we dare not breathe
so utterly precious was that moment.

But then your voice of love
broke into the stillness
and that grace
that bought us and brought
us to our knees
burst forth in a song of praise
from the very depths of our being.

Father,
when we consider all that you
have done for us in Christ
we simply cannot contain
the sacrifice of praise, that
if it is not released
it feels as if it would tear us apart.

How can we not praise you?
For you have lifted us
from the darkness
that was crushing out of us
the life you intended us to enjoy.
How can we not praise you?
For you have lit up our hearts
and minds and lives
with your renewing love
to us in Jesus.
All praise to you, our Father,
all praise now and for
evermore. **Amen.**

Confession

Judges 4:1

Lord, we never learn!
Again and again we make
our promises to you
only to break them even
before the words
have taken root in our hearts.

Lord,
we seek your forgiveness
for promises broken
and also promises we have
failed to make.
Come, Father, cleanse and renew us
that we may have the joy
of remaining in the freedom
of your grace
and live the kind of lives
that bring you glory.
For Christ's sake. **Amen.**

Intercession

Matthew 25:14

Think of someone just setting
out on the journey of life.
A newborn baby in its
mother's arms,
a child starting school
for the first time,
or a young person
at the doorway to a world
of rich experiences.
Let us ask the Lord to
journey with them.

silence

Think of someone whose
journey has begun.
Those setting out on their own,
those going to college or university,
and for those discovering the gifts
God has placed in their hands
and are now seeking ways to
use them to the full.

Let us ask the Lord to
journey with them.

silence

Think of someone whose
journey means starting
new relationships or
friendships or marriage
and for those whose journey
will mean singleness
as they experience fulfilment
in being themselves.
Let us ask the Lord to
journey with them.

silence

Think of someone whose journey
involves brokenness.
For those whose relationships
are damaged
or where trust is lost through
no fault of their own;
for those whose dreams
have failed to be fulfilled
on their journey
and for those too afraid to
risk making a new start.
Let us ask the Lord to
journey with them.

silence

Think of someone who journeys
with eyes that are blinkered.
For those who only have eyes
for the goal they have
set themselves,
which never allows them to see
the pain, suffering, and despair
of those who have fallen by the way
and for those who have
closed their ears
to the heartache and weeping
of their neighbour
and who quickly pass by
on the other side.
Let us ask the Lord to
journey with them.

silence

Think of someone whose
journey is almost over.
For those whose health is failing
and their weakness of
mind or of body
means their journeys are
all in their memories
and for those who still journey
in faith, hope, and love of their Lord
and for whom death is
no more than
a door to a new world in the
heaven of Christ's love.
Let us ask the Lord to
journey with them.

silence

Think of someone you know
with whom you share
the journey of life
and for whom you are
deeply concerned.

silence

Now let us think of ourselves
and the journey we have made,
the journey we are making,
and the journey yet to come.

Let us ask the Lord to
journey with us.

silence

We bring all our prayers in
the name of Jesus,
the one who has promised
to share every journey
to the end—
and beyond. **Amen.**

SUNDAY BEFORE ADVENT

Prayer of Approach

Psalm 95:1–2

This is the time to celebrate
as we prepare for the
coming of the King.
This is the time of hope
as we prepare to welcome the
Saviour of the world.
The is the time of anticipation
as we prepare our hearts
for the Christ-child.
This is the time to worship
for he is Immanuel, always
Immanuel. **Amen.**

Praise

Ezekiel 34:11

Father,
we praise you because you
are the God who speaks
and who longs to
communicate with us.
The prophets brought
us your words.
When they spoke in your
name they said,
'Thus says the Lord,'
and your people knew you
were meant to be heard.

Father,
we praise you that you are
the God who speaks.
Everywhere we hear your
voice ringing in our ears.
You speak through the beauty
of your creation
and the wonders of the vast universe;
every tree and every flower,
every hill and every mountain,
every planet and every constellation
shouts aloud that you are the God
of order and intricate design,
of plans and power and creativity
that blow our minds away.

Father,
it is with the coming of your Son
that we hear you speaking
most clearly.
As we stand on the
threshold of Advent
his coming amongst us, as one of us,
leaves us no choice
but to listen to him.
For in listening to him
we now know we are
listening to you.

Father,
we praise you, the God who spoke,
the God who speaks,
and the God who will
continue speaking
from now and until the
end of time. **Amen.**

Intercession
Matthew 25:40

Lord,
we pray for your troubled world,
where so many people are left
homeless and helpless
through their struggle to find
food for their family
or as they become refugees
fleeing from cruelty and war.
We pray for those who seek to
provide food and shelter
and strive to bring peace
in your world.
May the coming of the Christ-child
bring them hope.

Lord,
we pray for troubled people
in your world;
for homes where only angry
voices are heard,
where trust has been broken,
and for families living in poverty
through the lack of employment
or where the misuse of
drugs or alcohol
is undermining relationships
and abuse is destroying young lives.
We pray for social workers,
organisations that work with
families, and good neighbours
who seek to provide help
and support.
May the coming of the Christ-child
bring them hope.

Lord,
we pray for troubled young people
who leave school with
no qualifications,
no work, and no future;
for those with little or no
respect for authority,
other people, or themselves;
for those involved in gang culture
and those who to feed
their drug habit
enter a downward spiral
in a life of crime.
We pray for those who
give of themselves
to support young people
as they offer opportunities
to learn new skills
or discover themselves in
a sporting activity.
May the coming of the Christ-child
bring them hope.

Lord,
we pray for the old with their
particular troubles
as they try to continue to live
in their own homes
and for those whose health is failing
as they care for a loved one
that no longer knows who they are;
for families sinking under the
stress of responsibility
they have for their elderly relatives
or for those weighed
down with concern
for disabled members of their family
and are close to the point of breaking.
We pray for Age UK
and for all agencies of
care and support
for the elderly, the infirm,
and the disabled
and for all who still seek to
be a good neighbour.
May the coming of the Christ-child
bring them hope.

Lord,
we pray for those who are
troubled about your world;
for those who challenge us
about the damage to your creation;
for scientists and environmentalists
who warn us of
the serious impact that our
lives and our lifestyle
are having on God's good earth
and warn us that our failure to act
will affect the lives of our children
for generations to come;
for those who challenge us
to begin to trade fairly
and provide poorer nations
access to world markets,
that they may not need to rely
on the crumbs of aid
to fall from the tables of the rich.
We pray for world leaders
with a genuine concern for
those who are hungry
and a longing to end the
starvation of millions.
May the coming of the Christ-child
bring them hope.

Lord,
we pray for our troubled country;
for those whose lives are empty
and for those who live alone
and no one seems to care;
for the ever-widening gap
between the poor and the rich
and for those with no sense
of purpose or meaning
as each day is simply part
of the existence;
for those who focus their lives upon
what they can see or touch or prove;
and for those who find the security
in the false assurances of their
wealth and possessions.
We pray for every member of
every church in this land,
that we will take a step forward
in faith, hope, and love.
That we may have the courage
to begin to share our faith in the
presence and the power of God
and our trust in the coming
of the Christ-child
who himself is the hope
of the world.
May the coming of the Christ-child
bring them hope.

We bring our prayers in the
name of the Christ-child,
who is our hope and the hope
of the world. **Amen.**

YEAR B

FIRST SUNDAY OF ADVENT

Prayer of Approach

Psalm 80:3

Father,
we enter this house of prayer
in the hope of renewal,
the challenge of faith,
and with a deep longing to worship.
Fill us with your Holy Spirit
that your glory
will be the focus of all
we say and do.
For Jesus' sake. **Amen.**

Thanksgiving

1 Corinthians 1:4–6

Lord,
at times,
the joy of knowing we are
surrounded by your grace
is all but overwhelming
and the hope and thankfulness
your presence brings
give meaning and purpose to
the whole of our lives.

Since we began the walk with Jesus
we have faced many times of
difficulty and doubt,
but you have picked us up
when we have fallen
and held on to us when our journey
took us through a storm.

We give thanks for the assurance
that our value cannot be
measured in days or years
and that your coming in
the Christ-child
has given us a purpose that
is as vast as eternity.

Lord,
we overflow with a deep,
deep gratitude
for those whose Christ-filled lives
opened our eyes to your presence
and those whose joy in your
love touched our hearts.
We thank you for those whose
lives so reflected your love
that they became the
vehicle for your grace to
transform our minds.

We worship you that you saw fit
to come as our infant Lord
and we remember your advent with
its promise of your coming again.
We bless you for the way
your faithful people can be
a sign of your presence
and that you are longing to use even
us so that the world may believe.

Gracious, holy and loving Lord,
hear the prayer of our
thankful hearts.
In the name of Jesus. **Amen.**

Confession

Isaiah 64:1–3

Father,
we have yet to realise just how
much our lives offend you
and how our words and deeds
cause you such great sorrow.
Too often we compare
ourselves—our thoughts, our
words and our deeds—
to those around us, those who
have done evil things, and
those who ignore you.

You do not want to hear
our fine words
and you refuse to listen to our
finely scripted excuses.
You simply point us to Jesus and
suggest we stand next to him,
for he is the measure you
have prepared
and the microscope through which
you view our hearts and lives.

Father,
come touch our lives and our lips
with the fire of your grace
and, by your Holy Spirit,
transform every part of our lives
for your glory.

The Lord says,
'My word of grace still stands.
When you truly confess you
can know that I have made
you clean.' **Amen.**

Intercession

Mark 13:35–37

Father,
we want to talk to you about those
who have lost those they loved
and for the people everywhere
as they try to deal with
the outrages they face;
for those who planned and
executed the murders
of innocent people
and for those who hide their
evil deeds behind the
camouflage of religion.

silence

Father,
we want to talk to you about
those who have lost their way
and who are struggling to make sense
of what is happening in their lives;
for those who are facing life-changing
situations in their health;
and for those who feel all
alone as they experience an
unknown tomorrow.

silence

Father,
we want to talk to you about those
with no home of their own
and for those who sleep rough
on the streets of our town;
for those whose homes were
ripped apart by the bombs
of their neighbour
and for those migrants
who travel towards the
unknown, seeking peace.

silence

Father,
we want to talk to you about those
in positions of leadership
and for those who reject all authority
over their lives—except their own;
for those whose influence is marred
by signs of corruption and greed
and for those whose decisions
blight the lives of many
as they focus on the
enrichment of the few.

silence

Father,
we want to talk to you about
those who are concerned
about your world
and for those who call us to change
our ways before it is too late;
for those who warn us of the dangers
to the future of our planet
and for those whose lives
are being damaged by the
pollution we are creating.

silence

Father,
we want to talk to you about
those who accept cheating
and lying as normal
and for those whose behaviour
has darkened the world of
banking, sport, and politics;
for those in all parts of our
society who serve with
honour and integrity
and for those whose witness
for Christ in their workplace
is a challenge to us all.

silence

Father,
we want to talk to you about
those for whom we have
promised to pray.

silence

And for ourselves and the things
from the past that still hurt us,
the experiences that steal our
hopes for tomorrow,
and the fears, pain, and loneliness
that haunt us today.

silence

Father,
we bring these concerns in
the name of Jesus,
who showed us how to
talk to you. **Amen.**

SECOND SUNDAY OF ADVENT

Prayer of Approach

Psalm 85:1–2

Lord,
out of our brokenness, we
enter your wholeness;
from our despair, we come
to your fullness;
with all of our burdens, we come
to your throne of grace.

Lord,
as we worship you together,
overwhelm us with
the Spirit of wisdom and
of understanding,
the Spirit of counsel and of power,
the Spirit of knowledge and
the fear of the Lord
as your Holy Spirit rests and
remains upon us. **Amen.**

Praise

Isaiah 40:1–11

Father,
it is only when we sit in
your presence
and allow ourselves to be
touched by your nearness

that we are utterly overwhelmed
with the desire to praise you.
It is in those moments when you
break through our defences
and stir our hearts with a
renewed longing for you
that words of worship come
so easily to our lips.

And yet it is in those moments
that we find ourselves
lifted, blessed, and moved to offer
you more than mere words.
It is as if you have burst into
our act of worship
and transformed it into something
closer to falling in love.
No longer are we simply singing
hymns and saying prayers,
now we are talking to the
King of the universe
and the Lord of all things—
past, present, and to come.

Father,
how can we not praise you?
You are the one true, living God!
You have no beginning and
you have no end.
Our tiny, finite minds cannot
hope to comprehend
the wonder and the power and
the authority that are yours.

So we praise you, not simply
because of all you have done
but supremely because of
who and what you are.
You are the Lord, and we
will praise you!
You are our creator, and
we honour you!
You are our Saviour, and we
bow down before you!

Father,
when we felt we had said
everything about you
it was then that we realised you
can never be encapsulated
by our thoughts, our words,
or by our worship.
And yet, through your
Son, Jesus Christ,
you tore down the curtain
to your presence.
Through his life, death,
and resurrection
we have been granted a
glimpse of your grace
and promised a place before
your throne of love.

Father,
in humility, joy, and wonder we
dare to come and praise you
for you are our God and
you alone are worthy of
all our praises. **Amen.**

Intercession

Mark 1:1–8

Lord,
we pray for those in the
desert of fear
and for those overwhelmed by
their dread of the unknown;
for those who cannot give a
reason why they are afraid
and for those who are fearful of
what they are facing right now.
Lord of the kingdom of hope,
walk with us in the desert.

Lord,
we pray for those in the
desert of emptiness
and for those who feel drained
of hope, peace, and joy;
for those who have served and
are serving the kingdom
and for those for whom it is
time to learn simply 'to be'.
Lord of the kingdom of hope,
walk with us in the desert.

Lord,
we pray for those in the desert
of unanswered questions
and for those who are struggling
to make sense of their journey;
for those who want answers as they
hesitate on the threshold of faith
and for those whose courage and
peace are often the answers we seek.
Lord of the kingdom of hope,
walk with us in the desert.

Lord,
we pray for those in the desert of evil
and for those who spend their
days planning deeds of terror;
for those who have felt
the impact of evil
and for those torn apart by the
abuse they have suffered.
Lord of the kingdom of hope,
walk with us in the desert.

Lord,
we pray for those in the
desert of charity
and for those who want to
live before they die;
for those robbed of life-saving gifts
by the corruption of others
and for those who long for the
chance simply to trade fairly.
Lord of the kingdom of hope,
walk with us in the desert.

Lord,
we pray for those in the
desert of poverty
and for those who are low paid
but are labelled as scroungers;
for those who see the riches
that others take for granted
and for those who are part of the
'have nots' and not of the 'haves'.
Lord of the kingdom of hope,
walk with us in the desert.

Lord,
we pray for those in the
desert of injustice
and for those who have been
imprisoned for their faith;
for those who are facing the cost
of their commitment to justice
and for those who are paying
for their stand for truth
and democracy.
Lord of the kingdom of hope,
walk with us in the desert.

Lord,
we pray for ourselves and the
deserts we face in our daily lives
and for those times when life feels
empty and without purpose;
for those whom we meet on
the pathways of each day
and for the courage to
share our faith in the
opportunities provided.
Lord of the kingdom of hope,
walk with us in the desert.

Lord,
we pray in the assurance that
you will be with us
even in the desert places
of life. **Amen.**

THIRD SUNDAY OF ADVENT

Prayer of Approach

Isaiah 61:1–4, 8–11

Lord,
we come to lay down our lives
before the one who is from
eternity to eternity;
we come to declare your glory,
holiness, and sovereignty;
we come with open hearts and minds
to worship the one who is Lord;
we come to celebrate the King
who turns ends into new beginnings
and offers freedom to start
again to us all. **Amen.**

Praise

1 Thessalonians 5:16–24

We praise you, Father,
that by your grace
you enable us to see the world
in a whole new way.
Again and again you open our eyes
to the utterly endless opportunities
for giving you thanks and praise.
As you touch our lives
with your presence
we find a joy welling up within us
that we simply cannot contain.

When the way is strewn
with obstacles
and each day is coloured in
the darkest shades,
you flood our hearts with your peace.

When time is slipping
through our fingers
and our grasp on our
precious memories
is growing ever weaker,
you flood our days with your joy.

When all that is painful and
cruel causes us to stumble
and those things we held dear
are ridiculed and denied,
you flood our times
with your grace.

Father,
how can we not sing your
praises and take our stand
for your justice, mercy, and grace?

Come, Father, receive our songs
of thanksgiving for your Son.
Come, Father, and by
your Holy Spirit,
empower us for your glory. **Amen.**

Intercession

John 1:6–8, 19–28

Father,
we pray for those who lead the
way through pain and sorrow
and for those who help us to
find the light of Christ—
even on the darkest day.
When we are lost and alone
come, show us the way.

Father,
we pray for those who lead us
through the curtain of despair
when all hope seems hidden
from our sight
and for those who walk with us

in times of doubt, depression,
and anxiety
and assure us that we
are not to blame.
When we are lost and alone
come, show us the way.

Father,
we pray for those who
lead us to value
those we would so easily ignore
and for those whose giving of
their time and of themselves
we daily take for granted.
When we are lost and alone
come, show us the way.

Father,
we pray for those who challenge
us to care for your creation
and for those who remind us
that we live here in your
world by grace alone.
When we are lost and alone
come, show us the way.

Father,
we pray for those who are the
victims of terrorist atrocity
and for those who seek to
respond as they look for
the reasons for hatred and
the healing of wounds.
When we are lost and alone
come, show us the way.

Father,
we pray for those facing
the prospect of losing
their independence
and for those finding life harder
as they come to terms with
being unable to do what
once came so easily.
When we are lost and alone
come, show us the way.

Father,
we pray for those who
live by themselves
and for those whose singleness
by choice or by circumstance
means they often have no one
with whom to share their
hopes and their fears.
When we are lost and alone
come, show us the way.

Father,
we pray for your church in the world
and for those who live where to
be a Christian is dangerous
and they experience the true
cost of discipleship.
When we are lost and alone
come, show us the way.

Father,
as always, we bring our prayers
in the name of Jesus,
the one who promised to
be the way. **Amen.**

FOURTH SUNDAY OF ADVENT

Prayer of Approach

2 Samuel 7:1–11, 16

Lord,
teach us again that you
cannot be confined.
Our words, our thoughts,
and our churches

are simply far too small
to encapsulate
all that you are and all you will be.

You are disturbingly great
and you are infinitely glorious.
Your power, sovereignty, and
your utter holiness
simply blow our minds away!

So we gather with the
hosts of heaven
and all who have worshipped
the living God.
We join our praises in
one vast chorus
that declares your majesty,
glory, and love. **Amen.**

Praise
Romans 16:25–27

Father,
we praise you for the hope
that wells up within us
and for the assurance of your
presence that gives us courage.
Every time we remember
your grace to us in Jesus
we cannot hold ourselves back from
singing the song of heaven.

This is our God.
He heals our wounds and
forgives our wayward lives
and he comes looking for us even
when we turn our backs on him.
He is patient with us when we take
his faithfulness for granted
and he longs to speak to us of his
offer of unconditional love.

Father,
we praise you for meeting
us where we are
and that you are able to lift us
with nail-printed hands.
Thankfulness is our song
and deep-felt gratitude is the
message written on our hearts.

Your message of grace is not
a latter-day invention
but it is the life-blood that is
at the heart of all things.
The word has been on the
lips of your people from
the very beginning
and down the centuries it has been
the bedrock of all your messengers.

By your word of grace you
can do all things
and through your love you will
accomplish all your purposes.
Sovereign Lord, this message we
proclaim was not written by us
but was the indelible mark of
who and what you are.

Once you had revealed your
loving-kindness to us
you left us no alternative but to
surrender our all to you.
We can therefore do no other
than bring our praises
to the one true God
whose wisdom, glory, and authority
demands our worship.

In the name of Jesus, the
one through whom
your grace and truth are
made known. **Amen.**

Intercession

Luke 1:26–38

Father,
we pray for those who, like the angel Gabriel, sometimes bring unwelcome news
and for those who share the implications of tests the medical staff made;
for those who are journalists bringing us the reports of your broken world
and for those who are magistrates and judges giving the law's answer to the lawbreaker.
Our Father in heaven,
may your kingdom come.

Father,
we pray for those who live in communities who treat others differently
and for those where women are seen as property and of little value;
for those societies where women are denied the riches of education
and for those where wealth is in the hands of the few and the poor are hungry.
Our Father in heaven,
may your kingdom come.

Father,
we pray for those parents who are troubled about their children's future
and for those in developing countries where the next meal is their only worry;
for those who are concerned for their family as they face the stress of unemployment
and for those who see their child being trapped in a world of drugs and crime.
Our Father in heaven,
may your kingdom come.

Father,
we pray for those who see the change our lifestyle is bringing to your world
and for those who challenge us to act to protect God's creation;
for those whose homes and families are facing the dangers of flooding and violent storms
and for those now denied insurance cover because of the greater risk their homes face.
Our Father in heaven,
may your kingdom come.

Father,
we pray for our nation where many no longer see God at the heart of life
and for those who turn to anyone or anything to help them make sense of their lives;
for those who look to scientists, politicians, and medical research to solve all our problems
and for those who complain when they find human agencies don't have the solutions they need.
Our Father in heaven,
may your kingdom come.

Father,
we pray for those who, like Mary, are facing the total upheaval of their lives

and for those who see their
future strewn with confusion
and uncertainty;
for those whose dreams are
for a home and family
flooded with love and joy
and for those now facing singleness
through loss or broken promises.
Our Father in heaven,
may your kingdom come.

Father,
we pray for those like Mary
whose lives are being
transformed by God's love
and for those who are
discovering the power of God
to make all things new;
for those who, like Mary,
have been prepared to say
yes to the call of God
and for those who say yes even
when they do not know
what their yes will mean.
Our Father in heaven,
may your kingdom come.

Father, we have brought our
prayers in the name Jesus
in the assurance that your
kingdom will come. **Amen.**

CHRISTMAS DAY

Prayer of Approach

Psalm 89:1–4

Father,
our songs of praise join with
the angels in heaven
as we gather to celebrate
your faithfulness.
The praises we bring come from
hearts set on fire by your grace
and our worship is an expression of
the joy we feel in your presence.
But it is your promise of love to all
your creation that touches us deeply
and that today you burst into
our world in a dirty stable.
There in the manger we find
your promise fulfilled
and the wonder of Christmas comes
to us in the Christ-child. **Amen.**

Praise

Titus 2:11–14

Father,
we stand amazed in your presence!

We had heard that you were a
God of glory and authority
and we had assumed that we are
as nothing in your sight.
We hesitated at the very thought
of entering your presence
and we could only think of
you as King of creation
and Lord of all things.

Today you have invited us to peep
round the door of the stable
and discover for ourselves the
tangible expression of your grace.
For the first time, everyone,
everywhere can know the
truth of your love
and know they too are invited
to make room for the
Saviour of the world.

Father,
we stand amazed in your presence!

Your entry into our world
has changed everything
and we are beginning to realise
that you are changing us.
We praise you, our Father
and our God,
for making yourself known
to us in the humility and
poverty of the stable.

Father,
we stand amazed in your presence!

Your coming as one of us
heralds your intention to
transform our days
and to overwhelm our
thoughts, our hopes, and
our fears with your grace.
How can we not praise you
for the birth of Jesus
and for the promise that he
will return as Lord?

Father,
we stand amazed in your presence!

We will praise you now with
hearts overflowing with joy
and we look to the day when
we will praise you before
the throne of grace.
Come, Lord Jesus, come and fill
this Christmas with your glory
and may our transformed
lives demonstrate the
reality of your coming.

In the name of the Christ-
child. **Amen.**

Intercession

Luke 2:1–20

Lord,
we are concerned about those
who, like Mary, ponder
the meaning of life
and for those for whom life is
empty and has lost direction;
for those who are grieving
for the one they loved
and for those whose love for
you has grown cold.
Lord, we come in the name
of the Christ-child.
Amaze us now with your grace.

Lord,
we are concerned about those
who, like Mary, ponder
the meaning of justice
and for those who risk
everything for the needs of
migrants and refugees;
for those who are appalled by the
corruption in sport, in politics,
and in the courts of law
and for those in positions of
power who know the truth
but are unwilling to act.
Lord, we come in the name
of the Christ-child.
Amaze us now with your grace.

Lord,
we are concerned about those
who, like Mary, ponder
the meaning of peace
and for those who are content
to turn a blind eye to
preserve the status quo;
for those who only understand peace
to mean all the fighting is ended

and for those who long for
their neighbour to experience
the peace of God.
Lord, we come in the name
of the Christ-child.
Amaze us now with your grace.

Lord,
we are concerned about those
who, like Mary, ponder
the meaning of hope
and for those left behind by
the onward rush of the desire
for this life's possessions;
for those who place their trust
in science and technology to
answer all their problems
and for those who are finding
there are no satisfying solutions
at the end of this tunnel.
Lord, we come in the name
of the Christ-child.
Amaze us now with your grace.

Lord,
we are concerned about those
who, like Mary, ponder
the meaning of truth
and for those who will only
trust the truth of what they
can see, touch, or prove;
for those who are content
with the truth they have
created for themselves
and for those yet to look in the
manger and discover that
truth cannot be bought.
Lord, we come in the name
of the Christ-child.
Amaze us now with your grace.

Lord,
we are concerned about those
who, like Mary, ponder
the meaning of fairness
and for those in developing
countries where they are treated
unfairly by huge corporations;
for those who are told we all have an
equal opportunity in life to succeed
and for those who are finding
society's divisions mean they
must depend on the food bank.
Lord, we come in the name
of the Christ-child.
Amaze us now with your grace.

Lord,
we are concerned about those
who, like Mary, ponder the
meaning of Christmas
and for those for whom it is
all about Santa, a time for
children and presents;
for those who are left out of
the festivities as they have
no family to share it
and for those who will spend
Christmas, like Jesus, without
a home of their own.
Lord, we come in the name
of the Christ-child.
Amaze us now with your grace.

Lord,
we are concerned about those
who, like Mary, ponder
the meaning of love
and for those who have never known
what it means to feel wanted;
for those who have confused
love with needing to prove
themselves worthy

and for those who are discovering
God's love comes without
strings, unconditionally.
Lord, we come in the name
of the Christ-child.
Amaze us now with your grace.

Lord,
we are concerned about those
who, like Mary, ponder the
meaning of all things
and for ourselves as we ponder
before you those for whom
we are concerned.

silence

Lord, we come in the name
of the Christ-child.
Amaze us now with your grace.

Lord, we bring our concerns in
the name of the Christ-child.
We ask you to amaze us, now,
with your grace. **Amen.**

FIRST SUNDAY OF CHRISTMAS

Prayer of Approach

Psalm 148:1–6

Lord,
it's like joining the largest
choir that ever lived
as we come, all your
faithful people,
to praise the living God.
We are here with everyone of
every day and generation
to sing your glory.
Everyone who ever lived, is
living, or is yet to be born
will share in offering
thanks and praise,
O Lord most high. **Amen.**

Praise

Isaiah 62:1–3

Father,
there is a song we must sing
and a message of hope we
have to make known.
There is a word on our lips that
we can no longer hold in
and we know this is not the
time to remain silent!

Father,
it is the most amazing thing
that no matter who we are
you have adopted us
into your family
and whatever we have
done or failed to do,
like the prodigal son's father,
you welcome us home.
How can we keep quiet?
We want to shout it from
the rooftops:
you have made us your children
and we can know you as our Father!
Our cry comes from
hearts full of joy
and our songs of praise simply
cannot be contained within us.

We have done nothing at all to
deserve this bounty of grace
and there is nothing we
could have done
to win a place within the
family of heaven.
Such is your nature that you desire
that we should know you

and it is your will and purpose
that we should be known
as your children.
How wonderful it is to
call you Father
and to know, to really know, your
fatherly love in our hearts.
We praise you with songs of
love—we can do no other—
and we bow down before the Lord
of all things, who loves us.

Wonderful, wonderful Father,
help us to praise you
and, by your Holy Spirit, enable
us to praise you as you deserve.
May we praise you with our
lips and with our lives,
here and everywhere, always
and for ever. **Amen.**

Intercession

Luke 2:15–21

Lord,
we imagine that Joseph's mind must
have been in a state of confusion.
He was probably asking himself
what was happening and
what did it all mean.
It started out as a loving
relationship with Mary
and with thoughts of their future
life together in Nazareth.
But all their plans had gone
out of the window;
here they were in a stable in
Bethlehem, he had just become
a father—or had he?
We pray for those whose
lives are in turmoil;
the diagnosis of the doctor and
major surgery to be faced.
Lord of the stories of our lives,
help us to write them with you.

Lord,
it is hard to imagine what it
was like for the angels.
From before the beginning of time
this was the moment for which all
of creation had been waiting.
How those angels must have
been filled with joy and
the glory of God.
We pray for those for whom
life has been hard
and for whom each day has been
a struggle just to survive;
for those who now find it almost
impossible to find peace
and for whom there is no joy
and peace in their hearts.
Lord of the stories of our lives,
help us to write them with you.

Lord,
it is impossible to forget
the shepherds.
It was so utterly incredible that this
should have happened to them—
a group of nobodies, the
very ones that the good,
religious people ignored!
They probably didn't know
what to expect when they
arrived in Bethlehem,
but they still went—well, you
would if an angel told you to go!
We pray for those who know about
Jesus but have yet to meet him
and for those who each day close
their ears to the cry of the hurting
and their eyes to the pain of their
neighbour, in case Jesus may call.

Lord of the stories of our lives,
help us to write them with you.

Lord,
we can't imagine what the people
of Bethlehem thought
when they heard of the birth of a
baby with the animals in a stable.
They had probably all heard the story
but were too busy to go
there themselves.
We pray for those who fill
their days and their hours
with the things they think
are important
and for those who flood
their hearts and minds
with the things of earth
so that they leave no room
for the good news of the
doorway to heaven.
Lord of the stories of our lives,
help us to write them with you.

Lord,
we cannot think how the
parents of the children who
were murdered felt;
they were too overwhelmed with
grief and their devastating loss.
Their hearts had been torn apart
as anger towards Herod
welled up within them.
It was only much later they
discovered that it was
the Prince of Peace who
had been born.
We pray for families
whose pain of grief
is crushing hope and
life out of them
and for those who are
running for their lives
having lost home and family at
the hands of the terrorists.
Lord of the stories of our lives,
help us to write them with you.

Lord,
we can just imagine what
the people of Nazareth
would be thinking—
and it wouldn't be loving,
forgiving, or kind thoughts at all.
They knew that Mary
hadn't needed to journey
to Bethlehem—
it was their nasty tongues and
unfeeling condemnation
that sent her there.
We pray for those whose lives
have been damaged by
words spoken in anger
and for those who feel rejected
by the attitude of those who
should have helped them;
for those whose first response is to
belittle or insult their neighbour,
all because they are different
and not one of us.
Lord of the stories of our lives,
help us to write them with you.

Lord,
we really wonder how
Mary felt that night
giving birth in an old dirty stable.
She must have been weary
and frightened
and there wasn't a doctor on call.
But she has been called blessed
and highly favoured

and she had accepted the role
as the servant of the Lord.
We pray for those who
step out in faith
and are ready and willing to
face everything for Christ;
for those who thought following
Jesus would protect them
from all problems,
suffering, and shame
and for those who see
faith as risk-taking
in the service of the Saviour
of the world.
Lord of the stories of our lives,
help us to write them with you.

Lord,
in the stillness we bring before
you the story of our life
and the journey we are
taking each day.

silence

We pray that by your grace
we will remain faithful,
and whatever we face on the
road down which you lead us
we may know we are holding
the hand of the one
who will hold us now and
hold us for ever.
Lord of the stories of our lives,
help us to write them with you.

We bring our prayers in
the name of Jesus,
the one who is always
with us. **Amen.**

SECOND SUNDAY OF CHRISTMAS

Praise

Psalm 147:12–20

Lord,
it doesn't matter where we look
and it makes no difference
where we go;
always and everywhere we
see your fingerprints—
the signs of your presence at
the heart of your creation.

We praise you for your
sovereignty over all things
and your grace that oozes from
every fibre of the universe.
Again and again you have stamped
your will upon the fabric of life
and your signature is written
large to the eye of faith.

It is when your people
gather for worship
that in grace and truth you
reveal yourself so clearly.
It is then that our hearts
rejoice in your presence
and we are renewed by the
one who is of eternity.

Your word directs our path on
the journey of our life
and your gracious touch holds us
even in the midst of the storm.
The psalmist reminded us that there
is nowhere we can run from you
and wherever we go we
cannot hide from the love
that seeks to heal us.

Each time we pause to
consider who you are
a song of joy wells up within us
and when we place our
lives before you
your tender loving presence
renews our days.

Lord,
we praise you for who you are
and we celebrate all your
mighty works.
We rejoice in the discoveries of science
as they provide even more reasons
to offer you our worship.

We honour you, our great
and glorious God,
and we give you glory—
glory alone is due, to you the
Lord of all things. **Amen.**

Confession

Jeremiah 31:7–14

Father,
we confess that too often we try to
live each day in our own strength
as we find ourselves lost in the sea
of false ideas all around us.
When we look back we realise how
little thought we have given to you
and the days that have passed
without a thought of your
place in our lives.

There is no point being anything
other than honest with
ourselves and with you
for you know our deepest thoughts
and the motives of which
we should be ashamed.
We have sought to please
ourselves without bothering
to think of your glory
and we have planned our days as
if we could control the rising
and the setting of the sun.

Father,
like your people of old we
prepare ourselves for your
word of judgement
and we ready ourselves to face
the displeasure of our God.
Then, like the loving Father
that you are, what we receive
is grace upon grace
as you flood our lives with
forgiveness and you cleanse
our lives with your love.
Again and again you come to meet
your prodigal sons and daughters
as you envelop us in mercy
and take your rightful place
at the heart of our lives.

Father,
all we can do is to thank
you for your blessing
and seek, by your Holy Spirit,
to walk in your way in the
coming days. **Amen.**

Intercession

Ephesians 1:3–14

Lord,
we pray for those seeking
freedom from the things
that ensnare their lives
and for those who long to
escape the fighting in the war
zone that is their home;

for those whose days are
spent seeking food and
water for their children
and for those whose homes
and workplaces are where
the fighting never ceases.
Lord, in your mercy,
hear our prayer.

Lord,
we pray for those who yearn for
a real sense of belonging for
the first time in their lives
and for those whose experience
of isolation still colours
the whole of their days;
for those who are treated
differently because of their race,
their politics, or their faith
and for those who have attended
church all their life but for
whom Jesus remains a stranger.
Lord, in your mercy,
hear our prayer.

Lord,
we pray for those who are bursting
with desire to rejoice in the
wonder of your presence
and for those weighed down
by the worries they have
carried all their lives;
for those who have lost all
sense of the wonder of life
and the joy of friendship
and for those whose lives
exude a laughter and joy that
touches the lives of many.
Lord, in your mercy,
hear our prayer.

Lord,
we pray for those who need to
know that their value is not
measured by what they can do
and for those whose loss of
employment has robbed them
of their feeling of self-worth;
for those whose memories of abuse,
ridicule and failure still haunt them
and for those who are discovering
that God's grace gives them
the highest value of all.
Lord, in your mercy,
hear our prayer.

Lord,
we pray for those who spend
their lives striving for
acceptance by others
and for those who from their
earliest days were left feeling
their best wasn't good enough;
for those who still feel that their
worship, service, and prayers
are not acceptable to God
and for those who have found
that the Holy Spirit is God's
guarantee that they are accepted.
Lord, in your mercy,
hear our prayer.

Lord,
we pray for those who are troubled
by the things from the past
that are hurting them
and for those haunted by
memories of mistakes that are
still filling their minds today;
for those who find it so hard
to let go of the pain and
rejections they have suffered

and for those now reaching out
to grasp the hand of the God
who forgives and forgets.
Lord, in your mercy,
hear our prayer.

Lord,
we pray for those whose
opportunities are limited by
poverty, lack of education, or fear
and for those who neglect the
promises of God and are living
less richly than they could;
for those who have yet to discover
the wealth, hope, and joy
that flow from God's grace
and for those who seek to be a
blessing to others as they too
are blessed by the Holy Spirit.
Lord, in your mercy,
hear our prayer.

We bring our prayers in
the name of Christ,
the source of all grace. **Amen.**

FIRST SUNDAY IN ORDINARY TIME

Praise

Genesis 1:1–5

Lord,
how can we ever hope to
comprehend even the most
minuscule hint of your presence;
we know immediately we are out
of our depth when we seek
to understand your ways.
Every time we feel we have grasped
something more of your glory
it only makes us wonder how
you, the Lord of heaven and
earth, should care about us.

The truly amazing reality is that you
have left us to our own devices
and you simply do not expect
us to plumb the depths of
your limitless power.
From the very beginning you
had an intimate knowledge
of your creatures
and you designed us to have a
deep longing to experience
your living presence.
You are our incredible God!
You may be beyond our
understanding
but you have littered the world
with signs of who you are.
You have left your fingerprints
over everything you have made
and you have sent us off on
a journey of discovery,
for you are the God who wants to
be known by your creation!

Sovereign Lord,
we praise you not simply for
the mind-blowing universe
that speaks of your endless
rule and authority,
but we bow before the one who,
as evidence of your power,
was God before all things began
and you will be God when
all things cease to be.

It is then that it dawns upon us
that this truly amazing God
is a God whose love is always and
forever towards each one of us.

It is when we kneel at the
foot of the cross
and gaze into the suffering
face of the Son of God
that we know, deep down
within us, we are looking into
the human face of God.

Praise and glory, honour
and blessing, celebration
and endless worship
we offer to you in the knowledge
that the song of joy that
bursts from our lips
will be sung before your throne
of grace for all eternity.

Hallelujah, praise the Lord! **Amen.**

Confession

Psalm 29

Lord,
we sing your praises
and we declare our faith in you.
We speak of your greatness,
your power, and your glory
and we affirm that you are holy
and perfect in all that you are.
And yet, Lord, we have
little expectation
that you will be present and
active in our lives.
We rarely spend our days
expecting to meet you
in the faces of the lost and the
brokenness of the hurting.
We live each day with hardly
any expectation
that you will shake us and shock us
and that your Holy Spirit
will transform our lives.

The Lord says,
'You can always have great
expectations of my forgiveness,
and when you draw near to me you
will hear my words of grace:
your sins are forgiven and
forgotten.' **Amen.**

Intercession

Mark 1:4–11

Father,
we pray for those who, like
John the Baptist, are prepared
to live differently
and for those whose whole
way of life points to the
things that really matter;
for those who resist the headlong
plunge into possessing more
of the things of this world
and for those who invade our
homes and our minds with the
message of want and not need.
In the world of challenge
and change,
help us to live differently.

Father,
we pray for those who, like John the
Baptist, offered forgiveness to all
and for those who, like Jesus,
are ready to die to bring
freedom and hope;
for those whose lives have
been damaged by bullying,
ridicule, and abuse
and for those who at great cost
to themselves are teaching
us how to forgive.
In the world of challenge
and change,
help us to live differently.

Father,
we pray for those like John
the Baptist, whose focus
is not on themselves
and for those who are prepared
to live simply so that
others may simply live;
for those who put their lives at
risk serving as peacemakers
in the world's war zones
and for those who act as good
neighbours bringing hope to
the poor and the lonely.
In the world of challenge
and change,
help us to live differently.

Father,
we pray for those who, like
John the Baptist, go where
people are hurting
and for those who offer their
time to bring healing and
rescue wherever it is needed;
for those who serve around
the world sharing their skills
in hygiene, agriculture,
and medicine
and for those who reach out to
those whose home is a cardboard
box and newspaper their blanket.
In the world of challenge
and change,
help us to live differently.

Father,
we pray for those who, like
John the Baptist, demonstrate
a powerful humility
and for those whose concern
for the ones society has
forgotten touches us deeply;
for those who give of themselves,
caring for those struggling with
dementia and Alzheimer's
and for those whose care and
compassion enables many to
still live in their own home.
In the world of challenge
and change,
help us to live differently.

Father,
we pray for those who, like
John the Baptist, are a
signpost to life that is real
and for those whose lives are
a touchstone where the
presence of God is found;
for those whose whole way of life
is a challenge to the world's
greed, pride, and aggression
and for those whose endurance in
suffering and joy in adversity
is an example to us all.
In the world of challenge
and change,
help us to live differently.

Father,
we pray for those who, like John the
Baptist, teach the value of life
and for those whose concern for
the broken, the powerless, and
the disabled opens our hearts;
for those who fight all kinds
of injustice and who seek to
bring light in dark places
and for those whose words and
deeds are a source of hope
and beginning again.
In the world of challenge
and change,
help us to live differently.

Father,
in the stillness we pray for those
for whom we are concerned.

silence

We pray for ourselves, that, like
John the Baptist, we may
be signposts for Christ
and that we will take full
opportunity to share your love
with those to whom you send us.
In the world of challenge
and change,
help us to live differently.

We ask our prayers in
the name of Jesus,
the one who always lived
differently. **Amen.**

SECOND SUNDAY IN ORDINARY TIME

Prayer of Approach

Psalm 139:1–6

Father,
we do not have to speak of
entering your presence
for you are always there;
we are always and everywhere
in your presence.
It dawned on the psalmist
that there is nowhere we can
go but you are there.

Father,
Jesus has taught us that you
loved the world so much
that you gave your Son
for its renewal.
This means that there is no
God-forsaken place
and no God-forsaken person.

But we have come as your people
and we have deliberately entered
this place of worship
for you have promised that
as we gather together
we may experience your
presence anew.

Father,
by your Holy Spirit,
transform our songs, our
words, and our thoughts
into a vehicle of our heartfelt
thanks and praise.
In the name of Jesus. **Amen.**

Praise

Revelation 5:1–10

Lord,
we praise you because you are the
one with authority over all things.
Everything from the dawn of
creation owes its origin to you
and every living thing receives its
life by your sovereign will.
There is no one in the
whole of creation
that will not ultimately be
answerable to you.

Down the centuries and
across the world
many have given their
life for another.
But it is only you, Lord, who
died for the whole world
so that everyone, everywhere
can be liberated

from the things that damage
their relationship with you.

We praise you because you are
the one who is Saviour
and it is only you, through
your death on the cross,
who can wipe the slate clean
of the mess we have made.
Once we were locked out
of God's presence
with no hope of living
the kind of lives
that would allow us to enter
your holy presence.

Lord,
you have touched our lives and
by the power of your cross
we have known the freedom and
wonder of walking with you.
We have discovered that when
we place our trust in you
it is like switching on
a bright light
and we begin to see everything
in a whole new way.
We confess that we often do not
find it easy to walk in faith
until we realise that all you
are calling us to do
is simply to take the next step on
the stepping stones of hope.

In John's vision, the hosts of
heaven are concerned with
who will open the scroll
and reveal the message of
hope, grace, and heaven.
The steps of hope you are calling
us to take seem beyond us
but we have discovered that
we are not expected to
venture by ourselves.
You have shown us that
you alone can enable us,
by your Holy Spirit,
to 'expect great things from God,
attempt great things for God.'

We praise you, our holy, glorious,
and almighty Saviour,
who alone can lift us from the
depths of failure and despair,
that we too may reach the
heights of heaven.

In the name of the Lamb
of God. **Amen.**

Intercession
John 1:43–51

Lord,
every year we complain about the
commercialisation of Christmas
and that Santa Claus has replaced
the baby in the manger.
Each year there seems to be ever
more tinsel and crackers
as more people face credit card
doomsday come the new year.
As a church and as
individual Christians
we say we long to see Christ at
the heart of the real Christmas
but we find ourselves joining the
mad rush to spend even more.
Jesus called the disciples;
what are you calling me to do?

Lord,
we live in a world of injustice

where people are imprisoned
without a fair trial.
We are warned of nations
that flout human rights
and where women and
men are tortured
because of their belief in justice,
democracy, and Christ.
We feel helpless and pray that
someone will do something
and are deaf to Amnesty
International's appeals.
Jesus called the disciples;
what are you calling me to do?

Lord,
we know that Christians all
down the centuries
focused their lives on spending
time each day in prayer.
Reading the Bible and meeting
in groups to share faith
were vital parts of their mission
and ministry for Jesus.
It is unfortunate that so many of
us have become far too busy
and we are left squeezing in a
hurried whisper to God
instead of spending time
with our Lord.
It is said when we announce
that we might have been at a
prayer meeting if only it had
been arranged for another
time or another day.
Jesus called the disciples;
what are you calling me to do?

Lord,
we are surrounded by people
who live alone;
many are elderly with no
one who visits them.
Some have families who
live too far away
and others have families that
don't seem to care.
We are concerned for those
who are lonely
and for whom their four walls
have become the prison cell.
We know Age UK and ALONE
offer help to the elderly
but our neighbour receives
no help at all.
Jesus called the disciples;
what are you calling me to do?

Lord,
we listen to the challenge of scientists
who keep reminding us of the
dangers of climate change.
Again and again we are told of
the damage we are doing
and as Christians we know that
the earth is the Lord's.
We know that if the
planet is to recover
then the time has come for
action to be taken.
The scientists and world leaders
meet again and again
and we are left waiting for someone,
somewhere to respond.
Jesus called the disciples;
what are you calling me to do?

Lord,
we are told that religion is almost
finished in our country
and that life expectancy of the
church is in countdown.

But we cannot believe that the
people of God have no future
and that church as we know it
has reached its shelf life.
We are reminded that most
people who come to faith
do so because of a friendship that
was forged with a believer.
If only the church would
do something to attract
more people
and Christians would have the
courage to speak of their faith.
Jesus called the disciples;
what are you calling me to do?

Lord, Jesus called the disciples.
They had no idea where
following him would lead.
Help us to be like the disciples
and be ready to follow the
call of our Lord. **Amen.**

THIRD SUNDAY IN ORDINARY TIME

Praise

Jonah 3:1–5, 10

Lord,
we praise you that, like the
prodigal's father,
you long to embrace the
whole world.
We never cease to wonder at the
extravagance of your grace
and for the way you continually
reach out to gather a lost nation.

We may turn our backs on those we
assume have no interest in you
and remain content to celebrate
your love with the faithful.
But, like Jonah, you have not yet
finished with us or your world
and you are still longing for us to
fulfil the divine commission.

We praise you that you
have given us the most
important message of all:
that there is indeed room for
all in your kingdom,
and no one need ever feel
that they are excluded.
We may try to change our ways
and put our lives in order
but all you require is that we fling
open the door to our lives
and invite you to reign as Lord.

We live in a world where
achievement is the accolade
for which many long,
and the need to continually prove
ourselves is the task we embrace.
It is right that we seek to be
the best that we can be,
striving to reach the goals
you have set before us.
But the message we proclaim
is that Christ is the door
into the kingdom
and that it is by grace alone
that we can enter.

We praise you for the
message of Jonah,
that your word of hope is for all
and that even those we
dislike and despise
are offered a place in the
kingdom of God.
Our praises are for Christ, the
King of the kingdom,

and for the Father of love, who
delights in those who come home.
God's message of judgement
is in reality the opportunity
to be changed
and each of the warnings
in Scripture comes with
the grace of renewal.

How great is our God whose
love knows no end
and whose mercy is
offered freely to all.
How great is our Saviour who
died for the sin of the world
and whose grace is sufficient
to wipe every slate clean.
How great is the Holy Spirit whose
power can lift us to heaven
and whose presence brings
renewal and hope
from now to the end, and
beyond. **Amen.**

Confession

Psalm 62:5–12

Father,
we confess, in the presence
of your people,
that you are the source
of our strength.
It is by your grace that
we can stand firm
and it is your presence that
enables us to find peace.

We also confess that too often we
claim your gifts for ourselves
and we quietly forget that
what we have received, we
were meant to share.
You never intended that we should
selfishly devour your grace-gifts,
but offer them with open hands at
every opportunity you provide.

Forgive us, Father, and remove the
blockages of self-centredness
and make a clear path in our
hearts and lives for your
grace to flow freely.

In the name of Jesus, whose arms
on the cross still reach out
to a broken, hurting world. **Amen.**

Intercession

Mark 1:14–20

Lord,
we pray for those on the
journey of life
and for those at the start, setting
out with the thrill of it all;
for young people at school,
college, or university
and for those left without
qualifications and little
hope of a job;
for young people under pressure
from parents and peer groups
and for those seeking release
from their fears in drugs,
crime, or violence.
On every journey we take
be Lord of the way.

Lord,
we pray for those on the
journey of life
and for those who are walking a
road untroubled by problems;
for those who have all they
need and some to spare

and for those content to live out
their days in the comfort zone;
for those who can close their eyes
to the needs of their neighbour
and for those who shut their
ears to the cries of the
poor and the lonely.
On every journey we take
be Lord of the way.

Lord,
we pray for those on the
journey of life
and for those on a pathway
of health that is failing;
for those who are waiting in fear
of the doctor's diagnosis
and for those whose journey
tomorrow will not be
the same as today;
for those who cannot remember who
they are or where they are living
and for those who sit, still
sharing their journey
as if with someone they once knew.
On every journey we take
be Lord of the way.

Lord,
we pray for those on the
journey of life
and for those whose
pathway is poverty;
for those whose downward
spiral began with the
loss of employment
and for those who to care
for their family are left
depending on food banks;
for those who journey as part of the
growing multitude of refugees
and for those with no hope, no
purpose, and no future
with many unwilling to
offer a home.
On every journey we take
be Lord of the way.

Lord,
we pray for those on the
journey of life
and for those whose days
are a battlefield;
for homes where relationships
are at the point of breaking
and for those still seeking
a way to start again;
for those who wield power
to dominate others
and for those who are daily
in fear of their lives
being victims of marital
cruelty and abuse.
On every journey we take
be Lord of the way.

Lord,
we pray for those on the
journey of life
and for those near the
end of the journey;
for those for whom Christ's
presence brings them comfort
and for those who feel they are
facing an unknown future alone;
for those in a hospice being blessed
by the compassion they receive
and for those who lie alone
at home with no one
to share their days.
On every journey we take
be Lord of the way.

Lord,
we pray for those on the
  journey of life
and for ourselves and for
  the journeys we make;
for our journey with Christ as we
  discover the meaning of faith
and for the courage to trust in Jesus
  for the next step that we must take;
for a new infilling of the Holy
  Spirit's power and presence
and for the gifts and the fruit that
  will bring glory to Jesus our Lord.
On every journey we take
be Lord of the way.

We bring all our prayers in
  the name of Christ,
who is the way, the
  truth, and the life
for all the journeys we take. **Amen.**

FOURTH SUNDAY IN ORDINARY TIME

Prayer of Approach

Mark 1:21–28

Lord,
we come to sing, to pray,
  and to praise;
we come to listen to your word;
we come together as your people.
But it all remains an empty sound
signifying nothing—
until we remember you are
  the Lord of glory!

It is when we acknowledge
  your authority
that we can adore you.
It is when we confess all
  things are by grace
that we can praise you.
It is when we declare
  that Jesus is Lord
that we can worship you.

Fill us with the Holy Spirit,
that all we have and all we are
will make known the Lord of glory,
who alone is the centre and
  soul of our praises. **Amen.**

Praise

Psalm 111

For the joy of each new day
which is waiting to be filled
with fresh experiences of life
and the storing up of
  memories for tomorrow,
we thank the Lord
and we praise his name.

For the thrill of new discoveries
of the world around us
and exciting revelations
of worlds beyond our own,
we thank the Lord
and we praise his name.

For the work of scientists
who bring new insights,
a deeper understanding,
and the doorway to new
  possibilities,
we thank the Lord
and we praise his name.

For the gift of music and dance,
for poetry, art, and song
which enrich our days
and bring fulfilment and joy,
we thank the Lord
and we praise his name.

For green fields and meadows,
for flowers and trees of every kind
and for hills, mountains, and streams
which bring colour and
peace to our lives,
we thank the Lord
and we praise his name.

For the presence of family
and friends,
for those we meet and the
greetings we share,
for Facebook, Skype,
emails, and texting
that keep us in touch with
the people we know,
we thank the Lord
and we praise his name.

For the privilege of offering
praise and thanksgiving,
for worship in song, word, and deed,
for fellowship, faith, and believing
which fills each day with
meaning and purpose,
we thank the Lord
and we praise his name.

For the knowledge of God
that we find in Jesus,
for his life, death, and resurrection
and his reigning in glory,
for the promise of his presence
and his returning in power
which blesses our service and
lifts our eyes up to heaven,
we thank the Lord
and we praise his name.

For the presence and power
of the Holy Spirit,
for the experience of new life
his coming makes possible,
for the gifts he provides to
build up Christ's church,
changing how we see everything
now until Christ comes,
we thank the Lord
and we praise his name.

We bring our prayers in
the name of Christ,
the source and goal of all
our praises. **Amen.**

Intercession
Revelation 12:1–5a
I ask your prayers for those
gripped by the power of evil
and for those who believe
might is right;
for those who seek to
terrorise communities
and for those who preach violence
and murder without mercy.
In the name of Christ
we bring our prayer.

I ask your prayers for those who
give in to evil temptations
and for those obsessed with
pleasing themselves;
for those for whom words
meaning honesty and trust
are missing from their
dictionary of life
and those in the world of
politics, sport, or commerce
for whom the end seems
to justify the means.
In the name of Christ
we bring our prayer.

I ask your prayers for those on
 the slippery slope of evil
and for young people caught
 in a life of drugs, violence,
 and knife crime;
for those who see life as a
 lottery and buying a ticket
 as the way to freedom
and for those for whom
 life is a gamble and one
 they never can win.
In the name of Christ
we bring our prayer.

I ask your prayers for those
 trapped in the evils of poverty
and for whom each day is a
 struggle just to survive;
for those with no hope of
 meaningful employment
and for those who are being robbed
 of the little support they once had.
In the name of Christ
we bring our prayer.

I ask your prayers for those dying
 through the evil of hunger
and for those whose crops have
 failed and drought offers no hope;
for those in countries who
 depend on handouts from
 the rich man's table
and for those who simply
 seek justice and the
 chance to trade fairly.
In the name of Christ
we bring our prayer.

I ask your prayers for those
 who live under the evils
 of corrupt leadership
and for those struggling for
 liberty in a totalitarian state;
for those who live in lands of
 democratic justice and freedom
and for those who ensure
 that the cards are stacked
 in favour of the few.
In the name of Christ
we bring our prayer.

I ask your prayers for those who
 seek to fight evil of every kind
and for those who risk their lives as
 they seek help for the outsider;
for those with a burning
 desire to make known
 God's grace for us all
and for those who have lost home
 and family and freedom
for declaring that Jesus is Lord.
In the name of Christ
we bring our prayer.

We bring our prayers in
 the name of Jesus,
who died on the cross overcoming
 the evil of the world. **Amen.**

FIFTH SUNDAY IN ORDINARY TIME

Prayer of Approach

Psalm 147:1

Father,
we come before you as those
 in need of cleansing
and as those who long to be set free.
We come into your presence to
 acknowledge our weakness
and as those reaching up to
 receive your forgiveness.

We come, like the psalmist of
old, to confess your glory
and as those affirming that you
are Lord of all things.

We come before you with
hope and in faith,
excited to be here as we
offer you our worship.
We confess that we have no earthly
right to enter your presence
and we rejoice that we are here by
the invitation of heavenly grace.

Father,
we pray that you will
receive our praises
and that you will enjoy our worship.
We ask this in the name of Jesus,
in whose name alone we
can be set free. **Amen.**

Praise

Isaiah 40:21–31

Father,
we praise you that whenever we
turn to you with open minds
and come into your presence
with hearts on fire for you
you meet with us and overwhelm
us with your grace.
You astound us again and again
that we can know you
and that as our Father we
can experience the wonder
of your parenthood.

We praise you that you are
always so very near to us
and yet you remain far
beyond the grasp of the
greatest minds on earth.

The whole vast universe, whose
dimensions we cannot imagine,
is like a walk in the garden for the
one who is Lord of all things.

Even on the clearest day our view
is limited by our horizon
and though some have travelled
beyond our daily boundaries
their vision is curtailed by
their physical limitations.
Though we seek to plumb the
depths of our solar system
and to reach worlds beyond the
reach of sight and travel,
we praise you that your glory
reaches to the end of all things.

No wonder Isaiah asks, 'Do you
not know? Have you not heard?'
He challenges us to
remember we are here
to praise the Lord of all things;
to remember that our God has
no beginning and no end;
to stand in awe of the one who
is worthy of our praises;
to find in him the source of
hope, strength, and renewal.

Father,
we come in our weakness to be
lifted up on wings like eagles
and to celebrate that though
you are our Lord
you have, by nail-printed
hands, made it possible to
know you as Father.

So your children come with
heart-filled praises

and with songs of love for
your fatherly grace.

In the name of Christ,
our brother, Saviour,
and Lord. **Amen.**

Intercession

Mark 1:29–39

Prepare a set of nine candles. Light a new candle as you begin each prayer.

Lord, we light this candle
as we pray for those who suffer alone,
and for those whose
sense of isolation
only increases their pain.

silence

Lord, we light this candle
as we pray for those whose diagnosis
impacts on their whole life
as it numbers their days.

silence

Lord, we light this candle
as we pray for those who
struggle to care
for those entrapped by
their addictions,
to go on caring when
care is rejected.

silence

Lord, we light this candle
as we pray for those who
care for the sick;
for medics, pharmacists,
dentists, and ancillary staff
and for those for whom a call to
care is at the heart of all they do.

silence

Lord, we light this candle
as we pray for those who
care for the elderly;
for those who offer care
in a nursing home
and for those who enable others
to remain in their own home.

silence

Lord, we light this candle
as we pray for those who
offer care to the dying
and whose love, faith,
and compassion
bring peace and comfort to those
near the end of their days.

silence

Lord, we light this candle
as we pray for those whose
sickness cannot be seen,
and for those who seek
to bring hope
to those who are anxious, depressed,
and overcome with despair.

silence

Lord, we light this candle
as we pray for those whose
brokenness and sorrow
brings a need of healing deep
within their hearts and minds.

silence

We also light a candle for ourselves
as we seek healing of our
relationships with others
and with God.

silence

Lord, we bring our prayers
in the name of Jesus,
who alone can bring the light that
heals and restores. **Amen.**

SIXTH SUNDAY IN ORDINARY TIME

Prayer of Approach

2 Kings 5:1–14

Father,
we always have the feeling
that when we enter this
place of worship
we are simply coming home.

We come, not by right nor
by our own initiative
but by your gracious invitation.
Naaman did not come for
healing by his own choice
but simply by the word of
an unknown child.

Your invitation to come home
comes in different ways
and through many and
varied agencies—
but the invitation is
always from you.

By your Holy Spirit, may we
offer you thanks and praise
and experience healing and renewal
that are freely offered to all who
come at your invitation. **Amen.**

Thanksgiving

Psalm 30

Lord,
though our words cannot
lift you any higher
we want to shout your name
from the rooftops.
With the psalmist, we long to sing
glory, glory, glory to the
Lord Almighty
that the whole world would
come to declare your praises.

When we were at our lowest
and everything seemed against us
we found our hope in your presence
and our strength in your love.
When all our dreams came true
and no clouds appeared
on our horizon
we counted our blessings
and learned to trust the
giver and not the gifts.

When we knew we had
let you down
and our lives had fallen short
of bringing you glory
it was then that we rediscovered
the width of your love
and found once more the
unimaginable depths
of your grace.

To give thanks to you is one
of life's greatest pleasures
because we know it brings joy
to our hearts and to yours.

If we were to write down all for
which we should give thanks
it would be a book so huge not
all the libraries in the world
would be sufficient to hold the
volume of our praises!
You are our God and we
bring you the thanks
of hearts set ablaze by your grace
and the worship of our daily lives
as we are empowered by
the Holy Spirit.

With the psalmist, we will sing
the song of your grace
and declare glory, glory, glory
to the Lord Almighty,
that the whole world will come
to sing your praises.

In the name of Christ,
through whom all our worship
is offered. **Amen.**

Intercession
Mark 1:40–45

Father,
the story of Jesus and the
leper reminds us
that you are forever on the
side of the poor.
We pray for those who wonder
where they will find food
and for those who feed only on
their wealth and possessions.

silence

You call us to be reflections
of your love
to everyone we meet.

Father,
the story of Jesus and the
leper reminds us
that your heart reaches
out to the broken.
We pray for those with broken
hopes and dreams
and for those with minds and
bodies broken by war.

silence

You call us to be reflections
of your love
to everyone we meet.

Father,
the story of Jesus and the
leper reminds us
that you long to bring the
homeless home.
We pray for those whose
home is a cardboard box
and for refugees who are leaving
their homes in fear.

silence

You call us to be reflections
of your love
to everyone we meet.

Father,
the story of Jesus and the
leper reminds us
that you seek to hold those
who feel rejected.
We pray for those who aren't
valued because of their colour
and for those we deny our friendship
because they are different.

silence

You call us to be reflections
of your love
to everyone we meet.

Father,
the story of Jesus and the
leper reminds us
that your love flows out to
the sick and the dying.
We pray for those whose
days are numbered by
medical appointments
and for those who are just
counting their days.

silence

You call us to be reflections
of your love
to everyone we meet.

Father,
the story of Jesus and the
leper reminds us
how much you are seeking to
embrace those who are hurting.
We pray for those who are
estranged from their family
and for those who no longer
remember the names of
those who love them.

silence

You call us to be reflections
of your love
to everyone we meet.

Father,
the story of Jesus and the
leper reminds us
that you always reach out and
touch those who are honest.
We pray for journalists who
expose lies and corruption
and for ourselves to recognise
our need as we stand
before our Maker.

silence

You call us to be reflections
of your love
to everyone we meet.

Father,
the story of Jesus and the
leper reminds us
that you always reach out to
those we think are outsiders.
We pray for the whole life and
witness of [*name your church*],
that our whole focus will be
speaking and living the
grace of our Lord.

silence

You call us to be reflections
of your love
to everyone we meet.

We bring our prayers in
the name of Jesus,
who touched the leper
and seeks to touch us all. **Amen.**

SEVENTH SUNDAY IN ORDINARY TIME

Prayer of Approach

Psalm 41

Lord,
we are always in your presence
and there is nowhere we can hide
from the sight of your
grace-filled mercy.

Like the psalmist, we
are overwhelmed
just to be here before our
almighty God.
The truth dawns upon us
that you alone are worthy
to receive the worship
that flows from hearts and minds
set on fire by your love.

With all who, down the centuries
and across the world,
have gathered to worship the
one who is Lord of all
we cry, holy, holy, holy
to our Saviour.
With all the hosts of heaven
we cry, praise the Lord. **Amen.**

Praise

Isaiah 43:18–25

Lord,
we praise you that, through Jesus,
you have made a way
to take from us
the baggage of hurt and brokenness
that, for too long, has
ruled our days.

We have allowed ourselves
to be weighed down
by the worries and fears
that have haunted us
and we have attempted to
navigate our unaided way
through the mountains of problems
and the valleys of despair.

We look back to the struggles
we have faced
and the battles we have
fought and lost.
We promised ourselves that this
time it would be different
and we felt assured that our
turning over a new leaf
would at last bring us the
security of your presence.

Yet all the time you were
whispering in our ear,
'Trust me, hold my hand, for
I alone am the way!'
How foolish to have turned
our back on your grace
and to fail to recognise, in
Christ, the way home.

Lord,
there is a volume of praise
that wells up within us
and we cannot hold back the
floodgates of worship.
Once we knew, really knew,
the depth of your love
and that its wideness could
reach out to touch even us,
there was nothing else we could
do but to sing your praises!

Perhaps for the very first time
we are beginning to realise

just a little of the vastness of your
mercy, forgiveness, and grace.
Perhaps now we have arrived at
the threshold of worship
as we open our hearts and minds
to the glory of the King.

You are making a way in
the desert of our days
and you are creating streams of
living water in our lives.
Now you are doing the new
thing you promised
and you are doing it that we
might know you, love you,
and offer the praises of
grace-renewed hearts.

In the name of Jesus,
who alone is the way
through the desert
and the source of living water. **Amen.**

Intercession
Mark 2:1–12

As the men brought their
friend to Jesus,
we bring our nation to
the throne of grace.
We pray for our country that
is turning its back on God
and for our nation that
worships anything and
anyone but its Maker;
for those around us who seek to
find their meaning in life
without God at the centre
of everything.
It is in the breakdown of
our communities
we see the price that is
now being paid.
Lord, by your healing touch,
make all things new.

As the men brought their
friend to Jesus,
we bring your church to
the throne of grace.
We pray for the church of Jesus Christ
here and all around the world.
For Christians who are facing the
hostility of their neighbours
and persecution and death at
the hands of the authorities;
for churches that have lost their way
and become clubs for the religious
and for places where the
body of Christ is reaching
out and bearing fruit.
Lord, by your healing touch,
make all things new.

As the men brought their
friend to Jesus,
we bring the lost to the
throne of grace.
We pray for those whose addiction
to alcohol is wrecking their life
and for those who are turning
to crime to feed their
use of illegal drugs;
for those whose prospects for the
future were once shining bright
and for those who are now lost
amid the homeless on our streets.
Lord, by your healing touch,
make all things new.

As the men brought their
friend to Jesus,
we bring the poor to the
throne of grace.

We pray for those who have
sunk into poverty
and this through no fault
of their own;
for those whose loss of
employment is destroying
their home and their family life
and for those labelled
scroungers on the state
when there is no other help
except food banks.
Lord, by your healing touch,
make all things new.

As the men brought their
friend to Jesus,
we bring those who serve to
the throne of grace.
We pray for those who give of
their time to help others
and for those who reach
out to help those
who can no longer help themselves;
for those who staff night
shelters for the homeless
and for street pastors who
risk their lives
as they seek to support those
in vulnerable situations.
Lord, by your healing touch,
make all things new.

As the men brought their
friend to Jesus,
we bring world leaders to
the throne of grace.
We pray for the leaders of
nations around the world
as they face the problems of
corruption and lies;
for those who seem only concerned
to help their rich friends
and for those who are genuinely
working for peace between nations;
for those who speak up for the
poorest countries of the world
and for those who turn a
blind eye to human rights
and responsibilities.
Lord, by your healing touch,
make all things new.

As the men brought their
friend to Jesus,
we bring our family and friends
to the throne of grace.
We pray for the members
of our own family
and many of our friends who
do not know Jesus as Lord;
for those who have allowed
the faith they once had
to be crowded out of their lives
by work or by leisure;
for family and friends for whom
we are especially concerned.
In the silence, let us name them
in our hearts before God.

silence

Lord, by your healing touch,
make all things new.

As the men brought their
friend to Jesus,
we bring ourselves to the
throne of grace.
We pray for ourselves and the
problems we face each day
and for a new joy in worship,
fellowship, and service;
for a deeper walk in faith, knowing
Jesus is with us everywhere,

and for the power of the Holy Spirit
to enable us to bear fruit in his name.
Lord, by your healing touch,
make all things new.

We bring all things and all people
to the throne of grace
as we offer our prayer in the
name of the Lord. **Amen.**

TRANSFIGURATION SUNDAY

Praise

Psalm 50:1–6

Lord,
we have all done it.
We wander into church as if we
were doing the shopping
and we come without a thought
of what we are coming to do.
We make a greater Prayer of
Approach to meet some
important person
and we think about what
we might say or do.
How can we worship when we
arrive in the last minute
and the body of Christ is
unprepared to gather at
the throne of grace?

So let us pause and in the stillness
let us focus our minds on God
and seek again the power of the
Holy Spirit to worship him.

Wonderful, wonderful God,
your majesty stops us in our tracks
and your absolute holiness
challenges the shallowness
of our discipleship.
We are overwhelmed to be in
the presence of the one
whose power spans the ages
and whose sovereignty is
utterly complete!

Your glory stretches
throughout eternity
and your total knowledge of
all things is absolute.
You are the God whose rule has
no beginning and no end
and your wisdom, your power,
and your authority
are beyond the comprehension
of our tiny finite minds.

Glorious God!
Wonderful Lord!
Mighty Saviour!

We worship you because
you are Lord.

Lord,
the thing that leaves us stunned,
and we are left speechless when
we really think about it,
is that this mighty, holy,
independent, glorious God
is in love with his creation.

There isn't a moment when
he doesn't touch it
and a day never passes
but he longs to demonstrate his
love to people like ourselves.
We praise him because he is
worthy of all our worship
and we fall down in devotion
before him—

the one who is the greatest lover
the world has ever known!

In utter humility we offer
you the praises
of hearts that long to know you
and the songs of thanksgiving
from the lips of those who
are seeking to love you.

We offer our praises in
the name of Jesus,
who is forever and for all people
the emblem of our loving
God and Father. **Amen.**

Confession

Mark 9:2–9

Lord,
too often we find ourselves
going through the motions of praise
and simply uttering words
of thanksgiving.
We speak the words and
sing the songs
but our hearts are left untouched
by your presence.
We attend worship religiously
but our thoughts, our hopes,
and our dreams
are rarely focused on the
Lord of heaven.

Lord,
as your disciples were shocked
out of their complacency
by the revelation of your glory on
the mount of transfiguration,
so we confess that we too need to
be overwhelmed by your glory.
Forgive us that we take your
majesty for granted
and that we do not allow
ourselves to be bowled over
by the realisation that we are in
the presence of the living God.

Lord,
speak to us from the cloud
of your glory,
that grace will dispel the
mist of our apathy,
and by the revelation of
your sovereignty,
transform our words,
songs, and actions.
May they become a glorious
moment of worship
in the presence of the King of Kings
and the glory of the Lord
of all lords. **Amen.**

Intercession

Mark 9:2–9

Lord of transfiguration,
we pray for our divided nation.
Every day we become more aware
of the ever-widening gap
between those who have
everything they want
and those deprived of the
basic things they need.
Come, Lord, and move in all
our hearts and minds
that once more we may
become a people
whose concern for justice,
truth, and love
finds its source in a renewal
of faith in Jesus.
Lord, in your mercy,
hear our prayer.

Lord of the cloud of glory,

we pray for the life of
our community;
for those who find no reason to
give thanks for their blessings
and for those who offer praise
to anyone but their Maker;
for those who once walked
in faith and trust
and for those who have long
since ceased to be disciples.
As those three disciples discovered
the presence of God in their midst
so may your people be the visible
sign of your still being among them.
Lord, in your mercy,
hear our prayer.

Lord of the bright shining light,
we pray for those whose
lives are in darkness;
for those in the darkness of fear
and for those who are haunted by
the darkness of their memories
that still have the power to continue
to trouble them today;
for those imprisoned by the
walls of their home
and for those whose lives are
crippled and damaged
by the darkness of bitterness and
despair that still binds them.
Come, Lord, and shine the
light of your healing
and may the light of the empty
tomb set many free.
Lord, in your mercy,
hear our prayer.

Lord of the mountaintop,
we pray for those whose eyes
have been opened
and even now are longing to
know more of your glory;
for those who were found by
you in a moment of joy
and for those who found they
had been walking with you
at the table of communion and
in ordinary, everyday places.
By your Holy Spirit, enable us
to be channels of your grace
and give us courage to tell the
story of our walk with you;
may our words, lives,
and our service
enable the lost to find their way
to the mountain of the Lord.
Lord, in your mercy,
hear our prayer.

Lord of the valley,
we pray for those alone in
the depths of their pain
and for those whose whole world
has been turned upside down;
for those for whom the future
appears empty, bleak, and futile
and for those needing to come to
terms with their valley of change;
for those weighed down by
the baggage they have
carried for years
and for those who are victims
of life-sapping stress;
for those who offer the hand of
friendship and compassion
and for those who hold
the shaking hand
and promise to walk through
the valley with the broken.
Lord, in your mercy,
hear our prayer.

Lord of the disciples' questions,
we pray for those who are
still looking for answers
and for those who will search
anywhere but in the grace of God;
for those longing for a
solution to the things that
trouble them deeply
and for those content to blame God
for the sins of human beings;
for those who no longer ask any
questions of faith, hope, and love
and for those whose hearts are alive
to the Lord who loves them
as they use their minds that they
might know him more;
for those who through art, drama,
writing, teaching, and preaching
seek to open our hearts and
minds to the glory of Christ.
Lord, in your mercy,
hear our prayer.

Lord of the dangerous places of life,
we pray for those whose lives are
being transformed by grace;
for those you call to step out
of their comfort zone
and for those who now risk serving
in the places of danger;
for those who put their
lives in jeopardy for love
of their neighbour
and for those who offer their skills
of healing, rescue, and rebuilding
to those whose hopes have
been wrecked by sickness,
earthquake, and flood.
We pray, give us courage to step
out of our comfort zone
and bring hope to someone
as we share with them
the love of our Lord.
Lord, in your mercy,
hear our prayer.

We bring our prayers in
the name of our
crucified, risen, and ascended Lord,
whose presence changes
everything. **Amen.**

FIRST SUNDAY IN LENT

Thanksgiving

Psalm 25:1–10

Lord,
when we consider the blessings
with which you have filled our lives
and the hope with which you
have flooded our days
we are moved to offer you
heartfelt thanks and praise!

With the psalmist,
there are times when we feel
utterly overwhelmed
with the blessings with which
you have lavished upon us.
Again and again you have
soaked our lives with hope
and you have flooded our days
with your amazing presence.

In the moments when life is hard
and we do not know
which way to turn,
the memory of your
extravagant generosity
gives us the strength and the
desire to start again.

When the bottom drops
out of our lives
and our every dream seems to
slip through our fingers,
you are still there, reaching out to
hold us when we are hurting
and picking us up every
time we fall.

This is the reason that we
long to give you praise
and gives the urgency to offer
you heartfelt thanks.
Time and again we have
let you down.
Time and again we have pleased
ourselves and not you.
Time and again we have given in
to the smallest temptation.
Time and again we have been a
very poor example for Jesus.

And yet, Lord,
time and again you have loved
us, healed us, forgiven us
and by your grace you continue
to transform our lives.

Thank you, Lord, for being there
when no one else could be
and staying by our side when no
one else wanted to be there.
Thank you, Lord, that you forgive
us when we turn back to you
and that you love us even when
we are hopelessly in the wrong.

It seems almost too easy, but all we
can do is give thanks to the Lord
and offer him the praise of
hearts and lives made new
by his grace. **Amen.**

Confession

Genesis 9:8–17

Father,
you offered us a promise bond of love
but we confess that we have
lived to please ourselves.
You gave us a fantastic
world in which to live
but we have acted selfishly and
abused your generosity.
You planted your rainbow
of hope for all to see
but we have repeatedly failed
to trust your word.
You sought to have a new and
living relationship with us
but we turned our backs on you and
pretended you wouldn't know.

Father,
out of your great grace,
you have once more offered the
promise bond of peace
and opened our eyes to see all
things through your love.
In place of the rainbow you
have set before us the
cross of reconciliation
and in Jesus you declare us not
guilty as you welcome us home.
Cleanse, renew, forgive, and heal
us in the name of Jesus,
the emblem of hope and the
promise of grace. **Amen.**

Intercession

1 Peter 3:18–22

Father,
we pray for those who
carry heavy loads
and for those weighed down
by their burden of guilt;

for those whose crimes have
  landed them in prison
and for those whose
  misdeeds are known
only to themselves and God.
Lord of the cross of shame,
come heal our brokenness.

Father,
we pray for those who
  carry heavy loads
and for those who exist in an
  abusive relationship;
for those whose innocence
  was stolen in childhood
and for those whose lives still
  bear the scars of their youth;
for those whose actions have been
  the cause of much suffering
and for those who have yet
  to acknowledge the pain
  they have caused.
Lord of the cross of shame,
come heal our brokenness.

Father,
we pray for those who
  carry heavy loads
and for those whose burden
  is that of a single parent;
for those whose singleness is
  not by their own choice
and for those left alone through
  bereavement or divorce;
for those whose homes are
  a daily battlefield
and for those struggling to
  cope with the onslaught
of the power that seeks to control.
Lord of the cross of shame,
come heal our brokenness.

Father,
we pray for those who
  carry heavy loads
and for those who are facing
  the problems of ageing;
for those who can look to the future
  with hope and contentment
and for those overwhelmed
  with the reality of what
  their future may be;
for those for whom the doctor's
  diagnosis has numbered their days
and for those whose faith in Christ
  enables them to walk in hope.
Lord of the cross of shame,
come heal our brokenness.

Father,
we pray for those who
  carry heavy loads
and for those whose daily task is
  to find food for their family;
for those whose home and family
  has been swept away in a storm
and for those who long to
  flee the war zone that is
  engulfing their lives;
for those whose fear for their
  loved ones leads them to join
  the path of the migrant
and for those who arrive at the
  gate of their hopes to find
  it slammed in their face.
Lord of the cross of shame,
come heal our brokenness.

Father,
we pray for those who
  carry heavy loads
and for those who live on the
  streets of our cities with
  nowhere to call home;

for those whose loss of
employment has robbed them
of dignity and self-respect
and for those whose
wealth and position
insulates them from
understanding the poverty
of their neighbour;
for those who give of their
time and compassion in
support of the poor
and for those who work in
night shelters and food banks
for those in dire need.
Lord of the cross of shame,
come heal our brokenness.

Father,
we pray for those who
carry heavy loads
and for ourselves and the
burdens we carry each day.

In the stillness talk to God
about those you know
who are carrying loads too
heavy to carry alone.

silence

Lord of the cross of shame,
come heal our brokenness.

In the name of Jesus,
who through his death
and resurrection
was broken to offer healing
and hope to us all. **Amen.**

SECOND SUNDAY IN LENT

Praise

Genesis 17:1–7, 15–16

Father,
it is when we pause and
remember your glory,
and as something of
your almightiness
breaks into our thoughts
and touches our lives,
that we bow down in
wonder and adoration.
When we consider the huge
achievements of science
and the vast store of human
knowledge and understanding
it is then that we grasp just a little
of how wonderfully we are made.

But it is as we reflect on the
vastness of your power
and seek to focus our thoughts
on your creative word
that we find ourselves speechless
before the Lord of glory.
It is when we pause and allow
you to flood our thoughts
with your presence
and we open our hearts and
minds to your sovereign grace
that we come face to face with
the truth of your glory.

Now we confess, Father,
that the sum of all our knowledge,
the totality of our understanding,
and the entire store of
all our discoveries
are but a speck of dust on
the circumference of
your sovereignty.

Then comes the bombshell!
Now we are face to face with the
greatest truth in all of history
and we are utterly overwhelmed
by the love story
that is at the heart of all creation.
Though you are the sovereign
Lord of all things;
though you are the one with
no beginning and no end;
though you are utterly complete
in your own being;
though we are not worthy
to enter your presence;
though we have nothing
to offer you—
except that which we have
received at your hand—
we are blown away by the
grace-gift of your Son.
Now we know that you are not
only our sovereign Lord
but by grace we can know
you as 'our Father'.
How can we not praise you for
the wonder of your grace?
We find within our hearts a deep
longing to worship you.
Father, thanksgiving, honour,
and glory are yours
as we are lost in wonder,
love, and praise.
In the name of Jesus. **Amen.**

Confession

Psalm 22:23–31

Lord,
we confess that there are times
when you seem far away
and we experience a sense of
being lost and alone.
We confess that often we have
walked away from you
and, by our falling short
of your glory,
we have locked ourselves
out of your presence.
We confess that it is only through
the life, death and
resurrection of Jesus
that the doorway to new
life and renewal
is thrown wide open
when we come
confessing our need and
ready to receive
the forgiveness and cleansing
that comes through your
grace. **Amen.**

Intercession

Romans 4:13–25

Father,
we pray for those who hope
against hope for peace
and for those whose hearts and
minds can find no rest;
for the people who live in
the midst of a war zone
and for those who fear the
sickening work of terrorists.
In the midst of our days,
come, Lord Jesus, come.

Father,
we pray for those who hope
against hope for justice
and for those tortured and
imprisoned for the faith in Jesus;
for the work of Amnesty
International, who stand
with the oppressed,

and for those who daily make a stand
for freedom, truth, and democracy.
In the midst of our days,
come, Lord Jesus, come.

Father,
we pray for those who hope
against hope for healing
and for those whose days are shaped
by the treatments they face;
for those now coming to terms
with their life-changing illness
and for those who, though
they are not yet cured, are
experiencing healing.
In the midst of our days,
come, Lord Jesus, come.

Father,
we pray for those who hope
against hope for our planet
and for those who close their minds
to their own responsibility;
for those who warn us of the
damage our lifestyles are doing
and for those with the power
but not the will to act now.
In the midst of our days,
come, Lord Jesus, come.

Father,
we pray for those who hope
against hope for renewal
and for those who have allowed
their faith in Jesus to grow cold;
for those who mask their emptiness
with a veil of religion and service
and for those who long for
renewal but are afraid of what
the Holy Spirit may do.
In the midst of our days,
come, Lord Jesus, come.

Father,
we pray for those who hope
against hope for inclusion
and for the poor and the hopeless
who are left to struggle alone;
for those who reach out to care
for the lost and the homeless
and for those left behind as the army
of the wealthy move forward.
In the midst of our days,
come, Lord Jesus, come.

Father,
we pray for those who hope
against hope for revival
and for those who daily share God's
love with their neighbour;
for those who have committed
themselves to prayer
and to witnessing
and for those who are longing for
our nation to know Jesus as Lord.
In the midst of our days,
come, Lord Jesus, come.

We bring our prayers in
the name of Jesus,
the source and the goal
of all hope. **Amen.**

THIRD SUNDAY IN LENT

Praise

Psalm 19

Lord,
we cannot keep quiet any longer!
Deep within us there is
a song of praise
and it simply cannot be
controlled anymore.
It is as if the whole of creation
is shouting your praises

and everything we see challenges
us to join in the song of glory.

It is as if the vast universe
has been arranged
like a cosmic orchestra
where each of the suns,
moons, and planets
is there for the sole purpose
of making music for the
sovereign over all things.

Even when we look out across
our corner of creation,
somewhere deep inside we
find your praises
bubbling to the surface,
ready to offer adoration
with our voices lifted to the heavens.

As we pause, simply to
catch our breath,
it dawns upon us that we are
only offering praise
for what we can see and hear.
In the stillness with which we
are suddenly enveloped
our hearts are lifted once
more in thanksgiving
and our voices murmur
our overwhelming
sense of gratitude.

At last the truth blows us
away with its power
and our hearts are thrilled
by its simplicity.

We are loved!
We have always been loved!
We will be loved for ever!

We tear our eyes away from
the vista of creation
and now we focus on the sheer
audacity of re-creation.
In wonder, we find ourselves
confronted by a cross of wood
and we stand in awe before
an empty tomb.

Once again, Lord, you have
demonstrated your power
to thrill, to challenge, and
to come in mercy.
Again we know we cannot
keep quiet any longer
for deep within us there
is a song of praise
and it is a song that must be sung
by the whole of creation.

For Christ has died,
Christ is risen,
and Christ will come again.
Praise the Lord. Hallelujah. **Amen.**

Confession
Exodus 20:1–17
Father,
when you said, 'You shall not'
you were giving us boundaries
for our lives.
Your boundaries were never
intended to be a burden
but a blessing to guide us
into life that is real.

We confess that our record of
keeping within your boundaries
has never been very good and
we have paid the price in
broken lives,
broken promises,

broken hearts,
broken relationships,
and a broken world.
We confess that only through
Jesus can we begin again
and through his death
and resurrection
the way has been opened,
our brokenness has been healed,
and by your grace we can
begin again. **Amen.**

Intercession

John 2:13–22

Lord, we pray for those
prepared to be different
and for those for whom their
faith is their way of life;
for those ready to walk each day
in the footsteps of Christ
and for those who are not ashamed
to name the name of Jesus
as they willingly pay the cost
of being his disciples.
In the name of Christ,
we pray for them.

Lord, we pray for those
prepared to be different
and for those for whom public
service is the heart of their lives;
for politicians who follow
their conscience and not
simply the party whip
and for those who risk reprisals
by 'blowing the whistle'
on their employer
and the media who
expose the injustice and
corruption they find.
In the name of Christ,
we pray for them.

Lord, we pray for those
prepared to be different
and for women and men who seek
to act as role models for others;
for those who do not rely
on drugs to enhance
their sporting success
and for those in banking and
finance who reject the use
of underhand practices
as they use their power and
influence to condemn the
corruption they find.
In the name of Christ,
we pray for them.

Lord, we pray for those
prepared to be different
and for those whose lives are
a demonstration of their
commitment to God;
for Christians facing persecution
in countries around the world
and for those who are imprisoned
and murdered for their
belief in democracy
as they risk everything for
simply declaring the truth.
In the name of Christ,
we pray for them.

Lord, we pray for those
prepared to be different
and for those who face ridicule
and rejection because they
won't follow the crowd;
for young people who refuse
to poison their lives with
drugs and binge drinking
and for those who are
deliberately seeking ways of
fulfilment and satisfaction

as they are discovering opportunities
of caring and voluntary service.
In the name of Christ,
we pray for them.

Lord, we pray for those
prepared to be different
and for those whose lifestyle
speaks of a vision of life that
is more than possessions;
for those who use their expertise
to warn of the damage we
are doing to the planet
and for those who are committed
to changing their way of life
as they limit the demands they
make on earth's finite resources.
In the name of Christ,
we pray for them.

Lord, we pray for those
prepared to be different
and for those who are finding new
ways of dealing with the past;
for those who have carried the
scars of neglect, disability,
or abuse down the years
and for those looking forward in
hope and a sense of renewal
as they let go of the past
and, by God's grace, enter
the freedom he offers.
In the name of Christ,
we pray for them.

Lord, we pray for those
prepared to be different
and for ourselves, that the presence
of Christ may be seen in our lives.
In the stillness
let us pray for those whose whole
way of life speaks of God's love
and for the way they live, speak
and behave, which brings
honour to the name of Jesus.
In the name of Christ,
we pray for them.

We bring our prayers in
the name of Jesus,
who was always ready to be different
as he loved those who rejected
him and gave of himself
for a broken and fallen world. **Amen.**

FOURTH SUNDAY IN LENT

Prayer of Approach

Numbers 21:8–9

Lord,
we have come to worship you
and you alone.
We have come with the baggage
that we have carried all our lives.
We come to the source
of hope and peace
that we find in Jesus.
We come to lift up the name of Jesus
not only here, but through
all our days. **Amen.**

Praise

John 3:14–21

Lord,
we live in a world that we have
infected with our darkness.
You gave us a home filled with
the light of your love
and a world that overwhelms
us with its beauty.
Everywhere we look our eyes of
faith see your fingerprints
and the vast array of your creation
takes our breath away.

It is truly an incredible thing to
experience your splendour
and to be enthralled by the
sheer scale and wonder
of your universe.
Our minds are blown away
as we simply try to take in
something of your glory
and we are blessed by your
presence beyond anything
we can put into words.

Lord,
you designed this world as an
emblem of your grace
and as the arena where we
might experience your love.
We are thrilled that you provided
us with a place to know you
and with days and years in
which to love and serve you.

Yet you know that by our greed
we have damaged your world
and by our selfishness we have
flooded our lives with darkness.
Our thoughts, attitudes,
and self-centredness have
hurt those around us
and we have tried to close the
shutters of our hearts and
minds to your presence.

Lord,
we praise and worship you for your
grace always has the last word
and your mercy reaches down
and lifts the fallen.
We thank you that no matter
how far we fall we find the
arms of grace beneath us
and in Jesus' life, death, and
resurrection we know that
your grace is all in all.

Once again we find our
eyes lifted to the cross
and our hearts are enriched by its
light which floods our days.
We offer you heartfelt thanks that
the presence of Jesus gives us hope
and that his light will
always triumph over the
deepest darkness.

We bring our prayers of
praise and thanksgiving
for the light, mercy, and peace
we find in Jesus. **Amen.**

Intercession
Ephesians 2:1–10
Think of someone who is
experiencing times of doubt
and someone who feels
that God is far away.
Think of someone who is
battered and bruised by life
and someone who is hiding
their hurt deep inside.

silence

May the incomparable
riches of God's grace
renew their days.

Think of someone who
is experiencing a
breakdown of health
and someone who is afraid of
what their future may hold.

Think of someone whose thoughts
  are focused on their pain
and someone who feels
  ensnared by their troubles.

silence

May the incomparable
  riches of his grace
renew their days.

Think of someone who is experiencing
  a deepening of their faith
and someone whose eyes are being
  opened to the love of God.
Think of someone who is seeing the
  fingerprints of God in their lives
and someone who now looks at
  others through the love of Jesus.

silence

May the incomparable
  riches of his grace
renew their days.

Think of someone who is
  experiencing a time of great loss
and someone who has lost everything
  in [*name any recent tragedy*].
Think of someone whose loss
  of employment puts their
  home and family at risk
and someone who feels they have lost
  their value as a person of worth.

silence

May the incomparable
  riches of his grace
renew their days.

Think of someone who is
  experiencing the darkness
  of depression
and someone who feels
  guilty and ashamed when
  they are not to blame.
Think of someone whose
  every waking moment is
  wracked with anxiety
and someone who feels imprisoned
  by their fears within.

silence

May the incomparable
  riches of his grace
renew their days.

Think of someone who is
  experiencing a time of loneliness
and someone who lives alone with
  no one to share their days.
Think of someone who has many
  memories of days long ago
and someone who cannot
  remember who you are or
  what they have been.

silence

May the incomparable
  riches of his grace
renew their days.

Think of someone you know
  whose life is in turmoil
and someone you know by name
  who needs your prayers.

silence

Think of yourself and what you
are experiencing in your life
and think of what you will be facing
in the coming days of this week.
May the incomparable
riches of his grace
renew our days.

We bring our prayers in
the name of Jesus,
whose incomparable
riches of his grace
heal and hold us all. **Amen.**

FIFTH SUNDAY IN LENT (PASSION SUNDAY)

Prayer of Approach

Jeremiah 31:31–34

Father,
we are here because you
have called us
and we have come in
answer to your grace;
we are here because of your
love to us in Jesus
and we are here to worship
you, the source of hope;
we are here because you are
worthy of our praises
and we have come to give you the
offering of our thankful hearts;
we are here to celebrate our
new relationship with
the Lord of glory
and we have come because in Jesus
you have opened a way,
built by grace, into the
presence of the King.
We come in the name of Jesus
and his name alone. **Amen.**

Confession

Psalm 51:1–12

Lord,
whenever we remember we are
living in your presence
it feels as if the brightest
light in the universe
is pouring into every
crevice of our lives.
Your utter holiness overwhelms
every one of our excuses
and your boundless grace
picks us up when we fall.
Your love welcomes us home when
we have wandered far from you
and once again you make a
place for us in your family.

Lord,
we confess that we have made
a mess of our lives
and the poverty of our
commitment and our
failure to trust you
has left our lives empty and
our promises broken.
We confess that our days
are strewn with
selfish words, thoughtless actions,
and the fruits of our self-
centredness.
Come, Lord, forgive,
cleanse, and renew us
that we may walk in the way of
grace all our days. **Amen.**

Intercession

Hebrews 5:5–10

Father,
we want to talk to you about
those who experience rejection

and for those who always feel
  on the outside of life;
for those who are happy to have
  been adopted as a baby
and for those still seeking answers
  to their questions of identity.
Come, kneel at the foot of the cross,
the place where pain is shared.

Father,
we want to talk to you about
  those who experience
  domestic violence
and for those who daily live in fear
  for themselves and their children;
for those who suffer verbal and
  mental torment that no one sees
and for those whose every
  waking moment is a life
  of cruelty and control.
Come, kneel at the foot of the cross,
the place where pain is shared.

Father,
we want to talk to you about those
  who today are living in poverty
and for those who are struggling
  to keep their home and
  to feed their family;
for those who have none
  of the luxuries many of
  us take for granted
and for those hit hardest by loss of
  employment and benefit cuts.
Come, kneel at the foot of the cross,
the place where pain is shared.

Father,
we want to talk to you
  about those who daily face
  persecution for their faith
and for those who are paying
  the cost of their commitment
  to truth, love, and justice;
for those who refuse to remain
  silent, but long to share
  the love of their Lord
and for those who each day face
  the risk of losing their homes,
  their family, and their lives.
Come, kneel at the foot of the cross,
the place where pain is shared.

Father,
we want to talk to you about those
  who experience loneliness
and for those for whom the
  walls of their home have
  become their prison;
for those for whom their
  family was the source of
  their meaning in life
and for those feeling lost and
  broken now that they find
  themselves living alone.
Come, kneel at the foot of the cross,
the place where pain is shared.

Father,
we want to talk to you
  about those who face the
  restrictions of disability
and for those who feel locked
  out of a world designed
  for the fit and the able;
for those whose striving to live
  life to the fullest puts our
  feeble excuses to shame
and for those who face their
  disability with a smile and
  whose joy moves us to tears.
Come, kneel at the foot of the cross,
the place where pain is shared.

Father,
we want to talk to you about those
who are fighting injustice
and for those who expose the
cheating and corruption
in huge corporations;
for the work of Amnesty
International that makes us
aware of the world's injustices
and for those who even now
are languishing unjustly
in prison without trial.
Come, kneel at the foot of the cross,
the place where pain is shared.

Father,
we want to talk to you about
those we know whose lives
are filled with pain
and for those whose days are
weighed down with uncertainty,
grief, and sadness.

silence

We want to talk to you
about ourselves and the
burdens we carry within
and for the assurance that the
past is dealt with, tomorrow
is in your hands,
and today is your precious
gift to us all.
Come, kneel at the foot of the cross,
the place where pain is shared.

We have brought our concerns for
the world to the throne of grace
and we have done so in the
name of Jesus. **Amen.**

SIXTH SUNDAY IN LENT (PALM SUNDAY)

Prayer of Approach

Psalm 118:22–24

Lord,
our coming is an acknowledgement
of our need
and a declaration of your glory.
We know that we are always
in your presence
but our being here is our confession
that you are with us.
You alone are the foundation
of all that is true
and your authority marks the
path that we should walk.
Gathering here in the house of
God is a divine privilege
and our songs and prayers are
our response to your grace.

Lord,
your presence makes
every day special
and your love adds the colour
of hope to the darkest day.
Your grace overflows and
drenches our days
and we have come to lift up
your name in thanksgiving.

By your Holy Spirit, awaken our
hearts and recharge our voices
that we may sing the
songs of heaven
and worship the Lord
of glory. **Amen.**

Praise
Mark 11:1–11

Father,
we praise you that when
we speak of war
in Jesus you come in peace;
when we use words of greed,
selfishness, and hate
in Jesus you come in love;
when we feel we have nothing
to offer and are worthless
in Jesus you come in love.

How can we not praise you,
our Palm Sunday King,
for you are coming to
your coronation?
You will be crowned with thorns
on a cross of cruel agony
to bear the pain of all those for
whom the world has no room.
We praise you, Lord Jesus,
not only that you rode
into Jerusalem
but that you are ready and longing
to ride into our hearts and lives.

On that first Palm Sunday
the pilgrims and the
disciples gave thanks
and the crowds that lined
the way threw cloaks and
branches before you.
But their praises were empty
and the songs didn't last;
they quickly reclaimed their
temporary emblems of worship.
For the King they once praised
as the bearer of peace
they just as easily condemned
to bear his own cross.

Father,
we long to offer you the praises of
hearts touched by your grace
and the thankfulness of lives
enriched through the
poverty of your Son.
In Jesus we see one who by
his self-giving love
has turned the values of this
world on their head.
He challenges us all to look
beyond the here and now
and to seek the truth in the things
that we cannot touch or prove.
He promises not only to share
the joy and celebration of life
but to walk with us no matter
how dark the day feels.

Because of Jesus, the King
of Palm Sunday,
and Christ, the Lord of
the empty cross,
we can offer you praise
without ceasing
and experience hope that
literally has no end.
Come, Lord Jesus, come
touch our lips with words
for your glory
and our hearts and minds with
love for our Lord. **Amen.**

Intercession
Philippians 2:5–11

As in Christ God reached
out to the lost,
so we pray for those who
give of themselves
to walk with the homeless, the
no-hopers, the failures,

and those addicted to
alcohol and drugs.
We ask that you will walk with them
and teach us how to share
their journey.
Lord, in your mercy,
hear our prayer.

As in Christ God reached out
to the world in love,
so we pray for those who
give of themselves
to hold the broken, to
comfort the dying,
and to be Christ to those
who weep alone.
We ask that you will
walk with them
and teach us how to share
their journey.
Lord, in your mercy,
hear our prayer.

As in Christ God reached out
in compassion for all,
so we pray for those who risk
their lives far from home
and for those who give of
themselves to rescue people
from earthquake, fire, or flood
and to bring healing and hope.
We ask that you will
walk with them
and teach us how to share
their journey.
Lord, in your mercy,
hear our prayer.

As in Christ God reached out to a
world clothed with insecurity,
so we pray for those who
place their trust in their
wealth and possessions,
for those who never experienced
the joy of a loving home
and who are trapped by
the false promises of the
addictions that hold them.
We ask that you will
walk with them
and teach us how to share
their journey.
Lord, in your mercy,
hear our prayer.

As in Christ God reached out
to a world seeking hope,
so we pray for aid workers who
seek to rescue the hungry
and for those who are dedicated
to bringing health and healing
to those suffering the effects of
polluted water, malnutrition,
and HIV/AIDS.
We ask that you will
walk with them
and teach us how to share
their journey.
Lord, in your mercy,
hear our prayer.

As in Christ God reached out to
those haunted by their past,
so we pray for those in deep
despair for their future
and for those overwhelmed with
anxiety as they face today;
for those who are afraid of what the
doctor's diagnosis may reveal
and for those who already
know the struggles they
face in the coming days.

We ask that you will
walk with them
and teach us how to share
their journey.
Lord, in your mercy,
hear our prayer.

As in Christ God reached out to
build a people to bear his name,
so we pray for Christians everywhere,
that by the Holy Spirit
we may demonstrate what it means
to be the people of God.
By deeds of compassion, seeking
justice, and our love of Jesus
may we truly be the body of
Christ where we are.
We ask that you will walk with us
and teach us how to journey
in Jesus' name.
Lord, in your mercy,
hear our prayer.

We bring our prayers in
the name of Jesus,
who is forever reaching out to a
lost world in love. **Amen.**

EASTER SUNDAY

Prayer of Approach

Psalm 118:1–2

Lord,
we are here for one reason,
and for one reason only!
We are not here to receive a blessing
nor have we come out of habit.
We have come by an
inner compulsion,
a deep desire to give you
thanks and adoration.
We are here because your
love has drawn us
and your extravagant grace
is making us whole.
We have come so that together
we might declare your glory
and that we might sing
your song of praise.
We have a song in our hearts
that must be sung—
that the Lord is good and his
love endures for ever. **Amen.**

Praise

John 20:1–10

Lord,
truly you are the God of surprises!
Every time we think we
know who you are
and are certain of what you can do
you blow our minds away with
the power of your grace.

Lord,
truly you are the God of surprises!
Again and again you make
the impossible a reality
and what we thought was
the end of everything
you transform into the
beginning of all things new.

Lord,
truly you are the God of surprises!
When our hopes are dashed
and doubts overwhelm us
you walk alongside us
and ever so gently
you open our eyes to comprehend
truths beyond our searching.

Lord,
truly you are the God of surprises!
The disciples came to the
  tomb on Easter Day;
their faith had been broken
  and they had lost all hope
but their meeting with the risen
  Christ changed everything.

Lord,
truly you are the God of surprises!
We come with our praises
for the times when you
  blow our minds away
with the reality of your risen
  presence in our midst.

We come with our praises
for the moments when you
  entered our doubts
and by your grace renewed our hope.

We come with our praises,
that in the depths of our brokenness
you apply the healing touch
  of your resurrection.

We come with our praises
in the knowledge that death
  has been defeated
and that by the power of
  the Holy Spirit,
even now, you are making
  all things new—
even us!

Lord,
truly you are the God of surprises!
Come and surprise us all over again
and lift our hearts,
  empower our voices
that we might join with
  the hosts of heaven
and worship you, our risen
  and living Lord. **Amen.**

Intercession

1 Corinthians 15:1–11

Lord,
because you are risen
we pray for the peace of the world
and for those who work to
  bring an end to fighting;
for those who do not experience
  peace and contentment
and for those who have a house
  but not a home of joy.
Come, risen Lord,
and make all things new.

Lord,
because you are risen
we pray for a renewed concern
  for your creation
and a deeper commitment
  by all governments
to take action to safeguard
  the future of our planet;
for those whose activities
  destroy the habitat
of creatures large and small
and for those whose total
  disregard for our world
is daily threatening the future
  of endangered species.
Come, risen Lord,
and make all things new.

Lord,
because you are risen
we pray for those who
  live lonely lives

and for those whose home
has become their prison;
for those whose days are
spent in isolation
and for those who long for someone
to come and share their memories.
Come, risen Lord,
and make all things new.

Lord,
because you are risen
we pray for those whose lives
are filled with anger
and for those whose hatred brings
pain and suffering to many;
for those who plan and
commit acts of terrorism
and for those whose lives are wrecked
through the actions of those who
have been radicalised to hate.
Come, risen Lord,
and make all things new.

Lord,
because you are risen
we pray for those who are hungry
and for those who have no
food in a world of plenty;
for nations who spend billions
on weapons of destruction,
while today there are millions who
will be unable to feed their family,
and for those simply hungry to
know they are loved and accepted.
Come, risen Lord,
and make all things new.

Lord,
because you are risen
we pray for those who are hurting
as they weep for those they have lost
and for those whose hurt
is deep inside
as they are finding they
can weep no more;
for those who weep for dreams
that came to nothing
and for those who weep for
dreams they failed to have.
Come, risen Lord,
and make all things new.

Lord,
because you are risen
we pray for governments
who pay lip service
to the rights of human beings
and for those locked away from the
eyes of the world without trial;
for those who bravely take their
stand against injustice
and for global corporations whose
actions pollute God's world
as their workers are
treated like slaves.
Come, risen Lord,
and make all things new.

Lord,
because you are risen
we pray for those who
are losing hope
as the doctor's diagnosis reduces
the number of their days
and for those whose hopes of
parenthood have been dashed;
for those who have longed for
acceptance and friendship
but daily experience rejection
because of their colour, their
gender, or their nationality
and for those facing times of
doubt, despair, and depression,

blaming themselves when
they are not to blame.
Come, risen Lord,
and make all things new.

We bring our prayers in
the name of Christ,
our risen and living Lord. **Amen.**

SECOND SUNDAY OF EASTER

Prayer of Approach

Psalm 133

Father,
our coming together in worship
was always your plan for us.
Like a parent rejoicing as they see
their children enjoy each
other's company,
so may our gathering as your family
be a source of joy, glory, and praise
to our heavenly Father.

Father,
come smile upon your children
as we fill our lips with songs
of thanksgiving.
Give to us an overwhelming
experience of your presence
as by your Holy Spirit
you join our worship with
the song of heaven.
In the name of Jesus. **Amen.**

Praise

1 John 1:1–4

Father,
we praise you for the joy
with which you have filled our lives
and for the hope
of your living presence
enriching our days.

This is a joy that no longer depends
on the situation in which
we find ourselves—
around us or within us.
It is a joy that is almost
beyond words.
It holds us, overwhelms us,
and touches every facet of
our life's journey.

The joy we have within us
does not protect us
from life's sorrows, hardships,
and disappointments
but it is a fountain that
wells up within us
and brings healing, hope, and
thankfulness in its wake.

We praise you, Father,
for you are the source of our joy
and the wellspring of
hope brings us life.
Our joy comes
not from a call to follow;
not from a pattern in which
to mark our footsteps;
not from a blind obedience
requiring no thought.

This is the joy:
that you did not call us from afar
but in Jesus
you entered our world,
lived our life,
walked our pathways,
and entered into all that
life means to us.

This is the joy:
through Christ's life, death,
and resurrection

comes the promise of hope
  and eternal life.

This is the joy:
we do not simply know
about your holiness,
your glory,
your power,
and your authority
but in Jesus
we can call you 'our Father'
and for this
we praise you now
and we will praise you for ever.
In Jesus' name. **Amen.**

Intercession
John 1:5–7

Father,
we want to talk to you about
those in the darkness of loss;
for those who have lost
  those they loved
and are finding it hard to begin again.
Father, in the darkness,
come with your light.

Father,
we want to talk to you about
those in the darkness of worry;
for those whose concerns
  for tomorrow
prevent them entering
  the joy of today.
Father, in the darkness,
come with your light.

Father,
we want to talk to you about
those in the darkness of fear;
for those who live in a war zone
and each day face the reality
  of injury or death.
Father, in the darkness,
come with your light.

Father,
we want to talk to you about
those in the darkness of debt;
for those whose income
  has been lost
through unemployment or
  cuts to their benefits
and have bills they cannot pay
as they face the possibility
  of losing their home.
Father, in the darkness,
come with your light.

Father,
we want to talk to you about
those in the darkness of
  long-term illness;
for those for whom each day
  is a battle just to survive
and whose pain, frustration, and
  reliance on others for support
colours their days with resignation
and their future seems
  like an empty void.
Father, in the darkness,
come with your light.

Father,
we want to talk to you about
those in the darkness of loneliness;
for those whose disability brings
  a feeling of isolation
in a world designed and planned
  for and by the able
and for those who no longer have
  family and friends around them

as they long for a smile, a
visit, and a listening ear.
Father, in the darkness,
come with your light.

Father,
we want to talk to you about
those whose darkness
we find on the pages of
our newspaper
and in the images that we
see on the television;
for those we know whose struggles
are beyond our understanding
and for ourselves and the
darkness that won't go away.
Father, in the darkness,
come with your light.

Father,
we have talked to you about the
darkness in your world.
We pray, come, Lord Jesus,
come with your light
and drive away the darkness. **Amen.**

THIRD SUNDAY OF EASTER

Praise

Luke 24:36–48

Lord,
we cannot imagine the shock
on your disciples' faces
or their sense of confusion and how
unreal it must have seemed.
They had seen you die on the cross
and they knew your body had
been laid in the tomb.

Of course, they had heard
the women's story that
the tomb was empty
but hearing the story and
knowing it was true was
something very different.
Your coming, standing
in their presence,
must have been a life-
transforming experience
and the driving force in their
mission and service.

Lord,
we want to praise you for each
new day you grant to us
and how you fill them with
moments of joy and discovery.
Even in our times of doubt you
come ready to hold us
and when we are overwhelmed
by life itself
and we wonder just how we will
cope with the day ahead
your risen presence breaks
through the darkness.

Lord,
we praise you that as with
your disciples
you come when we least expect
you but need you most.
You light up our hearts and our
minds are thrown into turmoil
as you are there in the
compassionate smile of a friend
and the caring hug of
someone who cares.

We find you in the midst of
a busy supermarket
and discover you are there
as we read your Word.
In moments of pain, sorrow,
and deep hurt within

we experience the sense of being
held in loving hands.

Lord, surprising Lord,
we praise you for your capacity
to go on surprising us
and turning our life upside down.
You are not simply a
figure of history
nor have you left us with
simply a path to follow
and a set of rules we must obey
if we are to be accepted.
Your risen and living presence
demands our trust and
our obedience
because first we have learnt to
accept that we are accepted!

Come, Lord Jesus, come!
Come and go on coming to
transform who we are
that we may praise you now
and praise you for ever,
as by your living presence
you show yourself to be
our surprising Lord.
In Jesus' name. **Amen.**

Confession

1 John 3:1–7

Father,
we sometimes find
confession difficult
as we don't always feel that we
are living dreadful lives!
The problem is that we
measure ourselves
against what we see as the worst
examples of humanity.

Father,
because we have no murder
or adultery to confess,
we too easily forget how our
words and our attitudes
have damaged the lives of
those around us.

Father,
because we haven't robbed a bank
or our neighbour's property,
we forget that what we have
said and done has stolen
someone's good name
and we have kept for ourselves the
time we promised to give to you.

Father,
because we do not think of
ourselves as worshipping idols
we fail to see that the importance
we give to our possessions
and the value we give to
the things of earth
are replacing the place in our lives
that was reserved for you.

Father,
we are ordinary people who daily
make ordinary mistakes.
But we have an extraordinary
heavenly Father
whose extraordinary love reaches
out with his offer of forgiveness
to ordinary people who daily
make a mess of their lives,
often in such ordinary ways,
with such ordinary words,
and with such ordinary
thoughts. **Amen.**

Intercession
Acts 3:12–19

Lord,
we pray for ordinary people
with ordinary problems;
for those who enjoyed the hustle
and bustle of work and family life
and are now finding
themselves overwhelmed
by too much of the peace and quiet
for which they once longed.
God of surprises, open our
eyes to your presence
and touch us with your grace.

Lord,
we pray for ordinary people
with ordinary problems;
for those who are single by
their own personal choice
and for those who are alone as a result
of bereavement or the breakdown
of a relationship.
God of surprises, open our
eyes to your presence
and touch us with your grace.

Lord,
we pray for ordinary people
with ordinary problems;
for those who are dissatisfied
with their lives
and for whom each day feels the same
as they feel they are merely existing
and life is passing them by.
God of surprises, open our
eyes to your presence
and touch us with your grace.

Lord,
we pray for ordinary people
with ordinary problems;
for those who are trying to cope with
the loss of someone they loved
and have a hole left behind now that
the years of caring have ended,
as they regret the things they said
and the things they failed to do.
God of surprises, open our
eyes to your presence
and touch us with your grace.

Lord,
we pray for ordinary people
with ordinary problems;
for young people setting out on
the journey of adventure
and for those left behind with
few options of progress
as they experience a deep sense
of failure or disappointment.
God of surprises, open our
eyes to your presence
and touch us with your grace.

Lord,
we pray for ordinary people
with ordinary problems;
for those who are no longer
able to care for themselves
and for those whose failing health
and increasing weakness
brings the frustration of growing
dependence on others.
God of surprises, open our
eyes to your presence
and touch us with your grace.

Lord,
we pray for ourselves, for we
are ordinary people with
ordinary problems;
for the concerns we have for our
health, our family, or our future.

In the stillness let us talk to God of
the issues that trouble us deeply.

silence

God of surprises, open our
eyes to your presence
and touch us with your grace.

We bring our prayers in
the name of Jesus,
the one who promises, 'I am
with you always.' **Amen.**

FOURTH SUNDAY OF EASTER

Prayer of Approach

Psalm 23

Lord,
we are as foolish as sheep
and just as ready to wander
away, needing to be found.
We too need a quiet place to
rest and find renewal
as we struggle to find the
right path through life.
On days that are filled with
darkness and fear
we long for someone to respond
to our cries for help.

Lord,
we are as foolish as sheep
and yet, wonder of wonders,
you reach out to find us
and lead us home.
We have come to offer you
thanks and praise
with the invitation to
your heavenly party
ringing in our ears.

Lord,
we may be as foolish as sheep
but we worship you, our
loving shepherd,
for you gave your life for
your sheep. **Amen.**

Praise

Acts 4:4–12

Lord,
you never cease to amaze us
with the seemingly foolish
things you say and do
and you have the oddest way
in which you show us what
you value most.

When we think of the billions of
planets that fill the universe
we are utterly overwhelmed
by our sense of smallness.
Yet out of all the parts of your
creation you could have chosen
we find it almost beyond
belief that you selected
our insignificant world.
There must have been places more
deserving of your royal attention
than our broken, damaged,
selfish spinning globe.

Even more amazing is that
when you came it wasn't
in a blaze of glory
nor with the pomp and ceremony
we provide for our earthly rulers.
Your coming as one of us took
everyone by surprise
and the shockwaves of your birth
as the baby in Bethlehem
still ripple out across our world.

In the beginning it was only
a handful of people who
recognised your presence
though now your coming has
divided our history in two.

Lord,
you never cease to amaze us
with the seemingly foolish things
that Jesus said and did.
We might have expected him to
work through the religious people
and those who lived upright lives
and were looking for your arrival.
But from the start he spent his time
with the poor and the broken
and gave of himself to those
whom everyone else had
rejected as worthless.
When it all seemed to have gone
badly wrong, as Jesus died alone,
you still reached out to those
who would listen to the
wonder of resurrection.
Once again the audacity of your
plan takes our breath away
because instead of turning
to learned teachers
you foolishly relied on the witness of
uneducated, illiterate fishermen!

Lord,
we praise you for the value
you place on each of us
and we thank you that you
can use the simplest gifts
of the most ordinary people.
Jesus, we worship you, our
Lord and Saviour.
You are the Son of God, who
became a human being
that human beings might
become children of God.
May our praises ring through
this vast universe
and our songs of thankfulness echo
to the end of time. **Amen.**

Intercession
John 10:11–18
Lord,
we pray for those who are servants
of the Good Shepherd—
for those who know you
and those who don't.
For those who work in
homes for the elderly
and for those who offer support
for those with special needs;
for Macmillan nurses caring
for the terminally ill
and for those who provide
hospice care for those at
the end of their journey.
Jesus the Good Shepherd,
show us how to care.

Lord,
we pray for those who are servants
of the Good Shepherd—
for those who know you
and those who don't.
For those involved in medical
research to deal with disease
and for those who test the
safety of new treatments;
for those who take away the
rubbish from our homes
as they remove the cause of sickness
and infection at its source.
Jesus the Good Shepherd,
show us how to care.

Lord,
we pray for those who are servants
of the Good Shepherd—
for those who know you
and those who don't.
For those who reach out
to the homeless
and for those who care for those
whose home is a cardboard box;
for those who serve as street pastors
to those who are vulnerable
and for shopping centre chaplains
who meet people in need.
Jesus the Good Shepherd,
show us how to care.

Lord,
we pray for those who are servants
of the Good Shepherd—
for those who know you
and those who don't.
For those who give of their time
working in local charity shops
and for those who volunteer
to collect charity envelopes
in their street;
for those whose support enables the
elderly to live in their own home
and for those who are good
neighbours showing the
world the love of Jesus.
Jesus the Good Shepherd,
show us how to care.

Lord,
we pray for those who are servants
of the Good Shepherd—
for those who know you
and those who don't.
For those who travel across
the world to rescue
victims of earthquakes
and for those who risk their lives
to save those they don't know;
for those who serve as members of
the fire brigade or a lifeboat crew
and for those who are part of
a mountain rescue team.
Jesus the Good Shepherd,
show us how to care.

Lord,
we pray for those who are servants
of the Good Shepherd—
for those who know you
and those who don't.
For those who are chaplains to
prisons, education, and industry
and for those who share
their skills with those who
can't read or write;
for those who offer help
and support through
Alcoholics Anonymous
and for those who work
within Victim Support
and Citizens Advice.
Jesus the Good Shepherd,
show us how to care.

Lord,
we pray for those who are servants
of the Good Shepherd—
for those who know you
and those who don't.
For those we know who give of
themselves to help others
and for those who do so without
any thought of a reward;
for ourselves and for the
opportunity to show
unconditional compassion
and to demonstrate the love of
Jesus in all we say or do.

Jesus the Good Shepherd,
show us how to care.

We bring our prayers in
the name of Jesus,
the Good Shepherd who sends
his sheep out to care. **Amen.**

FIFTH SUNDAY OF EASTER

Praise

Psalm 22:25–31

Father,
we praise you as we gather
together in your name
and for the freedom to
celebrate your glory.
How can we not praise you,
the Lord of heaven,
and worship you for your
almighty power?

When we face times of
hardship and difficulty
it is the knowledge of your
sovereignty that keeps us strong.
In those moments when our
doubts almost overwhelm us
your loving presence holds us
and renews our trust.

Your word speaks to our hearts
and fills us with peace
that in the darkest times we
have the assurance of hope.
You are the God whom we
worship and no other—
for you alone are the Lord of
time and space and eternity.

We praise you for the promise that
the worship we offer on earth
will find its utter fulfilment
before the throne of grace.
Sovereign Lord, by your Holy
Spirit, so empower and renew us
that every moment of every
day will be lived as a
song of your glory.

Father,
may our praises find their out-
working in our care for the poor
and that your loving presence
will be seen in our compassion
for the hungry.
May our lives be so transformed
by your love that your grace
will touch our neighbour
and our words and deeds speak of
the source of our hope and joy.

Our songs of thanksgiving
are for you alone, the
Lord of all the earth,
and the worship we begin here in
the assembly of your people
will echo from here to the
end of time and beyond.
Our songs of your glory will never
cease in the ages to come
but will be gathered up and offered
in the name of your Son.

On that great day we will come
with all your people of all
times and from all places
before the throne of the King and
sing the song without end.
Come, Lord Jesus, come
and receive the praises
of your people
for you alone are worthy to receive
our song of your glory. **Amen.**

Confession

John 15:1–8

Father,
we confess that you have a great
deal of pruning to do in our lives
and that we still hold on to things
that do not honour you.

We confess that though we have
welcomed you into our hearts
too often we live lives that do not
speak of your love and compassion.

We confess that though
we have found hope and
renewal in your grace
we still harbour ill will to
our neighbour and find
it hard to forgive.

We confess that though we know
you are Lord of heaven and earth
even now we hold back
from allowing you to be
Lord of our lives.

We confess that though we have
received the gift of the Holy Spirit
our lives do not bear the
fruit of lives on fire that
you expected to see.

We confess that we can sing
of your lordship in the
midst of your people
yet we find it almost impossible
to name Jesus as Lord
to our neighbour.

We come, Father, making
our confession,
that in receiving your forgiveness
our renewed lives will
glorify your name.

Hear Jesus' word of grace:
'I have forgiven your sin
and made you whole.
Live in peace and declare
my name.' **Amen.**

Intercession

Acts 8:26–40

In the stillness ask God
to raise up those
who like Philip with the
Ethiopian will be open to
God's opportunities;
for those he is calling to
speak his word of grace,
that the lost may find
their way home.

silence

In the stillness ask God to
open the eyes of those
who like Philip with the
Ethiopian will respond to
God's opportunity;
for those with the heart of a servant,
that they may reach out to those
in need of compassion.

silence

In the stillness ask God
to raise up those
who like Philip with the Ethiopian
will be open to God's moment;
for those with the gifts and the
skills to help the despairing,
that they may bring food to the
hungry and peace to the broken.

silence

In the stillness ask God
to raise up those
who like Philip with the Ethiopian
will recognise God's planning;
for those with concern for the
lonely, the bereaved, and
those who are hurting,
that they may be agents of hope,
comfort, and healing.

silence

In the stillness ask God
to raise up those
who like Philip with the
Ethiopian understand God's
purposes for them;
for those who know what it
means to experience life-
threatening illness,
that they may use the blessing
of hope they received to
be a blessing to others.

silence

In the stillness ask God
to raise up those
who like Philip with the
Ethiopian will acknowledge
God's gift of timing;
for those who have
struggled with doubts and
unanswered questions,
that they may be a channel
of peace having found
Jesus to be the answer.

silence

In the stillness ask God
to raise up those
who like Philip with the
Ethiopian will respond
in ordinary ways to God's
ordinary purposes;
that he will use ordinary
people like ourselves
to be his extraordinary messengers
of hope to our neighbour.

silence

In the stillness thank God for those
whom he will raise up to serve him.
But remember to ask him if the
person he wants is you.

silence

We bring our prayers in
the name of Jesus,
who equips those he chooses to do
such amazing things. **Amen.**

SIXTH SUNDAY OF EASTER

Prayer of Approach

Psalm 98

Lord,
we have come to sing your praises
because all worship begins
and ends in song.
We sing a song of hope, of
joy, and of thanksgiving.
Our songs are not merely
words on a printed page
but a song that wells up
from within us.
This is not a song that we or
another has composed,

it is the song of love you wrote
in grace upon our hearts.
This is the song that we have
come to sing. **Amen.**

Praise

1 John 5:1–6

Lord,
our society loves to honour people
and often for the most
trivial of things.
The tributes we give are for
what they have done
and rarely are people blessed
for who they are.

When we gather for worship
it's the same mistake that we make.
We focus our praises on
your work in creation
and your fingerprints on
the beauty around us.

We praise and we thank you
for all you have done to
bring us home.
That from the beginning it
was always your plan
to make us your children through
new birth in your love.

It is right in our worship
that we remember our
Saviour and Lord,
that we never forget Jesus
died in our place
and rose again to open for us
the door of the kingdom.
In Jesus we have a Saviour to praise
and a debt of forgiveness
we can never repay.

Lord,
we must never forget not only
what Christ has done
but focus our worship on
the one who is Lord!
Our praises are lacking if
we fail to remember
he is the one who was sovereign
before time began.

We call you our friend, but what
a glorious being you are,
who has dared to walk beside
us and fill us with hope.
You are our Sovereign, King of
Kings, and Lord of Lords
and your glory and power are
from eternity to eternity.

To worship you, our loving
Saviour and Lord,
fills us with joy, hope, and
the promise of renewal.
It is when our eyes are opened
to the wonder of grace
that we are forced to confess the
truth of your heavenly birth.
To name you as Lord is much
more than a word;
it is the foundation on which
true worship is built.
In the presence of your glory,
your power, and authority,
our worship takes flight and
our hearts are lifted high.

Lord Jesus Christ, we praise
you for all you have done
and we worship you for
the Lord of heaven that
you truly are. **Amen.**

Intercession

Acts 10:44–48

I am a police officer
and I seek to break down barriers
by bringing criminals to face justice.
It makes me unpopular
with those who break the law.
I face danger every day of my life
as I seek to protect ordinary people.
Pray for me.

I am a politician
and I seek to break down barriers
by working for a fairer,
more just society.
It makes me unpopular
with those only interested
in themselves.
I face opposition from all sides
as I seek to bring hope to the poor.
Pray for me.

I am a social worker
and I seek to break down barriers
by supporting those who can't cope.
I am treated as a 'do-gooder'
by those who don't care for the lost.
I am ridiculed and blamed
for every mistake
as I seek to help the
vulnerable and weak.
Pray for me.

I am a refuse collector
and I seek to break down barriers
by removing the source of infection
along with your rubbish.
I receive no respect for
the work that I do
and am ignored by those
who rely on my help.
The service I give is for
rich and for poor,
for the source of disease
knows no barriers at all.
Pray for me.

I am a journalist
and I seek to break down barriers
that would hide privilege and wealth.
I create many enemies by
the work that I do,
exposing injustice and
abuse of the young.
I draw back the curtain on
bribery and corruption
whoever the person,
whatever the cause.
Pray for me.

I am a scientist
and I seek to break down barriers
that people build between
science and faith.
I face great opposition for
the work that I do,
rescuing God's creation from
the damage we do.
My faith is in God and I am
concerned for his world
as I reveal the action to be
taken before it's too late.
Pray for me.

I am a Christian
and I seek to break down barriers
that we build which cause
God's love to be hidden.
Those within churches seem
afraid things might change
whilst those on the doorstep
find our worship remote.

The task I am given means
opening our minds
in the life of the church
that all may find room.
Pray for me.

We bring our prayers in
the name of Jesus,
who through his life, death,
and resurrection
broke every barrier
down. **Amen.**

SEVENTH SUNDAY OF EASTER

Prayer of Approach

1 John 5:13

Lord,
we come to worship you
in the name of the one
who gives us hope
and we gather to
honour the one
whose promise of grace is true.

Lord,
you designed us for worship
and we were made to
sing your praises.
In Jesus you have given our lives
a purpose vast and wide.

Lord,
we celebrate the one in
whom we have new life
and we give glory to him who
is the door to eternal life.
The Son of God has promised
us his presence now
and we have his assurance of the
heaven of his love to come.
Come, let us worship the Lord,
for he is worthy! **Amen.**

Thanksgiving

Acts 1:21–26

Lord,
we are astounded that you
have always chosen
to work through imperfect
human beings like ourselves.
From the very beginning you
selected the very ones
who appeared to be least
worthy of your call.

When we read the stories of
Abraham, Isaac, and Jacob
we cannot help but wonder at
your seeming foolishness.
But the story of your choice flows
on through the Bible—
as we find you calling Moses,
Solomon, David, and Jeremiah.
We are amazed that you chose
Peter, Matthew, and Judas
as your disciples, whose fault
lines were obvious to all.

Lord,
we are thankful that you look
beyond our faults and weaknesses
and that you look deep within
not only to what we are
but what, by your grace,
we can become.
We know now that if you
could choose Judas
you can call anyone, even us,
into the service royal.

There is something overwhelming
about your call

for you choose the very ones no
one else would consider.
We are thankful that whilst the
world rejects many as no-hopers
these are the very ones you call
to build your kingdom.

Lord,
in those moments when we
feel lost, empty, and afraid
we are grateful that you hold
us and speak of your love.
When we feel we have wasted
our time and achieved little
we are filled with hope by the
value you place on our lives.

Our hearts overflow with
amazement and thanksgiving
that we should be named as
servants of the living God.
We awake each day ready to
serve the King of Kings
in the knowledge that nothing we
do in his name is ever wasted.

Lord,
we offer you our heartfelt
thanks and praise
for you have restored our hope
and rekindled our joy.
We will thank and praise you
now in the service we offer
and give glory at the throne
of grace to the Lord of
broken people. **Amen.**

Intercession

John 17:6–19

Father,
we want to talk to you about
your church on earth
and for those churches facing
terrible persecution;
for Christians who face danger
every day of their lives
and for those who risk prison for
meeting together for worship;
for churches whose members face
exile because of their faith
and for those who are ready
to suffer rather than deny
the name of their Lord.
For the sake of your
church on earth,
come, Lord Jesus, come.

Father,
we want to talk to you about
your church on earth
and for those churches that are
continuing to struggle;
for churches that find themselves
sowing seed on barren ground
and for congregations that
are dispirited as they
are facing decline;
for churches demoralised as their
efforts to witness come to nothing
and for those whose service to their
community has gone unnoticed.
For the sake of your
church on earth,
come, Lord Jesus, come.

Father,
we want to talk to you about
your church on earth
and for those churches that have
lost their sense of anticipation;
for churches who no longer are
aware of God's presence
and for those who are rediscovering
the Spirit's power for worship;

for those who have lost the vision
of being Christ's body on earth
and for those seeking an experience
of gifts and the fruit of the Spirit.
For the sake of your
church on earth,
come, Lord Jesus, come.

Father,
we want to talk to you about
your church on earth
and for those churches that
have lost their way;
for congregations that have
closed the door to outreach
and for those whose close-
knit, familiar fellowship
shuts out those who come searching
for hope, love, and faith;
for churches who simply sit
waiting for seekers to turn up
and for those neglecting
the command to go and
make disciples.
For the sake of your
church on earth,
come, Lord Jesus, come.

Father,
we want to talk to you about
your church on earth
and for those churches that
are your servants today;
for congregations that
see themselves as a
serving community
and for those who reach out to hold
the broken and find the lost;
for those who gather together for
praise, thanks, and communion
and for those whose concern
for justice is part of the
worship they offer.
For the sake of your
church on earth,
come, Lord Jesus, come.

Father,
we want to talk to you about
your church on earth
and for those churches
yet to be planted;
for the vision to build a new
fellowship of faith
and for the courage to grow
in unexpected places;
for the wind of the Spirit to come—
refreshing and renewing—
and the fire of God to cleanse,
inspire, and empower.
For the sake of your
church on earth,
come, Lord Jesus, come.

Father,
we want to talk to you about
your church on earth
and for those churches that
are growing and reaping;
for churches whose numbers
are increasing
and where there is an ever-
deepening spiritual maturity;
for congregations that
are experiencing rich
blessing from God
and for those who rely on Christ to
grow in faith, hope, and love.
For the sake of your
church on earth,
come, Lord Jesus, come.

Father,
we want to talk to you about
your church on earth
and for those churches that still
have their eyes on heaven.
In the stillness
we remember those whose
faithfulness brought us to faith
and those who are ready to walk in
faith to the end—and beyond.
For the sake of your
church on earth,
come, Lord Jesus, come.

We bring our prayers for the church
in the name of Christ, whose
body we are. **Amen.**

PENTECOST SUNDAY

Prayer of Approach

Psalm 104:35b

To gather as your people
brings a moment of joy,
and as we bring our praises
we find ourselves at the
gateway to heaven.

To sing of our love for you
lifts our hearts to the mountaintop
and as we celebrate your glory
your grace binds us ever closer
together as the body of Christ.

It is in your presence that
your Holy Spirit
bursts the floodgates of the
resources of our praises
and releases the pent-up
wonder of your glory
that is lying deep within us.

With the psalmist, the cry of
worship bursts from our lips,
overwhelms our hearts, and
transforms our whole being.
The joy surges forth as we
too sing with joy,
'Bless the Lord, O my soul,
and all within me, praise
his holy name.' **Amen.**

Confession

John 15:26–27

Lord,
you promised that the Holy
Spirit would come
to be our guide and our
encourager—
but we have preferred to
rely on ourselves.

You told us that he would
lead us into all truth—
but we have listened to the voices
of those who do not know you.

You assured us that he
would enable us
to share the good news of your
love and grace to all—
but we have allowed our deeds,
our words, and our lives
to be the focus of the attention
of everyone we meet.

So come, Holy Spirit, and fill our
hearts with your presence
and capture all we say and do,
transforming everything
into a vehicle for your glory.

In Jesus' name. **Amen.**

Intercession

Romans 8:22–27

Father, we want to talk to you
about those who ache for
those they have lost
and for those crying deep inside
for those they loved but
see no more.
Come, Holy Spirit,
and heal your world.

Father, we want to talk to you
about those who ache
for their broken hopes and
unfulfilled dreams;
for those whose failing
health is robbing them
of the freedom to live the
life they had planned.
Come, Holy Spirit,
and heal your world.

Father, we want to talk to you
about those who ache for peace
and for those who live out their days
in the midst of civil war and
the work of terrorists.
Come, Holy Spirit,
and heal your world.

Father, we want to talk to you
about those who ache
for forgiveness
for the things they have said
or done or thought
that have hurt you, other
people, and themselves;
for those who have been
hurt so deeply
that the price tag of letting the
pain go feels far too high.
Come, Holy Spirit,
and heal your world.

Father, we want to talk to you
about those who ache for the lost,
the broken, and the forgotten
and for those who feel they have
no hope and no future;
for those who live with
their memories
and long for someone with
whom they can share them.
Come, Holy Spirit,
and heal your world.

Father, we want to talk to you
about those who ache for the
hungry and the starving;
for those who ache for something
with which to feed their children
and for those whose work for
Christian Aid, Tearfund,
and food banks
is offering life and hope to the poor.
Come, Holy Spirit,
and heal your world.

Father, we want to talk to you
about the ache at the very
heart of our nation;
for its ever-widening gap between
the rich and the poor, the
'haves' and the 'have nots',
those who are honoured
and those who are treated as failures;
for those who have everything
this world considers of value
but who will arrive as empty-
handed paupers
at the doorway of eternity.
Come, Holy Spirit,
and heal your world.

Father, we want to talk to
you in the stillness
about those for whom our
hearts and minds ache.

silence

We want to talk to you
about the ache
that fills our lives and
colours our days;
that shapes our memories and
touches our relationships;
that comes from our yesterdays, is
waiting to meet us tomorrow,
and all but overwhelms us today.
Come, Holy Spirit,
and heal your world.

We bring our prayers in
the name of Jesus,
who comes to heal and
restore us. **Amen.**

TRINITY SUNDAY

Prayer of Approach

Psalm 29

Lord,
we hear your voice in the
power of the wind
and it speaks to us of your splendour.
We recognise your voice
in cold clear water
and it declares your holiness
and gentleness.

You are the one whose
majesty overwhelms us
and whose glory is beyond
words to describe it.

Nothing in all the vast universe
is greater than you
and no one ever will match
your sovereignty.

This is the God we
worship and praise,
the one who is enthroned in glory.
This is the one who is the
centre of our worship,
the God who reigns supreme over
all that he has made. **Amen.**

Praise

Isaiah 6:1–8

Lord,
what an amazing privilege
we have been given
that we can gather together
to sing your praises.
But you have granted
us a higher gift
for we can join our worship
with the song of the angels.

When Isaiah entered your presence
the adoration of your glory
had already begun.
He was overwhelmed by the
glory of your presence
and the mind-blowing experience
of adding his song to the
praises of heaven.

Lord,
we are told that even when two
or three of us meet together
the presence of Jesus will
transform our praises.
As we come to sing our hymns
and to talk to you in prayer

you reveal the staggering truth that
we do so with the hosts of heaven!

As Isaiah experienced the
glory that is yours alone
he came to a deeper understanding
of your holiness.
The sign that we are in the
presence of your majesty
comes when we are aware of
our utter unworthiness.

Then comes the act of
grace upon grace
as you reach out to touch
and to cleanse us.
We can enter your presence
only because of Jesus—
his life, death, and resurrection
has thrown open the door to
the kingdom of grace.

We praise you that no matter who
we are or what we have done—
no matter our mistakes, our
weaknesses, or our failures—
your grace makes it possible not
only for us to begin again
but, wonder of wonders, you call us
to be servants of the Servant King!

Lord,
we can hold back our
praises no longer
and our songs of thanksgiving will
echo across your kingdom.
We worship, honour and praise
you—Father, Son and Holy Spirit,
for all you are and for all
you have done.

Praise the Lord! **Amen.**

Intercession

John 3:3

Lord,
our world is tearing itself apart
as every day we hear of nations at war
and the work of terrorists
destroying peace.
We pray for those with the
power but not the will
to break down barriers to
peace and reconciliation.
Lord, pour out your Spirit
and make all things new.

Lord,
our nation is tearing itself apart
as the divisions of rich and
poor grow wider
and there is growing hostility
towards those who are different.
We pray for those with the
power but not the will
to break down barriers to equal
opportunity and hope.
Lord, pour out your Spirit
and make all things new.

Lord,
our churches are being treated
as relics of a bygone age
as the secular society spreads
its tentacles into every
part of our lives
and offers the false security
of wealth and the empty
promise of possessions.
We pray for those with the
power but not the will
to break down barriers to
faith and godly living.
Lord, pour out your Spirit
and make all things new.

Lord,
our world is being destroyed
by our reckless lifestyle
as we pollute the fabric of
the earth by our greed
and by our refusal to take
drastic action to reverse the
damage we are doing.
We pray for those with the
power but not the will
to break down barriers to heal our
world and restore its beauty.
Lord, pour out your Spirit
and make all things new.

Lord,
our world is divided into the
'have nots' and the 'haves',
the hungry and the well fed, the
powerless and the powerful
and we hear the cry of the voiceless
and those seeking justice.
We pray for those with the
power but not the will
to break down barriers to food
and justice for our neighbour.
Lord, pour out your Spirit
and make all things new.

Lord,
our towns and our cities
hide the thousands with
no home of their own;
many are sleeping rough,
wrapped in newspaper
and a cardboard box,
turning to drink or to drugs
to block out the emptiness
and pain that is theirs.
We pray for those with the
power but not the will
to break down barriers to
hope and to restoration.
Lord, pour out your Spirit
and make all things new.

Lord,
within our community there is
much suffering and despair,
where relationships are
broken, employment is lost,
and children abused,
and there are many with health
worries and fears for the future.
We pray for those with the
power but not the will
to break down barriers to healing,
peace, and reconciliation.
Lord, pour out your Spirit
and make all things new.

Lord,
in the silence of our own hearts,
we bring before you those who
are hurting, lost, or afraid.

silence

Lord, pour out your Spirit
and make all things new.

In the name of the Father, the
Son, and the Spirit. **Amen.**

EIGHTH SUNDAY IN ORDINARY TIME

Prayer of Approach

Psalm 103:1–2

Lord,
we prepare ourselves for worship
as we reflect on the gifts

with which you have
  flooded our lives.

You have given us life with
  all its opportunities
and each morning heralds a
  day of new beginning.
You have placed us in a world
of colour, change, and endless
  things to discover.

You have given us minds
with which to think, reflect,
  plan, and choose.
We have received hearts to
  love and to receive love
and the ability to reach out
  in forgiveness and hope.

You have given us yourself
and in Christ you came to be
  our suffering servant.
In him you granted us your
  grace, the greatest gift of all,
that, by your Holy Spirit, we
  may know and worship you,
who gave us all things.

Praise the Lord, O my soul. **Amen.**

Praise
Isaiah 43:19
Lord,
you are the author of life
and the source of new things.
Each day carries the promise
  of hope and renewal
as we open our hearts, minds,
  and lives to your grace.

When God's people were
  lost and afraid
and they wondered just how
  they would get home
your prophet Isaiah brought
  them your word of hope
that you are the author of life
and the source of new things.

We live in a generation
  that is obsessed with
new things, new discoveries,
  and new experiences.
Whilst many of the new things,
on which we have set our
  hearts, rarely last
and the promises they made often
  turned out to be worthless,
your word for today and
  every today is
that you are the author of life
and the source of new things.

The new thing you offer is
  life full of meaning
and joy and peace that
  simply never end.
For you specialise in finding the lost
and bringing them home;
in healing the broken
and making them whole;
in offering forgiveness
to those least deserving.

Lord,
we praise you for the wonderful way
you reach out to hold us
and to come looking
even when we were not
  aware we were lost!

You who gave us life
now long to overwhelm
  us with new life;

you who died in our place
now come as our risen Lord;
you who walked this earth
now open the door to your
kingdom of grace.

We praise you, Lord, for
you are the author of life
and the source of new things.

Come now and make all
things new. **Amen.**

Intercession

Mark 2:1–12

Father,
we want to talk to you about those
who live in a crisis of fear.
For those whose whole lives are
dominated by things they dread
and for those whose anxiety is
robbing them of the joy of life
that you are simply longing
to give them.
Lord, in the crisis,
touch us with your love.

Father,
we want to talk to you about
those in a crisis of despair.
For those living in Syria, Iraq, or
places dominated by ISIS,
whose homes and family
have been destroyed;
for migrants who set out in
hope of a welcome
but are finding the door
to a new beginning
is being slammed shut
in their faces.
Lord, in the crisis,
touch us with your love.

Father,
we want to talk to you about
those in a crisis of brokenness.
For those who have been deeply
hurt by those closest to them
as they are left feeling
vulnerable and alone,
and for those facing the loss
of someone they loved,
the loss of employment, or the
loss of meaning in life.
Lord, in the crisis,
touch us with your love.

Father,
we want to talk to you about those
facing the crisis of ageing.
For those who are discovering the
impact of the passing years
on their eyesight, their energy,
and their mobility,
and for those who are now facing
tomorrow's journey alone
as they no longer have the
family and friends who
once walked with them.
Lord, in the crisis,
touch us with your love.

Father,
we want to talk to you about those
who face a crisis of identity.
For young people overwhelmed
by the choices they must make
in the midst of the pressures to
succeed, as they struggle
with the feeling that
their whole future
depends on the results of a
few brief examinations,
and for those in danger of following
the crowd into a lifestyle

that will silently rob them of
their hopes and their days.
Lord, in the crisis,
touch us with your love.

Father,
we want to talk to you about those
facing a crisis of decision.
For those in positions of leadership
on whose shoulders
rests the world's hope for peace
and prosperity for everyone,
and for those who see only
their own status and glory
as they opt for short-sighted
solutions that suit no
one but themselves.
Lord, in the crisis,
touch us with your love.

Father,
we want to talk to you about
ourselves and the crises
that trouble our minds.
For our family and friends
who do not know Jesus
as Saviour and Lord
as they struggle with their
crisis for meaning and
purpose and peace,
and for those moments when
we are earnestly seeking
God's wisdom and direction
when the way still seems
so very uncertain.
Lord, in the crisis,
touch us with your love.

We have brought our concerns
to the Father of hope
and have done so in the name of the
one who loves us most. **Amen.**

NINTH SUNDAY IN ORDINARY TIME

Praise

Psalm 139:1–4

Lord,
we thought we knew who you were
and that our knowledge of
you was sufficient.
It seemed to us that you might be
all-knowing and all-powerful
but still we assumed there were
things we could hide from you.

We thought your knowledge was
like our understanding of things
and we somehow treated you as if
you were a cosmic Wikipedia.
We have yet to learn that your
comprehension goes far deeper
and that, disturbingly,
there is simply no limit
to what you know—
and know completely!

Lord,
we praise you that your knowledge
of people like ourselves
is utterly, absolutely,
frighteningly total.
We realise now how little we really
understand your authority
and how vast is the sum
of all you know.

You know our thoughts, our
plans, and our dreams.
You comprehend our doubts, our
fears, and our deepest longings.
You are fully aware of what we
are and what we are not.
You have stored our first thoughts
that followed our birth

and you will gather our final wish
before we meet you face to face.

Lord,
this knowledge you have is so
detailed and complete
and it is part of what makes you
sovereign Lord of all creation.
Our minds are blown away and we
stand in awe in your presence.
We have no words, no images,
and no examples with which
to speak of your glory.

Amazingly, your knowledge
of us gives us hope
for though you know us and
know us completely
still your love for us is also complete
and full and utterly free—
it comes 'free of charge' with
'no strings attached'.

Lord,
the psalmist was overwhelmed
by your knowledge of him
as he sang of the wonder and
power of your grace.
We pray, help us to offer the
worship you deserve
and that, empowered by
the Holy Spirit,
our praises will be worthy of
the one who is all in all.

It is your glory and authority
that stops us in our tracks
and it is your majesty and
almightiness that thrills our hearts;
it is your unconditional love
that touches us deeply
and it is your grace that
is the mainspring of all
our praises. **Amen.**

Confession

1 Samuel 3:1–4

Lord,
we know so much about
your love for us
and we are constantly thrilled
by the touch of your grace;
we are moved by the colours
of the rainbow
and our hearts are captured
by the changing seasons.

We find joy in singing your praises
as we gather together as
the people of God.
We experience a sense
of well-being
as we fulfil the service we
offer in your name.

Yet we are bound to confess that
we rarely listen for your voice
and we keep you at a distance
in case you call our name.
Unlike Samuel who heard
your voice even though
he did not know you
we who profess to be your adopted
children keep our ears closed.

Lord,
open our minds to your voice
behind the news headlines
and make our hearts receptive
to your word in Scripture.
By your Holy Spirit, enable
us to seek spaces each day

when we will be still—and
simply listen to the voice
of our Lord. **Amen.**

Intercession

Mark 2:27–28

Father,
we pray for those who don't
live by the rules
and for those who choose
to live differently;
for those who welcome the stranger
whatever their colour,
religion, or race
and for those who reach out
with the hand of friendship
to those facing prejudice,
abuse, and rejection.
In a world ruled by greed
and self-interest,
help us to live out your love.

Father,
we pray for those who don't
live by the rules
and for those who choose
to live differently;
for those who choose to care
for their neighbour
whether they live across the
world or down the street
and for those whose compassion
for others is costly
as they care for the lonely, the
homeless, and the forgotten.
In a world ruled by greed
and self-interest,
help us to live out your love.

Father,
we pray for those who don't
live by the rules
and for those who choose
to live differently;
for those who see giving as a
part of their daily life
and for those for whom sharing
is also their worship of God;
for those who give of their time,
their skills, and their money
and for those who keep no record
of what they have done.
In a world ruled by greed
and self-interest,
help us to live out your love.

Father,
we pray for those who don't
live by the rules
and for those who choose
to live differently;
for politicians who refuse to
simply toe the party line
and for those whose concerns are
for the poor and for justice;
for those who break all the rules for
the sake of the people they serve
and for those ready to stand up for
what they believe to be right.
In a world ruled by greed
and self-interest,
help us to live out your love.

Father,
we pray for those who don't
live by the rules
and for those who choose
to live differently;
for those for whom each day
is a close walk with God
and for those who seek to work out
their faith in the arena of life;
for those who live with their feet
firmly on the ground each day

and for those with their focus on
God's presence each step of the way.
In a world ruled by greed
and self-interest,
help us to live out your love.

Father,
we pray for those who don't
live by the rules
and for those who choose
to live differently;
for those in the world of
business and finance
and for those whose faith and
ethics impact their decisions;
for those whose task it is to create
the wealth of the country
and for those who know
they are answerable to
God and his kingdom.
In a world ruled by greed
and self-interest,
help us to live out your love.

Father,
we pray for those who don't
live by the rules
and for those who choose
to live differently;
for those who choose to live simply
that others may simply live
and for those who reject the
unnecessary gathering
of possessions;
for those concerned for our planet
and willing to play their part
and for ordinary people who
remember there is a limit
to the size of the cake.
In a world ruled by greed
and self-interest,
help us to live out your love.

Father,
we pray for those who don't
live by the rules
and for those who choose
to live differently;
for those who look for opportunities
to share their faith
and for those who are seeking
ways to speak of Christ;
for those who are always looking
for moments of mission
and for those whose gentleness and
conviction offers a message of hope.
In a world ruled by greed
and self-interest,
help us to live out your love.

We bring our prayers in
the name of Jesus,
the one who didn't live by
the rules. **Amen.**

TENTH SUNDAY IN ORDINARY TIME

Prayer of Approach

Psalm 138

We come to worship the
God who is faithful
and we celebrate the one who
is Saviour and Lord.
We open our lips to sing praise
to the Lord on high
and we give glory to the
one who is with us.

We worship because you are
sovereign over all creation
and every living being
owes its life to you.
Our songs are for the one, before
whom all rulers will bow,

and our words of praise
come from hearts set alive
by your grace. **Amen.**

Thanksgiving

2 Corinthians 4:13–18

Lord,
there is a song in our hearts,
a song of thanksgiving
and by faith we must sing it
to the one Lord of all.
Our song is of the Saviour
who died and rose again
and we worship the King
who reigns over all.

Our faith in Jesus prompts us to
give the thanks he deserves
and knowing him leaves us no
choice but to honour his name.
It is because of who he is and
what he has done for us
that thanksgiving and worship
flow out of our hearts.

Lord,
we thank you for the purpose
and meaning you have
given to our lives
and for the touch of your
grace through which we
have received new life.
Your presence in our lives
fills us with joy that
overflows into worship
and your mercy has opened
the way into life before
the throne of grace.

How can we not thank you
for the change you have
brought to our days
and for the promise of forgiveness
and hope we do not deserve?
Each day we experience the
renewing power of the Holy Spirit
and we have the joy of
knowing you are changing
us from the inside out.

Lord,
we give thanks that our hope and
our peace are in you alone
and that these are not rewards
we have won but are gifts
of unconditional grace.
We still face the problems
and the pain from living
in this fallen world
but nothing can outweigh the
wonder and blessings we are
receiving daily at your hand.

You have opened our eyes
to see all creation as signs
of your presence
and we praise you because you
have opened our eyes of faith
to find you in the love of a friend;
to see you in the face of the hungry;
to discover you again in the
struggles of the homeless;
to experience your compassion
in those seeking justice;
to acknowledge your grace in the
hearts of the peacemakers.

Because you are Lord and
because you have found us
we come with hearts flooded with
so many reasons to give thanks.
Come touch our lives again
and heal our brokenness,

that the song of thanksgiving
will reach to the ends of
the earth. **Amen.**

Intercession
Mark 3:20–35

Lord,
we pray for those who make
mistakes in their lives
and for those who fail to see where
their mistakes are leading;
for those young people away
from home for the first
time in their lives
and for those starting college,
university, or a new sphere
of employment;
for those in danger of
being led astray into the
world of illegal drugs
and for those making the mistake
of simply following the crowd.
When the path is uncertain
come show us the way.

Lord,
we pray for those who make
mistakes in their lives
and for those who fail to see where
their mistakes are leading;
for those who place the highest
value on things of the moment
and for those who make the
mistake of valuing
only what they can touch and prove;
for those who see no value in faith,
hope, and offering forgiveness
and for those so damaged by abuse
they do not value themselves.
When the path is uncertain
come show us the way.

Lord,
we pray for those who make
mistakes in their lives
and for those who fail to see where
their mistakes are leading;
for those who are making a mistake
about the purpose of life
and for those who see life is to be
lived and all for themselves;
for those who are focusing their
days on the accumulation
of possessions
and for those who will arrive
empty-handed and empty
of life before God.
When the path is uncertain
come show us the way.

Lord,
we pray for those who make
mistakes in their lives
and for those who fail to see where
their mistakes are leading;
for those who see their
Christianity solely in terms
of church on a Sunday
and for those who are quite content
to respond to Christ's teaching
as they foolishly forget what matters
is their response to the teacher;
for those whose faith hasn't
grown or deepened since
they left Sunday school
and for those longing for a
hope that will guide them
through the storm.
When the path is uncertain
come show us the way.

Lord,
we pray for those who make
mistakes in their lives

and for those who fail to see where
their mistakes are leading;
for governments who try to
ignore the needs of the poor
and for those who allow justice
to become the gift of the rich;
for those whose power has
been tainted and their
influence corrupted
and for those whose example has
been the downfall of others.
When the path is uncertain
come show us the way.

Lord,
we pray for those who make
mistakes in their lives
and for those who fail to see where
their mistakes are leading;
for those who are role models
whether they planned it or not
and for those whose behaviour and
addictions influence the young;
for those who abuse their
success, wealth, and fame
and for those who speak out about
the mistakes they have made.
When the path is uncertain
come show us the way.

Lord,
we pray for those who make
mistakes in their lives
and for those who fail to see where
their mistakes are leading;
for ourselves and the mistakes we
have made that no one else knows
and for the wrong choices, the faults,
and errors that only God sees;
for those moments when
our words and our deeds
failed him completely
and for the cleansing, renewal,
and forgiveness his grace
freely offers to all.
When the path is uncertain
come show us the way.

We bring our prayers in
the name of Christ,
who alone is the way, the
truth, and the life. **Amen.**

ELEVENTH SUNDAY IN ORDINARY TIME

Praise

Psalm 20

Father,
the psalmist is so aware of
your presence he simply
cannot stop praising you.
He trusts you completely
and this hope echoes
throughout his message.
He sees the whole world as a
sign of your goodness and
a promise of your love.
Wherever he looks your
fingerprints and your creative
touch are everywhere.

He praises you for the comfort you
gave when he was in trouble
and he rejoices in the protection
he has received at your hand.
His great longing is to know
and love you more
that he might declare your
compassion to all the world.

Father,
we come bringing our desire
to honour your name

and to celebrate your presence
wherever we find ourselves.
We praise you for those moments
when we were alone—and
you were there;
when we were struggling to make
sense of what was happening
to us—and you were there;
when we were afraid of the
future—and you were there;
when we had lost hope—
and you were there;
when we had lost our way—
and you were there;
when we were hurting,
doubting, longing for you—
and you were there.

Father,
we praise you, our faithful,
sovereign creator,
whose presence makes us whole
and your ever-flowing
grace delivers
hope, peace, and healing
into our hearts.
Your sovereign will goes ahead of us
and leads us into those things you
planned from the beginning
and whilst others may put their
trust in human agencies
we will trust the living God. **Amen.**

Confession

1 Samuel 16:7

Father,
we can make ourselves look smart
and we can stand in the
shower or take a bath
but these things only make
us clean on the outside.
Samuel tells us that you
don't look at what can be
seen on the outside,
you look deep into our hearts and
reveal what is in our minds.
We understand that you see
the angry thoughts and
the selfish intentions
because not one tiny scrap of our
lives can be hidden from you.

We confess that we have tried
to hide many things from
the gaze of our friends
and we have even hoped that
if we ignored them you
might ignore them too!
Now is the moment to seek
your healing touch.
Now is the moment when we
seek your forgiveness.
Now is the moment when we cry,
come, Lord, and make us new!
The Lord says,
'Now is the moment to accept that
you have been forgiven.' **Amen.**

Intercession

Mark 4:30–32

Lord,
where there is fighting,
war, and destruction
and innocent children and
families are killed
we pray for a seed of hope
to be planted
that will grow into a lasting peace.
Lord of the planted seed,
come, give us the harvest.

Lord,
where people are lonely and alone

and have no one to share the
store of their memories,
we pray for a seed of
compassion to be planted
that will grow into joy
and contentment.
Lord of the planted seed,
come, give us the harvest.

Lord,
where evil men peddle their
drugs of addiction
and young lives are being
damaged and broken,
we pray for a seed of
resistance to be planted
that will grow into lives
free and whole.
Lord of the planted seed,
come, give us the harvest.

Lord,
where churches have lost hope
and forgotten their purpose
and there is no vision of
renewal and recovery,
we pray for a seed of new
growth to be planted
that will become a people
vibrant in witness and faith.
Lord of the planted seed,
come, give us the harvest.

Lord,
where people are cold, hungry,
and living on our streets
and no one seems to care about
those who feel forgotten,
we pray for a seed of caring
action to be planted,
that those who were forgotten will
know they have been found.
Lord of the planted seed,
come, give us the harvest.

Lord,
where there are those who
are uncertain of what
the future may bring
and others await the doctor's
diagnosis with fear,
we pray for a seed of peace, joy,
and hope to be planted,
that whatever comes they will
know they won't face it alone.
Lord of the planted seed,
come, give us the harvest.

Lord,
where the lead weight of
doubt and depression is
robbing people of peace
and where anxiety rules,
trapping many in its shackles
around their lives,
we pray for a seed of
freedom to be planted
that will bring a new sense
of release, courage,
and life that is beginning again.
Lord of the planted seed,
come, give us the harvest.

Lord,
whatever problems and
difficulties that we are
finding hard to overcome
and where we feel at the end of
our tether or the bottom has
dropped out of our lives,
we pray for a seed of hope,
healing, blessing, and
joy to be planted
that will open a new pathway

where Christ is calling us to
walk in his strength.
Lord of the planted seed,
come, give us the harvest.

We bring our prayers, ready
to plant some seeds
that Jesus may reap a great
harvest. **Amen.**

TWELFTH SUNDAY IN ORDINARY TIME

Prayer of Approach

Psalm 9:9–20

Father,
we have come carrying
burdens that have weighed
us down for years
and we have come longing for
your love to set us free.
There are memories of
rejection that still hurt
and times of deep disappointment
that still linger, causing pain.

We have come with all the baggage
that has hindered our living
and the moments of sadness
and loss that won't go away.
The journey we have been on has
been littered with many barriers
and we have come to you, the
one who knows how we feel.

We have come to worship
you, the Father of grace
and as we draw closer to you, come
lift our burden and set us free.
May this be the moment,
as we experience your
unconditional love,
that we enter the freedom, hope,
and blessing we long for. **Amen.**

Praise

Mark 4:41

Lord,
your disciples answered your
call to follow you
and they witnessed how you
dealt with people in need.
They had seen you heal the
sick in body and mind
and they had listened to your
teaching and seen you
restore a lame man.
Your disciples had been there when
you fed over five thousand people
and they had enjoyed the way you
answered your opponents.

All those things had been
for someone else—
what happened didn't affect
them, they simply watched.
Unfortunately by just being
among the onlookers
they somehow failed to take in the
authority and the power of Jesus.

But now it was real, there in the
boat, and it was all about them;
they were no longer just watching—
they were deeply involved!
It must have been a terrible
storm for those hard-bitten
fishermen to be scared;
they were really frightened out there
on the lake in a sinking boat.

They did the only thing that
they could: they woke Jesus
up to keep them afloat

and it was then they discovered
something about their leader
that blew them away.
They knew from their scriptures
that it was God alone
who ruled the waters
for he had the power to create them
and the power to make them still.

It was then the disciples were
struck by the truth that it
was God in the boat
and his being there brought
them hope, peace, and
saving from death.
'Who is this?' they asked each other
as their faith began to grow
and they began a journey
with Jesus that brought
their trust to full bloom.

Father,
we praise you that when we
least expect it you enter
our moments of despair
and you reveal your
presence to heal, save, and
restore us to peace.
The truth is that it is only
when our need is personal
that our faith is tested
and your grace-filled presence meets
us when the hole is very deep.

Somehow it seems that only when
faith must be put into action
that it changes from a set
of beliefs to life-giving,
life-renewing power.

We praise you now and we
will praise you for ever
for you alone are the one who
meets our deepest need—
to find and use faith. **Amen.**

Intercession

1 Samuel 17:45

Father,
we want to talk to you about those
facing great obstacles in their lives
and for those struggling to
overcome the problems
they are experiencing;
for those whose illness is life-
threatening and they are
fearful about tomorrow
and for those whose condition
is life-changing and they
wonder how they will cope;
for those who know that their
number of days are now but a few
and for those finding courage
in the presence of God's
never-ending love.
In the name of the living God,
come, show us your power.

Father,
we want to talk to you about those
facing great obstacles in their lives
and for those struggling to
overcome the problems
they are experiencing;
for those whose homes have been
repeatedly bombed to destruction
and for those who grieve for the
family and friends they have lost;
for those whose lives have been
wrecked by the ruthless
action of terrorists
and for those who seek to wreak
terror, that their obstacle of
hate may be overcome.

In the name of the living God,
come, show us your power.

Father,
we want to talk to you
about those facing great
obstacles in their lives
and for those struggling to
overcome the problems
they are experiencing;
for governments around the
world faced with an ever-
growing tide of migrants
and for those seeking humane
ways of responding to the
multitude fleeing in fear;
for world leaders showing little
compassion as their people
reject their intentions to help
and for those who have risked all
to find safety and find the door
slammed shut in their face.
In the name of the living God,
come, show us your power.

Father,
we want to talk to you
about those facing great
obstacles in their lives
and for those struggling to
overcome the problems
they are experiencing;
for those imprisoned without
trial and who have little
expectation to be set free
and for those who keep their
names and their injustice
before the court of the world;
for those locked away from the
eyes of nations for their faith
in democracy and truth
and for those persecuted for their
faith and ostracised by their
family for naming Jesus as Lord.
In the name of the living God,
come, show us your power.

Father,
we want to talk to you about those
facing great obstacles in their lives
and for those struggling to
overcome the problems
they are experiencing;
for those without meaningful
employment who rely on
gifts from the food bank
and for those treated as
scroungers and find even the
benefits they need are cut;
for those in our nation of great
wealth who are sleeping rough
with a cardboard box for their home
and for compassion, action, and
hope to replace the silent shrug
of self-centred inaction.
In the name of the living God,
come, show us your power.

Father,
we want to talk to you about those
facing great obstacles in their lives
and for those struggling to
overcome the problems
they are experiencing;
for those with a secret that has
haunted the whole of their lives
and for those now finding the
courage to speak about the
abuse they suffered long ago;
for those whose attempts to build a
relationship have been thwarted
by the pain deep inside

and for those whose apparent
strength and the normality they
wear mask their suffering.
In the name of the living God,
come, show us your power.

Father,
we want to talk to you about those
facing great obstacles in their lives
and for those struggling to
overcome the problems
they are experiencing;
for those whose longings to
find faith hit the barriers
of doubt and despair
and for those seeking solutions
to all of their questions
before they can believe;
for those who are aware
of what it will cost once
they say they believe
and for those who are taking
the first step as they respond
to Jesus as Lord.
In the name of the living God,
come, show us your power.

In the silence, hold before God the
obstacles you and others are facing
and ask for courage, grace,
strength, and the hope that
comes from the Lord.

silence

In the name of the living God,
come, show us your power.

We bring our prayers to God,
who has the power, love, and
grace to save us all. **Amen.**

THIRTEENTH SUNDAY IN ORDINARY TIME

Prayer of Approach

Mark 5:36

Lord,
we come to be touched by you
and set free by your presence;
we come in our weakness
for your strength to renew us;
we come hurting inside—
a pain that only you see;
we come hiding in the crowd
for we long to remain anonymous;
we come overwhelmed by
concern for others
ready to cry out for those
all around us;
we come unwanted,
unclean, and rejected
knowing that your grace
embraces all;
we come as we are for we can
come no other way.
Our coming is a cry for help
that only you hear.

Lord,
we come in Jesus' name
to offer songs of worship
and prayers of hope.

Come meet us, Lord,
and set us free,
that we may worship you
here and everywhere
for the rest of our lives. **Amen.**

Thanksgiving

2 Corinthians 8:8

Father,
in our world of selfishness and greed

where self-interest and
personal aggrandisement
are the goals of so many
we rejoice to give thanks for
those who just give.

We thank you for those who
give of themselves
to serve others
and for those who are
working tirelessly
to bring health and healing to many.

We thank you for those
who risk their lives
preventing crime and
arresting wrongdoers;
for those who seek to act justly
in their role as magistrates,
probation officers,
and volunteers with
Victim Support.

We thank you for those who
open young minds
to the wonders of life
and to set them searching
for those things
still waiting to be found.
We thank you for those who use
their gifts of compassion
to listen to the pain people
have deep inside
and for those with a heart for
those who are less abled
as they help others reclaim
their meaning and value.

We thank you for those
who give sacrificially
for others around the world to
have food on their table
and for those whose research
and experiments
have brought hope to a sick world.

We thank you, Father, that
your love never varies
and that we can be certain
your grace is for all.
We thank you that those with
the gifts that were needed
were moved by your Spirit
to use what they had
for the good of their neighbour
and the glory of your name.

We thank you supremely for
your gift to us in Jesus—
freedom, forgiveness, and the
chance to start again.
The gift of your Son brought
us healing and hope
and we can never cease thanking you
for all that you are and for all
you have done. **Amen.**

Intercession

Psalm 130

Father,
we pray for those who cry
out from the depths
and for those who cry
for good cause;
for those who cry out from
the depths of loss
and for those who ache for those
they loved but see no more;
for those who regret what
they said and did
and for those who suffer remorse
for what they failed to do.
Lord, hear our voice
and answer our cry for hope.

Father,
we pray for those who cry
out from the depths
and for those who cry
for good cause;
for those who weep because
they feel unworthy
and for those trained from their
earliest days to fear failure;
for those who stopped trying to
avoid a deluge of criticism
and for those who now look back
to what might have been.
Lord, hear our voice
and answer our cry for hope.

Father,
we pray for those who cry
out from the depths
and for those who cry
for good cause;
for those who are sinking to
the depths of addiction
and for those who can't break
the shackles that bind them;
for those whose family have left the
merry-go-round of false promises
and for groups like Alcoholics
Anonymous that can help
addicts out of their hole.
Lord, hear our voice
and answer our cry for hope.

Father,
we pray for those who cry
out from the depths
and for those who cry
for good cause;
for those who languish in
prison as a result of the
mistakes they have made
and for their families bearing the
cost and suffering the shame;
for those who cry out from
their prison of loneliness
and for those who weep alone
where no one can see.
Lord, hear our voice
and answer our cry for hope.

Father,
we pray for those who cry
out from the depths
and for those who cry
for good cause;
for those who give voice to those
whose cries are not heard
and for those who weep for
those with no food for
their children today;
for those who cry from the
depths of their poverty
and for those who speak out against
corruption in high places.
Lord, hear our voice
and answer our cry for hope.

Father,
we pray for those who cry
out from the depths
and for those who cry
for good cause;
for those who cry aloud for
the saving of our planet
and for those who challenge
governments to act now;
for those who speak for the
earth's endangered animals
and for those with the power
but not the will to respond.
Lord, hear our voice
and answer our cry for hope.

Father,
we pray for those who cry
out from the depths
and for those who cry for good cause;
for those whose weak whisper is
heard from their hospice bed
and for those too young to be dying
but whose courage speaks to us all;
for those whose life-changing illness
is robbing them of their dreams
and for those whose smile from the
wheelchair gives hope to us all.
Lord, hear our voice
and answer our cry for hope.

Father,
we pray for those who cry
out from the depths
and for those who cry for good cause;
for those who cannot remember
our face or our name
and for those who no longer are
the people we once knew;
for those who treat us as a
member of staff or a stranger
and for those who weep deep
within for what has been lost.
Lord, hear our voice
and answer our cry for hope.

In the stillness, we pray for those
for whom we are concerned
and for ourselves and our own depths
of hurt, questions, and doubts.

silence

Lord, hear our voice
and answer our cry for hope.

We bring our prayers in
the name of Jesus,
who wept and weeps for
us all. **Amen.**

FOURTEENTH SUNDAY IN ORDINARY TIME

Prayer of Approach

2 Samuel 5:1–5

Lord,
we have come prepared
to meet the King
and to offer him the glory
that is his by right.
You are the king of all creation
and every creature on earth
owes its being to you.

On earth, monarchs seek to
divide and conquer
and to take land and
people by force.
You are King of all things
and all people by right
and your will is to make
all people one.

You are the Servant King
and you rule by serving your people.
You washed the feet of
your disciples
and shared a meal with the
lowest of the low.

You are King of a servant people
and our task is to
worship our Lord.
We are your people, your body.
Come, Lord, and enjoy the
praises we bring. **Amen.**

Praise
Psalm 48

What a privilege is ours!
To stand in the very presence
of the Almighty
and to speak with the one
to whom all things belong!

To not only stand in the
presence of the living God
but to experience being loved
in a way that is deeper, higher,
and more wonderful
than any love we have known before.

No worship is too extravagant
to offer the King of Kings
and there is no song that
has been written
that can possibly do justice
to your glory.
If we ask what is so amazing
about grace,
that answer is simple—you are!

The whole of heaven
and the fullness of the universe
are yours to command
and you could have
chosen anywhere
to be the centre of your operations.
But wonder of wonders—
you have made our hearts
your home base.

How can we not praise you for
the God of grace that you are?
How can we not raise our voices
in adoration of the King?
How can we not thank you for
adopting us into your family?
How can we not give you
our worship, our hearts,
and our lives?
They are a thank offering of glory to
the one who is all in all. **Amen.**

Intercession
Mark 6:6b–13

Father,
we pray for those who like
the disciples are setting out
on a new role in life;
for those recently married and are
discovering how two can be one
and for the new things about each
other, to love and to cherish;
for those who after many years
together are still learning
the meaning of love
and for those finding joy
in making space for each
other's plans and dreams.
You open the door
to a new way of living.

Father,
we pray for those who like
the disciples are setting out
on a new role in life;
for young people away from home
for the first time in their lives
and for those starting a new life at
school, college, or university;
for those leaving school seeking
to find their way in the
world of employment
and for those whose lack of
qualifications is causing them a
struggle in reaching their dream.
You open the door
to a new way of living.

Father,
we pray for those who like
the disciples are setting out
on a new role in life;
for those elected to serve their local
community as local councillors
and for those who have
been chosen to represent
others in parliament;
for those who are discovering
the power of vested interests
and for those who are struggling
under the weight of expectations.
You open the door
to a new way of living.

Father,
we pray for those who like
the disciples are setting out
on a new role in life;
for those who are starting out
on the road of parenthood
and for those for whom the
sense of responsibility
weighs them down;
for those who are thrilled with
their role of being grandparents
and for those who are struggling
to cope with the demands
of childminding.
You open the door
to a new way of living.

Father,
we pray for those who like
the disciples are setting out
on a new role in life;
for those who are suddenly alone,
having lost someone they loved
and for those who hide from the
pain by keeping themselves
as busy as possible;
for those who are recently retired
and are finding the time on
their hands a great burden
and for those whose redundancy
and unemployment have robbed
them of their own self-worth.
You open the door
to a new way of living.

Father,
we pray for those who like
the disciples are setting out
on a new role in life;
for members of the armed
forces who are finding new
strength and comradeship
and for those who signed up
to find a new purpose but
never expected to fight;
for those who find themselves in the
midst of the world's trouble spots
and for those who return
home disabled in body,
mind, and spirit.
You open the door
to a new way of living.

Father,
we pray for those who like
the disciples are setting out
on a new role in life;
for ourselves and the new
areas of voluntary work to
which you are calling us
and for those places of service
where you are sending us but
we would rather not go.
In the silence, pray for those
known to you who are facing
great changes in their lives.

silence

You open the door
to a new way of living.

We bring our prayers in
the name of Jesus,
who goes with us through every
door we face. **Amen.**

FIFTEENTH SUNDAY IN ORDINARY TIME

Prayer of Approach

Psalm 24

Lord,
there are times when we
forget why we are here
and our focus is on ourselves
and not on you;
our hearts and minds are
full of many things
but giving you glory is not
always the most important.

Lord,
prepare us now to desire
nothing but your honour
and to seek only that we may
worship you alone;
come now and renew our minds
that we may praise you
and empower us, by your Holy
Spirit, to meet with you.

You are the Lord of all things
we can see, hear, and touch
and even the whole world is not
a sufficient offering to you.
Come, cleanse our hearts and
set us free to praise you
and to offer the praises of lives set
on fire by your love. **Amen.**

Praise

Ephesians 1:3–14

Lord,
every time we are aware
of your presence we are
overwhelmed by joy
and to come together as your people
we feel the touch of your grace.
How easily we take you for granted
and fail to remember your glory
and the Holy Spirit reveals
the utter inadequacy of our
fine words of praise.

You alone are the source of every
blessing that enriches our days
and from you flows the everlasting
stream of power and glory.
We have done nothing to deserve
one scrap of your grace
and we can only come humbly
before confessing your mercy.

We have been given the awesome
privilege of calling you our Father
and the immense blessing in being
your children is dawning upon us.
How can it be that you who
need nothing and no one
choose to love us
and to love us so completely
that you have adopted
us by your grace?

Our songs of praise pour
out from hearts ablaze
with your Holy Spirit
and our prayers of thanksgiving
are shot through with great joy.
We cannot grasp the wonder
of your purposes for us

and we have yet to comprehend that
we were always part of your will.

In Christ you have touched our lives
in ways beyond our expectations
and in him you have bound us
ever more closely to yourself.
He is your word of life that
again and again reveals
the power of your love
and from before the dawn
of all things he alone was
your truth and mercy.

We praise you for the good
news of your gift of freedom,
hope, and renewal
as through his life, death, and
resurrection the door of the
kingdom was opened.
By your Holy Spirit, all your promises
of grace are fully guaranteed
and by his power we are enabled
to sing the song of heaven
here on earth. **Amen.**

Intercession

Mark 6:14–29

Father,
we pray for those like Herod who
live solely for themselves
and for those who make their
plans with little thought of
the impact on others;
for those whose positions of
power could bring hope
and opportunity to all
and for those whose deep-
seated corruption continues
to favour the few.
Lord of truth and justice,
touch us with your grace.

Father,
we pray for those like
Herodias whose bitterness
was consuming her life
and for those whose hurt and
sense of injustice are robbing
them of peace and love;
for those who have borne grudges for
mistakes and misunderstandings
long since forgotten
and for those whose relationships
have been damaged through
the failure to forgive.
Lord of truth and justice,
touch us with your grace.

Father,
we pray for those like Salome
who are weak and are pawns
in the hands of others
and for those who opt for the
easy way without a thought
of the deeper implications;
for those so focused on themselves
and their comfort that they
ignore the pain of their neighbour
and for those whose years of being
dominated and controlled has left
them with little life of their own.
Lord of truth and justice,
touch us with your grace.

Father,
we pray for those like the crowd
lulled into silence by drink,
lust, and the desire of power
and for those who know right
from wrong but whose inaction
adds to the evil that is done;
for those who refuse to stand up
and be counted and so contribute
to the power of injustice

and for those more concerned
to be in favour than to speak
out against what is wrong.
Lord of truth and justice,
touch us with your grace.

Father,
we pray for those like John the
Baptist who stood up for
what he knew to be right
and for those daring to pay the
cost of being a lone voice
against a growing tide of hate;
for those prepared to stand firm on
the truth of God in the midst
of the shifting sands of greed
and for those who have faced
ridicule, violence, and abuse rather
than deny naming Jesus as Lord.
Lord of truth and justice,
touch us with your grace.

Father,
we pray for those like John the
Baptist's disciples who did not
hide their commitment to him
and for those whose names and
faces are lost in the crowd but
who are God's salt to the earth;
for those who offer hope in words
only heard by the few and actions
that give strength to many
and for ourselves, that our lives,
words, and deeds will enable others
to enter the kingdom of grace.
Lord of truth and justice,
touch us with your grace.

We bring our prayers in the
name of the King,
that by his grace we may be part of
the answer to our prayers. **Amen.**

SIXTEENTH SUNDAY IN ORDINARY TIME

Prayer of Approach

Psalm 89:26

Lord,
you are the rock on which we stand
and this is the place where
we can begin again.
In you we find our hope
and in your presence we
have new strength.
You call us to yourself and declare
that you are our Father
and we are overwhelmed to be
called your precious possession.

Lord,
in the stillness look into our hearts
and reach down into our memories
that we may be clean.

silence

We stand before the Lord
of all creation
and we will worship our
Saviour and Lord. **Amen.**

Thanksgiving

Mark 6:30–34

Father,
we live such busy lives,
leaving ourselves little
time to be still.
From our youngest days we were
encouraged to work hard
and our earliest memories are of
doing more and more things.
We see life as moving from
one activity to the next
and we are left feeling guilty
if we have nothing to do!

We thank you that you created us
to be human beings and
not human doings.
It was never your plan that we
should be always on the go
but that to sit, to contemplate,
and to reflect are part
of our humanity.
We are told that you have a
purpose for each of our lives
and we have interpreted that to
mean even greater activity.

When we read of those who knew
you and served you in the past
we discover that they made time
and space to be with you.
Moses waited at the burning bush
and Isaiah came to worship
in the temple;
Elijah rested on Mount Horeb
and David wrote his
songs of praise.

Few people have been as
busy as Jesus—
healing, teaching, confronting
misuse of God's house.
He sent his disciples out on mission
and he rejoiced with them as they
reported what they had done.
Then, in the midst of their busyness
Jesus said it was time to be still.

We thank you that you not
only want us to serve;
you call us to be still in
your presence.
We thank you not only for
the command to go
but for the requirement to be
human and to walk with you.

We thank you for the gift
of rest and renewal
and that it is your will that
we live not as machines.
Our gathering to worship you
and meditate on your grace
is part of being your precious children
and disciples of Christ. **Amen.**

Intercession

Ephesians 2:11–22

Father,
we pray for those who often
do not feel included
and for those for whom there
is a barrier to overcome;
for those who are poor and
have limited resources
and for those whose poverty
restricts their opportunities;
for those who feel excluded from
the luxuries others enjoy
and for those whose daily concern
is feeding their family.
Lord of the broken barrier,
break down the walls we build.

Father,
we pray for those who often
do not feel included
and for those for whom there
is a barrier to overcome;
for those who are single in a
family-orientated society
and for those who live alone with
neighbours they no longer know;
for those who are now single
through bereavement or breakup
and for those for whom it is more
expensive now living alone.
Lord of the broken barrier,
break down the walls we build.

Father,
we pray for those who often
do not feel included
and for those for whom there
is a barrier to overcome;
for those for whom their colour
remains a barrier to inclusion
and for those whose ethnic origin
means they are facing abuse;
for those who came looking for
peace and not prejudice
and for those fleeing a war zone
only to face daily attack.
Lord of the broken barrier,
break down the walls we build.

Father,
we pray for those who often
do not feel included
and for those for whom there
is a barrier to overcome;
for those whose disability is
compounded by a selfish society
and for those struggling to live in
a world of the fit and the able;
for those who are daily neglected
by those who can see and hear
and for those who are shunned
and ridiculed because of
their mental illness.
Lord of the broken barrier,
break down the walls we build.

Father,
we pray for those who often
do not feel included
and for those for whom there
is a barrier to overcome;
for those who are Christians in a
nation that has lost its faith
and for those facing insults and
derision at work and also at home;
for those whose stand for
their faith in Jesus can
even put them in court
and for those around the
world facing persecution
and jail for their faith.
Lord of the broken barrier,
break down the walls we build.

Father,
we pray for those who often
do not feel included
and for those for whom there
is a barrier to overcome;
for those whose serious health
problems are locking
them out of life
and for those wracked with pain as
they struggle to cope each day;
for those whose anguish and pain
is a result of a broken friendship
and for those whose every
attempt at reconciliation
is rebuffed or ignored.
Lord of the broken barrier,
break down the walls we build.

Father,
we pray for those who often
do not feel included
and for those for whom there
is a barrier to overcome;
for those known to us whom
we long to be closer to God
and for those who no longer
meet for worship because of
the hurt they received;
for the barriers we erect to keep
God and his call at a distance
and for ourselves and the walls
we have built that keep
others out of our lives.

Lord of the broken barrier,
break down the walls we build.

We bring our prayers in
the name of Jesus,
who died and was raised to
make us all one. **Amen.**

SEVENTEENTH SUNDAY IN ORDINARY TIME

Praise

Ephesians 3:14–21

Father,
you are amazing! Utterly,
absolutely amazing!
We are blinded by your purity
and we are forced to our
knees by your majesty.
Your glory reaches across the
vast expanse of the universe
and it is your power that gives
life to all your creatures.
There is no other in all of creation
to whom we owe thanksgiving
and you alone are the source of
light in our darkest moments.

It is as the words of praise
form in our minds
that we realise that they do not
reach the heights of heaven;
there is no song we can sing that
can speak of your fatherly care
and we can only be left
wondering at your gentleness
and compassion.

This is our God: the one
who holds all things in
the palm of his hand.
This is our God: the one to
whom past, present, and
the future are one.
This is our God: the one whose
glory shines from one end
of eternity to the other.
This is our God: the one who
in Jesus speaks to us of a
love that is absolute.
This is our God: the one who
through his Son pours out
grace that is unconditional.
This is our God: the one who reaches
deep into our pain to set us free.
This is our God: the one who desires
that we call him 'our Father'.

Father,
we praise you for your desire
to go on reaching out
and reaching down
to lift us up, to set us on
our feet, and to lead us to
your throne of grace.
Your purposes for us are
greater than anything we
could ever have imagined
and your deepest desire is
that through your Son we
may grow closer to you.
Our hopes, plans, and dreams
are puny imitations of
your design for us
and we have experienced
nothing to compare with
your stupendous love.
Our only wish is that you will
hold us when we are falling
and that you will pick us up
when we are down.
May our lives be so touched
by your grace

that the whole world may
see your glory
and come and join in the song
for the glory of the King
whose name is Our Father. **Amen.**

Confession
Psalm 14
Lord,
the psalmist speaks of those
who are foolish.
Their foolishness is not that
they deny your existence
but that they discount your interest
or concern for your world.

We gather to declare our faith in you
and to offer our songs of
praise for your glory;
we rejoice in the hope
we have in Christ
and we come with thanksgiving
for your mighty grace.

Lord,
we come to confess that though
we worship you here
too often our praises end at
the door of the church
and our thanksgiving does not
flow out into our daily lives.
There are times when our lives do
not mark us out as people of faith
and too often our words of trust are
not borne out by our actions.

We are here that your Holy
Spirit might come as a
mighty rushing wind
and that the fire of your
cleansing might be evident
in our walk with Jesus.
May we so experience your
love, grace, and power in
the midst of our worship
that our daily lives will be
shot through with the joy
of your presence. **Amen.**

Intercession
John 6:1–15
Lord,
we pray for those who are
hungry for love
and for those who have never
known true compassion;
for those who never truly felt wanted
and for those simply longing for
unconditional acceptance.
Come, Lord, in your grace
and make us whole.

Lord,
we pray for those who are
hungry for faith
and for those who will only accept
the things they can prove;
for those filled with doubts,
uncertainties, and questions
and for those yet to discover
that you only want them
to take the first step.
Come, Lord, in your grace
and make us whole.

Lord,
we pray for those who are
hungry for forgiveness
and for those with hidden baggage
they have carried for years;
for those who feel too
unworthy for your cleansing
to reach down to them

and for those who still do
not realise you nailed their
sins to your cross.
Come, Lord, in your grace
and make us whole.

Lord,
we pray for those who are
hungry for hope
and for those for whom the bottom
has dropped out of their world;
for those for whom each day
seems darker than the last
and for those who long to
experience the light of
Christ in their hearts.
Come, Lord, in your grace
and make us whole.

Lord,
we pray for those who are
hungry for food
and for those who see their children
dying for lack of bread;
for those who cannot read and are
locked out of food for their minds
and for those who are desiring
renewal though the power
of the Holy Spirit.
Come, Lord, in your grace
and make us whole.

Lord,
we pray for those who are
hungry for power
and are willing to do anything
to reach their prized goal;
for those for whom power will
be a blessing to others
and for those for whom it will
ultimately bring corruption.
Come, Lord, in your grace
and make us whole.

Lord,
we pray for those who are
hungry for health
and for those whose every day is a
journey of pain and discomfort;
for those awaiting in great
trepidation the doctor's diagnosis
and for those who move us to tears
by the courage they demonstrate.
Come, Lord, in your grace
and make us whole.

Lord,
we pray for ourselves and
our hunger deep inside
and for the plans and dreams we
had that came to nothing;
for the questions that fill our
minds and rob us of our sleep
and for the hunger we have to
see others made whole
and brought to a knowledge of
Jesus as their Saviour and Lord.
Come, Lord, in your grace
and make us whole.

In the name of Jesus,
who always comes in grace. **Amen.**

EIGHTEENTH SUNDAY IN ORDINARY TIME

Prayer of Approach

Psalm 74:12–17

Lord,
you are our King of all the ages
and the sovereign over all things.
You are the source of all that is good
and the blessings we receive
come from your grace.

Lord,
you are our King of all the ages
and your holiness shines
in the darkness.
You are the creator of beauty,
love, and compassion
and we are overwhelmed when
we consider your generosity.

Lord,
you are our King of all the ages
and we have come to worship you.
You are the heart and
soul of our lives
and we delight to give you
all the glory. **Amen.**

Confession

John 6:24–35

Lord,
we have chosen the wrong bread.
You offered us the bread of heaven
but we have chosen the
bread of life.

Lord,
we have chosen the wrong bread.
You offered us the bread
that brings healing
but we have chosen a way that
damages your world.

Lord,
we have chosen the wrong bread.
You offered us the bread of
compassion for others
but we declared that charity
began at home.

Lord,
we have chosen the wrong bread.
You offered us the bread
of forgiveness
but we have refused to
forgive one another.

Lord,
we have chosen the wrong bread.
You offered us the bread
of faith in Jesus
but we have preferred to
trust in ourselves.

Lord,
we have chosen the wrong bread.
You offered us the bread
of a new beginning
but we have found it hard
to walk a new road.

Lord,
we have chosen the wrong bread.
You offer us love, hope,
and renewal.
By your grace alone we
chose to reach out
to take hold of your hand
that we may know
what it means to be made new.

This is God's word to us:
'The record of your wrong
choices has been wiped away.
Come now, and receive the
bread of eternal life.' **Amen.**

Intercession

Ephesians 4:11–13

Lord,
we pray for those with
different gifts
and for those whose gifts
we take for granted;

for those who are plumbers,
electricians, and joiners
and for those who clean windows
or bring mail to our door;
for those who design and
create new buildings
and for those whose gifts bring
comfort to our home.
Lord, may all your gifts be used
to bring you glory.

Lord,
we pray for those with different gifts
and for those whose gifts
we take for granted;
for those who are poets,
writers, and musicians
and for artists whose use of
colour enriches our days;
for those who are actors,
comedians, and filmmakers
and for their gifts which bring
new insights and challenge.
Lord, may all your gifts be used
to bring you glory.

Lord,
we pray for those with different gifts
and for those whose gifts
we take for granted;
for those who are porters,
secretaries, and technicians
and for those whose work in our
hospitals is largely unseen;
for radiographers, pharmacists,
and physiotherapists
as they use their skills to bring
healing and recovery.
Lord, may all your gifts be used
to bring you glory.

Lord,
we pray for those with different gifts
and for those whose gifts
we take for granted;
for those who drive road rollers,
bulldozers, and diggers
and for those who repair our
roads and our pavements;
for those who build sewers, lay
cables, and provide internet access
and for those whose gifts we rely
on for the utilities we need.
Lord, may all your gifts be used
to bring you glory.

Lord,
we pray for those with different gifts
and for those whose gifts
we take for granted;
for hymn and songwriters, organists,
and members of music groups
and for those who use their
gifts to enrich our worship
and our praise of God;
for those who ensure that
the church is warm, safe,
and in good repair
and for those who go in the name
of God's people to the sick, the
lonely, and the housebound.
Lord, may all your gifts be used
to bring you glory.

Lord,
we pray for those with different gifts
and for those whose gifts
we take for granted;
for those who work in shops
and the supermarket
and for those who stock the shelves
or meet us at the checkout;

for those who work in factories,
farms and offices
and for those bringing the things we
need in the wagons they drive.
Lord, may all your gifts be used
to bring you glory.

Lord,
we pray for those with different gifts
and for those whose gifts
we take for granted;
for those who volunteer to
work in charity shops
and for those who give of their
time with Citizens Advice;
for those who give of their time
in youth organisations
and for those who use their gifts
to help adults learn to read.
Lord, may all your gifts be used
to bring you glory.

Lord,
we pray for those with different gifts
and for those whose gifts
we take for granted;
for ourselves, that we may use
the gifts we have received
and for a new understanding that
God's gifts are only on loan;
for those we know who use their
time and skills to serve others
and for those who are serving Christ
even when they don't know him.
Lord, may all your gifts be used
to bring you glory.

We bring our prayers in the
name of the Servant King,
whose gifts we have received
to use for the glory of
his name. **Amen.**

NINETEENTH SUNDAY IN ORDINARY TIME

Praise

Psalm 130

Lord,
we praise you for being so
forgetful about our mistakes
and for the promise to wipe
the slate completely clean.
This is not because you don't
care what we say or do
nor is it a sign of any weakness
in your nature.

The Bible tells us that you are
an incredibly holy God
and that you are perfect beyond
any perfection we have known.
Your glory, splendour, and majesty
are outside our comprehension
and even the songs of heaven cannot
do justice to your authority.

We praise you that our holy
God was prepared to
stoop to the depths
and to reach down to lift us up
that we might stand before
the throne of grace.
For you are more than simply
our creator God who
designed everything
and you are greater than all the
vastness of your universe.

We praise you that this world bears
not only your fingerprints
but its very existence finds its origin
in your overwhelming love.
It is grace, your totally
undeserved self-giving,
that drives you to love

and we see that grace reaching
its zenith as your Son is
crowned on Calvary.

As the psalmist declared, if you
kept a record of this world's sin
there would be not one of
us who could stand before
you, our holy God.
But in Christ your grace comes in
the mightiest flood in all creation
and this is not a torrent of
judgement, it is the on-
rushing power of love.

Wonderful, wonderful God, we
praise you not only for your glory
but that your majesty is clothed in
the healing touch of forgiveness.
For the truth remains that whenever
we hear or feel your judgement
we know it is simply the
fanfare that heralds your
grace-filled love. **Amen.**

Confession

Ephesians 4:25–5:2

Father,
we confess that often the
things we say and do
fail to bring honour to your name
and our attitudes and behaviour
cease to be a sign of your
presence in our hearts.

Father,
we confess that often our lives
do not echo the love of Jesus
and our self-centredness
is a poor example
of how the people of God
were intended to live.

Father,
we confess that our insisting
on our own way
and our selfishness that
damages our fellowship
must break your heart and
make you weep.

Father,
we confess that we have used our
lips to speak angry words
and we have allowed our
ears to listen to gossip.
We have filled our minds
with unworthy thoughts
and we have ignored the cries of
those you sent us to help.

Father,
turn to us again and remake
us in your image
that every part of our lives
might speak of your glory
and our every thought be
focused on you.

The Father says that he has loved
us from the beginning
and he loves us still.
In Christ he shouts aloud
that we are forgiven
and in the Holy Spirit he gives the
power to be made new. **Amen.**

Intercession

2 Samuel 18:31–33

Father,
we pray for those who are
receiving unwelcome news
and for those whose lives are
being turned upside down;

for young people whose
  examination results are not
  what they hoped for
and for those whose plans for their
  future seem totally wrecked;
for those leaving further
  education with the
  qualifications they needed
and for those who are joining the
  fruitless search for employment.
Father, share their journey today
and give them hope.

Father,
we pray for those who are
  receiving unwelcome news
and for those whose lives are
  being turned upside down;
for those who have received
  their consultant's diagnosis
and for those who are facing
  a life-changing situation;
for those whose illness has huge
  implications for their lives
and for those confronted with
  a time of uncertainty.
Father, share their journey today
and give them hope.

Father,
we pray for those who are
  receiving unwelcome news
and for those whose lives are
  being turned upside down;
for those who face death
  every day as they live the
  midst of a war zone
and for those who are victims as
  they long for the fighting to end;
for those who face the constant
  threat of terrorist action
and for those whose peace has
  been lost by the atrocities
  of their neighbours.
Father, share their journey today
and give them hope.

Father,
we pray for those who are
  receiving unwelcome news
and for those whose lives are
  being turned upside down;
for those whose harvests
  have failed as the droughts
  have ruined their crops
and for those who have nothing
  with which to feed their children;
for those who watch helplessly as
  family and friends die of starvation
and for those who look to the
  tables of the rich hoping some
  crumbs may be given.
Father, share their journey today
and give them hope.

Father,
we pray for those who are
  receiving unwelcome news
and for those whose lives are
  being turned upside down;
for those whose loss of employment
  has brought stress to their home
and for those whose redundancy is
  robbing them of their self-respect;
for those for whom the loss
  of their home is becoming
  a very real danger
and for those needing several
  part-time jobs just to put
  food on the table.
Father, share their journey today
and give them hope.

Father,
we pray for those who are
receiving unwelcome news
and for those whose lives are
being turned upside down;
for those facing the pain of
losing someone they loved
and for those who dread returning
to their home that feels empty;
for those who have no one
with whom they can share
precious memories
and for those who are losing their
memories of places and people.
Father, share their journey today
and give them hope.

Father,
we pray for those who are
receiving unwelcome news
and for those whose lives are
being turned upside down;
for those whose hopes for a family
of their own have been dashed
and for those who weep inside when
they see others with children;
for those whose lives were torn apart
because of a broken promise
and for those finding it hard to
trust anyone because of the
abuse they have suffered.
Father, share their journey today
and give them hope.

Father,
we pray for those who are
receiving unwelcome news
and for those whose lives are
being turned upside down;
for those we know who are
struggling just to cope each day
and for those who are hurting with
a pain that no one ever sees;
for ourselves and the fears, doubts,
and worries that we carry inside
and for the courage to face
every day in the knowledge
we face it with Jesus.
Father, share their journey today
and give them hope.

We bring our prayers in
the name of Jesus,
who alone is the source
of all hope. **Amen.**

TWENTIETH SUNDAY IN ORDINARY TIME

Praise

Psalm 111

For the glory of his name
which transforms our lives
and the wonder of his love that
gives value to our days;
for the joy with which he fills
our hearts and our minds
and the song of thanksgiving
that springs from our lips;
let us praise the Lord.
We will praise the Lord.

For the wonder of his creation
which moves us to praise
and the love that brought
all things into being;
for the view from the mountaintop
that takes our breath away
and the beauty of quiet valleys
that fills us with joy;
let us praise the Lord.
We will praise the Lord.

For the thrill of reading
the Scriptures and his
message of hope
and the grace that flows from his
Word and changes our lives;
for the life, death, and resurrection
of Jesus that is his good news
and the fruit and the gifts of the
Spirit to bring renewal for all;
let us praise the Lord.
We will praise the Lord.

For the gift of life's journey
that begins each new day
and for those who have travelled
with us every step of the way;
for those we have loved who
made life so precious
and for those who loved us
when we were weak and
when we were wrong;
let us praise the Lord.
We will praise the Lord.

For the work of scientists who
work for the good of us all
and for the discoveries that
open our eyes and minds;
for the wonder we see in
the vastness of space
and for the beauty all around
us that enriches us still;
let us praise the Lord.
We will praise the Lord.

For the work of artists and
writers; for their use of
colour, shape, and words
and for those who enable
us to see the world in a
deeply enriching way;
for those who work in the media and
open our eyes to injustice and greed
and for those who draw
back the curtain on our
hungry, starving world;
let us praise the Lord.
We will praise the Lord.

For the promises of God and
the assurance of hope
and for more and more reasons
to offer our worship to him;
for hymns and for songs that
were written for his praise
and for the joy of singing together
as his precious children;
let us praise the Lord.
We will praise the Lord.

For those who have served him
here and around the world
and for those whose faithful witness
brought us to know him as Lord;
for those who are channels of
God's amazing grace
and for those whose lives speak
so powerfully of his love;
let us praise the Lord.
We will praise the Lord.

We bring our prayers of praise
in the name of Jesus,
whose name is the Lord. **Amen.**

Confession

1 Kings 3:1–3

Lord,
we find it so hard to stand
out from the crowd
and too often we take
the easy way out.

You call us to be a holy people
so that the way we live sets us apart
to serve you, and you alone.

But we live and work amongst
many who don't know you
and we are surrounded by those
who would rather trust
themselves and not you.
We find it so difficult to stand alone
and it is very costly to
face the ridicule
of our work colleagues,
neighbours, and friends.

All those years ago when
Solomon became king
he found it easy to pray to you
and also to worship idols.
He asked you for wisdom
for ruling your people
but he found it hard to be
faithful to you alone.

Lord,
we confess that too often
we seek our security
in the possessions we can hold
rather than to trust in our God
whom we cannot see.
We confess that too often our focus
is not always on you but on
the things we have made.
We confess that too often you
are not the centre of our lives
and we are happy to take your
place at the heart of our living.

Lord,
we seek your forgiveness,
renewal, and blessing
and the assurance that you are
welcoming us home. **Amen.**

Intercession

Ephesians 5:15

Lord,
we pray for those who look
at life differently
and for those who help us to see
things in a whole new way;
for those who look up and remind
us to give praise to God
and for those whose whole being
acknowledges God's glory;
for those whose words, deeds, and
actions are focused on worship
and for those whose purpose
each day is to live for the
praise of their Lord.
Lord of change and renewal,
come, make us anew.

Lord,
we pray for those who look
at life differently
and for those who help us to see
things in a whole new way;
for those who look back and
who teach us to be thankful
and for those who ooze with
gratitude for all they have received;
for those who with joy have
counted their blessings
and for those whose whole lives
are a song of thanksgiving.
Lord of change and renewal,
come, make us anew.

Lord,
we pray for those who look
at life differently

and for those who help us to see
things in a whole new way;
for those whose vision helps
them to see the whole world
and for those who challenge us
to hear the cry of the poor;
for those who work to bring hope
to the hungry and starving
and for those who open our
eyes to the homeless on
the streets of our cities.
Lord of change and renewal,
come, make us anew.

Lord,
we pray for those who look
at life differently
and for those who help us to see
things in a whole new way;
for those who look ahead and help
us to see where we are heading
and for those who challenge
our misuse and abuse
of God's world;
for those who speak out for those
who cannot speak for themselves
and for those who expose the
loss of our rainforests, and
animals facing extinction.
Lord of change and renewal,
come, make us anew.

Lord,
we pray for those who look
at life differently
and for those who help us to see
things in a whole new way;
for those who look with compassion
into the faces of the lonely
and by grace see something of the
hidden pain in people's lives;
for those who seek to embrace
the broken, the depressed,
and the abused
and for those who shed real
tears with those who are
frightened and hurting.
Lord of change and renewal,
come, make us anew.

Lord,
we pray for those who look
at life differently
and for those who help us to see
things in a whole new way;
for ourselves, that we may
open the eyes of our
neighbour to God's love
and for real opportunities to
become a channel of his
peace, joy, and hope;
for a new willingness to care
for those who are careless
and love the unloveable
and to be ready to offer forgiveness to
those who don't really deserve it.
Lord of change and renewal,
come, make us anew.

We bring our prayers in
the name of Jesus,
who lived, died, and rose again that
we might live differently. **Amen.**

TWENTY-FIRST SUNDAY IN ORDINARY TIME

Praise

Psalm 84

Lord,
every time we enter this place
it feels like we are coming home!

We know that there is no place
that we cannot find you
and your presence cannot be
restricted by time and space.

Yet here we have these precious
moments to worship you
and to focus our thoughts and
our longings on your glory.
To meet together as your people
brings joy to our hearts
and it feels like a foretaste of
joining your heavenly choir.

By your Holy Spirit, enable us to
bring you our thanksgiving,
that all we say, do, and desire may
honour your great name.
We pray that our songs of praise
will rejoice your heart
and that our prayers will be heard
before the throne of grace.

Great and wonderful God, it is our
greatest pleasure to worship you
for you alone are sovereign of
all things, even life itself.
You alone are God, for you rule
over the whole of creation,
and our world in its beauty and
richness praises its Maker.

To worship you is the greatest
task you have set before us
and to live for your glory is
our highest achievement.
Everything else that we
can do in this world
pales into insignificance compared
to singing of your love.

We praise you for who you are
and for all you mean to us
and we bring words of adoration
in response to your grace.
To walk with you through
the days of our lives
is to discover the true meaning of
fulfilment, joy, and thanksgiving.

Let us praise the Lord,
and all God's people said: **Amen.**

Confession

1 Kings 8:22–30

Lord,
we confess that we have set
boundaries to our worship
and we set times when we will
offer our thanksgiving.

We confess that we gather together
to offer you our praises
but our praises end as we
leave the church.

We confess that our lives often
sing a different song
and our days are not filled with
the glory of your name.

We confess that we treat
you like an elderly relative
we visit once a week
and we have forgotten that the
whole of creation is where
we must praise you.

We confess that too often our
words and our attitudes
deny your presence

and we have yet to learn that
our whole world cannot
contain your glory.

Forgive us for thinking we
can leave you behind at
the end of the service;
set us on fire so that we will be
unable to contain our songs of joy.

Come, Lord Jesus, come,
that we may worship here
and everywhere
now and for ever. **Amen.**

Intercession

Ephesians 6:10–20

Lord,
we pray for those for
whom life is a battle
and, in the silence, we remember
prison governors, prison
officers, and all involved
in working with convicted prisoners.

silence

The Lord hears our prayer.
Thanks be to God.

Lord,
we pray for those for
whom life is a battle
and, in the silence, we remember
members of the armed forces,
seeking to keep the peace
in dangerous places.

silence

The Lord hears our prayer.
Thanks be to God.

Lord,
we pray for those for
whom life is a battle
and, in the silence, we remember
those working for charity
organisations
as they seek to bring food,
water, and education
to the poorest places on earth.

silence

The Lord hears our prayer.
Thanks be to God.

Lord,
we pray for those for
whom life is a battle
and, in the silence, we remember
the work of Victim Support
as they care for those damaged
in body, mind, or spirit.

silence

The Lord hears our prayer.
Thanks be to God.

Lord,
we pray for those for
whom life is a battle
and, in the silence, we remember
members of the fire
brigade, the RNLI,
and mountain rescue as they risk
their lives to save others.

silence

The Lord hears our prayer.
Thanks be to God.

Lord,
we pray for those for
whom life is a battle
and, in the silence, we remember
research chemists and all who
work in laboratories
seeking to discover new drugs
and better treatments
for people longing to find
wholeness and health.

silence

The Lord hears our prayer.
Thanks be to God.

Lord,
we pray for those for
whom life is a battle
and, in the silence, we remember
police officers, judges,
and magistrates
in the stressful situations they face
and the integrity that is
demanded of them.

silence

The Lord hears our prayer.
Thanks be to God.

Lord,
we pray for those for
whom life is a battle
and, in the silence, we remember
ordinary people who struggle
with frustration
and battle to cope with bitter
disappointment and abuse.

silence

The Lord hears our prayer.
Thanks be to God.

Lord,
we pray for those for
whom life is a battle
and, in the silence, we remember
those for whom we are
especially concerned
and for ourselves and the
battles we will face
in the coming days of this week.

silence

The Lord hears our prayer.
Thanks be to God.

We bring our prayers in
the name of Jesus,
who is our strength for every
battle we face. **Amen.**

TWENTY-SECOND SUNDAY IN ORDINARY TIME

Praise

Psalm 45:6

Lord,
when we enter your presence it
is like stepping into eternity
and your glory wraps around us
with a hope too deep for words.
Your Word speaks to us of
your endless glory
and our hearts experience the joy
of your touch upon our lives.

You have given us eyes that
we may see the intricate
beauty of your creation

and you have filled us with
the desire to explore all
that you have made.
You have provided a world of colour,
design, and endless variety,
and you have granted us the
priceless gift of being able to
enjoy what you have made.

Your world is a reflection of
your nature as it echoes
your generosity of giving
and again and again your love
of truth and justice we see
woven into the fabric of life.
Your nature is wholeness and
your love is at the very
heart of all that you are.
When you speak it is to challenge
our sin, but what we hear
is a call to come home.

Wonderful, wonderful God,
how can we not praise you
with the whole of our lives?
From the very heart of our being
comes a desire to worship
the Lord of heaven.
It is our greatest pleasure to
offer you the thanksgiving
of our grateful hearts
and we find our deepest joy and
lasting hope in giving praise
to the glory of your name.

From the beginning it was
your purpose that all people
everywhere should worship you
and it has always been that
in giving you praise we
have been truly human.
Your will was that we should
find our purpose in living
our days for your glory
and each day takes on a deeper,
richer meaning when it
begins and ends in you.

Sovereign Lord of all things,
your power and authority
reach across eternity
and who and what you are—
your self-giving grace—is the
heartbeat of all creation.
We praise you most for the
supreme gift of your Son and
that in him there is life
and that he is the way, the
truth, and the life for all who
open their lives to him.

On the cross you reached
down to lift us up.
On the cross you reached
out to love us all.
On the cross you reached deep
within us to make us whole.

Lord,
we have come with our praises
as we declare your glory
and we do so in the name of your
Son who is our Saviour. **Amen.**

Confession

Mark 7:8

Lord,
it is so very easy to begin to make
excuses for our mistakes
and to think that because we have
not committed a great crime
you will ignore what we say and do.

We read of the horrendous things that
people have done to one another
and the awful way they have treated
their fellow human beings.
When we compare ourselves with
them we don't feel so bad after all
and we try to find comfort
in the belief that our sin
is our hidden secret.

Then the truth dawns upon us that
you know everything about us
and that absolutely nothing can ever
be hidden from your perfect gaze.
As Jesus warned us, we cannot
blame the impact of what
we have seen and heard
and we stand before you
knowing we are responsible
and answerable to you.

Lord,
we can do no other than make
our full confession to you
but we do so in the knowledge
that our all-just judge is
our loving Saviour.
We make our confession as we
kneel at the foot of your cross
and as we look up into your face,
we experience the freedom of
your forgiveness. **Amen.**

Intercession

James 1:25

Lord,
we pray for those who mistake
freedom for licence to
do what they want
and for those for whom there
are no ultimate things that
are right or wrong;
for those who allow their freedom
to remove any meaning
of decency and respect
and for those who feel free to
take someone's property,
peace, or good name.
True freedom comes from
the hand of the Lord;
may it be lived wisely.

Lord,
we pray for those whose experience
of freedom is not as you planned
and for those whose freedom
is limited by illness or by the
effects of their disability;
for those who look back
with fond memories to the
freedom of their youth
and for those whose freedom
seems to be fading with
the passing of the years.
True freedom comes from
the hand of the Lord;
may it be lived wisely.

Lord,
we pray for those who have lost their
freedom because of their faith
and for those who languish
in prison without trial
or hope of release;
for those who have bravely
taken a stand for their
freedom of conscience
and for those who have
willingly given their lives for
the freedom of others.
True freedom comes from
the hand of the Lord;
may it be lived wisely.

Lord,
we pray for those whose
enjoyment of freedom is
restricted by their poverty
and for those without the
resources to share in the things
others take for granted;
for those who feel their family
are robbed of freedom by
their lack of employment
and for those who daily hear,
read, and see examples of the
freedom they don't have.
True freedom comes from
the hand of the Lord;
may it be lived wisely.

Lord,
we pray for those who have
lost their freedom because
they have broken the law
and for those who will lose their
freedom again and again as
they return to a life of crime;
for those whose crimes are
a result of the addictions
that have trapped them
and for those who can see no way
to find the kind of freedom
they long to experience.
True freedom comes from
the hand of the Lord;
may it be lived wisely.

Lord,
we pray for those we call terrorists
but who see themselves
as freedom fighters
and for those who are
prepared to plant bombs
to murder and maim;
for those who seem to have no
compassion or concern for
their innocent victims
and for those so radicalised that
no cost for their freedom is
too high for others to pay.
True freedom comes from
the hand of the Lord;
may it be lived wisely.

Lord,
we pray for those for whom
we are concerned who are
still longing for freedom
and for those yearning to be
set free from doubt, fear, and
their feelings of shame;
for ourselves, that we might
experience a new sense of
freedom in living for Christ
and for the joy of entering
more fully into the freedom
he won for us on Calvary.
True freedom comes from
the hand of the Lord;
may it be lived wisely.

We bring our prayers in
the name of Christ,
the one who alone can
set us free. **Amen.**

TWENTY-THIRD SUNDAY IN ORDINARY TIME

Praise

Psalm 125

Father,
you meet us in the garden
of our lives
and you whisper to us as

we stroll through our days
of worry and concern.
You are there when we feel
the weight of the world
upon our shoulders
and your arms of love
enable us to stand
when we might have fallen.

We praise you that your mighty
presence fills the whole universe
and your grace-filled touch
transforms our days.
We thank you that you
hold our hands when the
pathway is uncertain
and your Holy Spirit provides
the strength to stand firm.
We praise you that we can
trust you completely
and that even the storms of life
cannot separate us from you.

Your goodness remains the
benchmark of your purposes
and it is always the touchstone
of your will for our lives.
We cannot hold ourselves
back from praising you
and our hearts are on fire as we
are touched by your grace.
There is a deep longing within us
to give thanks for your blessings
and there is a song of praise that
we simply cannot quench!

Sovereign Father, wonderful
God, you are our all in all
and we bring the worship
of our whole lives to
your throne of grace.

We stand utterly amazed
before the creator of our
unimaginable universe
and we are rendered speechless
that our God calls us his
precious children.
Receive our praises and accept
our heartfelt thanksgiving
for all your goodness
and enable us to go on singing
your praises every day
of our lives. **Amen.**

Confession

James 2:1

Father,
you made us to be one in Jesus
and it was your intention that
we should be your family.
From the very beginning
you showered your love
upon the whole world.
In your grace you placed no
restriction on your mercy
so that whoever turned to you
would find the welcome of
the prodigal's father.

Father,
forgive us that we are not as
welcoming as you are
and that we are very selective
in the ones to whom we offer
the hand of friendship.
Forgive us for our selfishness
and our reluctance to demonstrate
your accepting grace.
Forgive us for the ease
with which we judge people
and how hard we find it in our hearts
to forgive.

Come, Lord Jesus, come,
cleanse, renew, and reclaim us
and set our hearts ablaze
with your love. **Amen.**

Intercession

Mark 7:34

Father,
open our minds that we may
see your world as you see it
and grasp again the amazing
plan that we should be one.
Set nations and their leaders
free from selfish boundaries
that we may, by your grace, reach
out with the love of Jesus.
Father, touch us by your love
and make us channels of your grace.

Father,
open our eyes that we may catch a
fresh glimpse of your creation
and help us to see your fingerprints
in every part of your world.
Release all nations from the
greed that is plundering
your good earth
and help us all to understand
the damage that our
self-interest is doing.
Father, touch us by your love
and make us channels of your grace.

Father,
open our ears to the voice that
speaks to us of all your creatures
and teach us to value every
man, woman, and child
as you always do.
Challenge those nations who
keep hold of too much
of the earth's riches,
that we may all hear and respond
to the cries of the poor.
Father, touch us by your love
and make us channels of your grace.

Father,
open our hands to welcome
the stranger from around the
world or across the street
and give us the courage to
make the first move in being
a friend to the lonely.
Make our hands open, generous,
and filled with grace in
our giving and serving,
that the needs of the hungry,
the thirsty, the stranger,
the naked, the prisoner, and
the sick will finally be met.
Father, touch us by your love
and make us channels of your grace.

Father,
open our hearts that we may
know what it means to
fall in love with you
and overwhelm us by your
presence that our walk with
you may be flooded with joy.
Take from us any sense of duty
or drudgery in serving you
here or with our neighbour
and may the sheer wonder and
privilege of being your children
lift any burden we feel.
Father, touch us by your love
and make us channels of your grace.

Father,
open our lips to offer you
the worship of hearts set
on fire with your love

and keep our lips still when
we need to be silent as you
speak of your grace.
Give us the desire to offer words
of encouragement to those
who serve in your name
and may we have the courage
to take every opportunity
to speak of your love.
Father, touch us by your love
and make us channels of your grace.

Father,
open our lives to the power
of your Holy Spirit to
transform who we are
and by the grace of heaven
may our lives speak to all
of the love of our Father.
May we start each new
day claiming your
presence and power,
that the whole of our lives at
home, at work, or at leisure
will be part of our song
of thanksgiving.
Father, touch us by your love
and make us channels of your grace.

We bring our prayers in
the name of Jesus,
the one to whom all things
lie open. **Amen.**

TWENTY-FOURTH SUNDAY IN ORDINARY TIME

Praise

Psalm 19

Lord,
living in your world is like being in
a picture book of your glory—
every day we are surrounded by
glimpses of your presence.
It is as if the whole of creation
is one vast choir
and its purpose is to sing a song
to your praise and glory.

From lofty mountaintops, the
vista of creation lifts our hearts
and the rich colours of hidden valleys
and the silent ripple of streams
touch us deeply and bring
rest to weary lives.
Every night we crane our
necks to wonder at the
celebration of the heavens
and come the morning the new
day you have granted us
speaks of your desire to
make all things new.

We praise you that we are
so wonderfully made
and we have been designed to
be a reflection of your grace.
You have granted us the gifts
of creativity and reflection
as we are able to consider
who and what we are
and what we can become.

We praise you that from the first you
planned that we should know you
and in knowing you, have life!
This is the thing that takes
our breath away—
that our sovereign creator God
should desire our love.
It is something we cannot
understand.
For you are our God and you are
utterly complete in yourself.

But you have chosen to adopt us as
your precious children of grace
and, by your Holy Spirit, to see again
the wonders of your creation
and to see them with the eyes of faith.

Sovereign Lord, King of all creation,
receive our praises for we long
to give you the glory;
receive our songs of thanksgiving
for we are richly blessed;
receive our worship for all you
are and for all you made;
receive us for we come in
the name of Jesus,
who is the Lord of heaven
and earth. **Amen.**

Confession

Proverbs 1:20–23

Lord,
we think we are so clever
but we create more problems
than we solve.
We consider ourselves intelligent
but we say and do the
most foolish things.
We make our plans for the future
but we have no control over
the days to come.
We see ourselves as better
than others
but your grace is for all.
We think we are loving
but too often we are like a noisy gong
or a clanging cymbal.
We count ourselves wise
but we refuse to be fools for Christ.

Lord,
in your wisdom, grace, and mercy
touch our lives with your grace
and our hearts with your love.
Come, set us free to
honour your name
and by your Spirit come
cleanse and renew. **Amen.**

Intercession

Mark 8:27–38

Father,
we want to talk to you about those
setting out on the journey of life;
for young people faced with exams
that will shape their journey
and for those whose
prospects are bleak
as their lives are being damaged by
the choices they are making.
Lord of all creation,
walk with us today.

Father,
we want to talk to you about
those facing hardship on
the journey of life;
for those deeply troubled by
the life-changing illness
they now have to face
and for those whose hopes and
dreams have come crashing down
as the years and life's problems
are robbing them of their
precious memories.
Lord of all creation,
walk with us today.

Father,
we want to talk to you about those
whose lives have taken a detour;
for those who once served
you faithfully and knew
you as Lord of their lives

and for those who have allowed
the challenges of the journey
to steal them away
as they have permitted home
and family, work and leisure
to take your place.
Lord of all creation,
walk with us today.

Father,
we want to talk to you about those
whose lives are focused on you;
for those who make time each day
to be still in your presence
and for those who have rediscovered
joy in the coming of Jesus
as their hearts and lives have
been transformed as they
welcome Immanuel.
Lord of all creation,
walk with us today.

Father,
we want to talk to you about those
who are still on the journey;
for those whose lives are full
of questions and whose
doubts won't go away
and for those who long
for a Damascus road
encounter with Jesus
as they have yet to find his
presence in the ordinary
moments of their journey.
Lord of all creation,
walk with us today.

Father,
we want to talk to you about
those who are nearing the
end of their journey;
for those whose lives have
been a beacon of hope
and salt for the earth
and for those who know
that their earthly days are
now small in number
as they know they are homeward
bound, ready to meet their Lord.
Lord of all creation,
walk with us today.

We bring our prayers in
the name of Jesus,
the first and the last,
the beginning and the end of
all our journeys. **Amen.**

TWENTY-FIFTH SUNDAY IN ORDINARY TIME

Praise

Psalm 1

Lord,
you have blessed us with the
joy of your presence
as you have guided our footsteps
on our journey each day.
Walking in your company adds
such a richness to our lives
and we experience the thrill of
your love flowing over us.

Our hearts rejoice as we remember
your loving-kindness
and songs of happiness
flood into our minds.
We find such a sense of peace
just knowing you are there
and trusting you for each step
we take brings us hope.

We praise you for the lives
you have given to us
and for providing us with a
purpose, vast and wide.
For you have assured us that having
taken hold of your hand
you will lead us from where we first
met you to be with you for ever.

Our walk with you has made
many demands upon our lives
and there have been times when
our faith nearly faltered.
We have faced moments of testing
that cut deep into our hopes
and we have struggled with
doubts, questions, and fears.

We praise you, our Lord
and our Saviour, for you
have been faithful
and, just as you promised, you
have been with us always.
So our songs of praise cannot
be contained any longer,
for our deep sense of thanksgiving
of the life you have given us.

By your grace we have been blessed
way beyond our deserving
and we confess that our
joy, hope, and peace are
gifts from your hand.
We praise you for all that Jesus
means to us and for what we
receive through his love
as we offer heartfelt gratitude
for the blessings of life made
new in our Lord. **Amen.**

Confession

James 4:7

Lord,
we confess that temptation
is our daily experience
and that time and again we
have failed to stand firm.
We begin with such good intentions
of staying close to you
but our plans melt away in the
pressures and strain of each day.

Forgive our hasty words and
our thoughtless actions
which hurt you, other
people, and ourselves.

Forgive the things we have
neglected to do
and the promises we have yet
again failed to keep.

Forgive our lack of care and
compassion for others
and for selfishly demanding help
and support for ourselves.

Forgive us for treating
those closest to us
with an unkindness and lack
of respect we wouldn't
show to a stranger.

We confess that we have not read
your Word for a few days now
and it is ages since we last met
you quietly in prayer.

Forgive us, Lord, and reshape
our whole lives,
that as we submit ourselves
each day to you

we may receive the strength to
stand firm in your love. **Amen.**

Intercession

Proverbs 31:10

Think of those on whose
presence we depend
but who rarely receive the
value that is theirs.
Hold before God those who work
at the local shopping centre
and those who pull trolleys
full of goods as they provide
the services we need.

silence

Think of those on whose
presence we depend
but who rarely receive the
value that is theirs.
Hold before God your elderly
neighbours who are living alone
and those who still have wisdom
and experience to share.

silence

Think of those on whose
presence we depend
but who rarely receive the
value that is theirs.
Hold before God those who
keep our streets clean
and those who remove the
rubbish from our homes.

silence

Think of those on whose
presence we depend
but who rarely receive the
value that is theirs.
Hold before God the hospital
secretaries, porters,
and all the ancillary staff
whom we rarely see.

silence

Think of those on whose
presence we depend
but who rarely receive the
value that is theirs.
Hold before God those who
drive trams, buses, and trains
and the engineers and mechanics
on which they depend.

silence

Think of those on whose
presence we depend
but who rarely receive the
value that is theirs.
Hold before God all women
in paid employment
and those still seeking equal
opportunity and recognition.

silence

Think of those on whose
presence we depend
but who rarely receive the
value that is theirs.
Hold before God those with a
family responsibility of care
and those who give long-term support
to those in their own home.

silence

Think of those on whose
presence we depend
but who rarely receive the
value that is theirs.
Hold before God those who
volunteer as street pastors
as they seek to give aid in times
of someone's vulnerability.

silence

Think of those on whose
presence we depend
but who rarely receive the
value that is theirs.
Hold before God yourself; for those
times when you feel undervalued
and for someone on whom
you depend who may
not feel appreciated.

silence

We bring our prayers in
the name of Jesus,
in whom God showed his love
for the whole world. **Amen.**

TWENTY-SIXTH SUNDAY IN ORDINARY TIME

Prayer of Approach

Psalm 124

For the strength God gave
us in our weakness,
let us praise the Lord.
We will praise the Lord.

For the courage we received
when things were hard,
let us praise the Lord.
We will praise the Lord.

For the comfort that touched
our hearts in times of pain,
let us praise the Lord.
We will praise the Lord.

For the grace that loved us even
when we were wrong,
let us praise the Lord.
We will praise the Lord.

In Christ's name. **Amen.**

Thanksgiving

James 5:13–20

Father,
we thank you for the sense of
belonging we have here
and for the deep feeling of being
needed, wanted, and loved.
There is a fellowship we share
that is our strength
and our relationships with
each other in Christ that are
our hope and our peace.

We are only too well aware
that as your church we
are far from perfect
and our witness of your love is
clouded by the mistakes we make.
Our life together is often
coloured by our lack of
love and understanding
and too often we allow our
personal preferences to
damage the fellowship.

Yet, amazingly, we are still your
people, the body of Christ
and you go on calling us to
be the salt of the earth and
the city set on the hill.

We know that you designed
us to be the living example
of a renewed community
and that we can only fulfil
that commission by the
power of the Holy Spirit.

We thank you, Father, not only
for making us your children
but for creating us to be your
family on earth and in heaven.
It is not by our achievements or
a result of our deserving—
we are your people through
Christ and by grace alone.

You have given to us the
great privilege of being
your church on earth
but you have also given us the
responsibility of making
your love known.
You never intended us to open
the doors of the church and
wait for people to enter—
your command and commission
was to go out and bring
lost sheep home.

We thank you for all you have
done for us in Jesus
and we are here to give honour
and praise to him.
Now set your people ablaze with
the power of the Spirit
that our words, deeds, and
service will be a thank offering
in Christ's name. **Amen.**

Intercession
Mark 9:41

Lord,
we pray for those who give a
cup of water in your name;
for those on whom we rely
within the life of the church
and for those whose service
often goes unnoticed;
for those who clean the church
and keep it in good repair
and for those who are pastoral
visitors, treasurers, or stewards;
those who arrange the flowers,
welcome visitors, or
provide music for singing
and worship.
May their service bring
joy to their Lord.
Lord, in your mercy,
hear our prayer.

Lord,
we pray for those who give a
cup of water in your name;
for those on whom our
community relies;
for the staff at the local health
centre and for our dentists,
health visitors, and the staff
at the pharmacy;
for those who collect our
refuse and rubbish
and for those who work to
keep our streets clean.
May their service bring
joy to their Lord.
Lord, in your mercy,
hear our prayer.

Lord,
we pray for those who give a
cup of water in your name;
for those whose work is
demanding and dangerous
and for those we only hear of
when something goes wrong;
for social workers, probation
officers, and magistrates
and for the staff of young offenders
institutions and prisons.
May their service bring
joy to their Lord.
Lord, in your mercy,
hear our prayer.

Lord,
we pray for those who give a
cup of water in your name;
for those who care for the frail,
the elderly, and the infirm
and for those who work
in care homes
bringing peace and joy to those
who cannot live alone;
for those whose love,
compassion, and kindness
is a demanding ministry to
those with dementia
and for those who use their skills
of gentleness and listening
as they offer support to
the families of those
who no longer recognise the
faces of those they loved.
May their service bring
joy to their Lord.
Lord, in your mercy,
hear our prayer.

Lord,
we pray for those who give a
cup of water in your name;
for those who act as a good
neighbour in their community
and for those who seek to visit those
who are lonely and living alone;
for our local councillors who
are genuinely seeking to
serve the community
for the good of all and to the
very best of their ability;
for the 'lollypop' person who
gives of their time
to keep children safe on
their way to school.
May their service bring
joy to their Lord.
Lord, in your mercy,
hear our prayer.

Lord,
we pray for those who give a
cup of water in your name;
for those who serve us at the
supermarket checkout
and for the staff who fill up the
shelves with the things we need;
for those who deliver our mail
in sun, wind, or rain
and for those who bring the parcels
we ordered on the internet;
for those who every week give
of their time and energy
to run uniformed organisations
that help to develop young lives.
May their service bring
joy to their Lord.
Lord, in your mercy,
hear our prayer.

Lord,
we pray for those who give a
cup of water in your name;
for those who risk their lives to
bring peace in the midst of war
and for those who care for
the wounded in the face
of civil uprising;
for those who seek to use
diplomacy to bring an
end to the fighting
and for those showing kindness to
those forced to become refugees;
for those who give of
themselves as they show love
to the tide of migrants
and for those who are
offering a safe haven and
hope for the future.
May their service bring
joy to their Lord.
Lord, in your mercy,
hear our prayer.

Lord,
we pray for those who give a
cup of water in your name;
for ourselves, who have been
called and commissioned
to work out our faith in Jesus
in the way we lives our lives
and how we speak about him
in our words and deeds,
that others may know the love
of God for themselves.
May our service bring
joy to our Lord.
Lord, in your mercy,
hear our prayer.

We bring our prayers in
the name of Jesus,
that the cups of water we
give may bring glory and
praise to him. **Amen.**

TWENTY-SEVENTH SUNDAY IN ORDINARY TIME

Praise

Hebrews 1:1–4

Lord,
we have never really grasped
the majesty that is yours
nor have we truly understood
your power and authority.
At times we treat our
coming to worship
as if we are doing you a favour.

We have come because of the favour
with which you have welcomed
us into your presence.
We have come because your
glory insists we are here
and your grace throws open
the door of your kingdom!

We have come to lift high
the name of Jesus
and to declare to the whole
world his eternal lordship.
We have come because,
finally and completely,
you have stepped into our world
and we can know you in
Jesus your Son.

We praise you that you
loved your creation
and we are truly amazed that
you came to the earth.
In Christ you left all the
glory of heaven

that by grace, one day, we may
stand at your throne.

Lord, you have promised you
will never be far from us
and each morning we wake your
presence greets us with love.
You have prepared moments all
through the day to praise you
and around every corner comes
an opportunity to give thanks.

We praise you with words of
thanksgiving for all you truly are
and our songs take flight for
your glory, that the whole
earth may sing your praise.
We bring words, thoughts,
and celebration to honour
the King of the kingdom
and we call the myriad of the
hosts of heaven to join in
this song of praise. **Amen.**

Confession

Job 1:1

Lord,
we praise you for those whose
lives speak of you
and in whose days we
perceive you at work.
We are touched by the love
which we find in your people
and we are challenged by your
grace upon their lives.

We confess that we know just
how much we fall short
of living in the way that pleases you
and we are daily ashamed
that when people see us
it probably won't make
them think of you.

We confess that while you
have lifted our hopes to
the heights of heaven
too often our faith and our
expectations reach no higher
than what we think we
have achieved.
We confess that we rely
almost exclusively on
the things we can do
and close our ears to the
promise of power
that only the Holy Spirit can bring.

Come, Lord, and set us free
to live for your glory,
that we may more truly
reflect something of your
love and glory. **Amen.**

Intercession

Mark 10:13–16

I am a stranger,
you meet me everywhere.
Perhaps it's because my
hair is too long
or the ring in my lip
puts you off me.
I feel avoided wherever I go—
people's quick glances
tell me I am being judged
and classified.
Deep down, I want to
enter God's kingdom
but I find it hard to
come as a child.
Pray for me.

silence

I am a member of parliament
and unfortunately you associate me
with self-seeking,
and toeing the party line.
I am only too well aware
that many people are
put off by politics
and often our decisions
are not understood.
Deep down, I want to
enter God's kingdom
but I find it hard to
come as a child.
Pray for me.

silence

I am a migrant.
Exactly where I came from
really isn't that important.
I came here running away
from the bombs and the killing,
hoping to find peace
and a welcome.
My family and friends are all gone
and now I just want to be accepted.
Deep down, I want to
enter God's kingdom
but I find it hard to
come as a child.
Pray for me.

silence

I am a teenager.
Perhaps you can remember
what is was like being my age,
when your moods can
swing to extremes.
I am struggling to cope
with the mountain of decisions
that I know will impact
on the whole of my life.
Deep down, I want to
enter God's kingdom
but I find it hard to
come as a child.
Pray for me.

silence

I am a businessperson.
To many people that means
I'm greedy and simply
not to be trusted
and money is all that matters to me.
My role is creating the wealth
that is required to build
hospitals and schools.
I know that the resources
don't always find the places
they're most needed.
Deep down, I want to
enter God's kingdom
but I find it hard to
come as a child.
Pray for me.

silence

I am a scientist.
It is wonderful that so many people
are genuinely thrilled
by what we are trying to do.
I guess that it is also true
that scientists are not
always trusted
as we seem to undermine
the things that people believe.
Deep down, I want to
enter God's kingdom
but I find it hard to
come as a child.
Pray for me.

silence

I am a prisoner.
It was while I was completing
my sentence
that God entered my life
for the first time.
It feels like people don't trust me
and they think that my
finding God
is simply a cheap way to
find some acceptance.
I know my life is still in a mess
and living a new kind of
life won't be easy.
Deep down, I want to
enter God's kingdom
but I find it hard to
come as a child.
Pray for me.

silence

I am a person who once
came to church.
It is a few years now
since I took that brave step.
I crossed the church threshold
for the very first time
simply longing to find
faith and a welcome.
I was met with a stare and a voice
that told me I was sitting
in their place.
So I went home and
never returned.
Deep down, I want to
enter God's kingdom
but I find it hard to
come as a child.
Pray for me.

silence

We bring our prayers in
the name of Jesus,
the King of the kingdom
of God. **Amen.**

TWENTY-EIGHTH SUNDAY IN ORDINARY TIME

Prayer of Approach

Psalm 22:1

Lord,
we do not always feel
you are near us
and when we are facing
difficult times
it sometimes seems as if
we are coping alone.

There are moments
when it feels as if
the bottom has dropped
out of our world
and we look in vain for
your everlasting arms.

It is only when we remember
your promise
that you will never leave
us nor forsake us
that the clouds lift and we
glimpse signs of your grace.

We have come to meet
with you, Lord,
that we may speak to you
of our confusion
and so find that your
grace is indeed
sufficient for all our needs. **Amen.**

Praise
Hebrews 4:14–16

Lord,
we have come to praise you
for you are our great high priest.
You are the one who not only
opens the door to heaven—
you alone are the way to get there.

We praise you because through
your life, death, and resurrection
the pathway was prepared for
us to walk and not get lost.
Many have come and
proclaimed themselves as
teachers of a way of life.
You have not called us to
follow your teaching but to
trust you, the teacher.

Only you, Lord, have walked
this road that we call life.
Only you, Lord, have experienced
all that this life means to us.
Only you, Lord, have lived
the life of heaven.
Only you, Lord, have proved by
your sacrificial offering of yourself
that in and through you there
is a hope that is certain.

We praise you because you are
Son of Man and Son of God
and you really do know
our weaknesses and
our wayward lives.
You are the one we know
we can trust because you
have faced what we face
and on the cross you overcame
all things in your victory
of life and death.

We praise you for you are the
one who came from glory
and we celebrate your
sovereignty and authority as
you now reign in power.
It is in you that your will will
be realised when we stand
before the throne of grace
and join with all the nations
of the world, who will be
summoned to bow before you.

King of Kings, it is our greatest joy
to worship you as our Saviour
and Lord of Lords, with
hearts overflowing with
thanksgiving and adoration.
We join with the choir of heaven
to worship the Lord Almighty
and the sovereign over all things
in heaven and on earth. **Amen.**

Intercession
Mark 10:17–31

Father,
we pray for those who
walk a path of crime
and for those whose lifestyle
has landed them in prison;
for those whose antisocial behaviour
is wrecking communities
and for those who have been
abused and now abuse
themselves and others.
Lord of the cross of healing,
come and renew the earth.

Father,
we pray for those who walk
a path of loneliness
and for those who have no
one to share their days;

for those who long for peace
  and a space just to be
and for those who miss the
  constant noise of their family.
Lord of the cross of healing,
come and renew the earth.

Father,
we pray for those who walk
  a path of discovery
and for young people setting
  out on the journey of life;
for those faced with choices
  that will affect their future;
for those preparing themselves
  for further education
and for those whose studies
  have led to unemployment.
Lord of the cross of healing,
come and renew the earth.

Father,
we pray for those who walk
  a path of struggling
and for those for whom each day
is a battle with their health problems;
for those whose world is
  restricted by their disability
and for those with the
  power but not the will
to bring hope to the housebound
  and help to their carers.
Lord of the cross of healing,
come and renew the earth.

Father,
we pray for those who walk
  a path of singleness
and for those who feel excluded by
  our family-orientated society;
for those whose dreams of
  parenthood were never fulfilled
and for those who are now neglected
  by the children they had.
Lord of the cross of healing,
come and renew the earth.

Father,
we pray for those who walk
  a path of searching
and for scientists who seek new
  ways of healing and cure;
for poets, writers, and musicians
  who seek to open our
  eyes to God's world
and for those who are committed
  to helping us realise
our part in the damage being
  done to our planet.
Lord of the cross of healing,
come and renew the earth.

Father,
we pray for those who
  walk a path of faith
and for those who daily carry their
  cross in the name of their Lord;
for those who are paying the
  price of their obedience
in the persecution, suffering, and
  rejection by their community
and for those who are paying
  with their lives for being
  Christ's disciples.
Lord of the cross of healing,
come and renew the earth.

Father,
we pray for those who
  walk a path of love
and for those who reach out to the
  lost, the afraid, and the hopeless;
for ourselves, that we may fall
  in love with Jesus each day

as we seek to live out his
love in every word, every
thought, with everyone.
Lord of the cross of healing,
come and renew the earth.

We bring our prayers to the Father
in the name of Jesus,
who calls us to walk with him
on the road to the cross and
resurrection. **Amen.**

TWENTY-NINTH SUNDAY IN ORDINARY TIME

Praise

Psalm 104:1–9

Lord,
we have no words we can use that
will truly speak of your glory
and there is no way that we can
do justice to your power.
Your splendour is beyond anything
our minds can imagine
and your authority over your
creation is utterly limitless.

We praise you that your
being is outside anything
we have experienced
and there are no boundaries
by which your will can
ever be controlled.
You are not some godlike being that
our imagination has created for us
and your sovereignty over your vast
universe is utterly complete.

Not a blade of grass grows
without you knowing
and you know the name of
every plant and creature.
Your knowledge plumbs
the depths of space
and your understanding of our
world and worlds as yet unknown
is beyond comparison.

You see each raindrop fall and
you know where it will land
and you comprehend the design of
every snowflake that ever fell.
Your knowledge of the sun, moon,
and every star is staggering
and you know the fullest and deepest
truth of every cell and every atom.

Lord,
your knowledge of each of
us cannot be matched
anywhere or by any system
and you have a complete record of
our hopes and fears, our dreams
and our disappointments.
You witness the mess we make
of our relationships
and our moments of anger
don't escape you.
You weep with us when we
are hurting deep inside and
everything has gone wrong.

Amazing God, you share our
laughter and our tears
and you walk beside us
and hold our hand.
You entrust us with your
gift of freedom
and you are ready to help us pick up
the pieces when we get it wrong.
You have plans for us that we
have yet to grasp hold of
and you fill us with dreams of just
how fulfilling our lives could be.

No wonder the psalmist
sang your praises
and that he longed to find the
words to offer you his worship.
We join our song of
thanksgiving to his,
that the whole of creation
will sing your praises,
now and until the end of time—
and beyond. **Amen.**

Confession

Job 38:1–7

Lord,
when we enter the presence
of our almighty God
we have no alternative
but to confess our pride
and our arrogance.

When we enter the presence
of our holy God
we have no alternative
but to confess the mess we
are making of our lives.

When we enter the presence
of our all-knowing God
we have no alternative
but to confess the poverty
of our understanding.

When we enter the presence
of our sovereign Lord
we have no alternative
but to confess that we are less
than nothing in your sight.

When we enter the presence of
our God who is Immanuel
we have no alternative
but to confess our need of
our Saviour and Lord.

Lord,
touch our lives again with your grace
and reclaim us as your
precious children.
By the light of your love,
lead us out of darkness
to live lives that bring
you glory. **Amen.**

Intercession

Mark 10:42–45

Father,
we know that Jesus turns our
human values upside down.
In our world, the ones with the
loudest voices are followed—
we pray that those with gentle
words of wisdom will be heard.
Father,
turn the world the right way up
and make your glory known.

Father,
we know that Jesus turns our
human values upside down.
In our society, we are told
that money talks—
we pray that the voice of love and
compassion will change lives.
Father,
turn the world the right way up
and make your glory known.

Father,
we know that Jesus turns our
human values upside down.
In our priorities, we believe that
charity begins at home—

we pray that our lifestyle
will announce that charity
begins *from* home.
Father,
turn the world the right way up
and make your glory known.

Father,
we know that Jesus turns our
human values upside down.
In our education, we are often told
that our goal is gaining wealth—
we pray that the development
of our skills to serve
our community
will become the aim of learning.
Father,
turn the world the right way up
and make your glory known.

Father,
we know that Jesus turns our
human values upside down.
In our nation, we focus our
resources on those proven
to be successful—
we pray for a renewed commitment
to building one nation
in which everyone has an
equal opportunity.
Father,
turn the world the right way up
and make your glory known.

Father,
we know that Jesus turns our
human values upside down.
In our society, those with
money have an easier
access to healthcare—
we pray for a society where
everyone can find the medical
care that they need.
Father,
turn the world the right way up
and make your glory known.

Father,
we know that Jesus turns our
human values upside down.
In our world, we spend vast
sums on weapons of war
and mass destruction—
we pray for a change of focus
to feeding the hungry
and teaching everyone
to read and to write.
Father,
turn the world the right way up
and make your glory known.

Father,
we know that Jesus turns our
human values upside down.
In our own hearts and lives,
we find it too easy to
put ourselves first—
we pray that, by your Holy
Spirit, we will be transformed
into the people you always
meant us to be.
Father,
turn the world the right way up
and make your glory known.

We bring our prayers in
the name of Jesus,
who is for ever turning the
world upside down. **Amen.**

THIRTIETH SUNDAY IN ORDINARY TIME

Prayer of Approach

Job 42:1–6

Lord,
it is when we really look
that we see everything around
us in a new way;
it is when we really look in
that we find we are less
critical of others;
it is when we really look back
that we realise how thankful we are;
it is when we really look around
that we recognise the needs
of our neighbour.
But it is when we gather
for worship that
we see your glory,
sing of your majesty,
and give praise to our
living God. **Amen.**

Praise

Psalm 34:1–8

Lord,
it is in your presence that we find
the inspiration to praise you
and it is your touch upon our
lives that brings us great joy.
From the very depths of our being
comes the song of our worship
and our praises shout aloud of
your goodness and glory.

Yet wherever we travel, there is
something that speaks of you
and whatever we see, there is reason
to give thanks to our creator.
This world you have made gives
us praise songs to sing
and the people we meet
provide opportunities to
show you our gratitude.

We praise you for those whose
lives speak of hope
and offer thanksgiving for those
who spoke to us of your love.
Our hearts are thrilled each day
by your touch upon our lives
and the opportunities to make
your love and presence known.

We praise you for those
moments when fears and
anxiety had made life hard
and you came and held us
and promised to walk with
us the rest of the way.
It was when we had messed up our
lives with that so familiar sin
that you covered our shame and
despair with a forgiveness so real.

We praise you for the truths we can
learn from your word in the Bible
and for those parables of life and
faith that constantly surround us.
Our minds are overwhelmed by
your goodness and grace
and by your presence, which enriches
our days and floods us with hope.

We pray that the whole of our
lives will become a song
of praise for your love
and that every day will be
filled with signs of our
gratitude for your grace.

Come, Lord, in the busyness of life,

Come, Lord, in the
stillness of peace.
Come, Lord, and daily
claim us as your own.
Come, Lord, and live in our hearts,
that our whole being may
declare Jesus is Lord. **Amen.**

Intercession

Mark 10:46–47

Father,
we want to talk to you about those,
like blind Bartimaeus, who
cry out for healing;
for those who long for
healing of their sickness
and for those sick in body,
mind, or in spirit;
for those whose illness is
wrecking their lives
and for those for whom it is
numbering their days.
In the name of Jesus the healer,
come and make them whole.

Father,
we want to talk to you about those,
like blind Bartimaeus, who
cry out for healing;
for those who long for
healing of their fears
and for those who find life a
frightening experience;
for those who are always afraid
that something might go wrong
and for those who find it
hard to cope with the
uncertainties of life.
In the name of Jesus the healer,
come and make them whole.

Father,
we want to talk to you about those,
like blind Bartimaeus, who
cry out for healing;
for those who long for healing
of their loneliness
and for those who fondly remember
a home full of laughter;
for those who have no one with
whom to share their joys
and for those who have memories
and no one to share them with.
In the name of Jesus the healer,
come and make them whole.

Father,
we want to talk to you about those,
like blind Bartimaeus, who
cry out for healing;
for those who long for healing
of their anxieties
and for those who find it
almost impossible to journey
out on their own;
for those whose days are crippled
with a sense of uncertainty
and for those who feel guilty
about their anxiety, when
they are not to blame.
In the name of Jesus the healer,
come and make them whole.

Father,
we want to talk to you about those,
like blind Bartimaeus, who
cry out for healing;
for those who long for
healing of their sadness
and for those who are carrying
the pain of bereavement;
for those who shed tears deep
inside that no one else sees

and for those who cry for the one
who no longer knows who they are.
In the name of Jesus the healer,
come and make them whole.

Father,
we want to talk to you about those,
like blind Bartimaeus, who
cry out for healing;
for those who long for healing
of their doubts and despair
and for those who are losing
hope of ever being free;
for those whose journey has
been marked by depression
and for those whose days are all grey
and they yearn for rich colours.
In the name of Jesus the healer,
come and make them whole.

Father,
we want to talk to you about those,
like blind Bartimaeus, who
cry out for healing;
for those who long for
healing of their faith
and for those who once made a
commitment that was real;
for those who have allowed other
activities to steal in unseen
and for those who would come home
if someone would invite them.
In the name of Jesus the healer,
come and make them whole.

Father,
we want to talk to you about those,
like blind Bartimaeus, who
cry out for healing;
for those known to us who
are longing for peace
and for those who seek wholeness
in place of their confusion;
for ourselves and the healings of
friendship, hope, and love
and for an ever deeper walk with
Jesus as the Lord of our lives.
In the name of Jesus the healer,
come and make them whole.

We bring our concerns to God
in the name of Jesus, who longs
to make us all whole. **Amen.**

THIRTY-FIRST SUNDAY IN ORDINARY TIME

Prayer of Approach

Psalm 146

Lord, what a gift you have given,
what a treasure we hold.
What a fragile inheritance you
have entrusted to our care.
What a blessing is ours,
what a responsibility we have,
for freedom is your gift
and it must be handled with care.

Lord, we praise you
for the freedom we have to
think and to choose;
for the freedom to learn and
to share what we have;
for the freedom to discover
just why we are here;
and to allow you to freely use us in
ways we never dreamt possible.

Lord, the freedom you give is
what makes us what we are
and true freedom comes from
knowing Jesus as Lord. **Amen.**

Confession

Hebrews 9:11–14

Lord,
even before we say and do
the wrong thing
your offer of forgiveness
already stands.

When we are selfish and self-centred
your offer of forgiveness
already stands.

When what we say and do hurts
you, other people, and ourselves
your offer of forgiveness
already stands.

When our fall is deep and
painful and we wonder
how we can start again
your offer of forgiveness
already stands.

Your word touches us deeply
and your message of grace
calls us home;
that word and that message
is of forgiveness
because your offer of forgiveness
already stands. **Amen.**

Intercession

Ruth 1:1–18

Father,
we pray for those who
are strangers to us
and for those whose language and
customs we don't understand;
for those who choose to live close
to those whom they know
and for those who feel threatened
by those who are different.
May we love you and our
neighbour as we love ourselves.
Lord, in your mercy,
hear our prayer.

Father,
we pray for those who
are strangers to us
and for those we would
normally avoid;
for those who stand out because
of the colour of their skin
and for those who are
our fellow citizens
but are made to feel they
do not belong.
May we love you and our
neighbour as we love ourselves.
Lord, in your mercy,
hear our prayer.

Father,
we pray for those who
are strangers to us
and for those who belong to a
different church from ourselves;
for those whose style of worship
we sometimes find strange
and for those whose devotion
to God puts us to shame.
May we love you and our
neighbour as we love ourselves.
Lord, in your mercy,
hear our prayer.

Father,
we pray for those who
are strangers to us
and for members of our own family
from whom we are estranged;
for people at work we avoid because
they have made life difficult

and for fellow church members we
exclude from our circle of friends.
May we love you and our
neighbour as we love ourselves.
Lord, in your mercy,
hear our prayer.

Father,
we pray for those who
are strangers to us
and for those who sit on the
pavement hoping to receive
a few coins from us;
for those who look hungry,
cold, and a picture of
misery and futility
and for those who today will
sleep in a doorway as they
have nowhere to call home.
May we love you and our
neighbour as we love ourselves.
Lord, in your mercy,
hear our prayer.

Father,
we pray for those who
are strangers to us
and for young people whose words
we often find hard to understand;
for those whose way of life
and the way they dress can
seem like a barrier to us
and for those who delight us with
their acts of compassion and faith.
May we love you and our
neighbour as we love ourselves.
Lord, in your mercy,
hear our prayer.

Father,
we pray for those who
are strangers to us
and for those whom we find
difficult to befriend;
for those who have let us
down time and again
and for those who carry huge
burdens which we easily fail to see.
May we love you and our
neighbour as we love ourselves.
Lord, in your mercy,
hear our prayer.

We bring our prayers in
the name of Jesus,
the one who is every stranger's
friend. **Amen.**

THIRTY-SECOND SUNDAY IN ORDINARY TIME

Praise

Psalm 127

Lord,
we praise you because you
have set us free!
For most of our adult life we have
walked in our personal cocoon,
hearing the cries of our neighbour
but ready to close our eyes and
our ears to their pain.

We were satisfied and
content with our lot,
or at least we thought we were—
until the day Jesus walked
into our lives.

Perhaps we feel no sense of shame
for the way we have lived
but looking back we recognise
the hollowness of it all.
Now we can say that we
welcome each day with joy

and you bring us hope, even
on the darkest day.

So, Lord, we praise you
for the freedom
with which you have
touched our lives.
Now you have set us free to
become channels of freedom
to the hurting, the alone, and
the forgotten people
who live on the streets of
our cities. **Amen.**

Confession

Mark 12:43–44

Lord,
we confess that too
often our giving
does not reflect the generosity
of your giving to us.

We confess that we are slow to give
of our time, our skills,
and our resources.

We confess that we rarely give
out of what we have received
but from the little we
have left over.

We confess that sometimes
what we give of ourselves
is not what you expect of
those who love Jesus.

Forgive us our closed hearts
and our lack of self-sacrifice.
Come move in our hearts
and transform our willingness to
give in your name. **Amen.**

Intercession

Ruth 4:16

Lord,
as Naomi cared for Ruth's
baby in her old age
so you call us to show compassion
when we are just too busy.
When we learn of the hungry and
starving around the world
help us to hear your call
to give all we can.
When our neighbour is in need,
send us to care.

Lord,
as Naomi cared for Ruth's
baby in her old age
so you call us to show compassion
when we least expect to.
When people are fleeing in fear of
their lives as bombs continue to fall
help us to offer friendship and
help to those who are afraid.
When our neighbour is in need,
send us to care.

Lord,
as Naomi cared for Ruth's
baby in her old age
so you call us to show compassion
when we least expect to.
When we see the elderly and the
disabled struggling to cope
help us to respond with the
practical help we can give.
When our neighbour is in need,
send us to care.

Lord,
as Naomi cared for Ruth's
baby in her old age

so you call us to show compassion
when we least expect to.
When our neighbour is
facing sadness and loss
help us to demonstrate the
love and care of Christ.
When our neighbour is in need,
send us to care.

Lord,
as Naomi cared for Ruth's
baby in her old age
so you call us to show compassion
when we least expect to.
When we see people facing abuse
because of their colour or race
help us to show them our
compassion and solidarity.
When our neighbour is in need,
send us to care.

Lord,
as Naomi cared for Ruth's
baby in her old age
so you call us to show compassion
when we least expect to.
When new people enter
the life of the church
help us to offer a welcome
and friendship that is
genuine and costly.
When our neighbour is in need,
send us to care.

Lord,
as Naomi cared for Ruth's
baby in her old age
so you call us to show compassion
when we least expect to.
When we are faced with a time
of pain, sorrow, and hardship
help us to be ready to receive
what others seek to offer.
When our neighbour is in need,
send us to care.

We bring our prayers in
the name of Jesus,
who shows his love in the most
unexpected of ways. **Amen.**

THIRTY-THIRD SUNDAY IN ORDINARY TIME

Prayer of Approach

Psalm 16

Lord,
freedom is just a word,
unless we give it.
When we don't live in
it, we lose it;
when we abuse it, we forfeit it;
when we corrupt it, it
loses all meaning;
when we grasp it, it slips
through our fingers.

Lord,
freedom is just a word,
unless we share it.
When poverty limits our
neighbour's freedom
and wealth and opportunity
are the preserve of the few;
when commitment to
justice, peace, and to
trade fairly is broken
and freedom is used to disguise
selfishness, greed, and abuse—
then teach us again, Lord,
freedom is for all,
or it's not freedom at all. **Amen.**

Confession

Mark 13:9

Lord,
we confess that too often we put
our trust in the wrong things
and we seek to find strength
in the wrong places.

We have looked for security in the
things we can have and hold
and sought to find assurance in
the things we have achieved.

We have tried to find
peace by serving in the
church and the world
and we thought we would
discover hope in the
rituals of the church.

We expected to enjoy purpose
and meaning by obeying
Christ's teachings
and we assumed that by our
own efforts we could build
a pathway to heaven.

But, Lord, we confess that we
have been badly mistaken!
Our acceptance is not found
in things and security isn't
something we can achieve;
at least we have realised that
peace can't be captured
in the rituals we love.

We confess that it's by
trusting the teacher and
by following him
that we are set free, because he
has conquered our sin. **Amen.**

Intercession

Mark 13:5–8

Father,
we pray for those who work out
their faith on the battlefield of life
and for those for whom there
seems to be no way of escape;
for those who are the only
Christian in their whole family
and for those whose precious beliefs
are treated with apathy or scorn.
Lord, on the battlefield of life
keep us faithful and strong.

Father,
we pray for those who work out
their faith on the battlefield of life
and for those who seek to
follow Jesus in the midst
of a hostile community;
for those who find themselves
surrounded by people
of a different faith
and for those for whom it is
dangerous to worship or
name Jesus as Lord.
Lord, on the battlefield of life
keep us faithful and strong.

Father,
we pray for those who work out
their faith on the battlefield of life
and for those whose belief in
democracy is tested in the
midst of a totalitarian state;
for those who, because of their
commitment to truth, face
being denounced as a spy
and for those who are in prison
without trial because of their
concern for human rights.

Lord, on the battlefield of life
keep us faithful and strong.

Father,
we pray for those who work out
their faith on the battlefield of life
and for young people who
have dared to take a firm
stance against drugs;
for those whose faith in Christ
commits them to reject the
behaviour of their peers
and for those facing ridicule
and rejection from those they
thought were their friends.
Lord, on the battlefield of life
keep us faithful and strong.

Father,
we pray for those who work out
their faith on the battlefield of life
and for those who put
themselves at risk as 'Street
Angels' for the vulnerable;
for those who care for the lost
and the homeless, the drunks
and the drug addicts
and for those who discover they
are in constant danger of
physical and verbal abuse.
Lord, on the battlefield of life
keep us faithful and strong.

Father,
we pray for those who work out
their faith on the battlefield of life
and for those who are prevented
from living out their faith
in Jesus at work;
for those whose stand of
faithful obedience has
landed them in court
and for those treated as
criminals in our nation that
has created its own gods.
Lord, on the battlefield of life
keep us faithful and strong.

Father,
we pray for those who work out
their faith on the battlefield of life
and for those we know who are
facing abuse in their own homes;
for those longing to find
fellow Christians to support
and encourage them
and for those who are wondering
how much longer they can
cope with the battle.
Lord, on the battlefield of life
keep us faithful and strong.

We bring our prayers in the
name of Jesus Christ,
who has won the battle for all
who trust in him. **Amen.**

SUNDAY BEFORE ADVENT

Prayer of Approach

Psalm 132:1–12

You are our faithful God
and we will worship you.

You are our God who strengthens us
and we will worship you.

You are our sovereign Lord
and we will worship you.

You are our mighty Saviour
and we will worship you.

You are the reason for our praises
and we will worship you. **Amen.**

Praise

John 18:37

We bring our praises to the
King of the kingdom
and our thanksgiving to the One,
to whom all things belong.
We praise you, Lord, as we stand
on the threshold of Advent
and as we prepare ourselves for
the coming of the King.

Your coming had been designed
from before the dawn of creation
and your birth heralds the moment
when Immanuel was to be born.
From the very first it was the
fulfilment of God's purposes
and in Jesus the pathway has been
cleared for us to come home.

We praise you that Jesus came that
we might know the truth of God
and that we might experience
the overwhelming touch
of your grace.
His birth in Bethlehem is
the signal that the door to
heaven is wide open
because though he will be
born in a manger, he will be
dying to be our Saviour.

We praise you for Jesus, his life,
death, and resurrection
and for the assurance of God's
grace that his coming brings.
He is the King of the kingdom
and the Lord of all eternity
and we will praise him here, and we
will praise him for ever. **Amen.**

Intercession

Revelation 1:4b–8

Lord,
we pray for your church
here on earth
and for those in places
of persecution;
for churches who are paying
the price of following Jesus
and for those who remain faithful
to him no matter the cost.
Come
fill the church with your Spirit
for we are the body of Christ.

Lord,
we pray for your church
here on earth
and remember the churches
that are dying;
for those that are simply groups
of like-minded people
but who have lost the vision of
being the servants of Jesus.
Come
fill the church with your Spirit
for we are the body of Christ.

Lord,
we pray for your church
here on earth
and for churches that faithfully
proclaim the good news;
for churches where prayer
and the study of God's
Word are paramount
and for those whose focus
is on sharing God's love
in their community.
Come
fill the church with your Spirit
for we are the body of Christ.

Lord,
we pray for your church
here on earth
and for churches that
are open to all;
for those flooded with a
spirit of acceptance
and for those who never forget
that the church is a home
for all sinners.
Come
fill the church with your Spirit
for we are the body of Christ.

Lord,
we pray for your church
here on earth
and for churches all around the
world that are growing;
for those who are being blessed
with tremendous growth
and for those whose focus on
evangelism is bearing fruit.
Come
fill the church with your Spirit
for we are the body of Christ.

Lord,
we pray for your church
here on earth
and for churches alive with
the power of the Spirit;
for churches where the gifts and
the fruit of the Spirit are found
and for the Holy Spirit to be the
source of power for their worship.
Come
fill the church with your Spirit
for we are the body of Christ.

Lord,
we pray for your church
here on earth
and for the church here
in this place;
for the experience of the renewing
touch of God's grace
and for a sense of the
church on earth
being part of the church in heaven.
Come
fill the church with your Spirit
for we are the body of Christ.

We bring our prayers for the church
in the name of Christ, the
church's head. **Amen.**

YEAR C

FIRST SUNDAY OF ADVENT

Prayer of Approach

Psalm 25:1–10

Lord,
we come unready to
worship you;
our minds are too full of the
things we have left undone.
Our focus isn't completely on
giving you thanks and praise.
We carry so many memories of
hurtful words spoken to us.
We are finding it so very hard to
strip away all the distractions
and to clear our minds of the
things that trouble us deeply.

In the silence, come, Lord, and
refocus our thoughts on you
and by your grace we lay before
you the baggage of our lives.

silence

Lord,
by your Holy Spirit, enter
deeply into our hearts
and fill our lips with songs
of thanksgiving.
Now we are ready to give you
the praise that you deserve
and to honour your great and
glorious name. **Amen.**

Thanksgiving

1 Thessalonians 3:9–13

For home and for family
that bring us such joy
and for friends and for colleagues
who share our good days,
let us thank the Lord
and praise his name.

For those who stand by us when
life is full of problems
and for those who offer comfort
to friend and to foe,
let us thank the Lord
and praise his name.

For the beauty and variety
of our amazing world
and for those who open our eyes
to the wonders concealed,
let us thank the Lord
and praise his name.

For those who open young minds
to the discoveries of science
and for those who challenge us to
reach worlds beyond our own,
let us thank the Lord
and praise his name.

For those who remind us
of our responsibility of
care for God's earth
and for those who go on warning
us of the choices we must make,
let us thank the Lord
and praise his name.

For those who open our
eyes to the plight of the
poor and the starving
and for those who call on
governments to seek
justice for all,
let us thank the Lord
and praise his name.

For those who opened our hearts
to God's love all around us
and for those whose Jesus-filled lives
brought many prodigals home,

let us thank the Lord
and praise his name.

For the promise of Christ's coming
foretold by the prophets
and for the truth that rings out
through the days we call Advent,
let us thank the Lord
and praise his name.

For the blessings of love,
hope, and joy with which
Christ fills our days
and for the call to make our witness
to his love, power, and glory,
let us thank the Lord
and praise his name.

We bring our prayers in
the name of Jesus,
the hope and light of the
world. **Amen.**

Intercession
Luke 21:29–30
Lord,
we pray for those who look
for signs of peace
and for those whose world
lies in utter ruins;
for those who hide in
broken buildings
and for those driven from their
homes by the fighting.
May the coming of the Christ-child
be the sign of peace for the world.
Come, Lord Jesus, come.
Come, Lord Jesus, come.

Lord,
we pray for those who look
for signs of forgiveness
and for those who still bear the
scars of their mistakes;
for those whose prejudice,
abuse, and lies
have wrecked their homes and the
lives of those who loved them
and for those who carry a secret
no one knows but you.
May the coming of the Christ-child
be the sign of forgiveness
for the world.
Come, Lord Jesus, come.
Come, Lord Jesus, come.

Lord,
we pray for those who look
for signs of hope
and for those who wake up each
morning still in darkness;
for those who long to cry but
have no more tears to shed
and for those whose fears and
disappointments are deep inside.
May the coming of the Christ-child
be the sign of hope for the world.
Come, Lord Jesus, come.
Come, Lord Jesus, come.

Lord,
we pray for those who
look for signs of joy
and for those whose pain and
sorrow rob them of laughter;
for those who are single, with no
one to share their happiness
and for those who live alone,
longing for someone to
make them smile.
May the coming of the Christ-child
be the sign of joy for the world.
Come, Lord Jesus, come.
Come, Lord Jesus, come.

Lord,
we pray for those who look
for signs of grace
and for those who have been
made to feel like failures;
for those who have spent their
lives striving to be accepted
and for those hurt and
damaged in the past
and are longing to know they
are loved unconditionally.
May the coming of the Christ-child
be the sign of grace for the world.
Come, Lord Jesus, come.
Come, Lord Jesus, come.

Lord,
we pray for those who look
for signs of belonging
and for those who are always on
the outside of everything;
for those whose sense of
rejection runs very deep
and for those yet to
experience the wonder
of knowing they belong to
your eternal family.
May the coming of the Christ-child
be the sign of belonging
for the world.
Come, Lord Jesus, come.
Come, Lord Jesus, come.

Lord,
we pray for those who look
for signs of healing
and for those known to us
whose days are numbered;
for those whose sickness is of
the heart and the mind
and for those longing to
become the whole person
they know you designed them to be.
May the coming of the Christ-child
be the sign of healing for the world.
Come, Lord Jesus, come.
Come, Lord Jesus, come.

We bring our prayer in the
name of the one
who opens eyes and hearts
and minds in his love.
Amen.

SECOND SUNDAY OF ADVENT

Praise

Luke 1:68–79

Lord,
we come with our song of praise
for you are the God who
always keeps his word.
When the prophets
declared your truth
they did so in the full assurance
that it could be trusted.

Your word has touched nations
and changed lives
and your message of
compassion gives us hope.
In a world overrun with half-
truths, lies, and corruption
your word remains the rock on
which we can stand firm.

When evil appears to have
the world in its grip
you remind us that you will
always have the final word.

When life is dark and all
seems lost and futile

you reach out to take hold of
us and bring us home.

When our lives are broken and
peace is an empty dream
your word transforms the day
and renews our song of praise.

We praise you for you
are the Holy One
and everything you say and
do is perfect and right.
We sing our song of worship to
you, our Lord and our God,
and we will sing it now and
we will sing it for ever.

We offer you our adoration for you
bring light to the darkest day
and you offer the hope of renewal
where none seemed possible.
In you there is forgiveness and
the chance to begin again
and you show us the way of peace
and promise to walk with us.

We praise you, Lord
God Almighty, for you
alone are God.
We will worship you with our
songs and with our lives.
For you are the Lord who acts
in the most unexpected ways
and you call us all to do the
most unexpected things.

By your Holy Spirit, you call us,
challenge us, and empower us,
that our lives may be used
for your glory—
even when we least
expect it. **Amen.**

Confession

Malachi 3:1–4

Lord,
we had assumed that we knew
what you expected of us
and so long as we did our best that
would be sufficient for you.
We are only human, which we offer
as our excuse for our failures,
and we foolishly assume that you
will simply overlook our mistakes.

But we confess that your prophet
has shaken us out of our apathy
with his message of the necessity of
experiencing a deeper cleansing.
We confess that we had forgotten
that you are a Holy God
and we are beginning to
realise just how much we
need to be changed.

Lord,
come and purify our
hearts and minds
and make us clean within.

Lord,
come and transform who
and what we are
and make us what you
meant us to be.

Lord,
come like the refiner's fire
and burn away from our lives
everything that offends your glory.

Lord,
come and make us whole
that we may be your holy
people. **Amen.**

Intercession
Luke 3:1–6

Lord,
we want to talk to you about
the wilderness of our society
and for the breakdown of homes
and relationships all around us;
for our nation, where illegal drug
use is stealing young lives
and for our cities, where
many carry knives and even
children commit murder;
for the wilderness, where the
rich are getting richer
and the poor are simply
forgotten—and no
one seems to care.
Come, Lord of the wilderness,
and shake the foundations
of our broken world.

silence

Lord,
we want to talk to you about
the wilderness of corruption
and for the web of lies
and half-truths spun by
those in high office;
for the growing plague of
cheating to win at all costs
and for the damage athletes
are doing to themselves
and their sport;
for those who make their
decisions with no thought
for the moral consequences
and for those who see only
opportunities for profit and not
the communities they serve.
Come, Lord of the wilderness
of corruption,
and shake the foundations
of our broken world.

silence

Lord,
we want to talk to you about
the wilderness of faith
and for the impact of the media
who ridicule those who believe;
for the barrenness of our nation
that is shutting you out of its life
and for the damage this is
creating to people's sense of
meaning and purpose;
for churches that have
become like deserts where
no one goes to find life
and for those that have built a
stockade, keeping themselves
safe and new people out.
Come, Lord of the wilderness,
and shake the foundations
of our broken world.

silence

Lord,
we want to talk to you about
the wilderness of fear
and for the many no-go areas
of our towns and cities;
for estates where antisocial
behaviour is rife
and for those where crime and
gang warfare are endemic;
for places in our country that are
ruled by those dealing in drugs
and for our young people
being targeted with drugs
at the school gate.
Come, Lord of the wilderness,

and shake the foundations
of our broken world.

silence

Lord,
we want to talk to you about
the wilderness of our world
and for countries where war has
become a part of daily life;
for those places where
clean drinking water is a
luxury they don't have
and for governments who
spend more on weapons
than food for their people;
for those who export violence
and hatred that they have
tried to disguise as religion
and for those whose twisted
minds see suicide terrorism
as their gateway to heaven.
Come, Lord of the wilderness,
and shake the foundations
of our broken world.

silence

Lord,
we want to talk to you about the
wilderness of our own lives
and the struggles we face
making sense of the
journey we are taking;
for the times we have faced doubt,
despair, and depression
and for the crushing
moments when we have
lost someone we love;
for the concerns for our
families and friends who
have troubles of their own
and for the feeling of helplessness
when the bottom drops
out of our world.
Come, Lord of the wilderness,
and shake the foundations
of our broken world.

silence

Lord,
we come before you in repentance
for any part we have contributed
to the wilderness of your world.
Grant forgiveness and renewal
to the whole world,
that healing may begin for
your broken world.

We bring our prayers in the name
of the Lord of all creation,
who in Jesus shook the
foundations of the world—
and goes on shaking them. **Amen.**

THIRD SUNDAY OF ADVENT

Prayer of Approach

Zephaniah 3:14–17

We come to worship you,
our transforming God,
and we seek to lift up our voices
and to give glory
to the one who makes all things new.

You not only gave us life
but through Christ
we have been born again
and have been adopted
into your family of grace.

Now it is our joy and our delight
to offer you our thanks and praise

for all you have done for us in Jesus
and for the hope you
have set before us.

By your Holy Spirit,
fill our hearts with songs of praise
and our voices with words
of thanksgiving
as we join our worship
with the hosts of heaven. **Amen.**

Praise

Philippians 4:4–7

Father,
we have always been amazed by
the wonders of your creation
and by the utterly unimaginable
vastness of the universe.
We are left breathless as
microscopic creatures are
brought into view
and the seemingly endless variety
of animals and plants
are paraded before our eyes.

Our minds are awakened
as we learn of nations
we have never seen
and of races whose language and
customs are strange to our ears.
This is to say nothing of the beauty
of the blue planet we call home
and its mountains and valleys,
its oceans and seas, and
its rivers and streams.

Every day our lives are
touched by hundreds of
our fellow human beings
and through the media
the concerns of millions
bombard our thoughts.
We are beginning to realise just
how small is the spinning
ball on which we live
and how wide and deep, how
long and how high, our love
of our neighbour must be.

We praise you, Father, for
the challenge to respond to
the needs of your world
and to cease pretending
that we are ostriches that
hide from the truth.
We know that we share many
characteristics with the
rest of the animal chain
but you have granted us the
priceless gift of caring
for our neighbour
no matter who, no matter
when, and no matter
where they come from.

In our world, where we have
often been the cause of so
much pain and destruction,
you call us not to ignore the
suffering and hopelessness
of our neighbour
but to also celebrate what is good,
what is right, and what is lovely.

We praise you for opening our eyes
again to the good that people do
and to rejoice in the blessings we
and our neighbours receive.
We will not neglect to respond
to our deeply flawed
and troubled world
but we will praise you as
we refocus our hearts and
minds on those things

that are noble, right, pure,
lovely, admirable—that
by your Holy Spirit
they may be transformed into
launch pads for praise.

Father of peace, glory,
and authority,
we bring you our thanks
and praise. **Amen.**

Intercession
Isaiah 12:2–6

Father,
we pray for those who draw
from the wells of sadness
and for those whose tears have
never ceased to flow;
for those whose sense of loss is
still like an open wound
and for those whose pain is
too deep to cry anymore.
Father of life,
come quench our thirst.

Father,
we pray for those who draw
from the wells of anxiety
and for those whose lives
are restricted by risks
they can't face;
for those whose anxieties are like
boundaries they cannot cross
and for those who carry a burden
of shame for something
that isn't their fault.
Father of life,
come quench our thirst.

Father,
we pray for those who draw
from the wells of insecurity
and for those made to feel like
failures from their youngest days;
for those whose sense of
inferiority has limited
what they might have achieved
and for those who measure
themselves against others
as they forget that God has
a plan for them too.
Father of life,
come quench our thirst.

Father,
we pray for those who draw
from the wells of hunger
and for those whose whole day is
a never-ending search for food;
for those who watch helplessly
as their children are starving
and for those robbed of their future
by the impact of global corporations
upon their environment.
Father of life,
come quench our thirst.

Father,
we pray for those who draw from
the wells of superstition
and for those who see their lives
ruled by the stars and the planets;
for those trapped in a cycle
of behaviour that limits
the quality of their lives
and for those who trust in
touching wood and forget
to trust in its creator.
Father of life,
come quench our thirst.

Father,
we pray for those who draw
from the wells of hope

and for those who help us to see
God at work in his world;
for those whose walk of faith is
a light in the darkest places
and for those whose words,
deeds, and compassion for all
speak to us of their hope in God.
Father of life,
come quench our thirst.

Father,
we pray for ourselves and the
wells from which we draw
and for a commitment to
draw from the well of
your Word each day;
for our walk with you and an
openness to your will for our lives
and for a deeper experience talking
with you at the well of prayer.
Father of life,
come quench our thirst.

We bring our prayer in
the name of Jesus,
who meets us at the wells
of life. **Amen.**

FOURTH SUNDAY OF ADVENT

Prayer of Approach

Psalm 80:3

Lord,
we come to prepare
ourselves for worship
and to seek your blessing as
we gather in your name.
We long to experience the
renewal of your Holy Spirit
that we might stand before
you in holiness.
Come, make us clean.
Come, change our hearts.
Come, renew your
presence in our lives.
Come, Holy God,
and remake us as your
holy people,
set aside to live for your
glory. **Amen.**

Praise

Luke 1:46–55

Lord,
we join with Mary to
sing of your glory
and to declare your worth
to all who will listen.
There truly is no God like you
and there is most certainly
no God besides you.

You alone are Lord.

With Mary we echo the
praises of your people
and with all your people
across time and space
we give you the honour that
your name deserves.
Today we worship you
for who you are
and we glorify you for
all you have done.

You alone are Lord.

With Mary we stand amazed
by the way you have touched
and changed your people.
Ultimately your will is
done on earth
as it is in heaven.

Ultimately your presence
changes lives
and moves nations and their rulers.

You alone are Lord.

With Mary we are moved
when we remember
your compassion
and we are overwhelmed
by your constant offer of mercy.
Your grace reaches out
across the world
to every generation of every nation.

You alone are Lord.

With Mary we are
stunned by the way
you turn the values of the
world upside down.
Those who trust in their own riches
leave your presence empty-handed
but those who enter
declaring the poverty
of their lives—
you offer the riches of heaven itself.

You alone are Lord
and this is the reason
for our praises.
You alone are Lord
and this is why we come
to give thanks.
You alone are Lord
and you will be, now and
for evermore. **Amen.**

Intercession

Micah 5:2

Lord,
you are the God of small things
and we pray for those
who do things
that are not always recognised
or appreciated;
for those who volunteer
to be 'Street Angels'
as they care for vulnerable
young people
and for those who are shopping
centre chaplains
as they offer support
when it's needed.
Lord,
we bring our small gifts to you;
use them for your glory.

Lord,
you are the God of small things
and we pray for those
who do things
that are not always recognised
or appreciated;
for those who work in
hospital laboratories
as they enable the doctors
to make a diagnosis;
and for those committed
to medical research
as they seek to discover new
and better medications.
Lord,
we bring our small gifts to you;
use them for your glory.

Lord,
you are the God of small things
and we pray for those
who do things
that are not always recognised
or appreciated;
for those who keep our
roads in good repair

as they resurface those
damaged and pot-holed
and for those whose work is
to design new highways
as they strive to deal with
the demands of ever-
increasing traffic.
Lord,
we bring our small gifts to you;
use them for your glory.

Lord,
you are the God of small things
and we pray for those
who do things
that are not always recognised
or appreciated;
for those who are opticians,
dentists, or chemists
as they provide the healing
and care that we need
and for physiotherapists,
psychologists, and paramedics
as they respond to some of the
most urgent needs we have.
Lord,
we bring our small gifts to you;
use them for your glory.

Lord,
you are the God of small things
and we pray for those
who do things
that are not always recognised
or appreciated;
for those who write books that
bring enrichment to our lives
as they open our minds to the
colours and variety of life
and for those who bring the
world to our television screens
as they show us all of its plants
and creatures, great and small.
Lord,
we bring our small gifts to you;
use them for your glory.

Lord,
you are the God of small things
and we pray for those who do things
that are not always recognised
or appreciated;
for those who give of their
time and their skills
as they go to rescue those
trapped under earthquakes
and for those who are simply
seeking to be good neighbours
as they befriend the housebound and
the lonely in their community.
Lord,
we bring our small gifts to you;
use them for your glory.

Lord,
you are the God of small things
and we pray for those who do things
that are not always recognised
or appreciated;
for those who have been there
for us when we needed them
as they have provided strength,
courage, and hope
and for opportunities for our
homes to be a new Bethlehem
as they are transformed by the
presence of Jesus as Lord.
Lord,
we bring our small gifts to you;
use them for your glory.

We bring our prayers in
the name of Jesus,

whose birth amidst the
animals in Bethlehem
was the result of the promise of the
God of small things. **Amen.**

CHRISTMAS DAY

Prayer of Approach

John 1:14

Lord,
this is the day when the
world changed
and from this moment we count
our days from your birth.
As Jesus entered our world,
just as we do,
you challenge us to recognise
your presence in him.
It was always your plan that
we should know you,
that our whole lives would be
flooded with the light of heaven.

As we gather to hear the all too
familiar story of Christ's birth—
the journey to Bethlehem, the
birth among the animals,
and the shepherds, who were the
first apostles of his infant fame—
this day we join with them and
millions across the centuries
as we celebrate the coming of the
King who is Lord of all. **Amen.**

Praise

Isaiah 9:2–7

Lord,
it is as if you have turned
on the light of heaven
and the darkness of earth cannot
cope with its power.

We have come to sing the
songs of angels
and to celebrate that we are
surrounded by the glory of heaven.

There is still too much
darkness in your world
and there are so many places
where pain and hardship rule;
too many lives are wrecked by
greed, hatred, and selfishness
and people we know and
love are facing problems
that overwhelm them.

But the light has come!

We praise you, Lord, that nothing
can ever be the same again
for Christ is born,
for Christ is our Saviour,
for Christ is the Lord.

We praise you that your light
brings hope to the hopeless
and those at the end of their
tether are offered the
chance to start again.
The light of Christ not only
reveals the evil and wickedness
but it brings cleansing, renewal,
and a promise of hope
that doesn't deceive.

We praise you for the way that
the light of Jesus changes lives
and wherever it is experienced
darkness is put on notice
that ultimately its end has come!

Today we come as families to
become part of your family

that we may celebrate the wonder
and joy of Immanuel.
Today we remember that
the baby in the manger is
the man on the cross
and the man on the cross is our
risen Saviour and Lord.
Come, Lord Jesus, come—
come not as a baby born
in a manger!
Come, Lord Jesus, come—
come as the Lord of
our lives! **Amen.**

Intercession

Luke 2:1–7

Lord, we pray for your world
and all the hurting people in it;
for those who feel able
to talk about it
and for those who keep it
all locked up inside;
for those who have no one who
will listen to their pain
and for those whose painful
depression is only too real.
The Lord shares our hurt
and he feels our pain.

Lord, we pray for your world
and all the hurting people in it;
for those who are hurting
because of the wrong things
others have said and done
and for those still experiencing
the pain of the abuse
they suffered years ago.
The Lord shares our hurt
and he feels our pain.

Lord, we pray for your world
and all the hurting people in it;
for those who are hurting
because of civil war
and for those who suffer because
of fighting between nations;
for those fleeing the
dangers of a war zone
and for those who have
lost everything in their
search for peace.
The Lord shares our hurt
and he feels our pain.

Lord, we pray for your world,
and all the hurting people in it;
for those who are hurting
because of the wrong choices
they have made
and for those who are hurting
because they have nowhere to live;
for those who are hurting
because of the choices
others have made
and for those who have
come to the point
where they have no
choices left to make.
The Lord shares our hurt
and he feels our pain.

Lord, we pray for your world
and all the hurting people in it;
for those who live rough on
the streets of our cities
because they have nowhere to live
and for those who are hurting
because they have lost those
they have loved most;
for those who are filled with regret
because of what they did
or failed to do.
The Lord shares our hurt
and he feels our pain.

Lord, we pray for your world
and all the hurting people in it;
for those who are hurting
because of the mistakes
they have made
and for those who are hurting
because they are made to
feel they are failures;
for those who are hurting
because they are lonely
and for those who are hurting
because they just long to be loved.
The Lord shares our hurt
and he feels our pain.

Lord, we pray for your world
and all the hurting people in it.
We ask that those who are hurting
may come to know
that on the cross
you shared all their hurt and pain
and that because you are Lord
you still share all that
hurts them today.

Lord, we pray,
as Mary held you when
you were a baby,
come now as Immanuel
and in your gentle, healing,
loving hands
hold your hurting world.

We ask this in Jesus'
name. **Amen.**

FIRST SUNDAY OF CHRISTMAS

Praise

Psalm 148

Lord,
there are times when we seem
to have a misunderstanding
of worship
and we make the mistake
of thinking we can
confine our praises
to our time together, here
in your house.
We fall into the error of
assuming that our adoration
can only be expressed in
a formal setting
and we allow worship to be trapped
in our rituals and liturgies.

It is when we listen to the psalmist
that our minds are blown away
and our whole being is shaken
to the foundations.
It is as if he is giving us a
lesson in true worship
as he calls us to join in the
song of creation!

Lord,
we want to say, 'Wow!'
We never realised just how
exciting it is meant to be
giving praise to the King
of all creation.
We are only now
beginning to grasp
the wonder, joy, and the thrill
of being permitted
to give thanks and praise
to your holy name.

The psalmist opens our
eyes to comprehend
the utter vastness of the choir
that is singing of your glory.
From the heights of heaven to
the depths of the earth,
from the farthest reaches of space
to the mountains and
valleys of the earth,
everywhere is singing the
song of your glory!

Now comes the discovery
that the purpose of every
tree and every plant,
every bird, every creature
is to give you honour
and glory for ever.

Lord,
it is right that we assemble as
the people of your grace
to offer you wholehearted
thanks and praise.
Now teach us that the
song we sing here
has no beginning and no end.

We praise you that you are calling us
to go out into your world
determined to transform
everything we see, hear,
and experience
into lives filled with worship
and hearts focused on living
for your glory. **Amen.**

Confession

Luke 2:41–52

Lord,
we confess
that too often we rely on
ourselves and not on you
and that our attempts to follow you
are doomed to failure.

We confess
that we are not always
walking closely enough
to hear your voice
and we assume that we already know
what it is that you want of us.

We confess
that we do not make time
for you in our lives
and that we allow your Word
to grow dusty on the shelf.

We confess
that our time with you in prayer
is full of what we want to ask
so that we rarely allow your word
to enter our hearts and minds.

As Jesus needed to focus
on being with you,
so transform our priorities
that spending time in your presence
may become more precious
every day. **Amen.**

Intercession

Colossians 3:12–17

Lord,
we pray for those who
live differently
and for those who do not follow
the ways of the world;
for those who show great
compassion, especially
to strangers,

and for those whose
consideration for others
speaks loudly of God's
love for his world;
for those who work in busy A&E
departments of hospitals
and for those who enable the elderly
to remain in their own home.
Lord, help us to live differently,
that others may see Jesus in us.

Lord,
we pray for those who
live differently
and for those who do not follow
the ways of the world;
for those whose kindness is a
challenge to their community
and for those whose different
behaviour changes lives
as others witness the touch
of God's love;
for police community support
officers, who seek to bring
peace where they serve,
and for those who staff day
care centres providing
respite for families.
Lord, help us to live differently,
that others may see Jesus in us.

Lord,
we pray for those who live differently
and for those who do not follow
the ways of the world;
for those who value
people differently
and for those whose lives expose
the self-centredness of others;
for those who do not label the
poor as lazy scroungers
and for those who welcome
migrants as they flee in
fear for their lives.
Lord, help us to live differently,
that others may see Jesus in us.

Lord,
we pray for those who
live differently
and for those who do not follow
the ways of the world;
for those who do not allow
hatred to rule in their hearts
and for those who teach us the
wisdom of letting bitterness go;
for those who have experienced
the freedom forgiveness brings
and for those who offer
forgiveness to those who
have hurt them most.
Lord, help us to live differently,
that others may see Jesus in us.

Lord,
we pray for those who
live differently
and for those who do not follow
the ways of the world;
for those who think differently
about the real purpose of life
and for those whose attitudes
shout aloud of their
thankfulness within;
for those who are realising
that happiness isn't found
in wealth and possessions
and for those whose days are
enriched by their experience
of the love of God.
Lord, help us to live differently,
that others may see Jesus in us.

Lord,
we pray for those who
live differently
and for those who do not follow
the ways of the world;
for those who respond
with a gentleness that
turns away wrath
and for those whose genuine
humility marks them out
in a world of pride;
for those who treat others with a
grace they often don't deserve
and for those who take time
to listen so that others know
they have been heard.
Lord, help us to live differently,
that others may see Jesus in us.

Lord,
we pray for those who
live differently
and for those who do not follow
the ways of the world;
for ourselves and the way we live
and behave in God's world
and for a realisation that
our neighbours need
to see Jesus in us;
for an ever-deepening experience
of God's grace upon our days,
that we may daily ask the Lord for
an infilling of the Holy Spirit.
Lord, help us to live differently,
that others may see Jesus in us.

We bring our prayers in
the name of Jesus,
that our walk with him may
speak of his presence. **Amen.**

SECOND SUNDAY OF CHRISTMAS

Prayer of Approach

Psalm 147:12

Lord,
you have given us the most
important task in all the world
and the reward for its fulfilment
is beyond price.
Every time we gather together
we are reminded
that you have called us to lead the
whole world to worship you!

We have come that you
might prepare us for this
incredible purpose
and for the guidance of your hand
upon our words and deeds.
It is our greatest desire to worship
you, the Lord Almighty,
and to celebrate your extravagant
love for all the world.

Come, Lord, and fill us
with the Holy Spirit,
that we may worship you
and you alone. **Amen.**

Praise

Ephesians 1:3–14

Lord,
we find Paul so utterly amazing!
He has so much to say about
you and your glory;
it all cascades like a mighty
waterfall of praise.
He simply can't help himself—
his words of worship cannot
be held back any longer.

If only our praises were also
filled with such joy
and our songs simply overflowed
with thanksgiving.
We long for a renewed
experience of your glory
that we might be truly lost in
wonder, love, and praise.

It is easy to see why Paul was on
fire with his song of praise
and why the words of worship
flowed from his lips.
He had discovered the source
of powerful worship
and the secret he declared was in
his wonder at God's grace.

How can we not worship as we
realise something of your majesty
and how can we keep silent once we
know of your love and mercy?
The launch pad of our praises
lies in who you are and in
what you have done—
for you, the Lord of heaven, entered
our world to lead us home.

We praise you, Lord, that you
gave yourself on the cross
that we might walk in your
footsteps and celebrate
your compassion.
You are the King of glory.
You are sovereign over all things.
You left the glory of the angels.
You long to make your
home in our hearts.

Lord,
there is no song that is too
great to sing of your love
and there are no words that can
truly express your glory.
And—wonder of wonders—
you, by grace, have made
us your children
and you have called us your
precious possession.

But the song doesn't end there;
the message bursts forth:
the Holy Spirit has made himself
the guarantee of your love
and his presence in our hearts fills
us with the joy of your assurance.

Thanks be to you, our
wonderful Lord. **Amen.**

Intercession
John 1:1–9

Lord,
we pray for those
whose lives are trapped by
the darkness of fear;
for those facing a time of
uncertainty, illness,
and the fear that comes
from not knowing;
for those in hospital and those
undergoing unpleasant treatment;
for those who wait through
dark days of anxiety.
Lord, in the darkness,
come as the light.

Lord,
we pray for those
whose lives are filled with
the darkness of hate;
for those whose words and deeds
are the source of much pain,
sorrow, and despair;

for those whose whole way of
life is the enemy of peace
and whose attitude to their
fellow human beings
destroys their hope;
for those who cause terror
and assume the role of the
suicide bomber.
Lord, in the darkness,
come as the light.

Lord,
we pray for those
in the darkness of loneliness;
for those who are single in a
society designed for the family
and for those left alone now
that the family has gone;
for those who spend their days
in the prison of their home
and long for someone to visit
to break into the silence
of their aloneness;
for those who with the passing
years have only their memories
and no one with whom
to share them.
Lord, in the darkness,
come as the light.

Lord,
we pray for those in the
darkness of doubt;
for those who long to believe,
to have faith, and to trust;
for those with questions
they can't answer
and for those whose doubts are
simply tearing them apart;
for those whose ability to
trust has been damaged
by the behaviour of others
and for those whose faith
is all in their heads
and not in their hearts where
you meant it to be.
Lord, in the darkness,
come as the light.

Lord,
we pray for those in the
darkness of emptiness;
for those who have filled their
days and their hours
with the passing pleasures
of the moment
and are discovering that the security,
peace, and contentment
they promised
were but a mirage that
could never last
in the reality of the coming day;
for those whose riches account
for nothing of value
and for those whose hollowness is
bringing them pain and despair.
Lord, in the darkness,
come as the light.

Lord,
we pray for those in the
darkness of sin;
for those who today
will destroy a little more of themselves
through the addictions that
imprison their days;
for those whose selfishness brings
pain to their neighbour
and whose self-centredness
is building the wall ever higher
and locking the door
to the grace that would heal them.
Lord, in the darkness,
come as the light.

Lord,
we pray for those whose lives have
been darkened by disaster;
for those whose lives have
been destroyed
by the impact of earthquake,
flood, or fire;
for those who have lost
everything and everyone
that mattered to them
and for those facing hunger
and starvation
through no fault of their own;
for those struggling for existence
and for those who know that
they are losing the fight.
Lord, in the darkness,
come as the light.

Lord,
we pray for those who are facing
the darkness of the years;
for those who are in the
twilight of their days
and for those who have only
their 'might have beens'
and their 'if onlys' are still
causing them pain;
for those whose memories
still haunt them
and for those whose memories
are darkened and lost;
for those who can hardly
remember their name
and for those who have forgotten
the faces of those that they loved.
Lord, in the darkness,
come as the light.

Lord,
we pray for those whose lives have
been touched by your grace
and whose days are set
ablaze with your love;
for those whose faith in Christ
is daily being renewed
and the light of the Father's presence
fills them with hope, peace,
and joy from within;
for those for whom the
light of the Spirit
is the source of their strength,
compassion, and trust
and for those who are daily
committing themselves
to be beacons of light in
Christ's name.
Lord, in the darkness,
come as the light.

Lord,
we pray for those we know by name,
that the light of Christ will
bring them the joy
of renewal and refreshment.

silence

We pray too for ourselves,
that the light of Christ
will find its way
even into the darkest
corners of our lives
that we might walk in the
light of his love.
Lord, in the darkness,
come as the light.

We bring our prayers in
the name of Christ,
the light of the world. **Amen.**

FIRST SUNDAY IN ORDINARY TIME

Prayer of Approach

Psalm 29:2

Lord,
by your Holy Spirit, enable
us to give you glory
and by the power of your
grace may we worship
you as you deserve.
Your name is the Lord Almighty
and you reign over all things.
Teach us to sing your praise
as we join with the hosts
of heaven. **Amen.**

Praise

Isaiah 43:1–7

Lord,
how can we not sing
our song of glory?
How can we not give you
our heartfelt thanks and praise?
How can we not long to
know you more
and trust you with the
whole of our lives?

Lord,
we sing because you are
our great creator.
Everything we see and hear,
everything we touch and hold,
everything we watch and
think we understand,
everything that is good
and true and worthy
finds its origins in the
heart of our God.

Lord,
we sing because you are
our great sustainer.
Every moment of every day,
every breath we breathe,
every discovery we make,
every good deed and kindness,
every helping hand,
every time someone cares,
understands, and loves
finds its origin in the
heart of our God.

Lord,
we sing because you are
our heavenly Father.
Your almighty power and presence,
your compassion for all
that you have made,
your unfailing mercy
and forgiveness,
your love that reaches out
and welcomes us home,
your Holy Spirit who enables
us to begin again,
your coming to us in the one
who taught us to call
you 'our Father'
finds its origin in the
heart of our God.

Lord,
we come to sing our song of glory.
We come to give you our
heartfelt thanks and praise.
We come because we long
to know you more
and trust you with the
whole of our lives.
All praise and thanks to our God.
In the name of Jesus. **Amen.**

Intercession

Luke 3:15–17

Prepare a bowl of water and seven pebbles. Place a pebble in the water as you finish each prayer.

Lord,
your baptism was the sign of
your eternal sonship
and of your entering into all
that life means to us.
So we bring our prayers in the
knowledge of your glory
and in our experience of
your humanity.
Lord of the waters of baptism,
come and refresh your world.

Lord,
we pray for those who are
hungry in a world of plenty
and for those who have nothing
whilst others have everything;
for those who have lost all that
was precious to them
and for those whose hands reach
out for help to rebuild their lives.
Lord of the waters of baptism,
come and refresh your world.

Lord,
we pray for those who are
longing to learn
and for those with no one
to teach them;
for all teachers, lecturers, and
ministers of education,
that there will be equal
opportunity for everyone.
Lord of the waters of baptism,
come and refresh your world.

Lord,
we pray for those who care
for those in need
and for those whose life of service
brings dignity to others;
for those who give of themselves
in care homes and hospices
and for those whose lives are
enriched by their caring.
Lord of the waters of baptism,
come and refresh your world.

Lord,
we pray for those who serve the
nation as members of parliament
and for those whose faithful service
goes unnoticed by the media;
for those whose passion for truth
and for justice is undimmed
and for those in high office who
carry great burdens for us all.
Lord of the waters of baptism,
come and refresh your world.

Lord,
we pray for those who hold office
in the life of your church
and for those who work unseen
and unknown for your glory;
for those whose pastoral
care is an expression of
their love of Christ
and for those who share the love
of Jesus in all they do or say.
Lord of the waters of baptism,
come and refresh your world.

Lord,
we pray for those who work
for closer relationships
between churches

and for those whose daily
prayer and service are that
we may all be one;
for those who reach out across
the foolish barriers we erect
and for those whose life in the
Spirit destroys the stumbling
blocks we protect.
Lord of the waters of baptism,
come and refresh your world.

Lord,
we pray for ourselves
and our church,
that you will touch us and mould
us, hold us and love us.
We pray, renew your church in
the baptism of the Holy Spirit
that we may worship and witness
to the Lord of all glory.
Lord of the waters of baptism,
come and refresh your world.

In the name of Christ, Son of
God, source of grace. **Amen.**

SECOND SUNDAY IN ORDINARY TIME

Prayer of Approach

Psalm 36:5

Lord,
we simply can't help ourselves.
Every time we come into
your presence
we are bowled over
by the experience
of being loved.

Lord,
we want to hold our breath
and in the stillness
to wonder at the grace—
the undeserved love—
with which you utterly
overwhelm us.

Lord,
how can we not adore you—
our King,
our Prince of Peace,
and the source of all our hope?
Our hearts, minds, and lives
are touched by your grace
and healed by your love.

Wonderful, wonderful God,
for all that you are,
we offer you heartfelt
adoration. **Amen.**

Confession

Isaiah 62:1–5

Lord,
sometimes we wonder
if we can carry on much longer.
The strain of following Jesus,
of walking against the crowd
and seeking to serve in your name,
are taking their toll.

Lord,
we are dry, dying of thirst,
and hungry for refreshment
deep within.
The problem is, Lord,
that we have spent so long
serving, giving out,
sharing with others,
we have neglected
our own spiritual health—
we are like the parched ground
that the gushing rains simply
cannot penetrate.

Lord,
you must deal with us gently,
allowing your healing,
life-renewing grace
to seep down through the
fissures of our brokenness,
that, wholeness restored,
we may once more be
soaked in your love,
overflow with your grace,
and be pleased to name Jesus
as the source of our joy
and our hope. **Amen.**

Intercession
John 2:1–11

Lord,
we pray for families in need
of hope and renewal
and for those that are stressed
to the point of breaking;
for families where there
are arguments and
misunderstanding
and for those where listening
is now at a premium.
May the presence of Christ
change all things.

Lord,
we pray for families suffering
the effects of real poverty
and for those where depravation
is taking its toll;
for those who are bearing the
burden of the recession
and for those who are
losing their homes.
May the presence of Christ
change all things.

Lord,
we pray for families torn apart
by their parents' addictions
and for children living in an
atmosphere of violence and abuse;
for those whose choices are
symbols of hope to their family
and for those whose love and
faithfulness are the examples
their children need.
May the presence of Christ
change all things.

Lord,
we pray for families torn apart
by tragedy and disaster
and for those who have lost loved
ones in [*name any recent tragedy*];
for those now left with nowhere
to live and no work to do
and for those who look to people
like us for the help that they need.
May the presence of Christ
change all things.

Lord,
we pray for those recently
married or whose wedding
is soon to take place
and for those whose special
relationships have blossomed
over the years;
for those whose promise of
lifetime commitment has
been damaged or broken
and for those whose faithfulness
is a joy to us all.
May the presence of Christ
change all things.

Lord,
we pray for families torn apart by
the activities of their children
and for those whose love is
being stretched to its limits;
for those who feel disillusioned
and like failures as parents
when the fault is not theirs but the
result of choices made by others.
May the presence of Christ
change all things.

Lord,
we pray for the family of
the whole human race
and for its failure to live
together in peace, harmony,
and understanding;
for those whose actions bring
pain, sorrow, and terror
and for those who are God's
peacemakers on earth.
May the presence of Christ
change all things.

Lord,
we pray for the family
of your church
and for the damage our lack of
unity does to its witness;
for a renewal of the work of
the Holy Spirit in the life
of all of its members
and for a new focus on
mission and evangelism in
the name of our Lord.
May the presence of Christ
change all things.

Lord,
in silence, we pray for
our own family,
asking that God's presence
will renew every part
of our life together.

silence

May the presence of Christ
change all things.

In the name of Christ, the one
who is Lord of all. **Amen.**

THIRD SUNDAY IN ORDINARY TIME

Praise

Psalm 19:14

Holy, holy, holy Lord,
majestic, powerful, sovereign,
Saviour of the world.

Lord,
you are our God
and we give you all the honour.

Lord,
you are holy
and we lay our lives before you.

Lord,
you are majestic
and we offer you the worship
of our hearts and
minds and lives.

Lord,
you are powerful
and every corner of creation
is an emblem of your goodness
and the distant constellations
laugh at our thoughts
of your glory.

Lord,
you are our Saviour,
picking us up,
healing our wounds,
cleansing our sin,
transforming our lives,
and filling us with the Holy Spirit.

Holy, holy, holy Lord,
majestic, powerful, sovereign,
Saviour of the world.
We praise your holy name. **Amen.**

Confession

Luke 4:14–21

Lord,
our minds reel
as we try to grasp something
of the pain, sorrow, and suffering
that our sisters and brothers
face in your world.

Lord,
our hearts ache as we
ponder again
just what we can do
to heal the brokenness
of our neighbour.

Lord,
our lives lie open to you.
We wait quietly, patiently
as we focus again on your
unfailing love.
Help us to trust that
all these things
that are beyond our
understanding
or our power to resolve
are ultimately within
your grace. **Amen.**

Intercession

1 Corinthians 12:12–31a

Lord,
we pray for those who
need good news;
for those who know their lives
are poor reflections of what
their Maker intended;
for those who are poor because
their gifts and skills
are no longer required in our
post-industrial society
and for those whose poor health
has coloured every facet of their lives;
for those whose corrupt
government has robbed them
of the international aid
that would have changed
their whole lives.
Spirit of the sovereign Lord,
come and anoint your world.

Lord,
we pray for those who
need good news;
for those who are blind to the
wonder and the joy of each day
and for those whose negative
attitude closes their eyes
to the love of a child, the laughter of
hope, and the whisper of a smile;
for those in the media who
refuse to recognise
the damage their programmes
of violence and abuse
are doing to the young
and impressionable;
for those who are so focused
on their own petty needs,
unseeing, they pass by their
neighbour—across the street
or around the world.

Spirit of the sovereign Lord,
come and anoint your world.

Lord,
we pray for those who
need good news;
for those who are oppressed
by the weight of responsibility
that is heaped upon them
and for those who suffer in
silence behind closed doors;
for wives whose bodies, minds, and
spirits bear the scars of violence
and for those damaged for
life by the abuse they
experienced as a child;
for communities who are
oppressed by groups of vandals
and for nations who suffer at
the whim of their dictator.
Spirit of the sovereign Lord,
come and anoint your world.

Lord,
we pray for those who
need good news;
for those who have served in
the life of the church,
offering pastoral support, caring
for the property, the finances,
and the work with children
and young people;
for those who have given of their
time in the local community
as hospital volunteers, local
councillors, and charity workers;
for those seeking God's blessing
in the twilight of their days
and for those who long for
his guiding hand at the
start of their journey.

Spirit of the sovereign Lord,
come and anoint your world.

We ask our prayers in the
name of the One,
anointed by the Spirit of
the Lord. **Amen.**

FOURTH SUNDAY IN ORDINARY TIME

Praise

Psalm 71:1–6

Lord,
we will praise you
when the sun shines,
when the skies are blue,
and we don't have a care
in the world.
We will praise you too
when all is dark and grey
and the bottom has dropped
out of our world.

Lord,
we will praise you
when all our dreams come to fruition
and all we had hoped for
we hold in our hands.
We will praise you too
when our hopes are dashed
and the plans of yesterday
drip away like water through a sieve.

Lord,
we will praise you
in our hopes and in our fears,
through our joy and in the
midst of our sorrows.
We will praise you now.
We will praise you for all things.
We will praise you for ever.

In Christ, through Christ,
and for Christ. **Amen.**

Intercession

Luke 4:24

I am a care worker in a
home for the elderly.
It isn't the most exciting
job in the world
and it wasn't one that was high
on my list of possible careers.
You have no idea just how difficult
some of our residents can be—
I never get a moment's peace and
their demands are endless.
I am treated as their personal slave,
always at their beck and call.
The relatives, when they decide
to visit, are no better!
They are determined to find fault.
It would help if someone
said thank you.
It's as if I'm invisible—
I'm no longer a person
to be appreciated.
Pray for me.

I am the person who works at the
checkout at the supermarket.
You have no idea just how
boring this job is.
I pick up your shopping item by
item, pass them over the scanner,
and watch as you cram everything
into your array of shopping bags.
You don't know my name and
you never look at my face—
it's as if I just don't exist!
You never see me as I am:
a person in need of a kindly word,
a person longing for acceptance,
a person with hopes and
fears just like you,
a person!
Pray for me.

I am your doctor.
Have you ever thought what
it's like sitting there,
waiting for the next patient
with their endless list of
petty demands?
I sometimes wonder if
anyone would notice
if they were speaking
to a computer
rather than a real person.
No one ever asks how I feel
or gives a thought to my
needs or concerns.
I have been reduced to a
supplier of tablets
for those seeking instant cures.
Yet I'm in deep trouble if
something goes wrong
or if I make a mistake.
I have thought of wearing a badge
that declares I'm only human.
But I've become part of the
furniture of your life—
and you don't see me.
Pray for me.

I am the person who sweeps
up your rubbish.
This must be the most thankless
task in the world.
It is like painting the
Forth Bridge—
I never have the satisfaction
of knowing a job's done.
Perhaps you think that all those
sweet papers and cigarette ends

simply disappear from view
all by themselves,
they just vanish from your
sense of responsibility.
Not only do you never give
your litter a thought,
you do not see me—
you even avoid eye contact lest
you become contaminated.
You do not see me as a person
needing love and affection.
Pray for me.

I am a farmer.
No, you don't know me and
you don't know my name,
but if it were not for me
you would have no food
on your table
and you would have nothing
to give your family to eat.
You never give me a thought.
Do you ever wonder
who pays for the supermarket's
special offers?
The burden of their 'buy
one get one free'
is not a result of their generosity,
it's a price tag that always
lands at my door.
If only I wasn't hidden from
your sense of responsibility
and you could see me
and my family
struggling to make ends meet.
But you don't want to see me—
if you did it would cost
you too much.
Pray for me.

I am someone who works
in your church.
When you were looking
for a volunteer
I foolishly put up my hand
and everyone breathed
a sigh of relief.
Whatever I do—
pastoral care, youth work,
look after the property
or the finances—
I have disappeared from sight.
It never crosses your
mind to wonder
who opens the church and
gets everything ready.
You are perfectly happy to
worship when you feel able,
just as long as the work of the
church doesn't affect you.
Let me make it clear:
I really don't mind serving
my Lord as I do.
It is as if I've blended into
the background
and you've forgotten I'm here.
If only someone, one day
would stop and say thank you!
Pray for me.

I am me.
Whether at work or at home
I ceased to be a person—
I am known by the badge
I have been given.
I'm labelled retired, too
old, or too young.
I'm called married or single
or just unemployed.
I'm regarded as awkward,
difficult, or just plain daft.
I'm branded disabled,
dysfunctional, or
simply as terminal.

However I'm pigeon-holed—
in reality I'm still me!
I'm rather like Jesus in the
way that I'm treated
because they had labelled
him, his face didn't fit.
When you spare a thought for
the wonder of your Saviour
please spare a thought
and don't label me.
Pray for me,
pray for me.

Lord, in your mercy,
hear our prayer. Amen.

Dismissal

1 Corinthians 13:1

Lord,
send us out into your world.
For your glory, we will
speak in your name;
through your grace, we
will offer hope;
and in your presence, we
will be strong. **Amen.**

FIFTH SUNDAY IN ORDINARY TIME

Prayer of Approach

Psalm 138:1a

Lord,
we come with a sense of
joy and anticipation
for we have come to worship
the Lord of all creation.
Touch our hearts and set
our tongues free
that together we may praise
the Lord of glory. **Amen.**

Praise

Isaiah 6:1–8

Lord,
like Isaiah all those years ago,
we enter your presence with a
sense of awe and wonder.
To be permitted to offer
thanks and praise
to the Lord of all creation, the
sovereign Lord over all things,
is more than anything our
tiny, finite minds can
hope to comprehend.

Lord,
like Isaiah all those years ago,
we come with an overwhelming
sense of expectation.
You are our God—and
there is no other!
You are our sovereign Lord—
and we will have no other!
You are our Saviour, lover, and
friend—and you are all we need!

Lord,
like Isaiah all those years ago,
we come with a sense of our
own unworthiness.
How could it be otherwise,
when we are standing in the
presence of the supreme holiness?
It is here that perhaps we feel the
true weight of our sinful lives
and understand something of
your act of grace in Christ.

Lord,
like Isaiah all those years ago,
we praise you, not simply for
loving us but for loving
us unconditionally.

It was always your will that we
should find life in your presence
and it is through the life, death,
and resurrection of your Son
that we have been granted
the opportunity, by faith
in him, to begin again.

Lord,
like Isaiah all those years ago,
we come as we have always come
to give you our praises.
Come touch our hearts,
our minds, and our lives
with your Holy Spirit,
that as those cleansed, renewed, and
set free by his presence within
we may worship you all
our days. **Amen.**

Intercession

Luke 5:1–11

Lord,
we pray for those you call
to serve in caring for the
sick and the dying;
for doctors, nurses, and
all the ancillary staff in
a modern hospital
and for all who work in
our local health centres
and dental surgeries.
May they serve others as
they would serve you.
Lord, in your mercy,
hear our prayer.

Lord,
we pray for those still called
to be fishermen;
for those who risk their lives
reaping the harvest of the sea
and for those whose calling
is the lifeboat service.
May they serve others as
they would serve you.
Lord, in your mercy,
hear our prayer.

Lord,
we pray for those called to be
members of parliament;
for those who still serve with
a passion for truth and
honesty and integrity
and for those whose motivation
is their own personal
aggrandisement.
May they serve others as
they would serve you.
Lord, in your mercy,
hear our prayer.

Lord,
we pray for those called to
the legal profession;
for those who work as judges,
barristers, or solicitors
and for those who are members
of the police force.
May they serve others as
they would serve you.
Lord, in your mercy,
hear our prayer.

Lord,
we pray for those called to serve
their local community;
for those who are bus drivers, traffic
wardens, or local councillors
and for those who serve
in Citizens Advice.
May they serve others as
they would serve you.

Lord, in your mercy,
hear our prayer.

Lord,
we pray for those who are called to
serve those with special needs;
for those who work with the
disabled and the chronically
or terminally ill
and for those who are
chiropodists, occupational
therapists, and opticians.
May they serve others as
they would serve you.
Lord, in your mercy,
hear our prayer.

Lord,
we pray for those called to use
their gifts as musicians;
for those who are members of a
choir, orchestra, or rock band
and for those who offer their skills
in the enrichment of worship.
May they serve others as
they would serve you.
Lord, in your mercy,
hear our prayer.

Lord,
we pray for ourselves and all who
are called to discipleship;
for those who are working
out their calling at home, at
school, or in the world
and for those whose calling is
to call others to put their
faith in their risen Lord.
May they serve others as
they would serve you.
Lord, in your mercy,
hear our prayer.

In the name of Christ,
who calls everyone, everywhere
to follow him. **Amen.**

SIXTH SUNDAY IN ORDINARY TIME

Praise

Psalm 1

Wherever we are
and whatever we are doing;
whoever we are
and whatever we have been;
whatever our journey
and no matter our destination;
we praise you that
always and forever
we are in your presence.

Lord,
your will is our daily guide
and your purposes bring us hope.
As we walk seeking your company,
we experience a fullness of joy
that we find nowhere else in life.

There are many who
offer their advice
and we are surrounded by those
whose word would lead
us away from you.
There are many different
pathways of truth
which lead only to the cul-
de-sacs of our days.

We praise you, for you are
the Lord Almighty
and our experience of
your sovereignty
is the crown of life itself.
You are the King of all creation

and only in knowing you
can true wholeness be found.

You are the master of the universe
and to praise you is to
have a vision of life
which is truly vast and wide.
We praise you, our Lord,
and we honour you,
our creator, sustainer,
and the lover of our lives. **Amen.**

Confession
Jeremiah 17:5

Father,
we find words of faith come
to our lips so easily
and we can sing of your
goodness and faithfulness.
We can celebrate the lives of
those who have trusted you
and again and again we make
our promises to you.

It is in the hurly-burly
of our daily lives
that walking in faith
becomes really hard.
Too often what we say we believe
isn't matched by the way we
face our problems each day.

We confess that often our lives do
not speak of a person of faith
and we try to cope with our
fears often leaving you
out of the picture.
When we feel overwhelmed by
life and its twists and turns,
we fail to allow you to touch
us, hold us and comfort us.

So come, and in the midst of the
storm be the stillness we long for
and once again our lives will not
revolve around our problems
but, by your grace-filled presence,
may be focused on you.
We pray that we may become the
living witnesses to your love
that you designed us to be from
the very beginning. **Amen.**

Intercession
Luke 6:17–26

Lord,
we bring our prayers for
those who are poor in the
lands of the wealthy
and for those who suffer
most through the decisions
of governments;
for those who are ashamed of
the distress they have caused
those close to them
and for those who are only too well
aware of the poverty of their lives;
for those whose lives display all
the trappings of great riches
and for those whose lives
reveal their supreme paucity
in the eyes of God.
Lord, you promise a place
in your kingdom;
come now and lead us home.

Lord,
we bring our prayers for
those who are hungry
and for those who have no food
for their family today;
for those who are starved of love
and genuine compassion

and for those who long for
nourishment for their souls;
for those whose lives are empty
of any real sense of meaning
and for those whose deepest longing
is to know God more and more.
Lord, you promise a place
in your kingdom;
come now and lead us home.

Lord,
we bring our prayers for those
who weep for your world
and for those who care deeply about
the suffering of their neighbour;
for those who shed their tears
for those they have lost
and for those whose pain is so
deep they cannot cry anymore;
for those who cry for broken
promises and for relationships
that have ended
and for those who weep for those
who once walked with God
but do so no longer.
Lord, you promise a place
in your kingdom;
come now and lead us home.

Lord,
we bring our prayers for those
who are made to feel rejected
and for those who face the hatred
of the neighbours every day;
for those whose lifestyle marks
them out as different
and for those whose colour
or nationality is used as
a weapon of hate;
for those who daily face persecution
because of their faith in Jesus
and for those whose courage
and faithful witness is a
challenge to us all.
Lord, you promise a place
in your kingdom;
come now and lead us home.

Lord,
we bring our prayers for those
whose trust is in their wealth
and for those who find no need to
give thanks and praise to God;
for those who seek their security in
the possessions they can control
and for those whose sense
of fulfilment is found in
the things of the earth;
for those whose pride in
their achievements brings
great satisfaction
and for those whose eyes have
been opened to a heavenly
value yet to come.
Lord, you promise a place
in your kingdom;
come now and lead us home.

Lord,
we bring our prayers for those
who are a blessing to others
and for those whose lives of
generosity bring hope to many;
for those whose compassion touches
the lives of their neighbours
and for those whose walk with God
is seen in the joy they share;
for those whose lives are focused on
speaking of the blessings of grace
and for those whose words
and deeds reflect God's
presence in all they do.

Lord, you promise a place
in your kingdom;
come now and lead us home.

Lord,
we bring our prayers for
those for whom we are
particularly concerned
and for the poor in spirit,
the hungry for God, and
those feeling excluded;
for those who are longing
for someone to come
and share their tears
and for ourselves, that all we
do in Christ's name
may be a rich blessing for
our neighbour.
Lord, you promise a place
in your kingdom;
come now and lead us home.

We bring our prayer in the
name and for the sake
of Jesus, the Lord of the kingdom.
Amen.

SEVENTH SUNDAY IN ORDINARY TIME

Praise

Psalm 37:1

Lord,
you call us to sing your praises
in the midst of a people
who do not know you
and to sing our songs
of thanksgiving
whoever we are with
and wherever you send us.

May the kindness we offer
speak of your love
and may our words of hope
declare your glory.
May our generosity of spirit
be a sign of your grace
and may our gentleness
be a song of your presence.

Lord,
we praise you for every
opportunity
to worship you here with
your people of grace
and that we can honour you
with our lives and our lips
at home, at work, or out
in the community.

We praise you for you are
not only a great God,
you are the only Lord of all
things and everywhere.
When we look at the hills,
the mountains,
the rivers, streams, trees, and
flowers in the field
our song of praise simply
cannot be withheld!

The sheer vastness of space
and the history of all things
moves us deeply.
The joy on a parent's face
as they hold their newborn
baby for the first time
and the deep sense of peace
in the knowledge that we too
are loved unconditionally
flood our hearts with
an uncontrollable song of
praise and thanksgiving
bursting forth from our lips.

We praise you, Lord of all creation,
that our worship cannot be confined
and our songs must be unlimited.
By your Holy Spirit,
enable us to claim
every place as hallowed ground
and fill all places to which
you send us
with opportunities
for a glorious song of
thanksgiving. **Amen.**

Confession

Genesis 45:5–7

Lord,
we confess that often we treat you
like an elderly relative
that we visit every Sunday.
While we are here we focus
our hearts and minds
on giving you thanks and praise.
We share together in the
things we believe
and we commit ourselves to
put our trust in you.

The problem is that we
can go a whole day
and sometimes a whole week
without giving you a thought
or space in our lives.
It is as if we don't really
expect to find you
present in the everyday things of life.
We praise you as the
Lord of all things
but then we live our lives as
if you weren't there!

Lord,
Joseph enabled his brothers
to understand
how you had taken even
their evil plans
and transformed them into
hope for others.
It is only when we look back over
the days, weeks, and years of our lives
that we can discern your
guiding hand.

Forgive us for trying to leave
you behind in church
and come, make yourself know to us
in all the twists and turns
of our lives. **Amen.**

Intercession

1 Corinthians 15:35–36

Lord,
we pray for those who struggle to
overcome times of depression
and for those who are finding it
hard to make sense of their lives;
for those overwhelmed by the
problems they are facing
and for those whose days increase
the burdens they are carrying.
Lord
of new life and new beginnings,
be their hope.

Lord,
we pray for those who are facing
life-changing experiences
and for those who took their
health for granted but
can do so no longer;
for those now robbed of
the precious activities
they once enjoyed
and for those who are finding
it hard to come to terms
with their disablement.

Lord
of new life and new beginnings,
be their hope.

Lord,
we pray for young people
struggling to make the
transition to adulthood
and for those surrounded
by role models that are
making it even harder;
for those faced with critical life
decisions without understanding
what they will mean
and for those stressed beyond
reason as their future hangs
on the results of an exam.
Lord
of new life and new beginnings,
be their hope.

Lord,
we pray for those whose work is
taking over their whole life
and for those who may satisfy
their employer but are
neglecting their home life;
for those who feel the indignity
of redundancy and the
pain of unemployment
and for those content to do
nothing as they fritter away the
days they have been granted.
Lord
of new life and new beginnings,
be their hope.

Lord,
we pray for those whose days have
been strewn with times of sadness
and for those who still grieve for
those they loved but see no more;
for those whose days of loneliness
stretch out like an endless dream
and for those who are single
in a world designed for
those who are not.
Lord
of new life and new beginnings,
be their hope.

Lord,
we pray for those who once
walked very close to God as
they lived by faith in him
and for those who have allowed
the pleasures and things of the
world to steal them away;
for those who are finding it hard
to come to terms with a God of
love and a world of great pain
and for those who look for proof
of God's reality but fail to see his
fingerprints on the whole of life.
Lord
of new life and new beginnings,
be their hope.

Lord,
we pray for those we know who
are weighed down by their
responsibilities for others
and for those who are at the end
of their tether because of the
burdens they are carrying;
for ourselves and our own journeys
filled with times of great
sorrow, struggle, and stress
and for those moments when
we really need to know that in
Christ our end is his beginning.
Lord
of new life and new beginnings,
be their hope.

We bring our prayers in
the name of Jesus,
who is the alpha and the omega, the
beginning and the end. **Amen.**

TRANSFIGURATION SUNDAY

Prayer of Approach

Luke 9:29

Lord,
there is a song in our hearts,
a song of adoration.
We long to know you more
and experience your presence
every moment of every day.

Lord,
there is a song in our hearts,
a song of adoration.
We cannot contain our joy
as we look into the manger
or stand at the foot of
the empty cross
or the empty tomb.

Lord,
there is a song in our hearts,
a song of adoration.
Here and now
and everywhere we go
we will sing in the adoration
of your holy name. **Amen.**

Intercession

Exodus 34:29

Lord,
we pray for the world;
the hurt and pain,
the suffering and loss,
the deceit and the despair,
the success and the failures,
that are recorded on these pages.
Each report of robbery and violence,
every story of delight and disaster,
touches the lives of the famous
and impacts the days of
the unknown.

silence

Lord, we pray for your world,
that Christ may reign there.

Lord,
we pray for those who are hungry;
for those in a world of plenty
who have no idea when
they will eat again;
for those who daily depend
on the work of the aid agencies
for whatever food they are given
and for those who must
watch helplessly
as their children swell up and die;
for those who are being
robbed of their future
by corruption or civil war.

silence

Lord, we pray for your world,
that Christ may reign there.

Lord,
we pray for the elderly
and for those left behind
in a society that despises old age
and is designed for the
young and successful;
for those who feel they are forgotten
in a world that prizes
success at any price
and for those who through
the weakness of age

are experiencing the indignity
of dependency on others.

silence

Lord, we pray for your world,
that Christ may reign there.

Lord,
we pray for those who live
and die in isolation
in a world that thrives on
communication;
for those who by their disability
are trapped in their own
dark, silent world;
for those who have no
one who cares
what happens to them
and have no one with whom
they can share their hopes
and their fears.

silence

Lord, we pray for your world,
that Christ may reign there.

Lord,
we pray for those who are
ill or in hospital
and for those who work
to restore them to health;
for those who take
their continued health and
fitness for granted
and for those now robbed
of the years they thought
would be theirs;
for those faced with the
responsibility
of caring for loved ones
and for those who know they
may soon be alone.

silence

Lord, we pray for your world,
that Christ may reign there.

Lord,
we pray for those involved
in the world of education;
for teachers, lecturers,
writers, and students
and for all who are involved
in learning;
for those with no qualifications
and for those, who through
no fault of their own,
are unable to read or write;
for those whose skills are
no longer required
in our modern technological society
and for those marginalised
by the information highway.

silence

Lord, we pray for your world,
that Christ may reign there.

Lord,
we pray for those whose homes
are places of love, trust, and joy;
for those where there is
stress, anger, and bitterness
and for those being brought
to the point of breakup
or breakdown;
for those with no place to call home
and for those whose home
is a cardboard box

and whose bed tonight will
be the pavement.

silence

Lord, we pray for your world,
that Christ may reign there.

Lord,
we pray for all those we
know and love
and for any we know to
be in special need
of any kind.

silence

Lord,
we pray for any we know
who do not know you as
Saviour and Lord
and for those who once
worshipped with us,
that they may yet return to
the throne of grace.

silence

We also pray for ourselves
and all we are facing and
all we must face
in the days and weeks that lie ahead.

silence

Lord, we pray for your world,
**that Christ may reign
there. Amen.**

Dismissal
Luke 9:28
Lord,
it has been good for us
to be together on this
mountaintop of praise.
Go with us now, that we may
know your presence
when we walk through
the valleys of life
and we have no answer to
our deepest questions.
May your presence uphold us,
our Saviour renew us,
and the Holy Spirit fill us,
that you may transform us
daily more and more
into the likeness of Christ
our Lord. **Amen.**

FIRST SUNDAY IN LENT

Thanksgiving
Romans 10:13
Lord,
we thank you for being
the Saviour who has
walked where we walk
and has marked out the
path for us to follow,
and we bless you that he
himself is not only the way
but the power to walk it.

Lord,
we overflow with gratitude
that though Christ was your
Son from all eternity,
yet he stepped into our
world and added to his
knowledge of being divine

the experience of what it
  means to be human.

Lord,
we thank you that in Christ
we not only have the
  greatest example of victory
  over temptation
but a living Saviour, who is with
  us when we are tempted
and a Lord who picks us
  up when we fall.

Lord,
how can we not thank you for
  the love that overwhelms us
and for the joy, hope, and courage
  with which you flood our days?
We praise you for that grace
  that reaches out to find us
no matter how far we have wandered
  along paths of our own design
and we thank you for that loving-
  kindness that stoops down
  to lift us when we fall.

Lord,
you are sovereign over all things
and you hold every universe in
  the hollow of your hand.
There is nothing you do not know;
your understanding is total;
only your grace exceeds the
  bounty of your knowledge.
We praise you, our
  wonderful Father,
and we worship you, our
  amazing Saviour.
It is through your Holy Spirit
  that you have given us
  the tools of adoration
and the language through which
  we can give you glory.

Lord,
we thank you for being
  who and what you are
and we bless you that by your grace
we can become what you
  always meant us to be.

We bring our thanks and
  praise in the name of
  Christ the Lord. **Amen.**

Confession

Romans 10:9

Father,
we confess that we are not the
  people you meant us to be
and we do not live the kind of
  lives that bring you glory.

We confess our inner turmoil
  and our emptiness
and our daily struggle to live up
  even to our own poor standards.

We confess that we shall
  never reach the heights
  of your holiness
unless we walk in the
  footsteps of your Son.

We confess that to walk in his
  footsteps is only possible
because he was tempted just as we
  are, yet he never gave way to sin.

We confess that only through
  his sacrifice in the wilderness,
  in Gethsemane

and on the cross can we receive the
cleansing and renewal we long for.

We confess that only
through the life, death and
resurrection of Christ
and being filled with
the Holy Spirit,
can we hope to live the kind of lives
that bring you glory. **Amen.**

Intercession

Luke 4:1–2

Lord,
we pray for those who are
tempted to wreck their
lives with illegal drugs
and for those who are so focused
on the impact of the moment
that they give little or no
thought for the future health
they are sacrificing.
The Lord hears our prayer.
Thanks be to God.

Lord,
we pray for those tempted
to give up and give in
and for those for whom the
pressures of life have all
but overwhelmed them;
for those whose dreams
have come to nothing
and for those who have no
dreams because their fear of
failure strangles their days.
The Lord hears our prayer.
Thanks be to God.

Lord,
we pray for those who are tempted
to focus their lives on the
pleasure of the moment
and for those who see life
in terms of the material
possessions they treasure;
for those for whom all life
is seen as a gamble
and for those who have turned
their backs on the plans and the
purpose God has for them.
The Lord hears our prayer.
Thanks be to God.

Lord,
we pray for those who are
tempted to seek power
no matter the cost to
themselves and to others
and for those who are willing
to bend the rules to
achieve their own ends;
for those whose greed, pride,
and indifference wreck the
lives of many investors
and for those who refuse to accept
any accountability for the
wrong decisions they made.
The Lord hears our prayer.
Thanks be to God.

Lord,
we pray for sportsmen and women
who are tempted to cheat
to achieve personal glory
and for those who are
determined to remain honest
role models for others;
for those for whom winning
is everything

and for those who live out
their faith in Christ before
the eyes of the world.
The Lord hears our prayer.
Thanks be to God.

Lord,
we pray for those who are tempted
to dilute the Christian faith
proclaimed down the years
and for those whose trust has
been undermined by the
false teaching they hear;
for those who have stood
firm for the faith of Christ
crucified, risen, and ascended
and for those whose daily
walk with Jesus is an
inspiration to us all.
The Lord hears our prayer.
Thanks be to God.

Lord,
we pray for those in the media
who turn their backs on
the honesty of reporting
and for those whose work
helps to breed a culture
of violence and abuse;
for those with no concern
about what their work
does to the innocent
and for those with the influence
but not the responsibility to
run the life of the nation.
The Lord hears our prayer.
Thanks be to God.

Lord,
we pray for ourselves and the
daily temptations we face
and for the times when we
struggle with the important
choices that trouble us;
for those times when we are
weak as we try to deal with
temptation in our own strength
and for those moments when
we have stood firm, as we
placed our trust in the Lord.
The Lord hears our prayer.
Thanks be to God.

We bring all our prayers in
the name of Christ,
the one who has conquered
all. **Amen.**

SECOND SUNDAY IN LENT

Prayer of Approach

Psalm 27:14

Lord,
we live in a world of the instant,
a generation that demands
everything—now!
From instant coffee to news
wherever we are,
from immediate credit
to instant success;
we are surrounded by
signs of a society
that simply refuses to wait.

Lord,
teach us again to allow you
to change the focus of our lives
and the direction of our days.
Come, hold us gently
for we have been damaged;
be patient with us
for we have been broken

by our refusal to walk
in step with you.

We run ahead, Lord,
and we lose our way;
we drag our feet
and we lose sight of you.
The psalmist whispers in our ear
that the way to renewal is found only
as we wait for you
and hope is given
as we daily wait for you
to mark the path,
that we may place our steps
in yours. **Amen.**

Praise

Genesis 15:1

Lord,
we lie awake
and think of all we have done
with our lives today.
We remember the things
we have left undone,
the people we have let down,
the times we have failed you, Lord.

We think of the things
we've planned
and the dreams we've had.
We remember the people
we have known—
those who have cared
and the ones who have loved.

We think of the journeys
we have made
and the places
we have visited.
We return in our minds
to the times of joy
that have enriched our days
and those experiences
of God's presence
that have meant so much.

We think of those memories
that are precious
and those whose love
is still filling our lives.
We remember the times
we have spent with those
who matter most to us.

We remember the story
of Jesus
who loved us more
than anyone else
ever could.
We think of the one
who died as our Saviour
and was raised
as our living Lord.

Lord, we praise you
for the gift of memory
and that we can use it
to remember those things
for which we long
to give thanks and honour
to your wonderful name. **Amen.**

Intercession

Luke 13:31–35

Lord,
as you wept over Jerusalem, so we
weep for those with no home
and for those who tonight
will sleep on the streets of
our towns and cities;
for those whose home is
a cardboard box

and for those whose blanket is
a pile of old newspapers.
Lord, turn our tears into action
as we weep with you.

Lord,
as you wept over Jerusalem, so we
weep for those seeking peace
and for those fleeing a war
zone and finding the door
to hope slammed shut;
for those longing for the
chance to begin again
and for the world's refugees and
migrants praying to find a home.
Lord, turn our tears into action
as we weep with you.

Lord,
as you wept over Jerusalem,
so we weep for those who
care for our health
and for all who work in hospitals
and health centres who
are struggling to cope;
for patients whose appointments for
treatment are constantly cancelled
and for those with the power
but not the will to provide
the healthcare we need.
Lord, turn our tears into action
as we weep with you.

Lord,
as you wept over Jerusalem, so
we weep for those who cannot
live on the pay they receive
and for those who must have two or
more jobs to enable them to pay
the bills and feed their family;
for employers who are failing to pay
their workers even the living wage
and for those caught in the
uncertain trap of zero-hours
contracts where they may
have no work at all.
Lord, turn our tears into action
as we weep with you.

Lord,
as you wept over Jerusalem,
so we weep for those who
weep for the church
and for those saddened when
they find congregations who
have neglected their mission;
for churches empowered by
the Holy Spirit as they reach
out in the name of Jesus
and for churches where
congregations dwindle and there
is no vision for the future.
Lord, turn our tears into action
as we weep with you.

Lord,
as you wept over Jerusalem, so
we weep for those who are
weeping for their emptiness
and for those who shed tears for
the life they are losing to age
and the problems of health;
for those who cry all alone for the
mistakes they have made and
the people they have hurt
and for those who simply weep
for those they have lost with
whom they shared so much.
Lord, turn our tears into action
as we weep with you.

Lord,
as you wept over Jerusalem, so
we weep for those we know
whose situations are painful
and for those whose struggles
to cope with each day are
known only to a few;
for ourselves and the tears we
shed for relationships damaged
by misunderstanding
and for our silent weeping for
a world wracked by war,
injustice, and the impact
of global warming.
Lord, turn our tears into action
as we weep with you.

Lord, we bring our cries
for your world
in the name of Jesus, who
wept and still weeps the
tears of love. **Amen.**

THIRD SUNDAY IN LENT

Praise

Psalm 63:1–8

Father,
the knowledge of your
presence fills us with joy
and the more we know you, the
more we want to be with you.
We gather for worship, not
out of duty or habit
and certainly not because of
community pressure to do so.

As the psalmist reminds us, you are
the God who quenches our thirst
and you restore those who come to
you battered and bruised by life.
Our relationship with you is one
of pure grace upon our lives
and the love with which you
refresh our days comes
freely and unbidden.

To know you is better than
life itself as we rediscover
real life in your love
and experience deep within
us the joy of being loved
unconditionally.
Your glory is utterly beyond
anything our words
could ever describe
and your sovereignty blows
our minds away with
your glorious majesty.

We try to fill our lives with
the possessions we hope
will bring us satisfaction
only to realise, once again,
that in you alone can true
fulfilment be found.
It is when we find a quiet
corner of our lives and we
reflect on who you are
that we remember your
promise to hide us in the
shadow of your wings.

We are brought to our knees
as the joy of your love
overwhelms us each day
and we see the world around
us through the eyes of faith
and as a vehicle of praise.
It is our greatest pleasure to
offer you our thanks for
all your goodness to us

and we rejoice at every
opportunity to join our praises
with the song of heaven.

There is one more reason for
our praises, and one that
takes our breath away—
for you have taught us to call
you 'our Father' and to know
that we are your children.
You are no longer distant
or remote from us—you
are here in our midst
and we have come as your
family of grace to worship
our heavenly Father. **Amen.**

Confession

Luke 13:1–9

Father,
we can say our prayers of confession
but we find it hard to repent.
We can say we are sorry for
the way we have lived
but being sorry doesn't
cost us anything.
We can long to be free of the
guilt we carry within us
but we are reluctant to leave our
baggage of memories with you.

Father,
we know that you are not wanting
us simply to be sorry
and you are not satisfied with our
words of confession alone.
You long to see the fruit in our lives
that comes from the seeds
planted in repentance
and to know by the way
we live each day
we are now walking the path
you always intended. **Amen.**

Intercession

Isaiah 55:1–9

Father,
we pray for those who are
thirsty for justice
and for those longing for
their voice to be heard;
for those imprisoned for
years without trial
and for whom freedom is a
long-forgotten dream.
Come, all you who are thirsty,
come to the waters and drink.

Father,
we pray for those who are
thirsty for healing
and for those who are frustrated
as the years take their toll;
for those facing serious health
and life problems
and for those seeking a sense of
renewal and wholeness within.
Come, all you who are thirsty,
come to the waters and drink.

Father,
we pray for those who are
thirsty for refreshment
and for those who journey miles
every day for clean water;
for those whose lives are blighted
by common diseases
and for those who suffer
and die because what
they drink is unclean.
Come, all you who are thirsty,
come to the waters and drink.

Father,
we pray for those who are
thirsty for peace
and for those who are daily
surrounded by bombs,
fighting, and death;
for those who live with the shadow
of the terrorist hanging over them
and for those whose lives
are in turmoil and simply
want serenity within.
Come, all you who are thirsty,
come to the waters and drink.

Father,
we pray for those who are
thirsty for knowledge
and for those whose options
for learning are limited;
for those whose education is
restricted because they are women
and for those who received
little parental encouragement
to know more.
Come, all you who are thirsty,
come to the waters and drink.

Father,
we pray for those who are
thirsty for forgiveness
and for those who long to be free
from the burden of guilt;
for those needing to know that
the abuse was not their fault
and for those still needing to forgive
those who have hurt them most.
Come, all you who are thirsty,
come to the waters and drink.

Father,
we pray for those who
are thirsty for love
and for those desperate
to know they are
unconditionally accepted;
for those who have endured
humiliation at the hands
of a controlling partner
and for those who long to
experience mutual affection
that is given and not won.
Come, all you who are thirsty,
come to the waters and drink.

Father,
we pray for those who are
thirsty for hope
and for those who are finding in
Christ, light for their world;
for those whose journey of
life leads them through
many dark days
and for ourselves, that our
words of faith will bring
hope to our neighbour.
Come, all you who are thirsty,
come to the waters and drink.

We bring our prayers in
the name of the One,
who offers life-refreshing hope
to the whole world. **Amen.**

FOURTH SUNDAY IN LENT

Thanksgiving

Joshua 5:9–12

Lord,
you have given us no
mountain to climb
and there is no ritual for
us to complete;
you have not commanded that
we must visit special places

or that we are expected to be
worthy of your acceptance.

This is our God, the
God of all grace
whose mercy is utterly free;
your offer of cleansing and renewal
comes to us and is without price.

Lord,
we come with words of
thanksgiving,
knowing they can never do
justice to your love;
every sacrificial offering of service
can never, ever repay
the debt we owe.

When Joshua gathered
your people at Gilgal
it was a demonstration that their
freedom came from your hand;
from this moment on they
knew they were the people
of your promise
and the line had been drawn in the
sand on their past life of slavery.

Lord,
we thank you that in and through
Jesus our lives can be made new
and his life, death, and resurrection
are the doorway to new life.
We cannot put into words
the hope and joy we
experience in him
and we celebrate the overwhelming
sense of peace and freedom
that is your free gift to all
who open their hearts
to him. **Amen.**

Confession

Psalm 32:5

Lord,
we confess that like all
people of faith
we set out with great hope
and determination
to follow wherever you
might lead us.

But once we took our eye
from the light of Christ
we found ourselves
wandering aimlessly.
We almost forgot the reason
why we are here
and we lost sight of the
purpose of our lives.

Lord,
we confess that you are the
light of the world
and we commit ourselves to follow
in the footsteps of your wise men.
We know that only as we open our
hearts and lives to you once more
will our lives be engaged in
that purpose for which
you gave us life. **Amen.**

Intercession

2 Corinthians 5:16–21

Father,
we want to talk to you about
reconciliation in our world
where nations do not
trust each other;
for countries that export
acts of terrorism
and for a new desire to
see justice prevail

as there is an equal sharing of
the world's resources.
We pray for a new spirit
of reconciliation
and for a willingness to
listen and to learn.
Send your Spirit to revive us
and fill our hearts with healing.

Father,
we want to talk to you about
reconciliation in our families
and especially those facing
times of stress;
for homes where violent
words are often heard
and for those where violence
and abuse are found
as breakdown and breakup are
becoming real possibilities.
We pray for a new spirit
of reconciliation
and for a willingness to
listen and to learn.
Send your Spirit to revive us
and fill our hearts with healing.

Father,
we want to talk to you about
reconciliation in our nation
and the ever-widening gulf
between the rich and the poor;
for a country that appears
complacent at the plight
of the disadvantaged
and for the lives of those who
are just managing to cope,
as many turn to crime to feed
their addiction to illegal drugs.
We pray for a new spirit
of reconciliation
and for a willingness to
listen and to learn.
Send your Spirit to revive us
and fill our hearts with healing.

Father,
we want to talk to you about
reconciliation in the church
and for a renewal of
our commitment to
truth and justice;
for a new determination to declare
the good news of Jesus Christ
and for a rediscovery of
our purpose of making
disciples in his name,
as we affirm our responsibility
to witness to his promise of a
new relationship with God.
We pray for a new spirit
of reconciliation
and for a willingness to
listen and to learn.
Send your Spirit to revive us
and fill our hearts with healing.

Father,
we want to talk to you about
reconciliation in the workplace
and for places of employment
that have been tainted
with corruption;
for those whose working
environment is plagued
by bitterness and hate;
for those who are disabled
and often have little
choice of employment
and for many who do not
receive a wage on which
they can possibly live.

We pray for a new spirit
of reconciliation
and for a willingness to
listen and to learn.
Send your Spirit to revive us
and fill our hearts with healing.

Father,
we want to talk to you about
reconciliation with our planet
and for an honest understanding
of the damage we are doing;
for greater action to protect our
many endangered species
and for ways to reconcile the growing
demands on the human race
as we affirm that we are
simply stewards who are
answerable to our Maker.
We pray for a new spirit
of reconciliation
and for a willingness to
listen and to learn.
Send your Spirit to revive us
and fill our hearts with healing.

Father,
we want to talk to you about our
reconciliation with each other
and for a deeper desire to be good
neighbours to one another;
for a new spirit of acceptance
irrespective of a person's
colour or nation
as we seek to show the spirit
of the Samaritan as we
welcome those in distress.
We pray for a new spirit
of reconciliation
and for a willingness to
listen and to learn.
Send your Spirit to revive us
and fill our hearts with healing.

We bring our concerns in
the name of Jesus,
through whom all reconciliation
is wrought. **Amen.**

FIFTH SUNDAY IN LENT (PASSION SUNDAY)

Prayer of Approach

Psalm 126:3

Lord,
we come because we know you
and we are here because we
know you love us.
We have come to declare
our love for you
and we are here to hear again
the story of your love.

By your Holy Spirit, open our
ears to hear your voice
and unlock our hearts to
respond to what we hear.
Transform our time together
from an activity of worship
and let it become the energising
moment of our lives.

We have come, Lord, because
we long to give thanks
for the great things you have
done and are still doing
in our lives. **Amen.**

Praise

Isaiah 43:18–19

Lord,
we do not like change!
We look back to the things
we remember

and we dream of how
everything used to be.
We prefer familiar pathways
and we find it so very hard to
work in a different way.

There are times when we feel stressed
as change is forced upon us
and we try to erect a barricade to
ward off this enemy to our peace.
Our efforts to create a
memory of our golden-age
world fails miserably,
that is until we wear our double-
strength, rose-tinted spectacles!

Then the truth dawns upon
us: as the Scriptures tell us,
you make all things new!

We praise you that you are the Lord
of yesterday, today, and tomorrow
and though you do not
change, you are constantly
the source of renewal.
From before the beginning of all life
you were the agent of creation
and you provided the matter from
which the universe could explode.

When your people were enslaved,
lost, and far from home
you made a new way of hope
and joy through the desert.
We have discovered that every time
we think we have reached the end
you do a new thing and
transform our ends into
your new beginnings.

We praise you that when your
church seems to be withering away
you open our eyes to the renewing
power of the Holy Spirit.
When as Christians we feel
ignored, rejected, and
ridiculed by our society
you open doors to new ways
of worship, service, and
sharing our faith.

Lord,
there are times when we
lose our way on the
journey of discipleship
and we allow ourselves to become
negative and depressed.
Come, Lord, and remove the rose-
tinted spectacles from our eyes—
that as we praise you for
all that is past
we will trust you for all the new
things that are to come. **Amen.**

Intercession

John 12:1–8

Prepare a set of ten candles. Light a new candle as you begin each prayer.

We light this candle
for those whose lives are in
the darkness of pain—
of body, mind, or spirit;
for those who ache within
as a sign of their anguish
and deep concern.

silence

We light this candle
for those whose memories
are covered in darkness;
for those who are still
hurting inside

because of what was said
  or done to them
or denied them years ago.

silence

We light this candle
for those whose future
  looks very dark;
for those facing the cost
  of wrong decisions
and bleak horizons of
  emptiness and loss
through no fault of their own.

silence

We light this candle
for those who are overwhelmed
  by the darkness of the
  sickness within;
for those whose lives will
  never be the same
and for those who have
  little future left.

silence

We light this candle
for those who are darkening
  their lives with the addiction
to drugs, drink, or gambling;
for those whose lifestyle is clouding
  the lives of those nearest to them.

silence

We light this candle
for those who daily face the
  darkness of hopelessness;
for those who sleep rough
and for those on the downward spiral
  that is leading to a life on the street.

silence

We light this candle
for the darkness of nations;
for those who see no alternative
to violence and the terror it creates
in what they see as their struggle
  for justice and freedom.

silence

We light this candle
for those whose darkness is
  all in their minds;
for those who are so overwhelmed
by life and by living, they
  see only the darkness
that shuts out the light.

silence

We light this candle
for those who hide from the
  darkness and pretend all is light;
for those who close their eyes
to the hurt of their neighbour
  and the cry of the poor.

silence

We light this candle
for ourselves as we offer to God
  our darkness within;
we leave our unspoken hurt,
  sadness, and loss
with the one who is forever
  the light of the world.

silence

Lord,
you are the light in our darkness
and our hope in times of despair;
you are our courage when we
know we have failed;
you are the way when the
pathway is unclear;
you are our strength when
we might fall;
and you are our Lord and the
light that conquers the deepest
darkness of all.

We bring our prayers in
the name of Christ,
the world's light and ours. **Amen.**

SIXTH SUNDAY IN LENT (PALM SUNDAY)

Praise

Philippians 2:5–11

Lord,
there have been times when
we have failed to remember
that Jesus is your Son
and that we are in danger of
forgetting that he is Lord of all!
When we sing, 'What a
friend we have in Jesus',
we too easily neglect to
remember that he is the
Saviour of the world.

Wonderful, wonderful Lord,
break through the half-
truths of our worship
and transform all our songs
of praise by the glory of
the one we worship.
We too are unworthy to stoop down
and fasten the shoes on his feet
and yet he is the same
sovereign King who comes
as our suffering servant.

No words we can use will ever
do justice to his glory
and there are no phrases that
can worthily lift our worship
to the height of his throne.
You are the King of all creation,
the Lord of history, our
Saviour and our living Lord
and by the power and presence
of your Holy Spirit
we will join with the song
of myriad upon myriad of
the hosts of heaven.

On that first Palm Sunday the
pilgrims and the disciples
encompassed you with praise
as the crowds lined your journey
with spontaneous thanksgiving.
That day they welcomed you
as a conquering hero
but you were coming as
the Prince of Peace.
They thought you were
coming to your coronation
as the King of Israel
but you were coming to
be crowned with the
thorns of our Saviour.

We praise you that the day
is coming when the whole
world will sing your glory
and everyone whoever lived
or is living will bow in
adoration before you.
Incredible God, we praise
you for who you are

and we worship you for
all you have done
but we give honour to your
Son, through whom all things
belong to you. **Amen.**

Confession

Psalm 31:9–16

Lord,
when we are overwhelmed as we
remember our broken promises,
speak to us of your unbreakable
offer of forgiveness.

When we cannot rest because of
the ways we have failed you,
speak to us of your unbreakable
offer of forgiveness.

When our words have hurt you,
other people, and ourselves,
speak to us of your unbreakable
offer of forgiveness.

When we know that our selfishness
has spoilt our relationships,
speak to us of your unbreakable
offer of forgiveness.

When we try to live our lives our
own way and in our own strength,
speak to us of your unbreakable
offer of forgiveness.

When we feel rejected by those
around us and unworthy of you,
speak to us of your unbreakable
offer of forgiveness.

When we have walked far from you
and we cannot find our way back,
speak to us of your unbreakable
offer of forgiveness.

Lord,
we will trust no longer in ourselves
but in your mighty love and
certain forgiveness. **Amen.**

Intercession

Luke 19:28–40

Lord,
we pray for those like the
man with the donkey
who placed what he had into
the hands of Jesus;
for those who serve as chaplains
in hospitals, in prisons, in industry,
and in places of education
and for those who go where
people of all ages
are in need of a listening ear.
To the Lord who gave everything,
we offer what we have.

Lord,
we pray for those like the
man with the donkey
who placed what he had into
the hands of Jesus;
for those who give of their time as
they care for their neighbour
and for those whose names
we do not know
who show compassion to the lonely,
the broken, and the bereaved.
To the Lord who gave everything,
we offer what we have.

Lord,
we pray for those like the
man with the donkey

who placed what he had into
the hands of Jesus;
for those whose commitment
is a reflection of God's
love for the poor
and for those whose service
at food banks
enables many families to eat.
To the Lord who gave everything,
we offer what we have.

Lord,
we pray for those like the
man with the donkey
who placed what he had into
the hands of Jesus;
for those who work
tirelessly in support
of the silent sufferers in our society
and for those who raise our
awareness of the importance
of the research
that will bring hope to
those struggling with life-
changing illnesses.
To the Lord who gave everything,
we offer what we have.

Lord,
we pray for those like the
man with the donkey
who placed what he had into
the hands of Jesus;
for those unpaid heroes who work
with children and young people
and for those who share their
skills and their knowledge,
bringing hope to those our society
would prefer to ignore.
To the Lord who gave everything,
we offer what we have.

Lord,
we pray for those like the
man with the donkey
who placed what he had into
the hands of Jesus;
for those who travel the
world to use their skills
on behalf of people they don't know
and for those who risk their
lives to rescue those
trapped by the effects of
an earthquake
or by the impact of a
widespread epidemic.
To the Lord who gave everything,
we offer what we have.

Lord,
we pray for those like the
man with the donkey
who placed what he had into
the hands of Jesus;
for those who reach out to
those who sleep rough
on the streets of our towns and cities
and for those who demonstrate
the love of Christ
to those trapped in a world of
drugs and prostitution.
To the Lord who gave everything,
we offer what we have.

Lord,
we pray for those like the
man with the donkey
who placed what he had into
the hands of Jesus;
for ourselves and the wall of excuses
behind which we seek to hide
and for a deeper understanding
to recognise the gifts

of time, money, and skills God
gave for us to give away.
To the Lord who gave everything,
we offer what we have.

We bring our prayers in
the name of Jesus,
the source of all the gifts we can
offer in his name. **Amen.**

EASTER SUNDAY

Prayer of Approach

Psalm 118:14–24

Lord,
this is the beginning of
the day of hope
and it is the start of a journey
in your presence.
Come and surprise us with the
joy of your resurrection
and renew our worship with the
wonder of your presence.
Come, not to turn our
world upside down
but to put it back the right way up.
We have come to worship the
one rejected by many
and to adore the living Lord
of all creation. **Amen.**

Praise

Luke 24:1–12

Lord,
we looked everywhere
but we found no place to begin.
We searched high and low
but life still had no meaning.
We examined every avenue
but ultimately they all
led nowhere.
It was then we looked in the
most unlikely place
and we searched where we
were told it was futile.
But it was when we examined
the empty cross and the empty tomb
that it was there, hallelujah, and we
found what we were looking for.

The stone which the builders
had thrown away
because they decided it was useless
actually turned out to be the
very thing we really needed!

If only we had listened
to the angels—
they told us we were looking
in the wrong place.
It was all so obvious, looking for
the living among the dead—
of course it didn't make any
sense, then or now.

We praise you, our risen
and living Lord,
and we give thanks that your
borrowed tomb was really empty!
We cannot understand the
foolishness of the disciples
and why it took us so
long to understand
that your resurrection is
your promise to us all.

We still wonder at those moments
when your living presence
breaks into our hopes, our dreams,
and the experiences of our lives.
We find you there when we
least expect your company

and you gather us into your
arms when we are afraid.

We praise you that you turn every
day into an Easter experience
and that because you are alive
our ends are transformed
into your beginnings.
We come to learn again about
the tomb that was empty,
that our hearts may be
filled with hope
and our lives set on fire by
your grace. **Amen.**

Intercession
Isaiah 65:17–25
Lord,
you promised a new heaven
and a new earth
and that the things of yesterday
would be changed.
We pray for the leaders of nations;
for those who listen to the
cry of their people
and seek to do all they can
to bring them hope;
for those who close their ears
to the pleading of the poor
and for those whose only concern
is their personal glory.
Lord of the blessings of life,
come and make all things new.

Lord,
you promised a new heaven
and a new earth
and that the things of yesterday
would be changed.
We pray for those who find great
blessing in social media
and for those for whom it is a
constant window to friendship;
for those for whom
checking Facebook has
become an addiction
and for those who are finding Twitter
isolates them from real life.
Lord of the blessings of life,
come and make all things new.

Lord,
you promised a new heaven
and a new earth
and that the things of yesterday
would be changed.
We pray for the media and the
way it keeps us informed
and for the revealing of
lies and corruption
at the heart of government
and global companies;
for those who are damaged by the
intrusive action of some reporters
and for those parts of the media
more concerned for a story
than they are for the
people involved.
Lord of the blessings of life,
come and make all things new.

Lord,
you promised a new heaven
and a new earth
and that the things of yesterday
would be changed.
We pray for young people who
study hard for their future
and for those who are the sole
carer for their elderly parents;
for those who wreak havoc in
their local community

and for those without the
parental guidance they need.
Lord of the blessings of life,
come and make all things new.

Lord,
you promised a new heaven
and a new earth
and that the things of yesterday
would be changed.
We pray for those who
are volunteers,
who offer food and shelter
for the homeless,
and for those who open their
homes to frightened refugees;
for those who target their abuse
on people they see as different
and for those who believe
that charity begins
and ends at home.
Lord of the blessings of life,
come and make all things new.

Lord,
you promised a new heaven
and a new earth
and that the things of yesterday
would be changed.
We pray for all who work in the
National Health Service,
that they will receive the
resources they need
if they are to be able to
continue to care;
for those who have responsibility
for the health of society
and for those with the
power but not the will
to make it a reality.
Lord of the blessings of life,
come and make all things new.

Lord,
you promised a new heaven
and a new earth
and that the things of yesterday
would be changed.
We pray for ourselves and the
Easter joy we experience
and for the promise of renewed life
now and of heaven to come;
for those who seek to water down
the truth of the resurrection
and for those who have yet to
meet their living Lord.
Lord of the blessings of life,
come and make all things new.

We bring our prayers in
the name of Jesus,
the same yesterday, today,
and for ever. **Amen.**

SECOND SUNDAY OF EASTER

Praise

Revelation 1:4–8

Lord,
you are the alpha and the omega,
the beginning and the end.
We praise you that from before
the dawn of creation
you were God
and when this vast universe
is no more
you will still be God.
You are the alpha and the omega,
the beginning and the end.

Lord,
you are the alpha and the omega,
the beginning and the end.
We praise you for your total
understanding of all things

and that there is literally nothing
you do not fully comprehend.
Your knowledge of each
one of us is complete
and you hold all our days
in your hand.
You are the alpha and the omega,
the beginning and the end.

Lord,
you are the alpha and the omega,
the beginning and the end.
We praise you for your sovereignty
and we worship you because
you rule in righteousness.
Your grace-filled hands welcome
us into your presence
and your overwhelming love is ever
reaching out to draw us home.
You are the alpha and the omega,
the beginning and the end.

Lord,
you are the alpha and the omega,
the beginning and the end.
We praise you for the glory that
radiates through all creation
and for the glimpses of your presence
we find wherever we look.
The whole universe cries aloud
of your endless nature
and all over our world we
find the fingerprints of
your gracious design.
You are the alpha and the omega,
the beginning and the end.

Lord,
you are the alpha and the omega,
the beginning and the end.
We praise you that at the beginning
you had a purpose for your creation
and your plan was that all things
should know you and love you.
We praise you too that the end
of all things is in your hands
and that we will still be
safe in your hands
at the conclusion of our
own earthly journey.
You are the alpha and the omega,
the beginning and the end.

Lord,
you are the alpha and the omega,
the beginning and the end.
We praise you for being the
holy God that you are
and that you designed us to walk
in friendship with you.
You are great and glorious
in everything you say
and do and are.
You are not remote and
unknowable, you are
a God of grace—
in Christ's life, death, and
resurrection you have
made yourself known.
You are the alpha and the omega,
the beginning and the end. Amen.

Confession

Acts 5:27–32

Lord,
we confess that we are not
like the disciples
who spoke out before those
who were hostile to them.
We are chameleon Christians
and we prefer to blend into
our surroundings.
We do not want to stand
out as different

so we find it almost impossible
to speak up for Jesus.

Lord,
we confess that we are not
like the disciples
whose very way of life marked
them out as your followers.
We are chameleon Christians
and our values are often
indistinguishable from those
who don't know you
and our attitudes and our lifestyles
do not mark us out as Christians.
At times we seem content to allow
our society to write our agenda
and we find it almost impossible to be
the body of Christ in our world.

We pray that you will not
only forgive us
but that you will transform our lives.
We ask that we will be so
indwelt by the Holy Spirit
that being chameleon Christians
will no longer be an option.

Come, Lord, and renew and
empower your people. **Amen.**

Intercession
John 20:19–31
Hold before God those whose
days are filled with fear
and those who are too fearful to
venture out on their own;
those who are afraid because of
their uncertainties for the future
and those whose health problems
are causing them great distress.
Come, Lord Jesus,
and stand among us.

Hold before God those
whose disabilities lock
them out of daily life
and those who rely on the support
of carers to be there for them;
those whose anxiety and
panic attacks have trapped
them in their clutches
and those locked up in themselves
and no longer know who they are.
Come, Lord Jesus,
and stand among us.

Hold before God those who are filled
with times of doubt and despair
and those overwhelmed by life and
growing demands upon them;
those weighed down by
the responsibilities of
work and family
and those searching for
peace to rescue them from
their ocean of stress.
Come, Lord Jesus,
and stand among us.

Hold before God those whose
lives have lost purpose
and those coming to terms with
the loss of someone they loved;
those feeling empty as they
face living on their own for
the first time in years
and those needing hope
when all they had has been
washed away in the flood.
Come, Lord Jesus,
and stand among us.

Hold before God those
whose courage has been
an inspiration to many

and those whose dedication
to research has brought
healing to millions;
those whose faithful walk with
Jesus touched the lives of others
in ways they never knew
and those who obeyed the call
of Christ as he led them
along pathways of faith.
Come, Lord Jesus,
and stand among us.

Hold before God those whose
ministry of compassion spread
hope wherever they went
and those who use their
skills of healing and
caring in our surgeries,
hospitals, and hospices;
those who carry the pastoral
care of the church out into
the local community
and those who are street pastors
who offer help and support to
young people in our cities.
Come, Lord Jesus,
and stand among us.

Hold before God those who are
finding the journey of faith
strewn with difficulties
and those who fell by the wayside
when they sought proof when
they were challenged to trust;
those who allowed their walk
with Jesus to be diverted by the
demands of work and the world
and those whose faith, hope,
and love shout aloud of
their trust in their Lord.
Come, Lord Jesus,
and stand among us.

We bring our prayers in
the name of Jesus,
the one who always stands
among us. **Amen.**

THIRD SUNDAY OF EASTER

Prayer of Approach

Revelation 5:11–14

Lord,
we simply cannot keep silent
and there is no way our
tongues can remain still.
There is within us a deep longing
to sing your praises.
How can we not sing
when the whole of heaven
is pulsating with songs of glory?

Lord,
we do not sing alone
for the whole of creation was
designed for your praise.
This place of worship is filled
with the hosts of heaven
as we join in their tumultuous cry:

'Worthy is the lamb, who was slain,
to receive power and wealth
and wisdom and strength
and honour and glory
and praise!' **Amen.**

Thanksgiving

John 21:1–19

Lord,
we thank you for the way you
turn our lives upside down
and for the incredible way you
apply your grace to our lives.
We overflow with gratitude for the
times you have picked us up

and for those moments when
we had let you down
only to hear your words of
love and forgiveness.

We are truly blessed by your
presence and your compassion
and we are deeply touched by the
mercy you pour out upon us.
We have no right whatsoever
to assume that you
should care for us
and we should make no
assumptions as to the
depth of your goodness.

We stand before your cross and we
marvel at what you have done
and we are utterly lost for words
to describe our love for you.
We come empty-handed,
with nothing to offer as
payment for your sacrifice.
We come with only the baggage
of our lives to lay before you
that, in your love, you will
nail it to your cross, that
we might be free.

When you met Peter on the
beach that morning, you
did not reject him
and though he had badly let
you down, you reached
out to him in grace.
You did not remind him
of his dreadful failure as
one of your disciples
and you gently led him,
the lost sheep, back into
the fold of your love.

We thank you that as you
ministered to Peter, there
at his place of work,
you recommissioned him as a
servant of his servant Lord.
We are grateful that our
times of blessing are not
restricted to holy places
and that we can experience
your renewing mercy at any
moment of our lives.

We stand amazed that saints
and sinners are welcomed
into your service
and that there is literally no limit
to what your love can achieve.
We have yet to experience the
full measure of your love—
which never lets us off, never lets us
go, and never, ever lets us down.

We thank you that your presence
makes all things possible
and that your forgiveness can
wipe the dirtiest of us clean.
We bless you for the goodness
that gave us life
and we offer you thanks and
praise for the grace that
gives us new life. **Amen.**

Intercession

Acts 9:1–6

Lord,
we pray for those who are
longing for hope
and for those searching for
direction in the darkness;
for those for whom everything
seems to have gone wrong

and for those who feel they
cannot sink any lower.
Come and meet them on
their Damascus road
and shine the light of your
grace upon them.
Lord, in your mercy,
hear our prayer.

Lord,
we pray for those who
are far from you
and for those whose every step
is taking them further away;
for those who are asking the
big questions of life
and for those who are
beginning to wonder how
they can find you.
Come and meet them on
their Damascus road
and shine the light of your
grace upon them.
Lord, in your mercy,
hear our prayer.

Lord,
we pray for those who are
on the margins of life
and for those for whom each
day is a struggle to survive;
for those who rely on the gifts
they receive from the food bank
and for those who search rubbish
tips for scraps of food.
Come and meet them on
their Damascus road
and shine the light of your
grace upon them.
Lord, in your mercy,
hear our prayer.

Lord,
we pray for those who are at
the beginning of life
and for those young lives which
are being shaped by their peers;
for those who are living for
the moment without a
thought for their future
and for those who may have
no tomorrow because of
their lifestyle today.
Come and meet them on
their Damascus road
and shine the light of your
grace upon them.
Lord, in your mercy,
hear our prayer.

Lord,
we pray for those who simply do
not know which way to turn
and for those for whom the bottom
has dropped out of their world;
for those who are treated badly
by those once closest to them
and for those who are being crushed
by the burdens laid upon them.
Come and meet them on
their Damascus road
and shine the light of your
grace upon them.
Lord, in your mercy,
hear our prayer.

Lord,
we pray for those who know
they are approaching the
end of their journey
and for those filled with fear
as their days are slipping
through their fingers;

for those who are radiant with
hope and look forward with
joy to meeting their Lord
and for those whose faithful
witness to God's grace is a
blessing to everyone they meet.
Come and meet them on
their Damascus road
and shine the light of your
grace upon them.
Lord, in your mercy,
hear our prayer.

Lord,
we pray for those for whom
we are concerned as they
struggle through life
and for those we now name
in our hearts who need the
touch of God's grace.

silence

We pray for ourselves and
the burdens we carry and
the problems we face
and for those moments when
God is so real that our hearts
feel on fire with his love.
Come and meet us on our
Damascus road
and shine the light of your
grace upon us.
Lord, in your mercy,
hear our prayer.

We bring our prayers in
the name of Christ,
who always meets those on their
Damascus road. **Amen.**

FOURTH SUNDAY OF EASTER

Praise

Revelation 7:9–17

Lord,
we prefer our worship to be
offered in an orderly way
and our songs of praise to be
meaningful and holy.
We come to sing, to pray,
and to give you thanks
and we assume we can leave
unchanged by the experience.

To discover real worship we must
listen to John in his Revelation,
as he draws back the curtain on
the celebrations in heaven.
We are astounded by what seems
like worship that is out of control
and praises that clearly have
no beginning and no end.

The multitude that no one
could number come from
all over the world
and the Lamb is right in the
centre because he is the
focus of their praises.
We pray that, by your Holy Spirit,
you will transform our worship
that it might, by your grace,
become an echo of the
worship of heaven
and that Christ might be
the centre of all things.

Come, Lord, for you alone are the
reason for our thanksgiving
and we worship because of who
you are and what you have done.

You are our Saviour and
our risen Lord,
the one who makes all things new.

Come, Lord, and hold us
fast in your grace.
Come, Lord, and touch
us with your love.
Come, Lord, and by your
mercy set us free.
Come, Lord, and be the mainspring
of our songs and our praises.
May all we say and do here, and
as your people in the world,
become a glorious reflection of
the heavenly celebration.
May the songs we offer here and
the prayers we bring to you
flow out into everything we will face
every day of our lives. **Amen.**

Confession

Psalm 23

Lord,
we love the words of the psalmist
when he says you are our shepherd
and we find such a blessing in his
words about green pastures.
We rejoice in the knowledge
of your presence even in
our darkest moments
and we are comforted by the
promise of a place at the
banquet table in heaven.

But, Lord, we confess that we
are not very good at allowing
you to shepherd our days
and we find it not always to
our liking to be dependent
on you for guidance.
We are too self-centred to
be willing to trust you for
everything, every day
and we are only too well aware
that we are afraid of the
threats from an evil world.

The truth is that we are
grateful for the promise
of blessings to come
but deep down what we
really desire are your
richest blessings now!
We confess that the words of the
psalmist bring joy to our ears
but in our heart of hearts there
is still an empty void that
mere words cannot fill.
Come, Lord, and fill us
with your presence
and by your grace enable us
not only to love the words
but help us to experience
more of the reality of which
they speak. **Amen.**

Intercession

John 10:22–30

Lord,
we pray for those who
find faith hard
and for those who find it easier to
trust in what they have and hold;
for those who find it difficult
because they have too much
of this world's treasure
and for those, like the rich
young ruler, who find it
hard to lose control.
On the journey of life,
help us to walk in faith.

Lord,
we pray for those who find faith hard
and for those who have no time
for faith because they have
so little to hold on to;
for those whose days are spent
scavenging for food for their family
and for those so broken
by life that they struggle
simply to go on existing.
On the journey of life,
help us to walk in faith.

Lord,
we pray for those who
find faith hard
and for those who feel too
unworthy to see themselves
as loved by God;
for those whose lives are
ruled by their addiction to
drugs and to alcohol
and for those who from their
youngest days have never known
what it means to be loved.
On the journey of life,
help us to walk in faith.

Lord,
we pray for those who
find faith hard
and for those who demand
proof before they would
consider trusting in God;
for those who want to know all
the answers to their doubts
and their questions
and for those who have yet to
discover that they are invited
simply to take the first step.
On the journey of life,
help us to walk in faith.

Lord,
we pray for those who
find faith hard
and for those who believe that
Jesus asks too much of them;
for those who are content
to be a member of a
church congregation
and for those who are
afraid of what a personal
commitment might mean.
On the journey of life,
help us to walk in faith.

Lord,
we pray for those who
find faith hard
and for those for whom the
world and its problems
are a barrier to faith;
for those who cannot reconcile
God's love in Jesus with
a world of suffering
and for those who have yet to
discover the tears that God
is shedding over his world.
On the journey of life,
help us to walk in faith.

Lord,
we pray for those who
find faith hard
and for those we know who are
struggling with questions of faith;
for ourselves and the times of
doubt, fear, and uncertainty
that undermine our trust
and for a renewal of our walk with
Jesus as each day we seek to be
filled with the Holy Spirit.
On the journey of life,
help us to walk in faith.

We bring our prayers in
the name of Jesus,
the author and perfecter
of our faith. **Amen.**

FIFTH SUNDAY OF EASTER

Praise

Revelation 21:1–6

Lord,
we are told that you are
making all things new
and that nothing would
ever be the same again.
We expected to see everyone
living in peace
and that there would be no more
war and no more fighting.

We expected that everyone
would have enough food
and that no one would
ever be poor again.
We thought that the new
heaven and the new earth
would banish all greed,
selfishness, and evil for ever.

But we got it all wrong.

It was never your intention to
impose your authority on us
or to leave us no choice but
to submit to your will.
From the beginning you created
us to be truly human
and you built into your design
our freedom to choose.

We praise you that you are
the God of new things
and that in your hands all
things can be made new.
You have a glorious plan for
the whole of your creation
and your promise of a new heaven
and a new earth is true.

We praise you for the beautiful
new heaven that awaits us
and we worship you for the new
earth we can enter now.
For yours is the kingdom, the
power, and the glory
and we can experience the heaven
of your love here and now.

It was your touch that changed
our hearts so we could
hear the song of heaven
and as we open our lives to your
presence we see all things new now.
Your purpose from the first was that
we should fall in love with you
and that, day by day, we should
experience your life-renewing grace.

The new earth was created
in Christ's life, death,
and resurrection
and the new heaven is entered the
moment we place our trust in him.
We praise you that you are appointing
us as agents of the new earth
and for commissioning us to
point others to the doorway
of the new heaven.

All praise to the King and
glory to the Lord,
for the new heaven and the new
earth are in Christ. **Amen.**

Confession
John 13:31–35

Lord,
we have a confession to make
and we don't feel very
comfortable making it.
We know that you commanded
us to love one another
but the simple truth is, we don't.

We find it very hard to like
all the people we meet
and to be honest, loving them
seems utterly beyond us.
How could you expect us to keep
such an impossible order
and has there ever been a person
who could love without limit?

It is then that we look at the cross
and we realise that there was,
for you said 'Father, forgive' when
they nailed you to the cross.
Now we understand that there is
a cost to being your followers
and a price tag to naming you
as Saviour and Lord.

Lord,
we seek your forgiveness for being
such poor reflections of your grace.
We pray, fill us with your
Holy Spirit that we may live
as the body of Christ.
Your command was to love one
another, which we found
we were unable to do,
because it is only as we are filled
with your incredible love
that the impossible command
will be made possible as we
love in Jesus' name. **Amen.**

Intercession
Acts 11:1–18

Lord,
we pray for those who face
great barriers in their lives
and for those who find it hard
to be accepted as they are;
for those who feel rejected because
of their race or their colour
and for those who are avoided
because of their mental
or physical disability.
Come, Lord, and open our hearts
and break down the barriers.

Lord,
we pray for those who face
great barriers in their lives
and for those around the world who
receive little or no education;
for those denied the opportunities
of learning we take for granted
and for those enslaved by a
society that blocks every
avenue to learning.
Come, Lord, and open our hearts
and break down the barriers.

Lord,
we pray for those who face
great barriers in their lives
and for those who have no
access to the healthcare
they desperately need;
for those who watch helplessly
as their children die from
curable illnesses
and for those people who are
dying because the water
they drink is unclean.
Come, Lord, and open our hearts
and break down the barriers.

Lord,
we pray for those who face
great barriers in their lives
and for nations where people are
divided by class or by culture;
for those where governments pander
to the voices of the wealthy
and for those where the needs of the
poor with no voice are rarely heard.
Come, Lord, and open our hearts
and break down the barriers.

Lord,
we pray for those who face
great barriers in their lives
and for those who are simply longing
for freedoms that we still enjoy;
for those where freedom of
expression is legally forbidden
and for those imprisoned without
trial for challenging these laws.
Come, Lord, and open our hearts
and break down the barriers.

Lord,
we pray for those who face
great barriers in their lives
and for those who have built a wall
of bitterness around themselves;
for those for whom forgiveness is a
price they are unwilling to pay
and for those who continue to suffer
because of a hurt they can't let go.
Come, Lord, and open our hearts
and break down the barriers.

Lord,
we pray for those who face
great barriers in their lives
and for those who find it
hard to put the needs of
others before their own;
for those for whom the spirit of
altruism has been lost under
their greed and self-interest
and for our nation, where selfless
concern for others is buried in
the sands of self-centredness.
Come, Lord, and open our hearts
and break down the barriers.

Lord,
we pray for those who face
great barriers in their lives
and for those so hurt in the
past they are finding it hard
to trust again today;
for ourselves and the barriers
we face in a nation that
turns its back on God
and for the opportunity to
reach out in faith as we speak
of the Saviour we trust.
Come, Lord, and open our hearts
and break down the barriers.

We bring our prayers in
the name of Jesus,
who by his grace breaks every
barrier down. **Amen.**

SIXTH SUNDAY OF EASTER

Prayer of Approach

Psalm 67

Lord,
we are here for one purpose only
and we have assembled with
one desire in our hearts.
You are our great and
glorious God
and nothing in life matters
more than praising you.

We long to sing your praises
here in the world
that everyone, everywhere
may know of your love.
We have many concerns
in our daily lives
but there is nothing more important
than honouring your name.

May you bless us with your grace
that our lives will be a
reflection of your mercy.
May you bless us with your peace
that our days will echo
the song of heaven.
May you bless us with your love
that all we say and do and are,
speak of your presence. **Amen.**

Praise

John 14:23–29

What name shall we give him
and how shall he be made known?
We call him our friend
and our Saviour;
to us he is master and King.
Shall we declare him as
sovereign almighty
and the source of joy never-ending?

The God that we worship
is more than the sum of all
that we can proclaim.
His wisdom is too great
for mere finite minds
and his mercy leaves us
breathlessly asking for more.
His grace is utterly overwhelming
and his power is beyond
all we can imagine or sing.
But his love is the reason for
our peace and our joy
and his presence is the driving force
of the worship we offer.

What name shall we give him?
He is the Lord—
in whose name we offer
all our worship
and our prayers of praise. **Amen.**

Intercession

Acts 16:9–10

Lord,
we have a vision of the
hungry being fed.
They come to us with
outstretched hands.
We pray, help us to hear their cry
and show us how to move those
with the power but not the
will to feed them.
Lord, the vision is from you,
the answer is in our hands.

Lord,
we have a vision of those
who are lonely.
They live all alone and they long
for someone to share their memories.
We pray, teach us how
to care for them
as we demonstrate the love of God.
Lord, the vision is from you,
the answer is in our hands.

Lord,
we have a vision of those
on the fringe of faith.
They come with their doubts
and their questions

and often we do not
know what to say.
We pray, show us how to
walk with them
and how to share with them
our journey of faith.
Lord, the vision is from you,
the answer is in our hands.

Lord,
we have a vision of those
who are dying.
They look at us with fearful eyes
as the truth dawns upon them
that the days that remain for
them are few in number.
We pray, give us the courage
and compassion
to share the journey with them,
that our faith might be a
light for their path.
Lord, the vision is from you,
the answer is in our hands.

Lord,
we have a vision of the
world's refugees.
We hear them knocking on our
door and seeking help.
They come to us lost, afraid, and
feeling rejected by many nations.
We pray, help us to speak
out on their behalf,
that the countries of the world
may repent and show love.
Lord, the vision is from you,
the answer is in our hands.

Lord,
we have a vision of those who
have lost someone they loved.
They come to us, broken,
dazed, weeping deep inside
and with a feeling that it
all doesn't seem real.
We pray, enable us to be there for
them as we listen to their pain
and to be a source of hope in
the midst of their sorrow.
Lord, the vision is from you,
the answer is in our hands.

Lord,
we have a vision of your world
being reclaimed and restored.
We hear the cries of nations
already suffering the impact
of global warming
and the signs of climate change are all
around us and cannot be ignored.
We know that future generations
will ask why we didn't act
and you are wondering why we do
nothing to care for your world.
We pray, though we cannot
do everything,
help us to do what we can to
protect your good earth.
Lord, the vision is from you,
the answer is in our hands.

Lord,
we have a vision that you are
calling us into your service.
We come to you seeking your will
and longing to know your
purpose in our lives.
We come fearful of your call,
concerned of what it might mean
and knowing that you will
enable us to do
whatever you call us to do.

Lord, the vision is from you,
the answer is in our hands.

We bring our prayers in the
name of the One,
who alone is the source of all
true visions of hope. **Amen.**

SEVENTH SUNDAY OF EASTER

Praise

Psalm 97

Lord,
giving you praise is one of the
greatest joys and wonders of life
for there is nothing on earth that
provides us such eternal joy.
You are sovereign over all
that we can know
and you are the heart of
everything that really matters.

There are so many challenges to
your power and authority
and we are surrounded by those who
would love to take your place.
Deep down we know that there is
nothing in our vast universe
that could ever take the place of
its King and creator and Lord.

It is through Christ that we
can enter your presence
and by the Holy Spirit we are
empowered to stand before you.
You are our righteous God—who
does what is right and is right—
and Christ is our righteousness.
He is the one through whom
we have a right relationship
with the living God.

On life's darkest days the light of
your glory lights up our lives
and even when we feel
crushed and defeated, we
have victory in Jesus.
One day, all of creation will bow
the knee before its Lord
and he will receive the
honour, worship, and
praises that he deserves.

We sing our songs of praise for the
wonder of walking with you
and for the assurance that you will
never leave us nor reject us.
When we gather with those
who know and love the
Lord Almighty,
we briefly enter that experience
that one day will be eternal.

We will praise you now and
we will praise you for ever
and we will declare your glory now
and we will shout it for ever.
Lord, open our eyes to catch
a glimpse of your presence
in our daily lives:
unlock our ears to hear you speak
in the struggles of the poor;
speak your word of love in the
innocent life of a child;
touch us deeply as we
catch the sound of your
voice in the breeze;
and melt our hearts again with
the love that never lets us go.

Come, praise the Lord
for he is good
and his love, mercy, and
glory are eternal. **Amen.**

Confession
John 17:20–26

Lord,
it was your plan from the beginning
that we should be one
and it was Christ's prayer that
we should be his body.
You are the sovereign head
of the church on earth
and your people are gathered as
one around the throne of grace.

We confess that we are anything
but one people on earth
and that the body of Christ has
been divided again and again.
We confess that we are not
united in your Son
and that we do little to restore that
which you died to make whole.

We confess that Christ's prayer still
awaits its ultimate fulfilment
and that we continue to be
the stumbling block to
the church's healing.

Forgive us, Lord, and
heal your church.
Forgive us, Lord, and make us one.
Forgive us, Lord, and make us
the answer to Christ's prayer.
Forgive us, Lord, that the
world may see our oneness,
and believe. **Amen.**

Intercession
Acts 16:16–34

Lord,
we pray for those who seek to
work out their faith each day
and for those who do so before
a watching, waiting world;
for those who find it hard
to be a Christian at
their place of work
and for those expected to
turn a blind eye to things
they know are wrong.
May the presence of Christ
keep them strong
and his love uphold them.

Lord,
we pray for those who seek to
work out their faith each day
and for those who do so before
a watching, waiting world;
for those who seek to
share the love of God
with their neighbour
and also with those of a
different faith and those
with no faith at all.
May the presence of Christ
keep them strong
and his love uphold them.

Lord,
we pray for those who seek to
work out their faith each day
and for those who do so before
a watching, waiting world;
for those who are the
only Christian at home
or in their family
and for those torn apart
by the conflicts their
faith often brings.
May the presence of Christ
keep them strong
and his love uphold them.

Lord,
we pray for those who seek to
work out their faith each day
and for those who do so before
a watching, waiting world;
for young people at school who are
bullied because of their faith
and for those who are pressured
by their peers to conform.
May the presence of Christ
keep them strong
and his love uphold them.

Lord,
we pray for those who seek to
work out their faith each day
and for those who do so before
a watching, waiting world;
for those newly committed
to Christ who are now
ostracised by their family
and for those in need of the
love and support of their
new Christian family.
May the presence of Christ
keep them strong
and his love uphold them.

Lord,
we pray for those who seek to
work out their faith each day
and for those who do so before
a watching, waiting world;
for those in countries where it is
dangerous simply being a Christian
and for those facing torture,
imprisonment, or death
because of their faith.
May the presence of Christ
keep them strong
and his love uphold them.

Lord,
we pray for those who seek to
work out their faith each day
and for those who do so before
a watching, waiting world;
for those felt called by God into
the service of their community
and for those who are
teachers, councillors, or
who work in the NHS.
May the presence of Christ
keep them strong
and his love uphold them.

Lord,
we pray for those who seek to
work out their faith each day
and for those who do so before
a watching, waiting world;
for ourselves when it is hardest to
walk in the footsteps of Jesus
and for those times when we feel
challenged to name him as Lord.
May the presence of Christ
keep them strong
and his love uphold them.

We bring our prayers in
the name of Christ,
who always upholds us
with his love. **Amen.**

PENTECOST SUNDAY

Praise

Psalm 104:24–35b

Lord,
we praise you for your greatness
and we worship you for your glory.
Your splendour is beyond
our describing

and the light of your
presence dazzles us.

We praise you, the God
of all creation,
and we celebrate that before
anything came to be
you were already the sovereign
from all eternity.
Before the life of the
universe burst forth,
from the matter you created
you were the God we now worship.

The fingerprints of your
grand design
can be seen everywhere
by the eye of faith.

The seas and the oceans
and the streams and the waterfalls,
the mountains and the valleys,
and the trees and the flowers—
they sing the song of your creation.

The birds and the animals
and the fish and the reptiles,
the tiny things that fly or crawl,
and the planets we can see
and worlds far beyond our gaze—
they sing the song of your creation.

We too sing the song
of your creation
and praise you with the chorus
of our re-creation.
We give you honour, glory,
and thanksgiving,
that by the power of the Holy Spirit
we can sing the song of
heaven's glory. **Amen.**

Confession

Genesis 11:1–9

Lord,
we confess that too often we
have reserved our worship
for the things we have achieved
and we have celebrated the
wonder of what we have done
and failed to give you the
glory that was your due.

Lord,
we confess that too often our
words have caused division
and we have treated others
with too little respect.
We have hurt those closest to us
by our angry words and
our sullen silence.

Lord,
we confess that we are not the
people others think we are
and our walk with you is not
always what you intended.
Forgive us for all that we have
said and done and thought
that damaged our relationship with
you and with our neighbour
May the Holy Spirit's
fire make us clean
and his mighty rushing wind heal
our fellowship with you. **Amen.**

Intercession

Acts 2:1–21

Father,
we pray for those who feel
unworthy to enter your presence
and for those who are aware of the
things that are wrong in their lives;

for those for whom forgiveness
seems a long-forgotten dream
and for those who are ashamed
of the things they have said
and done and thought.
Come now in the silence and
with the fire of the Holy
Spirit, make us clean.

silence

Father,
we pray for those who long
for a deeper experience of
God in their daily lives
and for those who yearn for a closer
walk with their heavenly Father;
for those for whom the Lord
has been a remote being and
always far from them
and for those who seek
the new inner spiritual
strength of his presence.
Come now in the silence and
make yourself known in the
wind of the Holy Spirit.

silence

Father,
we pray for those for whom worship
is something they do every week
and for those for whom it is a
duty and rarely the delight
they know it should be;
for those who have yet to
experience the freedom and
joy in God's company
and for those who have never
been overwhelmed by
renewal in the Holy Spirit.
Come now in the silence and
flood our praises with the
power of the Holy Spirit.

silence

Father,
we pray for those whose
deepest desire is to be more
aware of you each day
and for those who close their
eyes of faith and do not see
your fingerprints everywhere;
for those who are blind to
God's activity in the lives
of those who know him
and for those who are unable
to see his action for good in
those who don't yet love him.
Come now in the silence
and by the Holy Spirit
open our eyes of faith.

silence

Father,
we pray for those who always
feel on the outside of
life, just looking in
and for those with little sense
of belonging at the heart
of the people of God;
for those who have offered great
service in the life of the church
and for those whose contributions
are too easily taken for granted.
Come now in the silence and
allow the Holy Spirit to
make us one in Christ.

silence

Father,
we pray for those who would
never feel able to push
themselves forward
and for those who know God
is calling them to be willing
to stand out in faith;
for those who lack the courage
to speak of what being a
Christian means to them
and for those who are simply too
afraid of being misunderstood
and made to look foolish.
Come now in the silence and fill us
with the power of the Holy Spirit.

silence

Father,
we pray for those who have
a new song in their hearts
and on their lips
and for those who have
experienced the renewing
presence of the Spirit;
for those who have found a
new joy and a new purpose
transforming their days
and for those with the privilege
and responsibility as they
answer the call of God.
Come now in the silence and,
with the joy of the Holy Spirit,
may we celebrate your grace.

silence

We bring our prayers in
the name of Christ
and in the power of the
Holy Spirit. **Amen.**

TRINITY SUNDAY

Prayer of Approach

John 16:12–15

Lord,
we come with open
hearts and minds
as we long to hear your word
and celebrate your love.
Your promise to us is that
the Holy Spirit
will make your purposes
known to us.

We pray that through
the word of God the Father,
the work of God the Son,
and the witness of the Holy Spirit
we may have the assurance
of your love
and the guarantee
that we are children of
your grace. **Amen.**

Praise

Romans 5:1–5

Lord,
we praise you for the difference
you have made in our lives
and for the way you have given
us a new sense of freedom.
In Jesus we find our days
transformed by his love
and in so many various ways you
make your presence known.

We praise you that, even in the
dark times, you surround
us with your grace
and when life is free from
pain, the light of your
love overwhelms us.

In the midst of times of trouble,
you change them into your
moments of opportunity
and when everything seems
to be going wrong, you
are there to hold us.

We praise you that when we
have lost our way and the
road ahead is uncertain,
the Holy Spirit comes to
flood our lives with joy and
our days with hope.
When you were simply a name
and we felt like strangers
in your presence,
it was then that in Jesus you
threw open the door that
leads to the throne of grace.

We praise you that even when
we knew we were utterly
unworthy of your love
you didn't hesitate to reach
out to us, and in Christ you
came to welcome us home!
We know that you didn't have to
love us but, in Jesus, you paid
the price that grace demands.
You are our amazing God and
we have discovered your
mercy knows no limits.

We praise you for those
who pointed us to follow
the way of your Son
and we honour you for those,
who through their lives, flood
your world with your peace.
We thank you that every
experience in our lives and
each journey we make
begins and ends in the love that
never lets us off, never lets us
down, and will never let us go.

Father, Son, and Holy Spirit,
we worship you now
and we will praise you
for ever. **Amen.**

Intercession

Psalm 8

O Lord, our Lord,
how majestic is your name
in all the earth!
We pray for the world that
owes its existence to you
and for its life which depends
on your sustaining power;
for our world, where many give
no thought to its Maker,
and for those who offer
worship to anyone and
anything but you.
Lord of all the earth,
hear our prayer.

O Lord, our Lord,
how majestic is your name
in all the earth!
We pray for our planet, which
we are silently engaged
in killing day by day,
and for our refusal to change
our selfish lifestyles as we
steal the earth's resources;
for a renewed commitment to end
our vandalising of God's world
and for a desire to offer our
good earth to God, as
part of our worship.
Lord of all the earth,
hear our prayer.

O Lord, our Lord,
how majestic is your name
in all the earth!
We pray for a deeper recognition that
every person is precious to God
and that we will treasure all women,
men, children, and young people;
for an end to modern slavery,
where human beings are
treated as goods for sale,
and for those enslaved in poverty
in a world of great wealth
in the hands of the few.
Lord of all the earth,
hear our prayer.

O Lord, our Lord,
how majestic is your name
in all the earth!
We pray for the children of our
world who are at risk when
they search the internet
and for those who are daily in
danger of being entrapped
by evil-minded people;
for those who in their innocence
are being groomed by those
with wicked intentions
and for those whose young
lives are ruined by the abuse
they suffer in secret.
Lord of all the earth,
hear our prayer.

O Lord, our Lord,
how majestic is your name
in all the earth!
We pray for those who are desperate
to live their lives in peace
and for those who seek to
change the world through
violence and terrorism;
for those who live within a
culture that allows them no
freedom of expression
and for those whose daily
lives are governed by the
stranglehold of a dictator.
Lord of all the earth,
hear our prayer.

O Lord, our Lord,
how majestic is your name
in all the earth!
We pray for those who because
of their greed are hunting
animals to extinction
and for those who are destroying
many creatures' habitats in
their desire for wealth;
for those for whom healthcare,
education, and justice are things
they can take for granted
and for those with no power
and no voice and who are
forgotten by all, except God.
Lord of all the earth,
hear our prayer.

O Lord, our Lord,
how majestic is your name
in all the earth!
We pray for those who are
committed to seeking the
health of their bodies
and for those who are doing
nothing to rescue the
health of their soul;
for those whose focus is on
this life and in living on
earth as long as they can
and for those who are spiritually
empty and in whose lives
God has no place.

Lord of all the earth,
hear our prayer.

O Lord, our Lord,
how majestic is your name
in all the earth!
We pray for ourselves and those
for whom we are concerned,
that our words, deeds, and
our way of life might praise
the name of our Lord.

silence

Lord of all the earth,
hear our prayer.

We bring our prayers
in the name of our
majestic God. **Amen.**

EIGHTH SUNDAY IN ORDINARY TIME

Praise

Isaiah 55:10–13

Lord,
we praise you for the assurance
that nothing we do in your
name is ever wasted
and that you can use the
smallest gift we can make.
There are times when we
feel our contributions
seem too small to make
a difference,
but in your hands you promise
they can do mighty things.

We praise you that you are the
God of transformation
and that your grace can bring
light into the darkest places.
You are the sovereign
Lord of all creation
and you have a purpose for
all that you have made.

We worship you for the way
you overcome our doubts
and for your power to gather
all things and all people
into your sovereign will.
Amazing God, we lift our
voices in thanksgiving
and we join in singing the
eternal song of your glory.

We await the day when everyone,
everywhere will give you glory
and we rejoice that the whole
of creation knows the song
sheet of your praise.
The whole vast universe
speaks of the endless power
at your command
and the seemingly endless variety
of our world and worlds
beyond cries out in joy.

You are the God who has no
beginning and no end
and your love and compassion
for your creation has
no limitation.
Great God Almighty, King of
all that you have made,
and Lord of all things and
all people near and far,
we worship you and lay
our hearts and lives
before you. **Amen.**

Confession

Luke 6:39–49

Lord,
we confess that we are very good at
highlighting the mistakes of others
but we are not so good at
recognising our own.
We can easily see where
others are going wrong
but we wander from the path of
obedience without noticing it.
We can offer many solutions
to the mess others are
making of their lives
but we do not appreciate
others pointing out where
we are going wrong.

Lord,
we ask your forgiveness for
our deliberate blindness
and that you will open our eyes to
our own catalogue of mistakes.
We ask your forgiveness
for assuming we had the
right to correct others
when we were in need of the
same correction ourselves.

Come, Lord, and make us clean.
Come, Lord, and make us whole.
Come, Lord, and fill us
with the Holy Spirit.
Come, Lord, and live in
our hearts. **Amen.**

Intercession

1 Corinthians 15:51–58

Lord,
we pray for those trapped
in an unending cycle of
hatred and crime
and for those whose lives are the
source of great anger to many;
for those who have been damaged
by the neglect and abuse of others
and for those whose bitterness causes
the spread of hurt and anxiety.
May they experience the victory
of Christ in their lives.
Come and touch us and heal us
and make our lives new.

Lord,
we pray for those lives which
are constantly filled with
fear and despair
and for those who do not know
what it is that makes them afraid;
for those whose days are an endless
path enveloped with worry
and for those whose anxieties
are triggered by the
uncertainties they are facing.
May they experience the victory
of Christ in their lives.
Come and touch us and heal us
and make our lives new.

Lord,
we pray for those for whom
every day is dark and empty
and for those who feel lost and for
whom life is miserable and grey;
for those who have given up
and have given in to a deep
feeling of hopelessness
and for those who know the
story of Jesus but not his living
presence in their hearts.
May they experience the victory
of Christ in their lives.
Come and touch us and heal us
and make our lives new.

Lord,
we pray for those who are
finding it almost too hard
to love their neighbour
and for those who have built a wall of
self-protection around their lives;
for those who have yet to
discover that they are required
to love themselves
and for those who need to
know they are accepted and
embraced by the God of love.
May they experience the victory
of Christ in their lives.
Come and touch us and heal us
and make our lives new.

Lord,
we pray for those whose lives
are filled with times of doubt
that overwhelms them
and for those who demand
verifiable proof before they
feel they can follow Christ;
for those whose uncertainties
are denying them every
opportunity to walk in faith
and for those who feel a huge
leap of faith is expected, when
only the first step is required.
May they experience the victory
of Christ in their lives.
Come and touch us and heal us
and make our lives new.

Lord,
we pray for those who are crushed
and broken by feelings of
guilt that won't go away
and for those who have made
their confessions but who
cannot forgive themselves;
for those who carry within them
the hurt, anger, and pain
they are unable to let go
and for those who have been
wounded so deeply they cannot
bring themselves to forgive.
May they experience the victory
of Christ in their lives.
Come and touch us and heal us
and make our lives new.

Lord,
we pray for those for whom
we are concerned, whose
lives are in chaos
and for those whose lives are
one long series of unending
problems and mistakes;
for those who realise that they
are not always as close to Jesus
as they know they should be
and for those who simply long to
be filled with the Holy Spirit in
the worship and service of God.
May they experience the victory
of Christ in their lives.
Come and touch us and heal us
and make our lives new.

We bring our prayers in the
name of the One,
who loves us now and will
love us for ever. **Amen.**

NINTH SUNDAY IN ORDINARY TIME

Praise

Psalm 96:1–2

Lord,
our worship can never reach
the heights of your glory

or sound the depths of
your love and mercy.
You are the Holy One, whose
greatness is beyond understanding
and whose grace enables us to
stand before the Lord.

You have put a new song
on our lips—
it is a song of Christ's
lordship over all things.
How can we not sing of
the love of our God
and why should we remain silent
about all you have done?

We use words to speak of the
wonder of your love
and our songs we offer to
declare your worth.
You are the God of all creation
and in and through you we have
received our purpose in life.

Lord,
at last the truth has dawned upon us
that our songs of worship
are to be sung here and
everywhere and for ever.
This is to be the greatest
hymn ever sung.

For you have given us
the gift of life
and the beauty of your creation.
You have granted us the privilege
of being your new
creation in Christ.

We praise you that you are the one
for whom worship has no
beginning and no end.
The whole of our lives and
every part of life itself
are to be a holy celebration
of the King of Kings.

Lord,
hold us in your grace,
lift us by your mercy,
and may the awesomeness
of your name
transform our praises for
your glory. **Amen.**

Confession
Galatians 1:1–12

Lord,
we stand before you and find
it hard to raise our heads.
We feel ashamed that so often
and so easily we let you down.
There must be times when you
are disappointed in us,
when once again we have failed
to be faithful to you.

We confess that we find the path
that Christ calls us to follow
is strewn with obstacles that
make us stumble.
We find our days littered
with temptations that
can lead us astray
and there are pitfalls into which
we plunge time after time.

The problems we face are
not always so obvious
and the challenges to our
discipleship sneak up
on us unnoticed.
We find it so much easier to
blend in with those around us

and it is so costly to stand out, to be different, and to stand for Jesus.

Forgive us, Lord, and take our hand when danger is near
and lead us by your grace that we might experience your victory once more. **Amen.**

Intercession

1 Kings 18:20–39

Lord,
we pray for those who are employees in large and multi-national companies
and for those who put their future at risk when they challenge illegal activity;
for those who because of their faith in Christ seek to speak out on behalf of their colleagues
and for those who offer words and deeds of hope and reconciliation to others.
Lord, come walk with those
who stand firm in your name.

Lord,
we pray for those who take a stand against malpractice in the National Health Service
and for those who blow the whistle because of their faith in the God of truth;
for those who are vilified by people in the media and also by their colleagues
and for those who, at great personal cost, reveal the truth that was meant to be hidden.
Lord, come walk with those
who stand firm in your name.

Lord,
we pray for members of parliament who take a stand for what they believe is right
and for those whose consciences will not allow them to unquestioningly follow the party line;
for those who are willing to pay the price of humiliation and the loss of political progress
and for those for whom the best interests of the whole nation are of paramount concern.
Lord, come walk with those
who stand firm in your name.

Lord,
we pray for those who daily face attacks on their property for their stand against racism
and for those who suffer physical abuse for seeking to protect those of a different colour;
for those who speak out when their neighbours face verbal confrontation at work or at home
and for those who risk their lives because they believe we are all equal before our Maker.
Lord, come walk with those
who stand firm in your name.

Lord,
we pray for those who take their stand against injustice wherever it is found
and for those who challenge the legal system whenever they believe it to be wrong;
for those whose utter determination to never give up forces them to face huge opposition

and for those who continue the
struggle until those wrongly
imprisoned are set free.
Lord, come walk with those
who stand firm in your name.

Lord,
we pray for athletes around the
world who take a firm stand
against the use of drugs
and for those who would rather
lose than rely on substances to
enhance their performance;
for sportsmen and women who
speak out against drug abuse,
whatever its purpose or form,
and for those whose faith requires
them to be good role models
to the next generation.
Lord, come walk with those
who stand firm in your name.

Lord,
we pray for those who take
their stand for Christ in
ways that few will ever see
and for those who refuse to
cheat and to lie, even when it
would be so less demanding;
for our young people, that they
will stand firm in the face of
peer pressure to conform
and for ourselves, that we will take
every opportunity to take our
stand in the name of our Lord.
Lord, come walk with those
who stand firm in your name.

We bring our prayers in
the name of Christ,
who stood firm for the
kingdom of God. **Amen.**

TENTH SUNDAY IN ORDINARY TIME

Praise

Psalm 146

Lord,
you are worthy of all our praises
and no worship we can
offer is too great.
You are the Holy One
and you are perfect in
everything you do.

Our praises come from the
very depths of our hearts
and we will sing songs of
adoration all our days.
We thank you, sovereign Lord, that
we can trust you completely
and we affirm that only you
can transform our lives.

We are moved by the
beauty of your world
and we are thrilled by the
wonder of all we see.
From sunrise to sunset, the earth
is filled with your glory
and every facet of your creation
speaks of your mighty power.

From the flowers in our gardens to
the mighty oaks of the forest,
we are moved to stand in awe
of our creator God.
From the tiny wren to the
wondrous eagle,
we find reasons to give
thanks to our God.

From the newborn baby to the
person near the end of their days,
we see signs of your constant love.

From the early parables of creation
to the message of re-creation,
we are overwhelmed with a
longing to bless your name.

You are the God of life and
the source of new life
and we find peace and hope
in your presence.
We praise you for the life, death,
and resurrection of your Son
and we sing our song of
thanksgiving for adopting
us into your family.

From now and until we stand
before your throne of grace,
we will praise your holy name and
honour you all our days. **Amen.**

Confession

Galatians 1:21–23

Lord,
we never realised
how small the world was
until we saw those pictures of earth
taken from space.

We never understood
just how loving you are
until you told us
to love our enemies.

We didn't know how real you are
until you touched our lives,
challenged our values,
and restored our hope.

Lord,
thank you for Jesus,
who made it possible
for us to be changed
by the discoveries
that he has opened our
eyes to see. **Amen.**

Intercession

1 Kings 17:7–24

I am an employer—and
I am hurting.
My business has been successful
and I have always tried to be
a good employer towards my staff.
When times are hard
and recession raises its ugly head
I find it extremely painful
to make members of my
workforce unemployed.
Pray for me.

I am a person struggling
with bereavement—
and I am hurting.
We have shared so many
years together
and our home was always
filled with laughter.
We made it our business
to support each other when
we needed help.
But now I'm on my own
and the house is empty
when I come home.
The laughter has gone
and though I don't tell anyone
it doesn't get any easier.
Pray for me.

I am a person in prison—
and I am hurting.
I know I did wrong
and I deserve to be locked up.
I'm deeply ashamed
of the mess I've made of my life

but I long to make amends to
  those I have hurt most.
I think of how, by my foolishness,
I have thrown everything away.
I long for the chance to
  make a new start.
Pray for me.

I am a doctor—and I am hurting.
I chose to study medicine because
  I wanted to help people
and serve in the NHS.
It never occurred to me
that I would be required to
  ration my services.
I find it painful to cancel
  the treatments
that my patients were expecting.
Those with the power to
  make a difference
don't seem to understand
the serious consequences
  the delays are causing.
Pray for me.

I am a young person—
  and I am hurting.
The mounting stress levels are agony
and I don't have a life
  outside of my studies.
I have no real idea what I
  want to do with my life
but I am forced to make choices
that will impact my future.
Many of my friends are opting
  out of the struggle
and I am facing the
  pressures of my peers
who tell me to 'get a life'.
But I still want to be
  the best I can be
whatever the cost.
Pray for me.

I am a hungry person—
  and I am hurting.
Everything was fine and
  we had a good life,
with a nice home and the
  trappings of success.
We had our holidays
and there were school trips
  for the children.
But I lost my job in the recession
and everything has gone wrong.
Now we depend on the food bank
otherwise we know we wouldn't eat.
I feel ashamed, rejected,
  angry—and hungry.
Pray for me.

I am a church leader—
  and I am hurting.
Whether you call me a vicar,
  minister, or lay worker
I have tried to encourage my people
to pray, to read God's Word,
and to share the love of Jesus
  in word and deed.
But many seem content just
  to gather for worship
and to silently ignore any call to
  give their personal witness.
At times, I feel I am
  wasting my time,
and it hurts.
Pray for me.

We bring our prayers in
  the name of Jesus,
who promised to hold us when
  we are hurting. **Amen.**

ELEVENTH SUNDAY IN ORDINARY TIME

Thanksgiving

Galatians 2:15–21

Lord,
we thank you for the way you
constantly reach out in love
and for the way you open the road
into your heavenly kingdom.
Like the prodigal son's father,
you come looking for us
and you begin your search even
before we acknowledge we are lost.

You do not even seem to take
account of who we were or
how we became lost—
your entire focus is reclaiming
us and holding a party to
welcome us home.
We thank you that you have not set
a mountain of rules for us to obey
and our acceptance into your
family comes even before
we can say we are sorry.

We know that if our acceptance
had depended on what kind
of lives we are living
then we would still be standing
outside with the door to the
kingdom slammed shut in our face.
We thank you that our welcome
as your children depends
on your grace alone;
we praise you that Christ has
died for us and is himself the
key to the kingdom of God.

We thank you most of all that our
life in the kingdom is focused
on Christ living within us
and that his presence is taking
the place in our hearts of all
that once led us astray.
This means that any signs of
our becoming the persons
you meant us to be
are the marks of Christ's
living presence and power
at work in our lives.

We thank you, Lord, for the
freedom with which you are
constantly flooding our days
and the hope, joy, and
fulfilment we experience in
the service of the King.
To have been touched by the love
of God is the most wonderful
thing we could know
which gives us the assurance
that, every step of every
journey, you are still with us.

Lord,
to offer thanksgiving for the
things you have done and
are doing in our lives
seems such a small thing to
do—but our gratitude comes
straight from our hearts.
We praise you for your promise
to prepare for us a place in
the heaven of your love
and we give you all the glory that
when we meet you face to face it
will be by grace alone. **Amen.**

Confession

1 Kings 21:1–10

Lord,
we confess that too often we turn
a blind eye to corruption

and we hope that no one is hurt by
the malpractices in high places.
We are aware that the
economical use of the truth
is acceptable today
and that the great sin is not what
was done but being caught!

We pray for ourselves and
our society whenever moral
concerns are ignored
and for times when governments
choose what will work
and not what is right;
for industry and commerce
for whom half-truths are
used to cover many lies
and for the life of the church
that has allowed things for
which it too needs to repent.

We confess that we have not
always cared for the hungry,
the lonely, and the poor
and that we can walk by
unmoved by the person hoping
for a coin to buy a warm drink;
for our prayers of concern
without action for
those struggling to feed
their own family
and for our worries, but lack of
action, for the plight of the
world's countless refugees.

Lord,
we pray not only for forgiveness
but for the renewing power
of the Holy Spirit
and for a total transformation of
our own lives and the life of the
nation to which we belong.
Come, Lord, and make
all things new.
Come, Lord, and renew our days.
Come, Lord, and reclaim us
by your grace. **Amen.**

Intercession
Luke 7:36—8:3
Lord,
we pray for those who have carried
a burden of guilt for many years
and for those who have a
memory of the secret that
has darkened their days;
for those who have confessed
their weakness but still
hold on to its pain
and for those whose sense of
unworthiness has dogged
every step of their lives.
Christ has died for our sin
and we can be forgiven.

Lord,
we pray for those who have no sense
of guilt or the need of forgiveness
and for those whose consciences
have been hardened so that
they see no reason to confess;
for those who measure their lives
against a standard they foolishly
have set for themselves
and for those whose environment
in childhood has inoculated
them to resist signs of weakness.
Christ has died for our sin
and we can be forgiven.

Lord,
we pray for those who have
been damaged by the lack
of unconditional love

and for those who from their
earliest days have been taught
that acceptance must be won;
for those who embrace the
truth that Christ died for
the sin of the whole world
and for those who still find it
almost impossible to accept
that they are accepted.
Christ has died for our sin
and we can be forgiven.

Lord,
we pray for the leaders of nations
whose policies have ruined
the lives of their people
and for those who have forgotten
God's bias to the poor in their
plans to favour the rich;
for those whose corruption and
violence are making them the
enemy of truth and justice
and for those who turn a
blind eye to the trust and
responsibilities laid upon them.
Christ has died for our sin
and we can be forgiven.

Lord,
we pray for those who find
it hard to pray, 'Forgive
our sin as we forgive …'
and for those who have
been badly damaged by
someone they had trusted;
for those who still carry within
them anger and bitterness
they cannot let go
and for those who are finding the
strength to let go, that Christ's
love enables them to do.
Christ has died for our sin
and we can be forgiven.

Lord,
we pray for those who have
been made to feel guilty for
something that wasn't their fault
and for those overwhelmed by
the memories of shame for
someone else's little secret;
for those who continue to
experience the scars of
deep hurt for the abuse
they have suffered
and for those who need to
feel the love of Jesus as
he tells them they were
truly not to blame.
Christ has died for our sin
and we can be forgiven.

Lord,
we pray for those we know
who were once at the
heart of the life of faith
and for those who have
wandered far from the
path of discipleship;
for those who are finding their
lives being touched once
again by God's invitation
and for those who are longing for
someone to come, take their
hand, and lead them home.
Christ has died for our sin
and we can be forgiven.

We bring our prayers in
the name of the One,
who said to the Father,
'Forgive.' **Amen.**

TWELFTH SUNDAY IN ORDINARY TIME

Praise

Psalm 42:1–11

Lord,
no day is ever complete
without you—
it is simply knowing you are there
that makes all the difference.
To know we are surrounded
by your power
provides us with the strength to face
whatever the day may bring.

The palmist spoke of his
deep longing for you
and that it was as if his whole
being was focused on your love.
He reminded us that being
uncertain of your being with us
is like the desperate desire for
water in an endless desert.

Lord,
we depend on food for
our physical bodies
to keep us healthy, active, and alive.
But we rely on your grace
to nourish our souls
and without your Holy
Spirit's touch
we would lose any sense
of wholeness.

How great is our God and
how majestic you are—
for you alone are the Lord
of our vast universe.
It is your glory that is the
source of our praises
and your authority over all
things that fills us with awe.
You are the centre of our hope
and the joy of all our days
and your sovereign will colours and
shapes our deepest longings.
We praise you, great and wonderful
God, for all that you are
and we bless you for the way
that your presence shines
through the gloom.

Whatever happens and whatever
we are called upon to face,
we will put our hope in you
and in the midst of the
storms of our days,
we will offer praises to your
holy name. **Amen.**

Intercession

1 Kings 19:1–15a

Lord,
we pray for those who have no food
and for those who will
not eat today;
for those who scavenge
on rubbish tips
and for those who commit
crime to feed their family.
As you sent help to Elijah,
so send us to help those in need.

silence

Lord,
we pray for those who
live by themselves
and for those who have no
one to share their fears;
for those who are single by choice
and for those who are alone
through bereavement
or broken promises.

As you sent help to Elijah,
so send us to help those in need.

silence

Lord,
we pray for those facing racial attacks
and for those whose home is
becoming their prison;
for those on whom we depend for
their work in our hospitals
and for those who came looking
for peace and found hatred.
As you sent help to Elijah,
so send us to help those in need.

silence

Lord,
we pray for those who are
just managing to cope
and for those whose several jobs do
not provide a living income;
for those who are exhausted
by the struggle to survive
and for those with none of the
luxuries we take for granted.
As you sent help to Elijah,
so send us to help those in need.

silence

Lord,
we pray for those whose days are a
series of medical appointments
and for those whose illness is
a closely guarded secret;
for those who need the comfort
of someone who comes
to pray with them
and for those whose pain impacts
the whole of their days.
As you sent help to Elijah,
so send us to help those in need.

silence

Lord,
we pray for those with no family
and who feel alone in the world
and for those whose greatest need
is simply to know they belong;
for those who feel alone in
the midst of a crowd
and for those whose deafness
or blindness can bring
a sense of isolation.
As you sent help to Elijah,
so send us to help those in need.

silence

Lord,
we pray for those we know
who have problems of
which no one knows
and for those who have
trusted you enough to
tell you their story;
for ourselves and the hurt
we feel inside that painful
memories can bring
and for those missed
opportunities and 'might have
beens' that haunt our days.
As you sent help to Elijah,
so send us to help those in need.

silence

We bring our prayers in
the name of Jesus,
who, by grace, meets all
our needs. **Amen.**

Dismissal

Luke 8:26–39

We came into your presence to
 give you thanks and praise.
You send us out to announce
 the wonder of your name.

We came to worship you with
 heart and soul and strength.
You send us now with songs
 of praise in our hearts.

We came because you are
 worthy of all we can offer.
You send us out now to prove your
 power to make all things new.

We came unworthy, alone,
 and still seeking.
You send us out as those
 you have found,
as those made worthy,
and as those no longer alone.

We were called by the power and
 the presence of the Holy Spirit.
You send us out in name of Jesus,
 our Saviour and Lord. **Amen.**

THIRTEENTH SUNDAY IN ORDINARY TIME

Praise

Psalm 77:1–2, 11–20

Lord,
in times of great darkness
 you come as the light
and when we feel as though
 our lives are breaking
you hold us in your grace.
In our weakness you
 are our strength
and when we lose our way you
 are our beacon of hope!

You never promised us a
 trouble-free life
or that our faith in Christ would
 protect us completely.
But when our world is
 turned upside down
and we are sinking beneath
 waves of despair
you reach out once more and
 lift our feet to the rock.

We praise you for your
 almighty purposes
and we give you glory that your
 love will never be defeated.
How can we not worship you—
 great God that you are,
and how can we not trust you—
 the sovereign Lord of life?

When everything in our
 lives had gone wrong
and we didn't know which
 way to turn,
it was then we had to stop
 our wandering
and remember that you were
 always there for us
and how you have loved us
 all down the years.

We praise you for the memories
 of your grace-care
and how you have sustained
 your people down the ages.
We worship you for the stories
 of your faithfulness
and we give you thanks for the
 way you have reached down

and surrounded those who
put their trust in you with
your unending love.

Holy and glorious God, in
awe and wonder we raise
our voices in praise
and we bless you that in your
faithfulness you put our feet
on the rock of Christ.
We give you glory that when
no one else could be there
and when no one else
wanted to be there
you came and held us
and gave us hope.
We praise you, our wonderful
God of all grace. **Amen.**

Confession

2 Kings 2:1–2, 6–14

Lord,
we confess that our
commitment is weak
and too easily we fail to
stand firm for you.
We find it so hard to walk
with you each day
when those around us are
walking a different path.

Forgive us for our lack of vision
and that we do not always
look to the light.
We think we can hide our
secrets in our hearts
and we forget that you see into
the depths of our lives.

Forgive us, Lord, and draw
us back closer to you
and teach us again to open
our hearts to your grace.
Come, Lord, and cleanse us that
we might stand in your presence
and heal our broken lives
that we may live to bring
you glory. **Amen.**

Intercession

Galatians 5:1, 13–25

Lord,
we pray for those who long for
freedom to do anything
and for those who desire to be
free to do what they like;
for those who have little concern
for the rights of other people
and for those whose misuse of their
freedom brings suffering to many.
May we always remember
that freedom is your
priceless gift to us all.

silence

Lord,
we pray for those who keep
longing to be free from fear
and for those who fill their
days with endless worries;
for those whose lives are
overwhelmed by concerns
for their future
and for those whose days pass
in anxiety about things
that never happen.
May we always remember
that freedom is your
priceless gift to us all.

silence

Lord,
we pray for those who long to be free
  of the addictions that hold them
and for those whose craving
  for illegal drugs has led
  to a life of crime;
for those desperate to be free
  of their habit because of its
  effects on their health
and for those who are dealers
  and drug pushers with no
  concern for their victims.
May we always remember
  that freedom is your
  priceless gift to us all.

silence

Lord,
we pray for those whose greatest
  wish is to be free from
  their painful memories
and for those who look back
  and remember with shame
  the things they have done;
for those whose pain and
  shame were caused by those
  whom they trusted
and for those who know they
  will only be free when they
  find the strength to forgive.
May we always remember
  that freedom is your
  priceless gift to us all.

silence

Lord,
we pray for those who need to
  be set free from the bitterness
  that fills their hearts
and for those whose deep-
  seated prejudice is destroying
  their lives from within;
for those whose relationships
  feel the impact of the
  need for total control
and for those who have yet to
  discover that real freedom
  comes in the colour of love.
May we always remember
  that freedom is your
  priceless gift to us all.

silence

Lord,
we pray for the freedom
  Christ offers to all who
  open their hearts to him
and for those, who by the
  power of the Holy Spirit, are
  bearing fruit in his name;
for those who know that their
  freedom is eternal and was
  a grace-gift from you
and for those who are reaping
  the fruit of heaven as they
  walk ever closer to you.
May we always remember
  that freedom is your
  priceless gift to us all.

silence

Lord,
we pray for those we know who
  are locked up in their pain, their
  sorrow, and their questions
and for those who have yet to
  realise that, through your
  love, they can be set free;

for ourselves, as we remember
before you those things that
still hold us in their grasp
and for the infilling of the Holy
Spirit, bringing us renewal,
peace, and the freedom to love.
May we always remember
that freedom is your
priceless gift to us all.

silence

We bring our prayers in
the name of Christ,
who through the cross has
set us free. **Amen.**

FOURTEENTH SUNDAY IN ORDINARY TIME

Praise

Psalm 30

Lord,
our deepest desire is to
lift up your name
and to offer you the kind of
worship that is worthy of you.
We long to focus our lives more
on you every day of our lives
and to live in such a way that
we may bring you glory.

We praise you for who you
are, our almighty God,
and we bless you for you are holy
beyond our understanding.
You have demonstrated
your immense power
across the universe
and we are humbled by
your majesty which has
no equal anywhere!

We bow before you as we are
overwhelmed by your authority
and our finite minds can
but scratch the surface
of your infinite glory.
Your understanding of all things,
we simply cannot comprehend,
yet we can praise you that, in Jesus,
you made yourself known to us.

Lord,
we worship you for all you
have done for all people
in all the world
and we give thanks for the way you
have blessed and guarded us.
You are the one who brings
the healing our hearts
long to receive
and you have offered us an
experience of hope that
transforms our days.

You fill our days with songs
of praise and our lives with
hymns of thanksgiving
as we find our lives encompassed
by your presence and
touched by your grace.
We praise you that in Jesus
we have a hope of your
free gift of eternal life
and through his death and
resurrection we receive the
assurance of forgiveness.

You are the Lord who hears
our cries of pain, of
sorrow, and despair
and we give thanks for your
promise to hold us, to comfort
us, and to walk with us.

We celebrate the wonder of
your presence and your
mercy gives us peace
as we declare that you are the
living God, and we bless you
for your loving-kindness.

We will praise you now, we
will praise you tomorrow
and all our tomorrows
as we will join with the hosts
of heaven to praise the
Lord of all glory. **Amen.**

Confession

Galatians 6:1–10

Lord,
we confess that too often we are
aware that we have fallen into sin
and that our lives are not
bringing you the glory
that is yours by right.
We find ourselves giving in to
the same temptations that
tripped us up yesterday
and our self-centredness
and self-interest conquers
us again and again.

We know that you have promised us
strength as we walk with Christ
but we allow ourselves to be
led astray along the paths
where we are weakest.
What makes it all the harder
is that we know deep down
what we should be doing
and we of all people have
received your promise of the
power of the Holy Spirit.

Come, Lord Jesus, come!
Come and set us free!
Come and heal our broken lives!
Come and make us whole!
Come and make us clean!
Come and pour your
forgiveness over us!

Come, Lord Jesus, come. **Amen.**

Intercession

2 Kings 5:1–14

Lord,
we pray for the healing
of the nations
and for those whose plans and
policies bring division;
for those that breed hatred,
bitterness, and terror
across the world
and for those who reject
the hand of friendship
and reconciliation.
Lord, in your mercy,
hear our prayer.

Lord,
we pray for the healing
of relationships
and for homes where angry
words are often heard;
for families damaged by
physical and verbal abuse
and for those where there
is domination and the
imposition of control.
Lord, in your mercy,
hear our prayer.

Lord,
we pray for the healing of creation
and for a genuine desire to reverse
the damage we are doing;

for a deeper acceptance
of our responsibility to
care for God's earth
and for a willingness to pay the
price of healing the harm
our greed has created.
Lord, in your mercy,
hear our prayer.

Lord,
we pray for the healing
of our nation
and for an honest recognition of
the need to heal the growing
divide in our country;
for those with the power to
provide an equal opportunity for
everyone to reach their potential
and for a more compassionate
people, who remember that
God is on the side of the poor.
Lord, in your mercy,
hear our prayer.

Lord,
we pray for the healing
of your church
and for a new spirit of love and
acceptance between those
of all denominations;
for a longing to demonstrate to
the world a church that is the
model of his new creation
and for a commitment to offer
the hand of reconciliation to
all who name Jesus as Lord.
Lord, in your mercy,
hear our prayer.

Lord,
we pray for the healing of sickness
of body, mind, or spirit
and for those who await the doctor's
diagnosis in fear and trepidation;
for those who unnecessarily
blame themselves for their
times of depression
and for those who are finding
it hard to cope with the loss
of someone they loved.
Lord, in your mercy,
hear our prayer.

Lord,
we pray for the healing of
those known to ourselves
and for those for whom each day is
filled with burdens they carry alone;
for ourselves and for the
healing of those scars which
have marred our days
and for an opening of our whole
being to the Holy Spirit, that
we might be made whole.
Lord, in your mercy,
hear our prayer.

In the name of Jesus the healer,
we bring our prayers. **Amen.**

FIFTEENTH SUNDAY IN ORDINARY TIME

Praise

Psalm 82

Lord,
we praise you for you are
great in holiness
and abounding in truth and power.
There is no God like you
and there is no God besides you.

We praise you for the way
you rule over all creation

and that you are the one with
authority over all things.
You majesty reaches to the
end of time itself
and your understanding is
utterly without limit.

We honour you that you call us
into your ministry of care
and that it is through people
like ourselves that your
compassion flows.
You call us to be channels of your
love to those in greatest need
and to be open-handed in our
giving that all may be fed.

Your compassion drives
us to care for the weak
and the dispossessed
and your mercy compels
us to challenge those
whose plans are evil.
In your name, you require us to
speak for those with no voice
and by your grace you call us to
hold the broken with gentleness.

We praise you for your love for
all that you have made
and we thank you that your
mercy is without end.
You are sovereign over
your vast universe
and your power will shake the
foundations of the world.

We praise you that ultimately you
hold all things in your hands
and that nothing and no
one will ever be beyond
the reach of your love.

We worship you, our living
God, and we thank you for
your goodness to us.
We stand in the midst of
your people knowing we
are surrounded by the
hosts of heaven.

We bring our prayers of praise in
the name of your Son. **Amen.**

Confession

Amos 7:7–17

Lord,
to be honest, we didn't really
feel we were terrible people
and so we often found it hard to
find something to confess.
When we compared ourselves
to other people
we were not really aware of
being dreadful sinners.
We thought of ourselves as
normal, ordinary people
when we measured our
behaviour against our work
colleagues and friends.

But Amos has warned us
about your plumb line,
against which you
measure our lives;
and when we consider
the life of Jesus
it is then we realise how far
short we have fallen.

It is when we are challenged
by your Son
that we come and fall
down before you.
It is in the light of your holiness

that we know we must confess
our need of your grace.

We pray, Lord, come with
your cleansing love
and transform our lives and
our way of living.
Teach us to measure
ourselves against Jesus
and then pour out your renewing
mercy upon us. **Amen.**

Intercession

Luke 10:25–37

Lord,
who is my neighbour?
Is it the person who is a refugee,
one of those fleeing the
dangers of a war zone?
Is it one of those of
whom people say,
'They are stealing our jobs'?
Lord, help us to love our
neighbour as ourselves.

silence

Lord,
who is my neighbour?
Is it that group of teenagers
who frighten the elderly
and who are responsible for
antisocial behaviour?
Is it those children who use
such terrible language
and are hostile when you
try to speak to them?
Lord, help us to love our
neighbour as ourselves.

silence

Lord,
who is my neighbour?
Is it the people I see on the television
who look as though they
are very hungry?
Is it those parents who
appear to have
no food for their family and
who seem to be dying?
Lord, help us to love our
neighbour as ourselves.

silence

Lord,
who is my neighbour?
Is it the people who live next door
whose lifestyle is immoral
and who I'm sure are taking drugs?
Is it that old lady who lives
across the road
and looks to be very lonely?
Lord, help us to love our
neighbour as ourselves.

silence

Lord,
who is my neighbour?
Is it that young man who
I don't think
has washed himself in weeks,
as he sits all alone hoping I
will throw him a coin?
Is it that old man whose
blankets are newspapers
and his home a cardboard box?
Lord, help us to love our
neighbour as ourselves.

silence

Lord,
who is my neighbour?
Is it the family who live
down the road,
the way they dress and their
language and their behaviour
which mean for us they
stand out as different?
Lord, help us to love our
neighbour as ourselves.

silence

Lord,
who is my neighbour?
In the silence, let us take
time to ask God
whom we should think of
as our neighbour
and how we can show God
is love to them.
Lord, help us to love our
neighbour as ourselves.

silence

We bring our prayers to God,
that we may learn to love
our neighbour. **Amen.**

SIXTEENTH SUNDAY IN ORDINARY TIME

Praise

Amos 8:1–12

Lord,
we praise you because you had
the first word in all creation
and we know that yours will be the
final word at the end of all things.
There are times when it feels that
the world is out of control—
until we remember that
yours is the kingdom, the
power, and the glory.

We praise you that you seek
our worship not simply as
we assemble in church
but for the whole of our lives to
be a song of thanksgiving.
You are the Lord who deserves
the very best that we can offer
and that begins as we make space
in our lives to honour you.

We are aware that there are
times when we allow other
things to crowd you out
and we give the commitment
to different activities that
we had promised to you.
Amos spoke about the way
they were squeezing you
out of their days,
as they neglected to offer every
part of their lives for your glory.

We praise you for longing to be the
Lord of the whole of our lives
and for your desire to receive our
songs of praise in every situation.
We owe you so much for the way
you pick us up when we fall
and how you gently set our
feet back on the road
of the kingdom.

You are the sovereign Lord who
calls us by name to worship you
and your call comes to us today, for
the time is ripe for your glory.
How merciful you are and how
gracious in all your ways

for you know our weaknesses
and still you come to hold
us with hands of grace.

We praise you for your power
and we thank you for your mercy.
We worship you for your glory
and we thank you for your
everlasting love. **Amen.**

Confession
Luke 10:38–42
Lord,
Luke tells us that Martha allowed
herself to become distracted
and that she was trying to impress
you with her hard work.
There was Mary sitting
quietly at Jesus' feet,
making time and space in her
heart and life for you.

Lord,
we find it so hard to keep
focused on you
and our minds are full of so
many different things.
We allow our lives to be filled
with the busyness of life
and somehow we leave less
and less time for you.

We confess that we are weak
when we do not focus on you
and that our days lack the joy and
peace your presence brings.
Hold us firmly in your grace-filled
hands and draw us to yourself
and, by your Holy Spirit,
give us a deeper desire to
be with you. **Amen.**

Intercession
Colossians 1:15–28
Lord,
we pray for those who make
the invisible God, visible
and for those whose lives open
our eyes to your presence;
for those who work in a home
for the frail and the elderly
and for those who care for
those who no longer
know who they are;
for those who serve in the tranquil
setting of the local hospice
and for those who seek to
be a channel of Christ's
compassion and peace.
Lord, come make yourself known
that the world might believe.

Lord,
we pray for those who make
the invisible God, visible
and for those whose lives open
our eyes to your presence;
for scientists who open our eyes to
the wonders of your creation
and for those who are teaching us
the need to care for God's world;
for those who open our
minds to the riches that
abound in your world
and for those who bring
the wonderful images
right into our homes.
Lord, come make yourself known
that the world might believe.

Lord,
we pray for those who make
the invisible God, visible

and for those whose lives open
  our eyes to your presence;
for those who offer their
  time and their skills in
  places of greatest need
and for those who offer their
  medical skills across the
  world to fight a pandemic;
for those who work in the local
  health centre providing support
  and care in the community
and for the doctors, nurses,
  and support staff who enable
  good care to be given.
Lord, come make yourself known
that the world might believe.

Lord,
we pray for those who make
  the invisible God, visible
and for those whose lives open
  our eyes to your presence;
for those who risk their
  lives to rescue those who
  are in great danger
and for mountain rescue
  teams and lifeboat crews;
for those who volunteer to
  use their time and their
  skills to save strangers
and for those putting their lives
  in danger rescuing people
  trapped after an earthquake.
Lord, come make yourself known
that the world might believe.

Lord,
we pray for those who make
  the invisible God, visible
and for those whose lives open
  our eyes to your presence;
for those who have dedicated
  themselves to medical research
and for those striving to
  discover new ways to combat
  serious conditions;
for those who are applying
  technology to bring freedom
  and hope to many
and for those who are bringing
  sight to the blind and
  hearing to the deaf.
Lord, come make yourself known
that the world might believe.

Lord,
we pray for those who make
  the invisible God, visible
and for those whose lives open
  our eyes to your presence;
for those who are finding
  practical ways of bringing
  relief to the poor
and for those whose work in
  a food bank brings food
  to the table of many;
for those who serve on the
  streets of our cities where
  they find real need
and for those who offer food,
  friendship, and faith to
  those that many ignore.
Lord, come make yourself known
that the world might believe.

Lord,
we pray for those who make
  the invisible God, visible
and for those whose lives open
  our eyes to your presence;
for those who reached out to us
  when our lives were falling apart

and for those who didn't try
to give us advice but held us
in arms of compassion;
for those we know who are broken,
sad, depressed, and living alone
and for a willingness to share
their journey, as we make the
invisible God, visible again.
Lord, come make yourself known
that the world might believe.

We bring our prayers in
the name of Jesus,
the one who made the invisible
God, visible. **Amen.**

SEVENTEENTH SUNDAY IN ORDINARY TIME

Praise

Colossians 2:6–19

Lord,
we never really understood
the wonder of your glory
and even now it is as though
we have caught a glimpse
of your sovereignty.
To us you were a powerful God
and the King of all creation
but you remained a distant,
unknown and unknowable being.

It was then we met you as if
for the very first time,
when we saw you in the face
of your Son, Jesus Christ.
Now when we look at his life we
find ourselves entering into life
and as we remember his death we
experience a sense of acceptance.
But it is when you confront
us with the power and
truth of his resurrection
that you break down our
false defences and flood
our hearts with hope.

We praise you that all the fullness of
your divine glory is found in him
and we discover that through
his sovereignty he rules
over all things.
It is in Christ that we are
welcomed home to share
in the heavenly banquet
and through grace alone we
find forgiveness and the
renewal of our lives.

We thank you that in him
you have removed every
obstacle to our acceptance
and for your promise of the
power that alone will enable
us to walk with him.
You leave us totally astounded
by the freedom you are
offering to us in him
for in Christ you have opened
the door of the kingdom to
all who come in faith.

Words of thanksgiving are easy
to use but they do not truly
express the joy we feel
and our songs of praise barely
scratch the surface of how
we wonder at your grace.
Our real praises are locked
deep inside as we remember
your majesty and glory

for in you our lives are being made new and our love of Christ grows ever deeper. **Amen.**

Confession

Psalm 85

Father,
we come to confess that our lives are not worthy of you
and yet again we have turned away from all that pleases you.
So many times we have repented, only to fail you again.
Our Christian witness is a poor reflection of your love.

Our thoughts are certainly not your thoughts
and our ways are far from what you had expected of us.
We have spoken of having faith in you
but our attitudes and our behaviour say that we don't.

We come to you, Father, because deep down we do believe in your grace
and though we constantly live to please ourselves and not you, we are sorry.
The psalmist believed that you are a forgiving God, we believe that too;
so we kneel before you and ask that by your grace you will make us new. **Amen.**

Intercession

Luke 11:1–13

Father,
we remember Jesus taught us to call you 'our Father'
and we are overwhelmed with joy every time we do so.
We pray for those whose experience of earthly parents
has damaged them so much that 'Father' is a word that still hurts.
Come,
Father, and heal our wounds
and set us free to pray.

Father,
we remember Jesus taught us to hallow your name
and that our lives should be focused on bringing you glory.
We pray for those whose sole motivation is their own success
and for our society, where wealth, possessions, and fame are the goal.
Come,
Father, and heal our wounds
and set us free to pray.

Father,
we remember Jesus taught us to seek your kingdom
and to give you first place in all our thoughts, plans, and lives.
We pray for those whose days are ruled by their addictions
and for those who once knew you but now serve the kingdoms of the world.
Come,
Father, and heal our wounds
and set us free to pray.

Father,
we remember Jesus taught us to ask you for our daily bread

and that life is more than
the things we can touch,
see, or prove.
We pray for those who are
so poorly paid they cannot
support their family
and for those who today will
go without food that their
children might be able to eat.
Come,
Father, and heal our wounds
and set us free to pray.

Father,
we remember Jesus taught us
to come in faith seeking
your forgiveness
and that the sign that we are
forgiven is when we too
are ready to forgive.
We pray for those whose lives are
broken by unconfessed sin
and for those whose hope of
peace is lost in the bitterness
they harbour within.
Come,
Father, and heal our wounds
and set us free to pray.

Father,
we remember Jesus taught
us to avoid places where
temptation lurks
and to be alert to moments
of weakness when the
tempter is close at hand.
We pray for those who today are
being tempted to cheat and to lie
and for those who blame you,
Father, when they have
made the wrong choice.
Come,
Father, and heal our wounds
and set us free to pray.

Father,
we remember Jesus taught us to
give you the power and glory
and that the whole purpose
of our lives is to bring
honour to your name.
We pray for those whose lives
of compassion are part of
their worship of you
and for those whose words and
deeds shout aloud of your
presence in all their days.
Come,
Father, and heal our wounds
and set us free to pray.

We bring our prayers in
the name of Jesus,
who taught us to call you
'our Father'. **Amen.**

EIGHTEENTH SUNDAY IN ORDINARY TIME

Praise

Psalm 107:1–9

Father,
the psalmist said,
'Give thanks to the Lord,
for he is good;
his love endures forever.'

We are here to give you the
praise that is yours by right
and we reach out to you with
our hymns of thanksgiving.
Our hearts are bursting with
the joy of worship

and we experience a deep and
lasting peace in your presence.

The closer you draw us to
yourself our hope increases
as we experience the touch of
your grace upon our lives.
Every time we turn to you in
praise and thanksgiving
we find ourselves renewed and our
walk with you richly blessed.

You are truly the God who
fills our days with hope
as you lead us gently ever deeper
into your overwhelming love.
As your Word reminds us, we did
not choose you, you chose us
and you have, by your grace,
made us members of
your eternal family.

We praise you that even when we
have wandered far from you
we discover that you are continually
seeking to lead us home.

When we were hungry for love—
in Christ you gave us love
without limit.
When we were in deep trouble—
in Christ you became our hope.
When we were lost and
far from home—
in Christ you came looking
for the missing sheep.
When we were thirsty for peace—
in Christ you gave us
endless satisfaction.

We praise you for your
love that never fails
and for your grace which
never lets us off,
never lets us down,
and never lets us go.

Sovereign Lord, you are the centre
and the heart of our praises
and we come to offer
you our thanks
for who you are and for all
you have done for us.
Come, Lord, and receive
our worship
and, by your Holy Spirit,
enable us to honour you
all our days. **Amen.**

Confession

Luke 12:13–21

Father,
forgive us that we often
allow our focus
to be on anything or
anyone but you.

Forgive us that there are times
when we seek to find our
security in our possessions.

Forgive us for those moments
when we walk away from you
and please ourselves.

Forgive us when our eyes see
only the things of earth
and we fail to look to the
glory of heaven.

Forgive us when we feel we
have done enough

and that we have already reached
the goal of our pilgrimage.

Forgive us when we are self-
satisfied and act as if we
are self-sufficient
and we turn our eyes from looking
to Jesus and relying on his grace.

Forgive us and, by your
Holy Spirit, remake us
in your own image
that we may be living examples
of grace-renewed lives for
your glory. **Amen.**

Intercession

Hosea 11:1–11

Father,
we have a story to tell
you of a small boy.
Both of his parents have been
killed in the civil war;
he has no one to help or
to care for him
and every day he is hoping
for someone to love him.
We pray that he will know you
will never give him up.

silence

Father,
we have a story to tell you of an
old man whose wife has died.
It's nearly a year ago now and
everyone has forgotten his pain
and his loneliness is written
all over his face.
He goes home to a cold
empty house
and there is no one to share
his sadness and tears.
We pray that he will know you
will never give him up.

silence

Father,
we have a story to tell you of a
boy who is bullied at school
and he is ridiculed whenever
he opens Facebook.
There is also the girl who innocently
has fun in a chat room,
totally unaware that she is
being groomed by men—
all for their own pleasure.
We pray that they will know you
will never give them up.

silence

Father,
we have a story to tell you of a man
who exercises power at home,
where everyone dreads his presence
and the torment he brings.
To those outside of their family, they
appear to be happy together—
but it's the frightened faces and the
bruises that tell the real story.
We pray that they will know you
will never give them up.

silence

Father,
we have a story to tell you of a
young woman who is anxious
about her appearance.
She is so afraid of being fat she has
almost stopped eating completely.

Her stay in hospital was a
traumatic experience for her
but her anorexia is responding
well to the treatment
and she is learning to love
herself as she is.
We pray that she will know
you will never give her up.

silence

Father,
we have a story to tell you of a
man who all his life has been
made to feel like a failure
and he cannot remember ever having
been loved unconditionally.
He never pushes himself
forward and always assumes
he will be rejected.
His deepest longing, that
rules his every thought, is
to know he is loved.
We pray that he will know you
will never give him up.

silence

Father,
we have a story to tell you of
the people we know who
are facing great problems
and of how they isolate
themselves with angry
words and selfish actions.
We pray that they will know you
will never give them up.

silence

Father,
we have a story to tell you
which is the story of our
own hearts and lives
and of the deep-seated fears
and the memories of our
mistakes that won't go away.
We pray that we will know
you will never give us up.

silence

We bring our stories and our
prayers in the name of Jesus,
who is the proof that his Father's
love will never give up. **Amen.**

NINETEENTH SUNDAY IN ORDINARY TIME

Praise

Psalm 50:1–8

Lord,
we come before the judge
of all the earth
whose knowledge of all
things is complete.
There is nothing you do not know
and everything in the whole
universe is open to your gaze.

We praise you for the awesome
God that you are
and our worship springs from
our desire to honour you.
You rule over all that you
have lovingly designed
and you alone know the purpose
for which all things were created.

How can we describe you
and what words will do
justice to who you are?
What pictures can we draw
that will be your likeness?
The truth remains: there is
nothing on earth to which
we can compare you
and we can search the
universe in vain to discover
your true image.

Your sovereign will rules
all living things
and for ever and ever you
will have the final word.
You alone are the judge and
jury that we will face
and majesty will allow no
rivals to your glory.

We praise you that your
judgement is soaked in mercy
and that your word of truth
is the source of our hope.
In Christ we caught a glimpse
of the divine love
and in him our feet were set on
the path to the throne of grace.

We come to praise the Lord
of heaven and earth
and to celebrate the one whose
glory blows our minds.
But it is in Christ that you
have revealed your mercy
and through him that you have
dazzled us with your love.

We will praise you now with
our songs of worship
and our prayers come
direct from lives set on
fire by your presence.
We long to join our thanksgiving
with the choirs of heaven
and we are here to praise
the Lord of all glory and
power and grace. **Amen.**

Confession

Isaiah 1:1, 10–20

Lord,
you have made us an
incredible promise
and it is an offer we simply
cannot refuse!
We are amazed at the
assurance you have given
and that it comes with no
strings attached.

You have told us that even
when we have made a
mess of our lives;
when we don't deserve
your forgiveness;
when the way we live
deeply offends you;
and when we cannot
forgive ourselves;
by your grace you will
make us clean.

For you have said,
'Though your sins are like scarlet,
they shall be as white as snow!'

Lord,
there is nothing we can say or do
that can make us clean
and there is no ritual
we can perform

that will make us worthy
of your grace.

So we simply stand before you,
seeking your pardon,
longing for forgiveness,
and claiming your promise
of grace. **Amen.**

Intercession

Hebrews 11:1–3, 8–16

Let us hold before God those he
has used to bring us to faith
as we remember their words that
spoke to us of the Father's love.
We give thanks for their lives, which
opened our eyes to God's grace,
whose whole way of life was flooded
with the presence of Christ.
On our journey of faith,
we will hold the hand of God.

Let us hold before God those
for whom faith is a struggle
as they seek to make sense of a God
of love in a world of suffering.
We pray for those who daily weep
with God, who weeps for his world,
as they seek justice for the poor, the
forgotten, and those with no voice.
On our journey of faith,
we will hold the hand of God.

Let us hold before God those whose
faithfulness enriches the life of faith
as we pray for writers, painters,
and musicians, who open
our eyes to God.
We bless you for those who
help us to catch fresh
glimpses of his nearness
as they lead us into ever
deeper hope, faith, and love
in our walk of trust.
On our journey of faith,
we will hold the hand of God.

Let us hold before God those
who are nearing the end
of their faith journey,
as they prepare themselves
to enter finally into the
presence of the King.
We praise you for their faithful
discipleship which has
marked their footsteps
with lives that have borne the
fruit of the Spirit as they
exercised the gifts that he gave.
On our journey of faith,
we will hold the hand of God.

Let us hold before God
those whose faith led them
into Christ's service
as they answered the call
to go wherever and to
whomever he sent them.
We pray for those who close
their ears to God's call
to speak of his love
and for those who are his
agents of grace across the
world or across the street.
On our journey of faith,
we will hold the hand of God.

Let us hold before God those
whose faith shines as a
light in the darkness
as they work out their faith
where people are broken and
the darkness is deepest.

We pray for those who
risk their lives to rescue
people in great danger
and for those who challenge us
to remember the poor, the
hungry, and the oppressed.
On our journey of faith,
we will hold the hand of God.

Let us hold ourselves before
God as we seek the next step
in our walk with Christ,
as we look to discover what
it might mean to walk by
faith and not by sight.
We pray for the guidance of the
Holy Spirit, that we may not
lose our way on the journey
and that by God's grace we may
live always to bring glory
and praise to his name.
On our journey of faith,
we will hold the hand of God.

Lord, in your mercy,
hear our prayer. **Amen.**

TWENTIETH SUNDAY IN ORDINARY TIME

Praise

Hebrews 12:1–2

Lord,
the Bible tells us of the great
cloud of witnesses,
those who have given their all for
you—and suffered for you.
We are told of those who paid a
great price in their discipleship
as they struggled against great
opposition to remain faithful.
We hear of those who trusted you
implicitly no matter what
and were prepared to live out their
faith before their enemies.
The stories of those who
have achieved great
things in your name
sometimes uplift us, but often we
are overwhelmed by their faith.

We praise you that we can turn
to you, our living God,
and offer you ourselves, not
what others have done.
The walk of faith is hard enough
without these giants
we are left feeling that we are
required to emulate.

We praise you that you call
us not to follow others
but to fix our eyes upon Jesus!
To know that we are
accepted just as we are
and that we are welcomed,
loved and valued
takes us to the very heart of life.

We praise you that the benchmark
of all our discipleship
is measured only against
Jesus Christ himself.

We praise you more that
you do not demand
that we should attain faithfulness
in our own strength.
For you have said that your grace
is sufficient for all our needs
and your call is to keep Christ
at the centre of our lives.

We come before you as we are:
with our weakness;
with our fears;
with our frustrations;
with our failures;
with our brokenness;
with our tears;
with our sinfulness;
with the promise of your
love ringing in our ears
and flooding our hearts with
joy, peace, and hope.

Lord,
we praise you that though not
all of us may be your giants
and capable of breathtaking acts
of trust and obedience,
you receive us like the prodigal
Father that you are!
By your Holy Spirit, empower us,
not always to leaps of faith,
but to take the step on the
next stone across the river
of discipleship. **Amen.**

Confession

Isaiah 5:1–7

Lord,
you have given us everything.
In Christ we have received
countless blessings
and through him we can enter
your holy presence.
You have set us free to
live for your glory
and the gift of your Holy Spirit
means we can live fruitful
lives for your glory.

We confess that too often we
have neglected your gifts
and we have focused our attention
on pleasing ourselves.

We confess that we have not
borne fruit for your praise
and we have selfishly hidden your
love from our neighbour.

We confess that at times our words
have not spoken of your grace
and our daily lives have rarely
demonstrated your presence.

We confess that we have
wasted opportunities to
speak of your Son
and we have failed to live by the
faith we claim to believe.

Lord,
come and enter our lives
all over again
and sweep our hearts clean of
the rubbish you find there.
Touch us with your grace
and remove the weeds
of self-centredness
and apply to us the cleansing
work of Christ that we may
bring you glory. **Amen.**

Intercession

Luke 12:49–56

Lord,
we long to see peace
in your world
and for nations to cease
fighting one another.
Our hope is that innocent
men, women, and children
will no longer be pawns in the
power games of their leaders.

Come, Prince of Peace,
and change our hearts.

Lord,
we long to see peace in
the minds of those
whose work is stressful and
consumes their lives
and for those who are depressed
and at their wits' end
as their search for employment
has come to nothing.
Come, Prince of Peace,
and change our hearts.

Lord,
we long to see an end to antisocial
behaviour in communities,
where people's lives are ruined
by the activity of the few;
for places where children
are no longer safe to be
out on their own
and for communities which are
victims of drug-related crime.
Come, Prince of Peace,
and change our hearts.

Lord,
we long to find peace in
homes where only angry
voices are heard
and where no one seems
willing to be the first to
say they are sorry.
We pray for children who
often feel that they are the
cause of the problems,
as their childhood is damaged
through no fault of their own.
Come, Prince of Peace,
and change our hearts.

Lord,
we long to see peace in the
lives of those who turn
to drugs or to alcohol
to fill the void and the sense of
failure that surrounds their days
and for those who are addicted
to gathering ever more of
the earth's possessions
in an increasingly futile hope
they will bring peace,
contentment, and happiness.
Come, Prince of Peace,
and change our hearts.

Lord,
we long to see peace in
the hearts of those
who are carrying the baggage
of their disappointments,
as they sink deeper into times
of regret for the opportunities
they have missed;
for those who reflect on what
might have been and the
mistakes they have made
and who are finding it hard to
receive the forgiveness offered
freely to them in Christ.
Come, Prince of Peace,
and change our hearts.

Lord,
we long to see peace in the hearts
and lives of those known to us
as they worry about their growing
weakness of today and its
implications for the future;
and for ourselves and our
continuing on the journey
as disciples of Christ,

that the grace-blessings we
receive can become a blessing
of hope to others.
Come, Prince of Peace,
and change our hearts.

We bring our prayers in
the name of Jesus,
the source and the channel
of all peace. **Amen.**

TWENTY-FIRST SUNDAY IN ORDINARY TIME

Prayer of Approach

Psalm 71:5

Lord,
your name is honoured
in all the world
and your praises will last for ever.
By your Holy Spirit,
may we offer worship to
the King of Kings
and celebrate the glory of your
wonderful name. **Amen.**

Praise

Hebrews 12:18–29

Lord,
you are the great and glorious One,
who alone is sovereign
over all things.
You have no beginning
and no end
and there is nothing you
do not know.

You are the majestic and
the holy One
and your absolute glory shines
through the universe.
Your purity is beyond our
comprehension
and the light of your splendour
is overwhelming.

In times past your people
avoided your presence
and were too afraid to come
near to your glory.
They were so dazzled
by your radiance
that they hid their eyes and lived
in dread of your authority.

Lord,
you have opened our eyes and
set us free from all our fears
and you enabled us to catch a
glimpse of your presence.
In Christ we discovered no
longer to be afraid of you
as you revealed yourself to be our
God whose love is immense.

We praise you that we can enter
your presence as we are
and that you welcome us home
as the children of your grace.
Your mercy takes our breath away
as you freely wipe our slate clean
and you pour out your
richest blessings upon us
even before we ask.

We celebrate the wonder of your
grace and the power of your word
that has opened our hearts
to discover your purpose
for our lives.
We worship you for your promise of
a place prepared for us in heaven

and we offer ourselves as a sacrifice
of thanksgiving for your love
to us in Jesus. **Amen.**

Intercession
Jeremiah 1:4–10

Lord,
we pray for ordinary people
living ordinary lives
whom you call to serve you, even
when they don't know it;
for those whose gifts are applied
to the world of business
and for those whose work is
in pensions and finance.
May they serve with honesty
and for the good of all.
Lord, your call comes to us all,
even when we least expect it.

Lord,
we pray for ordinary people
living ordinary lives
whom you call to serve you, even
when they don't know it;
for those who through play groups
prepare children for learning
and for teachers and lecturers
who open young minds
to your world.
May they serve with honesty
and for the good of all.
Lord, your call comes to us all,
even when we least expect it.

Lord,
we pray for ordinary people
living ordinary lives
whom you call to serve you, even
when they don't know it;
for journalists who bring us
news from around the world
and for musicians and actors
and all who use their
gifts in the media.
May they serve with honesty
and for the good of all.
Lord, your call comes to us all,
even when we least expect it.

Lord,
we pray for ordinary people
living ordinary lives
whom you call to serve you, even
when they don't know it;
for those who work in the
world of technology
and for those who give us access
to knowledge and discovery.
May they serve with honesty
and for the good of all.
Lord, your call comes to us all,
even when we least expect it.

Lord,
we pray for ordinary people
living ordinary lives
whom you call to serve you, even
when they don't know it;
for those who remove the
rubbish from our homes
as they protect our health by taking
away the source of disease.
May they serve with honesty
and for the good of all.
Lord, your call comes to us all,
even when we least expect it.

Lord,
we pray for ordinary people
living ordinary lives
whom you call to serve you, even
when they don't know it;

for architects and builders who
provide our new homes
and for plumbers, electricians, and
joiners who do our repairs.
May they serve with honesty
and for the good of all.
Lord, your call comes to us all,
even when we least expect it.

Lord,
we pray for ordinary people
living ordinary lives
whom you call to serve you, even
when they don't know it;
for our health centre staff and
the pressures they face
and for our chemists and
opticians who offer their care.
May they serve with honesty
and for the good of all.
Lord, your call comes to us all,
even when we least expect it.

Lord,
we pray for ordinary people
living ordinary lives
whom you call to serve you, even
when they don't know it;
for those who translate the Bible
into ever more languages
and for those who share the
Scriptures so everyone
can hear God's Word.
May they serve with honesty
and for the good of all.
Lord, your call comes to us all,
even when we least expect it.

Lord,
we pray for ordinary people
living ordinary lives
whom you call to serve you, even
when they don't know it;
for those known to us
personally whose
service we value
and for those whose lives are a
daily offering of God's love.
May they serve with honesty
and for the good of all.
Lord, your call comes to us all,
even when we least expect it.

We bring our prayers in the
name of the One,
who calls and who offers his
presence and power to those
in his service. **Amen.**

TWENTY-SECOND SUNDAY IN ORDINARY TIME

Praise

Psalm 81:1

Lord,
what a song we have to sing—
it is a song of your glory.
Our song comes from
lips filled with joy
and we sing with hearts on
fire with your love.

Lord,
what a song we have to sing—
it is a song of the wonder
of your creation.
Our song is a sign of our gratitude
and it overflows with thanksgiving
for all you have made.

Lord,
what a song we have to sing—
it is a song of great blessing.

Our song is a result of the way
you have changed our lives
and it is sung in honour of the one
who has made all things new.

Lord,
what a song we have to sing—
it is a song of your mighty strength.
Our song is about the powerful
love that made us
and we cannot hold back from
singing the song of your grace.

Lord,
what a song we have to sing—
it is a song that must echo
around the world.
Our song is sung by every
part of your creation
and we your people add our
praises to this mighty theme.

Lord,
what a song we have to sing—
it is a song of compassion
and justice.
Our song speaks of your grace-
blessing offered to all,
as we sing with joy that the
whole world might share
in our song. **Amen.**

Confession

Hebrews 13:15–16

Lord,
it is when we look within our hearts
that we discover we have
left you no room
and it is then that we
are led to confess
that yet again we depend
on your mercy.

We come remembering the good
things we have failed to do
and we cannot forget those
things which have not
reflected your glory.
We have so easily taken your
mercy for granted
and we have said sorry because
your grace has found us out.

We are aware of missed
opportunities to share your name
and the ways in which our
words and deeds have
hidden your grace.
This is why we are here,
that you will lay your
hands upon our lives
and that the peace that passes all
understanding will set us free.

In the silence we make our
own confession to God.

silence

Hear the promise of God:
If we confess our sin, he is
faithful and loving
and will forgive us our sin
and heal our broken relationship
with him. **Amen.**

Intercession

Jeremiah 2:11–13

Lord,
you told us that if we want
to experience peace and
wholeness of life
we must allow nothing and no one
to take your place in our lives

and that we are to love you with
everything we have and are.

We pray for those who place greater
value on their possessions
than they do on knowing and
loving you with all their hearts;
for those who fill their homes
with this world's good things
but have nothing of real
worth in this life to take
into your presence.
Lord, come and take
possession of our lives
and make us whole.

We pray for those for whom
their family is the total
focus of their lives
and who are unable to lift
their eyes to see the needs
of their neighbour;
for those who judge everything by
its impact on their own children
and seem unwilling to hear the cry
of the children around the world.
Lord, come and take
possession of our lives
and make us whole.

We pray for those who place
enormous importance
on their security
as they place their trust
in investments and
insurance policies;
for those whose days are
controlled by their fears of
what the future might bring
and for those who are dominated
by the earth's security
and not by heaven's.
Lord, come and take
possession of our lives
and make us whole.

We pray for those who
place great value on their
worldly achievements,
as they seek to bolster their personal
image in the eyes of others;
for our world, where those
with the most significant
qualifications are honoured
and those with the gifts of
love, compassion, and faith
are too easily ignored.
Lord, come and take
possession of our lives
and make us whole.

We pray for those who seek
to fill their lives with the
pleasures of the moment
and have yet to discover the
hollowness they are creating
within themselves;
for those like the psalmist who
foolishly ignore the reality
of the presence of God
as in their self-centred lives
they continue to declare,
I will live it my way.
Lord, come and take
possession of our lives
and make us whole.

We pray for those who
place immense value on
seeking justice for all
as they challenge poverty,
injustice, and exploitation
wherever it is found;

for those who do not allow
us to hide our eyes from
the hungry and starving
as they force us to accept
our responsibility to
ensure that all are fed.
Lord, come and take
possession of our lives
and make us whole.

We pray for those whose daily walk
is in the footsteps of Christ
as they desire to know his presence
and power at work in their lives;
for those who wrestle daily
with doubts and questions
they can't answer
as they trust in the grace
of God to hold them to
the end, and beyond.
Lord, come and take
possession of our lives
and make us whole.

We bring our prayers in the
name of the Lord Almighty,
who desires to be the true focus of
the whole of our lives. **Amen.**

TWENTY-THIRD SUNDAY IN ORDINARY TIME

Praise

Psalm 139:1–6, 13–18

Lord,
we simply cannot take it in
that you know absolutely
everything about us—
but that you still love us.

Every time we reflect on
how utterly complete
is your understanding of
each one of us—
we are simply awestruck.

Lord,
we praise you for your
boundless compassion
and your grace which
knows no limits;
your sovereignty sends us to our knees
before the throne of the King
who rules over all things.

But that this mighty God
should trouble himself
with the intimate knowledge
of our thoughts, our feelings,
and our failings
takes our breath away.

Your presence brings us a
deep, deep peace
and your grace transforms
our whole being.
Your love reclaims us
and lifts us when we fall,
as you set us on our feet
that we may walk with you again.

We praise you that you knew us
before we were even born
and it was your will from
the very beginning
to hold us in your grace.
We are indeed most
wonderfully made
for we have been designed to
offer worship to you alone.

We praise you now
and we will praise you for ever.
We will worship you now

and we will worship
before your glory
for ever and ever and ever. **Amen.**

Thanksgiving

Philemon 1–21

Father,
we thank you for being who
and what you are
and we bless you for those
through whom
you have ministered your grace to us
as they told us the story
of Jesus with their lives
and with their lips.

We give thanks for those
who have gone before
and for those who fought the fight
and have won the crown;
for those who have kept the faith
and have won the prize
as they stand before the
throne of grace and love.

We give you thanks for those
who have shared our journey
and who have held us when
our tears overwhelmed us;
for those who have loved,
guided, and prayed for us
even when the mistakes we
made caused them pain.

We thank you for those whose faith
is a light shining in the darkness
and whose walk with
Christ illumines even the
most terrible place;
for those whose sacrificial
compassion has healed
broken hearts
as they reached out to the lost, the
lonely, and the least deserving.

We thank you for the beauty we
experience in this world;
for those who use their
gifts and skills,
their time and their energies,
to open our eyes and our minds
to creation's intricate wonders.

We thank you for the joy of
fellowship with your people
and for the richness of worship
together with the people of God.
We bless you for the promise of
hope beyond our imagining
and the eternal celebration
in the life of the world
to come. **Amen.**

Intercession

Jeremiah 18:1–11

Lord,
we pray for those whose
lives are made of clay
which has been made brittle by
the abuse they have faced—
that in the hands of the
master potter
they may be set free from the shame
that has engulfed their hearts.
Lord, we come as supple clay
ready to be moulded.

Lord,
we pray for those whose
lives are made of clay
which is being shaped by the
example of those around them—
that in the hands of the
master potter

they may stand firm in the face
of ridicule and rejection.
Lord, we come as supple clay
ready to be moulded.

Lord,
we pray for those whose
lives are made of clay
which they are determined to
fashion by their own ideas—
that in the hands of the
master potter
their hearts and minds may be
opened by the love of God.
Lord, we come as supple clay
ready to be moulded.

Lord,
we pray for those whose
lives are made of clay
which has been impaired by the pain
and sorrow they have endured—
that in the hands of the master potter
their brokenness may be healed and
their damaged lives restored.
Lord, we come as supple clay
ready to be moulded.

Lord,
we pray for those whose
lives are made of clay
as they use their power and authority
to control the lives of others—
that in the hands of the master potter
your grace may restore to wholeness
the anger deep inside.
Lord, we come as supple clay
ready to be moulded.

Lord,
we pray for those whose
lives are made of clay
as they allow their lives to be
remoulded by the grace of Christ—
that in the hands of the master potter
they may bring light, hope,
and forgiveness to those
who need it most.
Lord, we come as supple clay
ready to be moulded.

Lord,
we pray for ourselves, for our
lives are made of clay,
as we struggle with the challenge
of being Christ's disciples—
that in the hands of the master potter
the Holy Spirit will empower us to
live for his glory, and his alone.
Lord, we come as supple clay
ready to be moulded.

We bring our prayers in the
name of the master potter,
that his hands of grace will
remould broken hearts
and lives. **Amen.**

TWENTY-FOURTH SUNDAY IN ORDINARY TIME

Thanksgiving

1 Timothy 1:12–17

Lord,
the old song told us to count
our many blessings
and to give each one of
them a number
so we wouldn't forget to remember
just how blessed we are.

There are times when we do
count our blessings

and we are utterly overwhelmed
by the bounty of your hand.
Our lives have been filled to
overflowing with reasons
to give you thankfulness,
honour, and praise.

Perhaps we aren't the richest
people in this world
but we have received
grace upon grace.
We may not have fulfilled
all our dreams
but you have flooded our
days with your presence.

We may not have the gifts we
see in the lives of others
but by the Holy Spirit you have
used us in extraordinary ways.
We do have many things which
have brought us sadness
but the joy of the Lord himself offers
us peace beyond understanding.

We may not have lived greatly
successful lives in this world
but you have promised us a place
in the heaven of your love.
We often have times of doubt,
fear, and of feeling lost
but you are the Good Shepherd
who comes to bring us home.

How can we not be thankful
when, like Paul,
we have so much to be thankful for?
He has shown us that not even
the mess we make of our lives
can stop you loving us even
for a moment in time.

Our thankfulness finds
its focus in Jesus,
the one who lived, died, and was
raised again to make us whole.
Your patience with us is completely
beyond our comprehension
and your mercy gives us hope
beyond our wildest dreams.

Come, Lord, and receive
our thanksgiving,
that our prayers of gratitude
may bring you joy.
Come, Lord, and strengthen
us with your Holy Spirit,
that our lives may be a song
of thanksgiving—
now and for all eternity. **Amen.**

Confession

Psalm 14

Lord,
the psalmist told us
that the person who doesn't
believe in you is a fool.

We confess that he meant that
we too are foolish ones
who claim to believe in you
yet resist your plans to
change our lives.

We confess our foolishness
when we declare that you
are a God of love
yet we fail to trust you in
times of darkness.

We confess that what
we sing and pray
is often very different
from how we live

and our words of faith
are built on sand
and not on the rock-solid
foundation of Christ.

Come, Lord,
forgive, change, and renew
our life of faith
that we may stand firm in the
storms of temptation. **Amen.**

Intercession
Luke 15:1–10

Lord,
we want to talk to you about
those who have lost everything
as the impact of earthquake,
fire, or flood has
destroyed their lives;
those whose most precious
possessions have been swept away
and whose loss of family and
friends has left them all alone.
Come, Lord of the lost,
and hold them in your love.

Lord,
we want to talk to you about those
who have lost their freedom
as they now languish in prison
because of their faith in Jesus;
those who spoke out for justice
and freedom of speech
and those imprisoned without
trial or knowing the
charges against them.
Come, Lord of the lost,
and hold them in your love.

Lord,
we want to talk to you about
those who have lost hope
as they hear of the work of terrorists
destroying innocent lives;
those who struggle to cope with the
images of the world's refugees
and those who weep for those
with no food and no future.
Come, Lord of the lost,
and hold them in your love.

Lord,
we want to talk to you about those
who have lost those they loved
as they give thanks for their
memories and the help
they have received;
those who are finding it hard
to cope as they are now
living on their own
and those who are filled with regret
for what they did or failed to do.
Come, Lord of the lost,
and hold them in your love.

Lord,
we want to talk to you about those
who have lost their memories
and those who cannot remember
where they are or who they are;
those for whom their family and
friends appear to be strangers
and those who are totally
dependent on others
for all their needs.
Come, Lord of the lost,
and hold them in your love.

Lord,
we want to talk to you about those
who have lost their faith in God
and those who once met with us
in his worship and service;

those who have given their
allegiance to their wealth
and their possessions
and those who allowed their lifestyle
to silently steal them away.
Come, Lord of the lost,
and hold them in your love.

Lord,
we want to talk to you about
those who have lost the health
they took for granted
and those who are facing a time
of uncertainty as they await
the doctor's diagnosis;
those who are concerned
for the well-being of their
family and friends
and those who live in fear of
tomorrow because they know
the number of their days.
Come, Lord of the lost,
and hold them in your love.

We bring our prayers in
the name of Christ,
who always holds us in
his love. **Amen.**

TWENTY-FIFTH SUNDAY IN ORDINARY TIME

Praise

1 Timothy 2:6

Lord,
there is a song of praise that
wells up within us
and the words on our lips are
designed to bring you glory.
We stand utterly amazed at
the love with which
you have touched our lives
and the grace that has
captured our hearts.

We have praised you as
our sovereign Lord
and have given thanks that
you are King of all things.
We have sought to worship
you, our living Lord,
and we have been overwhelmed
by who and what you are.

Just when it seemed that there
was nothing left to say
and that there were no
reasons remaining to offer
you our praises—
it was then that you opened
our hearts and minds
to reveal all that you have done for
us in and through your Son.

In Jesus, you have broken down
the barrier we had erected
and through his death
and resurrection
you have created a new way for each
of us to enter into your presence.
It is in him we have one who stands
before our sovereign Lord
and pleads for us in your
eternal love.

We praise you that by grace you
look not on our damaged lives
but you see only his nail-
printed hands.
We worship you for you do not
dwell on our selfishness
but your focus is on the marks
of his crown of thorns.

We praise you for Jesus, who
died and was raised again
to bring renewal to us and
to all your creation.
We will praise you now and
we will praise you for ever
and we will praise you before your
throne of endless grace. **Amen.**

Confession

Psalm 79:9

Lord,
the psalmist reminds us that our
sin is not a private issue
as it is not only our own
lives that are affected.
Our selfishness damages our
relationship with you
as we allow ourselves to drift
further and further away
from living the kind of lives
that bring you glory.

We confess that the choices we
make often offend you
and there are things on
which we place a high
value of importance
that must be a great
disappointment to you.
There are times when
our attitudes
undermine our relationships
with one another
and our thoughts create a
barrier to your grace.

For the glory of your name,
we seek your forgiveness,
that our lives might bring
you honour.

We ask for the infilling
of the Holy Spirit
for the renewal of our lives. **Amen.**

Intercession

Jeremiah 8:22

Father,
we pray for those in need of
your healing balm of grace
and for those who are struggling
with serious ill-health;
for those whose illness is ruling
the whole of their lives
and for those who are longing
simply to be made whole.
For those in need of healing,
we bring our prayer.

Father,
we pray for those in need of
your healing balm of grace
and for our nation as it turns
further away from you;
for our country as it closes its
eyes to the needs of the poor,
as it saves its preferential treatment
for the rich and the able.
For those in need of healing,
we bring our prayer.

Father,
we pray for those in need of
your healing balm of grace
as we remember those whose lives
are blighted by their addictions;
for those whose antisocial behaviour
is destroying communities
as the lonely and the fearful
are left to struggle without
the help of a neighbour.
For those in need of healing,
we bring our prayer.

Father,
we pray for those in need of
your healing balm of grace
as we watch the pain and the
suffering of nations at war;
for the twisted minds of those
who murder the innocent
as they seek to terrorise men,
women, and children.
For those in need of healing,
we bring our prayer.

Father,
we pray for those in need of
your healing balm of grace
as we hold before you those
who daily live in fear;
for those who are afraid of what
tomorrow might bring
and for those whose lives are
gripped by unknown anxieties.
For those in need of healing,
we bring our prayer.

Father,
we pray for those in need of
your healing balm of grace
as we think of the damage
our lifestyles are doing
to your creation;
for your grace to touch
the hearts and minds of
those with the power
but not the will to act, that
our good earth may be
healed for your glory.
For those in need of healing,
we bring our prayer.

Father,
we pray for those in need of
your healing balm of grace
as we remember those in need
of your presence and power.

silence

And for ourselves as we remember
the baggage we carry within,
that we may experience
what it means to be made
whole by your love.
For those in need of healing,
we bring our prayer.

We bring our prayers in the
name of Jesus the healer,
the one who makes us
whole. **Amen.**

TWENTY-SIXTH SUNDAY IN ORDINARY TIME

Prayer of Approach

Psalm 91:2

Lord,
we have come to worship you,
the source of our strength
and our hope.
We have come not to escape
from the problems and
stresses of daily life
but to place the burdens we carry
at the foot of your cross of grace.
We come not to run away
from life in the world
but to bring our concerns
for the world
to the one in whom we have
placed our trust. **Amen.**

Praise

1 Timothy 6:12

Lord,
we praise you for those whose
words light up your world
and for those whose deeds bring
hope to their neighbour.
We thank you for your touch
on the lives of those
whose generosity is a sign of your
peace within their hearts.

We praise you for the
life of your Son,
whose self-giving is the signpost
to your forgiveness.
It is in him that we are richly blessed
and the world is granted a
glimpse of your grace.

We thank you that Jesus' words
are the pathway to life
and that his deeds are the highway
to the heaven of your love.
His presence gives us hope
and joy beyond measure
and his touch upon our lives
brings us renewal and peace.

We praise you for the inner
contentment which grace
brings to our lives
and for the experience of a
joy so deep that nothing
can take it away.
We thank you for those whose
lives demonstrate your goodness
and whose peace speaks of your
presence within their hearts.

Come, Lord, and invade our
hearts with your amazing grace
and transform our lives with your
overwhelming offer of mercy.
We thank you that through the
power of the Holy Spirit
even we can become channels
of your love to a lost and
broken world. **Amen.**

Intercession

Luke 16:19–21

Lord,
we pray for those whose
focus is all in the past
as they rest on the laurels
of their achievements;
for those who still carry the
pain of broken dreams
and whose lives are coloured by
memories of sadness and loss.
Come, Lord Jesus, come
and be the focus of our lives.

Lord,
we pray for those whose focus
is simply on today
and who rarely give a thought
to their tomorrows;
for those who take no responsibility
for the impact of their actions
on the lives of the generation
yet to be born.
Come, Lord Jesus, come
and be the focus of our lives.

Lord,
we pray for those whose
focus is on the now
as this is all they can focus on;
for those who can no longer recall
the names of their loved ones

and for whom even family and
  friends are treated as strangers.
Come, Lord Jesus, come
and be the focus of our lives.

Lord,
we pray for those whose focus
  is totally upon themselves
as they seek to live in a world in
  which they are the centre;
for those who filter everything
  by its impact on their lives
and whose self-centredness means
  they ignore the needs of others.
Come, Lord Jesus, come
and be the focus of our lives.

Lord,
we pray for those whose focus is
  on having and wielding power
and for governments around
  the world who exercise
  control over their people;
for those who seek to
  dominate others in business
  or in their home
and for those who have been
  crushed and damaged by
  the insensitivity of others.
Come, Lord Jesus, come
and be the focus of our lives.

Lord,
we pray for those whose focus
  is on the things they possess
and whose trust is only
  on those things they
  have and can hold;
for those who focus their hopes
  on the things of earth
and have yet to open their
  hearts and minds to find
  their hope in God's love.
Come, Lord Jesus, come
and be the focus of our lives.

Lord,
we pray for ourselves, for
  those times when we
  lose our focus on you
as we allow feelings of
  being worthless to
  dominate our lives;
for a rediscovery of the value you
  have placed on all our lives
as we focus our lives again on
  your love, praise, and glory.
Come, Lord Jesus, come
and be the focus of our lives.

We bring our prayers in
  the name of Jesus,
the true focus of life lived by
  the power of God. **Amen.**

TWENTY-SEVENTH SUNDAY IN ORDINARY TIME

Praise

Psalm 137

Father,
we praise you for the gift of life
  with which you have blessed us
and for the world of challenge,
  change, and all-consuming joy.
How easily we take our days
  on earth for granted
and assume ownership of your
  glorious world as our right.

May we never forget the privilege
  of not only being alive

but of being alive in a world rich in
colour and the variety of species.
Your world not only has an
abundance of trees and flowers—
of hills, valleys, mountains,
and mighty waterfalls—
but we have the priceless gift
of being able to enjoy all
that you have made.

Father,
we know that the psalmist
wept because he was
exiled from his home
and felt unable to offer you
praise and thanksgiving in
the midst of strangers.
The songs of worship he had once
sung with joy and gladness,
he had failed to take with
him and to sing them out
of his comfort zone.

Teach us again that there can be no
end to the worship we offer you
and that you have placed
no boundaries to where
we can adore you.
We are beginning to discover that
our homes and our friendships,
our places of work and leisure,
you have declared to be
spheres of thanksgiving.

Father,
open our eyes, our minds,
and our hearts to see
everything and everywhere
with a new desire to recognise
places of awe and wonder,
of joy and blessing.

By your grace, so transform
our lives that we may
enter each new day
and every unknown situation
seeking your presence
and giving you glory.

Almighty God, Father of
our Lord Jesus Christ, you
cannot be encapsulated
by our words or by our ideas as
you meet us at unexpected
times and in surprising places.
The whole universe is not large
enough to contain your majesty
and only by the power of the
Holy Spirit can our praises
reach the heights of heaven.

Father,
come fill our hearts with your grace
and our lives with your love
that we may celebrate the
King of Kings and the
Lord of glory. **Amen.**

Confession

Lamentations 1:1–6

Lord,
we live out our lives in the
midst of a battlefield
as we are daily confronted with
those opposed to our faith
and the test of our
endurance brings us to
the point of breaking.

We confess that we need
your presence as we battle
with temptation

and it is only by your strength
that we can overcome
our spiritual enemies.
We too lament our weakness in
the face of the daily onslaught,
as we seek to stand firm in the
name and the power of Jesus.

Our battle is not against
human foes but the
spiritual forces of evil
which is the reason why we cannot
rely on our own strength.
In our weakness, we turn to Christ.
In our foolishness, we
trust his presence.
In our brokenness, we
seek his wholeness.
In our failures, we long for
his rescuing grace.

We confess that we have fallen
and that only by your grace
can we be made new.
We confess that we have failed you
and only by the power of the Holy
Spirit can we be restored.

Come, Lord, and reclaim
us as your own
that we, by your
strengthening presence,
may overcome all the powers of evil
and stand firm in Christ
our Lord. **Amen.**

Intercession

Luke 17:5–10

Father,
we pray for those whose faith is
no bigger than a mustard seed
and who go on applying it to
every part of their daily lives;
for those who by their
trust in God face great
trials with courage
and who conquer their problems
walking hand in hand with God.
May their demonstration of faith
open our eyes to your glory.

silence

Father,
we pray for those whose faith is
no bigger than a mustard seed
and whose words and deeds are the
source of great riches for our lives;
for writers, painters, teachers,
and scientists who open
our eyes to God's glory
as they challenge us to
demonstrate our thankfulness in
the way we care for our planet.
May their demonstration of faith
open our eyes to your glory.

silence

Father,
we pray for those whose faith is
no bigger than a mustard seed;
for those who have experienced a
life-changing accident or illness
and whose faith enables them
not to give up or give in;
for those whose child has serious
physical or mental difficulties
and who treat them as valued
persons still reaching
for their potential.
May their demonstration of faith
open our eyes to your glory.

silence

Father,
we pray for those whose faith is
no bigger than a mustard seed
as they seek to work it out
in the service of their
local community;
for those who are councillors
or serve in Citizens Advice
and for those who are volunteers
bringing hope and leadership
to young people.
May their demonstration of faith
open our eyes to your glory.

silence

Father,
we pray for those whose faith is
no bigger than a mustard seed
and for those who risk their lives
to share their faith in Jesus;
for those whose faith means
they face the hostility
of their community
and for those tortured and
imprisoned without trial
because of their beliefs.
May their demonstration of faith
open our eyes to your glory.

silence

Father,
we pray for those whose faith is
no bigger than a mustard seed
and for those who rescue
people trapped following
an earthquake or flood;
for those who risk their lives as
members of a lifeboat crew
and for those who volunteer
to use their medical skills
around the world.
May their demonstration of faith
open our eyes to your glory.

silence

Father,
we pray for those whose faith is
no bigger than a mustard seed
and for those we know who
work out their faith in caring
for their neighbour;
for ourselves, that we may
allow God to lead us into
new paths of service
as, by his grace, our faith is no
longer a set of beliefs but a
tool in the service of God.

silence

Father,
we bring our prayers in
the name of Christ,
the source and the goal of all
our faith-living. **Amen.**

TWENTY-EIGHTH SUNDAY IN ORDINARY TIME

Praise

Psalm 66:1–12

Lord,
we stand utterly amazed
in your presence
and we are overwhelmed by
your power and authority.
We are thrilled that we are
permitted to offer you worship

and we are blown away when we
discover that you love us.

You are the glorious sovereign
of this vast universe
and your power and glory
simply know no bounds.
No wonder the psalmist
couldn't restrain his voice
and that he longed for the whole
world to bring you praise.

We praise you as we see
your fingerprints spread
across your creation
and we rejoice in the wonders of
the world that you have made.
We cannot keep silent and our
voices will not be still
for we must praise you, our
sovereign, Saviour, and Lord.

Lord,
you have tested our lives and
prepared us for your worship
as we bring to mind the beauty
of the world in which we live.
Everything, everywhere writes new
verses to our song of thanksgiving
and our hearts are set ablaze by the
grace-filled hands that hold us.

You held us when we were
in danger of falling and
loved us when we fell
and you picked us up that,
in Christ, we might
begin all over again.
It is in and through Christ that we
have been set free to praise you
and through his life, death,
and resurrection,
you have written the new song
of joy in our hearts and lives.

Lord,
by your Holy Spirit, enthuse
and empower us
that the whole of our lives will be
shot through with worship.
May the song of praise we sing here
reverberate around the world
that everyone, everywhere may sing
the song of your salvation. **Amen.**

Confession

Luke 17:11–19

Lord,
we confess that too often we
fail to say thank you
and we appear to take your
blessings for granted.
When kindness is shown
which we didn't deserve
we rarely remember to give
thanks to you as its source.

We confess that we are part
of a selfish generation
that is aware of what it
considers its rights
but too easily neglects its
responsibilities.
We have received so much
more than we deserve
but our minds are set on
gaining even more.

We confess that our greed
and indifference
are damaging the world
in which we live
and that our lives and
our lifestyles

speak volumes of our deep-
seated ingratitude.

Come, Lord God, and
cleanse our hearts;
come and renew the very
centre of our being;
come and transform our
attitudes and our values;
come and make us whole. **Amen.**

Intercession

Jeremiah 29:7

Lord,
you call us to pray for the
community in which
you have placed us
and to hold before you those among
whom we spend our days;
for the doctors, nurses, and
receptionists who staff our
local health centres
and for dentists, opticians,
and clinics who provide
the help we need.
In the name of the Lord,
we pray for our community.

Lord,
you call us to pray for the
community in which
you have placed us
and to hold before you those among
whom we spend our days;
for the lonely, the alone, the
frail, and the housebound
and for those who live in
silence who have no one
to share their days.
In the name of the Lord,
we pray for our community.

Lord,
you call us to pray for the
community in which
you have placed us
and to hold before you those among
whom we spend our days;
for families who are stressed
by the need to support
those close to them
and for care workers who
enable many to remain
in their own home.
In the name of the Lord,
we pray for our community.

Lord,
you call us to pray for the
community in which
you have placed us
and to hold before you those among
whom we spend our days;
for those who are struggling
with the mounting debts
they cannot repay
and for those who daily live in fear
of what their future may hold.
In the name of the Lord,
we pray for our community.

Lord,
you call us to pray for the
community in which
you have placed us
and to hold before you those among
whom we spend our days;
for those in a nation of great
wealth who are forced to rely
on gifts from a food bank
and for those who sell us *The
Big Issue* as they attempt
to sort out their lives.

In the name of the Lord,
we pray for our community.

Lord,
you call us to pray for the
community in which
you have placed us
and to hold before you those among
whom we spend our days;
for those whose actions disturb
the peace of the community
and for those whose activities
are leading them deeper
into a life of crime.
In the name of the Lord,
we pray for our community.

Lord,
you call us to pray for the
community in which
you have placed us
and to hold before you those among
whom we spend our days;
for those who come as strangers into
our community seeking a new life
and for those who face
hostility from those they
counted as neighbours.
In the name of the Lord,
we pray for our community.

We bring our prayers in the
name of the Lord,
who sends us out to love our
neighbour as ourselves. **Amen.**

TWENTY-NINTH SUNDAY IN ORDINARY TIME

Praise

Jeremiah 31:27–34

Faithful Lord,
you are the God of promises—
promises that we can utterly rely on.
We praise you that you not
only make promises of
eternal proportions
but again and again you offer us
a hope that is everlasting.
You alone are the one who not
only gives us your word
but you have the authority to
assure us of its fulfilment.

Sovereign Lord,
your presence transforms our days
and your glory enriches our lives.
Your mercy renews our hope
and your faithfulness
overcomes our fears.

Creator Lord,
your fingerprints are over
all of your creation
and our minds feast on the
glory of all you have made.
Our minds are blown away by
the vastness of your universe
and we have no words to describe
its unimaginable wonder.

Renewing Lord,
you offer us an even greater gift,
one that overwhelms our
wildest dreams.
You made us a pledge to change
the colour of our tomorrows
and to open our hearts and
minds to your presence.

Promising Lord,
your prophet Jeremiah told
us of your promise
which you fulfilled in the life, death,
and resurrection of your Son.
In him you have offered us
a new relationship with
the King of heaven
and through your grace we have
become a new creation.

All praise and thanks to
our living God,
who makes all things new. **Amen.**

Confession

Psalm 119:97–105

Lord,
you gave us your word of grace
but we have followed the
ways of the world.

You called us to meditate on
the word from heaven
but we have allowed our busy
times to crowd you out.

You offered us the word of love
but we have filled our minds
with selfish thoughts.

You called us to obey the
word that gives life
but we have preferred to
trust ourselves.

You longed for us to walk the path
that your grace had planned
but we have pleased ourselves
in the pathways we have
chosen to walk.

By your grace you provided
a lamp for our feet
but we have chosen to
walk in darkness.

You remind us of the power of your
word to transform our days
but we have neglected to
listen to the voice of the
Lord of all creation.

Come, Lord, touch our hearts
and plant within us a deep
desire to love your word.
Come, Lord, and make
all things new,
even as we turn to you, seeking
your forgiveness. **Amen.**

Intercession

2 Timothy 3:16

Lord,
we pray for your world
which daily walks further from
the path of your design.
You lent us your creation
as your gift to us all
but we have treated it as our
personal possession.
You gave us freedom to care for
your world and everyone in it
but we have allowed a few
to become rich at the
expense of the poor.
You made us all equal in your
presence and purposes
but we have turned a blind eye to
the evil of human trafficking.
Lord, by your grace,
help us to change your world.

Lord,
we pray for our nation
which daily walks further from
the path of your design.
You made us a people rich with the
skills of design and invention
but we created wealth to be enjoyed
by an elite and not by us all.
You gave us the skills to widen the
ways by which we communicate
but we have allowed social media to
poison the lives of the vulnerable.
You were once at the heart
of our nation's life, its
decisions, and values
but we are paying the price in
broken lives, by choosing
to please ourselves.
Lord, by your grace,
help us to change your world.

Lord,
we pray for our community
which daily walks further from
the path of your design.
You made us to live by the golden
rule—to love our neighbour
but we prefer to live in isolation,
cocooned from people's problems.
You surrounded us with the joy of
the next generation in our midst
but we have done little to
protect them from abuse,
addiction, and apathy.
You designed us to build a
community of trust, hope,
and thankfulness
but we have closed our doors and
our hearts to the needs of others.
Lord, by your grace,
help us to change your world.

Lord,
we pray for your church
which daily walks further from
the path of your design.
You chose us to be a people who
lived for the kingdom of God
but we have built petty empires that
have brought you no joy or glory.
You designed us to be a
living example of Christ's
presence and love
but we have often seemed
little different from the
world outside our doors.
You gave us an absolute
command that we should live
as spokespersons for Jesus
but we have sealed our lips
and rarely live as Christ's
body in the world.
Lord, by your grace,
help us to change your world.

Lord,
we pray for ourselves
as we daily walk further from
the path of your design.
You gave us life to be lived for
your praise and glory
but we have preferred to
live for ourselves and our
self-centred dreams.
You have enriched our lives with
the gift of the Holy Spirit
but we seek to make our own
decisions and close our
ears to his prompting.
You have overwhelmed us with the
grace of the Lord Jesus Christ
but we have become a
bottleneck to the love of God
reaching our neighbour.

Lord, by your grace,
help us to change your world.

We bring our prayers in
the name of Christ,
who alone can enable us to
change the world. **Amen.**

THIRTIETH SUNDAY IN ORDINARY TIME

Praise

Psalm 65

Lord,
we have come ready to sing
our song of praise—
a song we pray will bring
joy to your heart.
We have come to gather together
every whisper of glory
and each murmur of thanksgiving
that has touched our minds
that we might present them
to you, our mighty God
and our awesome Saviour.

Lord,
we gather in your presence with
hearts overflowing with joy
and our pulses racing as
we acknowledge
the creator of our vast
universe is in our midst.
It is with gratitude that we sing of
the multitude of your blessings
with which you have
touched our days
and we worship you for your
endless stream of grace
that transforms the pathways
in which we journey.

Lord,
our song is of the utter
abundance of your love
and our praises are our confession
that we are unworthy of the
mountain of grace-gifts
with which you flood our days.
It is as if the whole of creation
can contain itself no longer—
like an ever-flowing torrent,
our thanksgiving,
worship, and honour
break forth before its Maker
as everything, everywhere, for ever
joins in the song of eternal
praise. **Amen.**

Confession

Luke 18:9–14

Lord,
there comes a moment
to be honest with you
and with ourselves.
The truth is that too often
we use a crooked rule
to measure the straightness
of our paths.
There are times, like the
Pharisee in Jesus' story,
when we are tempted to make
ourselves feel better than we are
as we compare ourselves against
life's worst examples of humanity.
This enables us to
reassure ourselves
that you may not notice
our foolishness.

But, Lord,
now the moment has come
to be honest with you and
with ourselves.

We have measured our thoughts,
our words, and our lives
against the life of Jesus Christ—
and we know now just
how far short we fall
compared to him.
We confess that
we are not the people
we pretend to be
nor are we the people
others think we are.
We are weak, fallen, selfish,
and self-centred
and we are not the people
you planned for us to be.

Come, Lord,
cleanse, renew, and forgive us
and by your life-renewing grace
make us whole again. **Amen.**

Intercession

2 Timothy 4:6–8

Father,
we want to talk to you
about those who are
fighting for justice
and for those who are risking
everything to bring hope
and freedom to others;
for those around the world who
share in the struggle for liberty;
for those enslaved by
corrupt systems
and for those who stand firm
for the rights of human
beings everywhere.
May those who have
fought the good fight
keep the faith and win the prize.

Father,
we want to talk to you about
those who are fighting
sickness and disease
and for those who are seeking
new treatments to improve
the health of nations;
for those who refuse to give
in to the life-changing
illness that afflicts them
and for those who
transform our lives
by the way they rise above their
pain and their disabilities.
May those who have fought
the good fight
keep the faith and win the prize.

Father,
we want to talk to you about
those who are fighting to
bring hope to the poor
and for those who speak out
for those who can no longer
speak for themselves;
for those who strive to rescue
those with no home, no
hope, and no future
and for those who battle to break
down the growing divide
of extreme wealth and ever-
deepening poverty.
May those who have fought
the good fight
keep the faith and win the prize.

Father,
we want to talk to you about
those who are fighting
for the needs of your broken world
and for those actively
seeking to bring peace

in the theatres of war
around the world;
for those who are literally
risking their lives
as they try to protect people
from their violent aggressors
and for those who are dynamic
examples of non-violent resistance
to evil and corrupt democratic
and totalitarian regimes.
May those who have fought
the good fight
keep the faith and win the prize.

Father,
we want to talk to you about
those who are fighting the
emptiness of atheism
as they offer the fullness and hope
of the presence of Christ
and for those whose walk with
God is a living challenge,
a life lived for selfish ambition,
personal wealth, and possessions;
for those who show themselves
as disciples of Jesus
as they name him as Lord on
the battlefields of their lives
and for those whose gentle words
and unselfish compassion
for the weak, the lost,
and the forgotten
speak powerfully of God's
bias to the poor.
May those who have fought
the good fight
keep the faith and win the prize.

Father,
we want to talk to you about
those who are fighting to
care for their family
and for those who have lost
everything and everyone in
[*name any recent tragedy*];
for those who battle the pain of
loneliness, emptiness, and loss
and for those who begin each
day ready for the fight
in a life of depression and anxiety
for which they are not to blame.
May those who have fought
the good fight
keep the faith and win the prize.

Father,
in the stillness we want to
talk to you about ourselves
and those known to us
and the battles we still fight against
temptation, worry, and fear.

silence

May those who have fought
the good fight
keep the faith and win the prize.

We bring our prayers in
the name of Christ,
who shares every battle
with us. **Amen.**

THIRTY-FIRST SUNDAY IN ORDINARY TIME

Thanksgiving

Psalm 119:137–144

Lord,
our minds are filled with words
that are designed for your glory
and our hearts sing for joy
every time we remember

that praise and thanksgiving
are yours by right!

Deep down we know that no
matter the words we bring
and whatever fine phrases we use
not one of them can ever reach
the heights of your majesty.

You are the King of creation.
You are sovereign over all things.
You are the Lord of life,
Lord of history—
for you are Lord of all!

As the psalmist revealed to us,
you are the God who is utterly holy
and you are righteous in
everything you do.

We have discovered that your
word is the pathway to life
and that as we place our trust
in it we find hope.
When we obey your word
it becomes the road to
healing and renewal.

When we put our faith
in your promises
your presence is our strength in the
midst of the storms we face.
When we hold fast to your word
our lips are filled with songs
of thanksgiving
and we are set free to walk
with you all our days.

Lord,
how can we not offer you
the thanksgiving
that wells up within us and longs
to burst forth in worship?
Your almighty power demands
our celebration of your glory!

In every circumstance
we will thank you
and in every situation we
face we will praise you.
On the hills of joy and in the
valleys of disappointment
your presence fills us with
songs of hope.

On every journey we will
seek your guidance
and in the workplace and the
marketplace we will praise you.
When we are alone we will sing
our song of thankfulness
and when we gather as your
body we will praise you,
our crucified and risen Lord. **Amen.**

Confession

Habakkuk 1:1–4

Lord,
we confess that we find
it much easier
to complain than to give thanks;
to criticise someone or something
comes quite naturally to us;
we have to try so much
harder to show
our appreciation for all the
good things we receive.

We confess that we readily
excuse ourselves
of the faults we highlight in the
lives of those around us;

we reject any accusation of
seeking personal praise
but we are often deeply offended
when we receive no thanks.

Worst of all, Lord, we confess that
we are quick to criticise even you
and that we feel let down when we
fail to receive everything that
we somehow think we deserve.
It is then that, like spoilt children,
we neglect to give you grateful thanks
for the wonder of your grace.

Come, Lord of grace, and
heal our critical hearts
and transform our complaints
into songs of praise and
thanksgiving. **Amen.**

Intercession

2 Thessalonians 1:1–4, 11–12

Father,
in your presence, we remember
those facing times of stress.
We pray for parents who
are struggling
to guide their children
through the maze
of peer group pressure to conform
and a society that worships
anyone and anything except
their heavenly Father.
Lord, may your will be done
and your name be glorified.

Father,
in your presence, we remember
those facing times of stress.
We pray for those in
positions of leadership
in national or local government
and for those with the
huge responsibility
of reflecting God's bias to the poor
in the decisions they are making.
Lord, may your will be done
and your name be glorified.

Father,
in your presence, we remember
those facing times of stress.
We pray for those serving
on the front-line;
for Amnesty International,
seeking freedom for
prisoners of conscience and
those held without trial,
and for those who risk their
lives and their freedom
as they challenge corrupt
governments around the world.
Lord, may your will be done
and your name be glorified.

Father,
in your presence, we remember
those facing times of stress.
We pray for those who
have lost everything
as their homes and families have
been washed away in floods
all over again—the price
they are paying
as the earth's climate is changing—
and for those who ignore
the evidence
and who refuse to act now
to reduce the impact of
global warming.
Lord, may your will be done
and your name be glorified.

Father,
in your presence, we remember
those facing times of stress.
We pray for those leaving
everything behind
as they flee for their lives
from the dangers of a war zone
and for those with the power
but not the will to give them hope.
Lord, may your will be done
and your name be glorified.

Father,
in your presence, we remember
those facing times of stress.
We pray for those whose lives
have been wrecked by the
indiscriminate and evil
work of the terrorist,
who sees only the cause for
which they are fighting
and not the innocent person,
and for those who daily live in fear
of a knife or acid attack or abuse
because of their nationality
or religion.
Lord, may your will be done
and your name be glorified.

Father,
in your presence, we remember
those facing times of stress.
We pray for those we know
who have been devastated by
their doctor's diagnosis
that has changed their lives
and for those torn apart
by the loss of those they loved
and on whom they depended.
Lord, may your will be done
and your name be glorified.

We bring our prayers to the Father
in the name of his Son,
Jesus Christ. **Amen.**

THIRTY-SECOND SUNDAY IN ORDINARY TIME

Prayer of Approach

Psalm 98

Lord,
we are here to join the hosts of
heaven to celebrate your glory
as we sing of the wonder of your love.
We will not be silent in
your presence
for we have come to declare
your sovereignty!

Yet, Lord, as we remember
your power and authority,
our voices are stilled as we
contemplate your awesome
mercy towards us.
Our lips fall silent and our
song of praise is drowned
by the overwhelming sense
of your greatness.

Come, Lord, and fill us
with the Holy Spirit,
that in song and in silence
we may worship you,
the King of all glory. **Amen.**

Praise

Psalm 145:1–5

Lord,
our greatest joy is to
sing your praises
and there is nothing that
gives us greater pleasure

than to declare your
everlasting glory.

You are our God, the ultimate
authority in the whole universe,
and there is no one, nor has
there been, nor ever will be
from before the dawn of creation,
that could match your sovereign
power and glory.

If we could gather up every song
that has been sung in your praise,
they would fall hopelessly short
of declaring your worth;
and if we could assemble every
prayer of thanksgiving
that from before the world began
has been offered in your name,
they would languish as
an empty mumble
instead of an echo of
heaven's eternal song.

Lord,
to say you are great is a
vast understatement
and to celebrate the wonderful
things you have done
would be little more than a
whimper in the wind
rather than an unrelenting
storm of thanksgiving
that is yours by right.

And yet, Lord, the thing that
blows our minds away
and the truth that thrills us to
the depths of our hearts
are that though our praises fall
so far short of your glory
still you receive our songs
of praise with joy!

With the psalmist we declare:
'Great is the Lord and most
worthy of praise;
his greatness no one can fathom.'

This is the song of our hearts
and we will sing it here
and we will sing it everywhere
and will sing it for ever
to the glory of our sovereign
King and Saviour. **Amen.**

Intercession

Luke 20:27–38

Lord,
we pray for those who are
facing hard questions;
for doctors, nurses, and all
who serve in the NHS
as they face the difficult choices
of the use of limited resources
and questions of life and death.
May those facing the
questions that are hard
know your guidance today.

Lord,
we pray for those who are
facing hard questions;
for young people who are stressed,
knowing the choices they
are making today
will impact on the rest
of their lives,
and for those confronted by
peer pressure to conform.
May those facing the
questions that are hard
know your guidance today.

Lord,
we pray for those who are
facing hard questions;
for those diagnosed with
a form of dementia
and for those who share the
journey with them;
for those faced with a life-
limiting illness
and the questions they have as
to what their future may be.
May those facing the
questions that are hard
know your guidance today.

Lord,
we pray for those who are
facing hard questions;
for those facing difficult options
in their discipleship
and for those who are struggling
to work out their lives
in a society that still has
no room for Jesus.
May those facing the
questions that are hard
know your guidance today.

Lord,
we pray for those who are
facing hard questions;
for churches who refuse to
accept decline as normal
but are truly seeking ways
to shape their mission
to their local community
and for churches standing
firm for the gospel
in the face of pressure to change.
May those facing the
questions that are hard
know your guidance today.

Lord,
we pray for those who are
facing hard questions;
for national leaders faced
with decisions
that will impact the future
of our planet
and for those for whom narrow
political considerations
matter more than
protecting the earth.
May those facing the
questions that are hard
know your guidance today.

Lord,
we pray for those who are
facing hard questions;
for those who find themselves
seeking answers
to the deep questions of life—
What does life mean?
What is its purpose?
What is my place in it?—
and for those who are
beginning to ask,
How can I allow God to be
at the heart of my life?
May those facing the
questions that are hard
know your guidance today.

Lord,
we pray for those who are
facing no hard questions;
for those who do not ask the
questions of life that really matter
as they are simply content to
drift through their days
and for ourselves and the hard
questions and the challenges
we face every day of our lives.

May those facing the
questions that are hard
know your guidance today.

We bring our prayers in
the name of Christ,
who alone is the answer to all
our questions. **Amen.**

THIRTY-THIRD SUNDAY IN ORDINARY TIME

Prayer of Approach

Isaiah 12:1–6

Lord,
we have come to give thanks
and to praise your name.
We are the people of your grace
and you have commissioned us
to invite the whole world
to sing a song of your glory.

Come, Lord of our strength,
and fill us with hope.
Come, Lord of our salvation,
and receive our thanksgiving.
Come, Lord of our healing,
and empower us to worship
you alone. **Amen.**

Praise

Isaiah 65:17–25

Lord,
you make all things new
and you alone are the source
of new life, new hope,
and new peace.

Your promise takes our breath away
and we are left with nothing to do
except to praise your holy name
and to give thanks for your glory.

Our world is ruled by selfishness
and by selfish ambition.
Our world is where the
loudest voice is heard
and the strongest is honoured
above all others.
Our world is where the
weak go to the wall
and the gentle are treated
as of no value.
Our world is where we do our
best to ruin your creation
and by our greed we ravage
that which belongs to
future generations.
Our world is where you
are largely ignored
and your presence is rarely
acknowledged.

But you are the God who
ultimately cannot be ignored!
Your presence is from
before time began
and will be when time is no more.
Isaiah declares the amazing truth
that you break into our lives
when we least expect it
and you come to reclaim your
world for your glory.

We praise you for transforming
our darkness into light
and you come to fill our
emptiness with hope and joy.
Your grace is like a shaft of bright love
that promises everlasting renewal
for everything, everywhere,
and for everyone.
Come, Lord, and claim your own.
Come, Lord, and shed your light.
Come, Lord, and receive our praises.

Come, Lord, and come now. **Amen.**

Intercession
Luke 21:5–19

Lord,
we pray for those whose lives
are filled with fear
and for those who cannot rest
because of the burden they
have carried all their days;
for those whose past still
continues to haunt them
and for those whose fears of
rejection, abuse, or failure,
experienced in childhood, have
never really left them.
Lord, come with your healing grace
and touch all our lives.

Lord,
we pray for those whose lives
are filled with fear
and for those for whom the future
appears as deep darkness
or an empty, frightening void;
for those overwhelmed by anxieties
that limit their vision,
ruling their lives with
uncontrollable worry,
and for those only too aware of the
troubles, sorrows, and heartache
that they know tomorrow
holds for them.
Lord, come with your healing grace
and touch all our lives.

Lord,
we pray for those whose lives
are filled with fear
and for those whose todays
are times of doubt
as disillusionment clouds
their minds;
for those whose days are
crippled by indecision
and for those whose sense
of inferiority,
leading to a fear of failure,
means each day ends with
little accomplished.
Lord, come with your healing grace
and touch all our lives.

Lord,
we pray for those whose lives
are filled with fear
and for those overwhelmed with
a sense of impending doom;
for those who see a world at
war and lives destroyed
by the ever-spreading reach of
the terrorist's evil work
and for those deeply moved by
the plight of the hungry
and as their lives are strangled by
times of their own uncertainties.
Lord, come with your healing grace
and touch all our lives.

Lord,
we pray for those whose lives
are filled with fear
and for those whose fears
are extremely real
as they face the pain and the
suffering of injustice;
for those who quake at the sound
of the knock on their door,
which signals the moment
that steals their hope,
and for those for whom something
died within them long ago

as they witnessed everything they
valued taken from them.
Lord, come with your healing grace
and touch all our lives.

Lord,
we pray for those whose lives
are filled with fear
and for those finding it
almost impossible
to cope with the demands and
responsibilities laid upon them;
for those who are afraid
for their family,
growing up in a world that
lives for the moment,
and for parents who worry for
the future of their children
in a society that teaches them there
are no absolute rights and wrongs.
Lord, come with your healing grace
and touch all our lives.

Lord,
we pray for those whose lives
are filled with fear
and for those known to
us personally
as they struggle with times
of sadness and loss;
for those who are facing
dark days in their lives
which suffocate their hopes
and their dreams
and for those for whom
life seems to be
a step from one tragedy
to the next—
a step they are facing alone.
Lord, come with your
healing grace
and touch all our lives.

We bring our prayers in
the name of Christ,
who comes to heal all
our lives. **Amen.**

SUNDAY BEFORE ADVENT

Praise

Colossians 1:11–20

Lord,
if our songs of praise could reach
the ends of the universe
they would still be too small;
if they could touch the
edge of eternity
they would not be wide enough;
if every hymn of praise were sung
and every song of thanksgiving
were celebrated
they would be a poor
offering for your glory.

There is absolutely nothing and
no one in the whole of creation
that is greater than you, Lord.
You are the King of Kings
and the Lord of Lords.
Before the dawn of time—
Christ already was!
Before the foundations of
the world were laid—
Christ already was!
Before all things came to be—
Christ already was!

We praise you that Jesus
came as the Son of God,
that in him we might glimpse
the Lord of heaven.
We worship the one who is the
exact image of the Father!

There is no one in the whole of
history greater than him
and across the world there has
never been his equal.

We praise you that Jesus
was born among us,
that he lived our life and
died in our place.
We worship you with
hearts set on fire
by the joy of his resurrection.
We give thanks that in his coming
he has opened the door to
the heart of the Father.
He is Lord and Saviour,
redeemer and healer of the nations.
He is Lord of all!

When we try to praise him we
simply run out of words
and when we seek to
declare his majesty
our words sound like an
empty echo of his worth.
By his power all things in
heaven and on earth
find their purpose in him.
Through him we receive
peace with God
and the promise of a place in
the heaven of his love.

It is in Christ that life receives
its true meaning
and through his grace we enter
the life that is eternal. **Amen.**

Confession

Luke 23:34

Father,
we come carrying the baggage
that has burdened us all our lives.
We have tried in vain
to set ourselves free
from the shackles of our sin
that hold us fast.
We were at the point of despair
as we had assumed that
we were locked out
of your holy presence
and that we would never
find the key
that would open the door
to your kingdom.

Into the midst of our
anguish, Christ came
and into the heart of our
struggle, he spoke.
His word gave us hope:
'Father, forgive.'
Just that; it said it all
and it meant so much.

There was no mention of
us trying harder,
that there was a standard to reach,
or that we should make
ourselves worthy
before these prodigals
could come home.

Jesus said it all: 'Father, forgive.'
Now we know that entry
into the kingdom
isn't something we could
ever deserve.
It is your free gift of grace
and it sets us free and
welcomes us home.

Thank you, Father. **Amen.**

Intercession
Psalm 42:10

Lord,
we pray for those whose
lives are in turmoil
and for those who are struggling
to cope with life;
for those deeply affected by the
news of a world in chaos
and the problems in their own
lives and the lives of others.
In the silence, remember
the promise:
'Be still and know that I am God.'

silence

Lord,
we pray for those whose lives
are spent keeping busy
and for those for whom it is a
cloak to hide their pain;
for those who are simply wanting
to prove their worth
and for those who find it impossible
to acknowledge their weakness
that no one else sees.
In the silence, remember
the promise:
'Be still and know that I am God.'

silence

Lord,
we pray for those who have
made a mess of their lives
and for those for whom the
cost has been great;
for those who can't forgive
themselves for what they did
or failed to do
and for those who have
been hurt so much
they find it almost impossible
to offer the forgiveness
that is needed.
In the silence, remember
the promise:
'Be still and know that I am God.'

silence

Lord,
we pray for those who lives
are lived out in loneliness
and for those who long for someone
to come and share their memories;
for those who never allow anyone
to get past their defences
and for those who are afraid
of dying all alone.
In the silence, remember
the promise:
'Be still and know that I am God.'

silence

Lord,
we pray for those who find it
hard to make decisions
and for those whose days
are filled with
'if onlys' and 'might have beens';
for those who try to hide
their painful insecurity
and for those who are highly
critical of other people
as they unwittingly seek to
disguise the sense
of their own inferiority.
In the silence, remember
the promise:
'Be still and know that I am God.'

silence

Lord,
we pray for those whose
lives are empty
and for those who seek
to fill the void
with ever more possessions they
know they don't need;
for those who seek satisfaction
in the things of this world
but who deep down are aware
they will arrive empty-handed
at the great throne of grace.
In the silence, remember
the promise:
'Be still and know that I am God.'

silence

Lord,
We pray for those who are lost
on the journey of life
and for those who have tried
every side turning
which the world in its foolishness
is happy to supply;
for those who are determined
to put their faith
in the things they can see,
touch, and prove
and for those who need
someone they trust
to help them find faith in Jesus,
which is the beginning of life
as God meant it to be.
In the silence, remember
the promise:
'Be still and know that I am God.'

silence

Lord,
we pray for ourselves and
the baggage we carry
and for the opportunity
to experience
the reality of freedom in Christ;
for the presence of Christ
to release us
from the anger within and the need
to lay the blame for everything
on anyone other than ourselves.
In the silence, remember
the promise:
'Be still and know that I am God.'

silence

We bring our prayers in
the name of Jesus,
in whose presence we
can know God
and experience the joy of being
his precious child. **Amen.**

APPENDIX

CHRISTMAS EVE

Prayer of Approach

John 1:14

Majesty, majesty, majesty!
Lord, we adore you
and proclaim your majesty.
Holy, holy, holy!
Lord, we adore you
and worship you in your holiness.
Glory, glory, glory!
Lord, we adore you
and celebrate your glory.
Father, Son, and Holy Spirit!
Lord, we adore you
for all that you are
and all that you will be.
O come let us adore him,
Christ the Lord! **Amen.**

Praise

John 1:5

Lord,
a long time ago,
through your prophet, you promised
that the people who
walked in darkness
would see a great light.

Today we praise you for
the light of Christ;
born in a manger;
walked on earth;
healed the sick;
revealed the love of the Father;
died on the cross
and was raised in power and glory.

Lord,
we praise you
for the light that has
enriched our lives
and changed the course of history;
for the light that has
renewed our hope
and challenged the darkness
of the world;
for the light that has
searched us deeply
and brought peace to the world
when none seemed possible;
for the light that streams
from your Word
and reveals your love
at the heart of all your creation.

Lord,
you are the light that came,
the light that comes,
and the light that keeps on coming.
We praise you in the name of Christ,
the light of the world. **Amen.**

Intercession

Luke 2:8

Lord,
we pray for those like the shepherds
who feel excluded by their lifestyle
and for those who have no place
at the table of the rich.
May the Prince of Peace
draw them to himself.

silence

Lord,
we pray for those like the shepherds
whose work leaves them no
time or space for worship,
and for those for whom the
pressures of life remain an excuse.
May the Prince of Peace
draw them to himself.

silence

Lord,
we pray for those like the shepherds
who have been left out by the
  formality of our praises
and for the willingness to offer
  worship that is open to all.
May the Prince of Peace
  draw them to himself.

silence

Lord,
we pray for those like the shepherds
who have been touched by the
  grace and the glory of God
and for those still setting the agenda
  by which they insist that you act.
May the Prince of Peace
  draw them to himself.

silence

Lord,
we pray for those like the shepherds
who discovered your presence
  changes everything
and for those who take the step of
  faith to meet the Christ-child.
May the Prince of Peace
  draw them to himself.

silence

Lord,
we pray for those like the shepherds
who came with their doubts
  and honest uncertainties,
that they may go home filled with
  laughter, joy, and wonder.
May the Prince of Peace
  draw them to himself.

silence

Lord,
we pray for those like the shepherds
who are prepared to come empty-
  handed and to come as they are,
that their lives may be touched
  by grace and by glory.
May the Prince of Peace
  draw them to himself.

silence

Lord,
we pray for those like the shepherds
to whom you have spoken
  your word of love
but who are unable or unwilling
  to step out in faith with you.
May the Prince of Peace
  draw them to himself.

silence

Lord,
we pray for those like the shepherds
who hear the great things God
  has done and is doing
but have yet to discover the joy of
  sharing the wonderful story.
May the Prince of Peace
  draw them to himself.

silence

Lord,
we pray for those like the shepherds
who are challenged to look up to
  their Lord and out to his world
but for whom the truth of God's
  coming in the Christ-child

is lost in the tinsel and
trappings we call 'Xmas'.
May the Prince of Peace
draw them to himself.

silence

Lord,
we pray that we too may
be like the shepherds
and that we too may welcome the
coming of the Christ-child.
In his name and for his glory. **Amen.**

MAUNDY THURSDAY

Prayer of Approach
Psalm 116:1–2

Lord,
on this Maundy Thursday
we gather as your disciples
did so long ago
to listen to your voice;
to experience your presence;
to be moved by your deep emotions;
but most of all, just to be with you.

Our being here is a sign that
you have called us
and our joy in your presence
knows no bounds.
Your are our Lord
and though we can never
really know
what these moments of fellowship
and sharing mean to you
we would not wish to be
anywhere else but here,
offering our praise to you our Lord,
and worshipping the one who
holds us in his grace. **Amen.**

Confession
John 13:1

Lord,
we confess that until we met you
we had no real understanding
of what love really meant.
Our minds still find it
so hard to take in
the wonder and meaning of
your act of self-giving.

You who are the Lord of creation
yet you have come to
wash us clean;
you who are the Lord of history
yet you have come to gather
us up into your story;
you who are sovereign of
time and eternity
yet you have come that we might
share all things with you.

What kind of costly love is this?
It is too extravagant for
us to comprehend.
What kind of peace is this
that you are offering
that longs for us to be at
one with the Father?
What kind of joy is this that
will pay any price
that we may enter your
grace-filled kingdom?

Lord,
when we see your love for us,
we know that we have betrayed
you all over again;
when we hear your voice,
we are aware of the hurt our self-
centred lives are causing you;
when we gather in your name,

we are reminded of the
opportunities of fellowship
we have ignored;
when we receive the bread and
wine of your communion,
we confess our utter failure to
be vehicles of your love.
Come, Lord, and welcome
even us to your table;
come and, by your
unbreakable grace,
cleanse, renew, and infuse
us with your mercy
that we may know the joy of
your forgiveness. **Amen.**

Thanksgiving
1 Corinthians 11:23
Prepare bread and wine to share.

Lord,
our every breath overflows
with thanksgiving
as we are filled with the
joy of knowing you, our
Lord and Saviour.
From the beginning of all things
the whole of creation has been
like a song of praise
and every living thing a hymn
to the glory of your name.
**We add our voices to the
song of praise.**

There has never been a moment
when you were not worthy
of our worship
and there will never be a time
when you have received all the
honour that is your due.
**We will worship you now
and praise you for ever.**

As we gather to remember your dying
and to give thanks for your
sacrificial death,
we are overwhelmed with
a thankfulness
that is too deep to put into words.
**You died for us that we
might live in you.**

The shadow of your cross
is for ever captured
in the bread we eat and
the wine we share.
They speak to us of a love
that knows no limit
and a grace that encompasses
all things.
**Because of your grace we
can be made whole.**

The whole of heaven sings
a song of praise
and every part of your creation
echoes the hymn of glory.

**Come, Holy Spirit, and
set us free to offer
worship, thanks, and everlasting
glory to our God
and blessing upon the
name of his Son.**

On the night of Judas'
act of betrayal,
Jesus gathered with his disciples
for the Passover meal.
He gave thanks for the bread
and after breaking it
gave some of it to each of them.

'This represents my body,' he said,
'which will be broken for you.'

Then he took the cup of wine.
He said, 'This represents my blood,
which I will shed for you.'

The bread is broken and the wine poured out.

May the Holy Spirit make
this holy meal
a true sharing in the life
and death of Christ.

We eat the bread and
drink the wine.
**It is the sign that we
belong to Christ.**

The bread and wine are shared.

Lord,
once more we have met at your table
and received grace at your hand.
We have joined with the
hosts of heaven
and given thanks for our
Saviour and Lord.
This meal has been a picture
of your limitless love
and a sign of your eternal
invitation to us all. **Amen.**

Dismissal

Exodus 12:1–3

The Lord says go!

This is not the end but
the beginning;
this is not the finale but an overture;
this is not the conclusion
but the launch of a life of
praise and thanksgiving in
Christ's name. **Amen.**

GOOD FRIDAY

Prayer of Approach

Psalm 22:1–2

Lord,
your cry from the cross
echoes the emptiness and
the frustrations we feel
and your words of desolation
touch us deeply.
You are no remote being—
one untouched and unmoved
by our anguish
with no real understanding of
what it means to be human.

We come to worship you
in the knowledge
that you have walked where we walk.
We come to praise you
in the assurance
that you have experienced all that
it means to be a real person.
We thank you for being a real-
life, flesh-and-blood Saviour
and our crucified Lord
of glory. **Amen.**

Praise

Isaiah 53:5

Lord,
it is absolutely wonderful to
know just how precious
we are in your sight;
to know that we matter so much
is the most awe-inspiring thing
in the whole world.

How can we not praise you,
our life-giving and life-
renewing God?
How can we not flood the whole
world with thanksgiving

once we have experienced
your life-changing grace?

We so easily take for granted
that you should love us
and that you should do
everything to make us clean.
As someone once said, 'You forgive,
because that is your business.'
But we forget that you
are a holy God
and our self-centred lives
must hurt you deeply
and our selfish attitudes
create a barrier we cannot
climb on our own.

We praise you because you are
not simply our creator God
but the one who in Christ pays the
ultimate price of our renewal.
It is utterly impossible for
us to put into words
the joy you have kindled within us
and the hope that is, by your grace,
emblazoned across this day.

Sovereign Lord, through
Christ's death on the cross,
you have wiped the slate of
our wayward lives clean.
You have welcomed us
into your presence
and claimed us as your own.

Almighty God, Father of hope,
and Lord of history,
how is it possible that you
should whisper in our ear
that you would have us
as your children?

Born not of human desire
or human endeavour
but by the death of Christ and
through the Holy Spirit,
we now belong to you.
On this Good Friday we affirm
with thankful hearts
that Jesus is Lord of our
hearts and lives.

Thanks be to God who has
done marvellous things—
by his grace all things—even
we—are made new. **Amen.**

Meditation

John 19:1–30
Verse 10

They say that ultimately all
power is from God,
and that how we use or abuse
it is our responsibility.
It's true; I do like to win
whatever it costs
and of course I wouldn't want
to neglect justice—
but I do like a quiet life doing
the things I like best.
It's so important that we reach the
goals we have set ourselves;
it's simply unfortunate if others
get hurt along the way.
I wouldn't want to be
misunderstood;
I'm all for living out the
Christian way of life—
but surely it's up to me if
I want to get angry,
and should I always be expected
to offer forgiveness
especially when it clearly
isn't deserved?

I suppose it is true that ultimately
all power is still from God—
but surely how I use or
abuse it is up to me.

Verse 15

Why is it that being swayed
by the loudest voice
comes so easily to us?
I imagine that there were
some in the crowd
that remained silent to
avoid facing ridicule.
It's sad that neglecting the
poor and the homeless
is something to which we
hardly give a thought.
The truth is we would never
willingly sacrifice our integrity
unless, of course, it cost us
the approval of others.
It's all very well putting our hope
in the kingdom of God,
but we do live in the real
world where financial
security is all-important.
I know we should speak
up for those who can't
speak for themselves,
but I'm quite sure that God can
always call someone else.
When we hear him knocking
but refuse Christ entry into
our lives—we crucify Christ.

Verse 15

I think it is very unfair to
criticise the Jewish leaders.
It was perfectly reasonable to
declare their commitment
to the Emperor
as I am quite sure that had a bigger
impact than speaking about God.
We all would want to say
that Christ is our King,
just so long as the cost of
following him isn't too high.
I would be the first to confess
Christ as my Saviour,
but of course it's how I live
that really matters.
I can't be expected to mention
Jesus by name.
It goes without saying
that Jesus is Lord,
but it does depend on how much
of my life he wants to have.
I can't be expected to step
outside my comfort zone,
so it's only reasonable
for me to choose
whom we will love and
whom we will forgive.
Naturally, Christ is our
King—just so long as we
can sit on the throne.

Verse 18

It was always the same with Jesus,
he just didn't seem to care
whom he was with.
He never cared where
people came from
and he didn't bother to
consider if they were fit
company for a rabbi.
But then, that was what caused
so much trouble for him.
He healed a leper and let a
disreputable woman wash his feet.
On one occasion he even went to
a party of dropouts and losers.

I'm sure many good people would
have taken him more seriously
if he'd only been a little more
selective about his friends.
But what can you expect of
someone born in a stable
and whose parentage was a
little bit questionable?
So it was hardly surprising
that when he was killed
it was with those for whom
he said he had come.

Verse 19

They said he was the
King of the Jews.
Pilate even put up a sign to that effect.
But he didn't look like a king.
He didn't have a crown—
unless you count that thing the
soldiers stuck on his head!
And where was his kingdom,
his palace, his throne,
and his servants?
You know, I don't think he
was the kind of king we
had ever seen before.
He seemed to think he could
be everybody's King
and that his kingdom had no
boundaries or time limits.
Perhaps that was why Pilate wrote
his sign in so many languages.

Verse 23

I guess if you are a soldier you
can get used to a crucifixion.
When you've seen one, what
does another one matter?
You could tell just by looking
at the four of them—
they weren't taking any
notice of Jesus.
But then, why should they,
if he was just another one
on just another cross?
Like millions before and
many more since
they probably said they were
just doing their duty.
The amazing thing was that though
they had their share of his clothes,
I rather think that they could
have received more from
him than they realised.

Verse 25

Crucifixion is a terrible way to die.
You could see the agony of it
tearing the life out of him.
But it's his mother I feel sorry for.
I cannot imagine how she
must have felt—
watching her son suffer
and die like that,
to say nothing of the shame
he had brought upon her.
There's no smoke without fire.
He must have been a bad lot
to end up on a cross.
And yet he spoke so kindly
to his mother and to
one of his disciples.
They say he even forgave those who
were responsible for his death—
makes you think, doesn't it?

Verse 30

It is finished!
What is finished? His life, certainly.
But somehow he didn't seem to
be thinking of his own life.

It was as if he was picturing
a jigsaw puzzle
and as he died it was like
putting in the final piece.
I guess it was like being given
an important task
and when you say, 'It is finished,'
what you mean is you have
completed everything
you were asked to do.
It sounded as if he was saying
that his dying like he did
meant that there was nothing
anyone could add or take away
from the great work he
had just completed.
I just wonder, who did he
think would benefit from
what he came to do?

Dismissal

Hebrews 10:16

This is the truth
and it is absolutely amazing!
Because of Christ and his cross
there is nothing left for us to do
and there is nothing we can add
to what he has done for us.
In faith, welcome the crucified
healer into your heart
and accept that you are accepted.
Know that he lives within you
and each day he writes the law of
his love all over your life. **Amen.**

ABOUT THE AUTHOR

David Clowes, born in Ellesmere Port, left school at fifteen following a secondary modern education. In 1965 he committed his life to Christ at Heaton Mersey Methodist and in 1967 he received God's call into the Methodist ministry. He trained at Hartley Victoria College and gained a degree in theology at the University of Manchester.

David served in a number of churches in the northwest of England before retiring in 2010 after thirty-five years in active ministry. His first book, *500 Prayers for All Occasions*, began as a spiritual exercise during a sabbatical. This was followed by *500 More Prayers for All Occasions*. His third book of prayers, *500 Prayers for the Christian Year*, is based on scriptures from the Revised Common Lectionary.

David is married to Angela, and they have two married sons, a foster son, and four grandchildren.